BEL CANTO
A History of Vocal Pedagogy

In this well documented and highly readable book, James Stark provides a history of vocal pedagogy from the beginning of the *bel canto* tradition of solo singing in the late sixteenth and early seventeenth centuries to the present. Using a nineteenth-century treatise by Manuel Garcia as his point of reference, Stark analyses the many sources that discuss singing techniques and selects a number of primary vocal 'problems' for detailed investigation. He also presents data from a series of laboratory experiments carried out to demonstrate the techniques of *bel canto*.

The discussion deals extensively with such topics as the emergence of virtuoso singing, the *castrato* phenomenon, national differences in singing styles, controversies regarding the perennial decline in the art of singing, and the so-called secrets of *bel canto*.

Stark offers a new definition of *bel canto* which reconciles historical and scientific descriptions of good singing. His is a refreshing and profound discussion of issues important to all singers and voice teachers.

JAMES STARK is a singer, voice teacher, and musicologist, with a lifelong interest in vocal pedagogy. He has taught at the University of Colorado, the University of Western Ontario, and, for the last twenty-five years, at Mount Allison University in Sackville, New Brunswick.

JAMES STARK

Bel Canto:
A History of Vocal Pedagogy

UNIVERSITY OF TORONTO PRESS
Toronto Buffalo London

© University of Toronto Press Incorporated 1999
Toronto Buffalo London
Printed in Canada
Reprinted in paperback 2003, 2008

ISBN 0-8020-4703-3 (cloth)
ISBN 0-8020-8614-4 (paper)

Canadian Cataloguing in Publication Data

Stark, James A. (James Arthur), 1938–
  Bel canto : a history of vocal pedagogy / James Stark

  Includes bibliographical references and index.
  ISBN 0-8020-4703-3 (bound)   ISBN 0-8020-8614-4 (pbk.)

  1. Singing – History.   2. Bel canto.   I. Title.

  MT823.S795 1999   783'.043'09   C99-931643-5

University of Toronto Press acknowledges the financial assistance to its
publishing program of the Canada Council for the Arts and the Ontario
Arts Council.

This book has been published with the help of a grant from the Humanities
and Social Sciences Federation of Canada, using funds provided by the Social
Sciences and Humanities Research Council of Canada.

University of Toronto Press acknowledges the financial support for its
publishing activities of the Government of Canada through the Book Publishing Industry Development Program (BPIDP).

Canadä

It is the definition of a beast,
that he does what he does not understand.

Guido d'Arezzo on singers (ca. 1030)

Contents

x   Contents

Preface

This book presents a brief history of vocal pedagogy, from the beginnings of the so-called *bel canto* tradition of solo singing in the late sixteenth and early seventeenth centuries to the present. It is intended primarily for voice students and teachers who may need a scholarly road map in order to navigate through the maze of materials that bear upon the subject, but it is equally suitable for anyone who has a serious interest in singers and singing. The critical method is to seek a *rapprochement* between historical and scientific views of good singing – that is, to extrapolate backwards in time our current understanding of the physiology, aerodynamics, and acoustics of singing as a means of reinterpreting historical vocal practices. Musicologist Carl Dahlhaus defined history as 'memory made scientific' (1983, 3); fellow musicologist Leo Treitler said, 'understanding takes place in the fusion of the horizons of present and past' (1982, 71). My purpose has been to attempt such a fusion in the history of vocal pedagogy. The focal point in this attempt is the vocal method of Manuel Garcia II, first published in the mid-nineteenth century, that served as a watershed between tradition and science in the history of vocal pedagogy. His works are considered by many to be the key to an 'old Italian school of singing,' as well as the springboard for modern voice science.

Each of the first five chapters presents a pedagogical concept regarding one aspect of vocal technique (including glottal closure, voice colour [*timbre*], registers, breath support, and vibrato) and examines that concept from both the historical and the scientific points of view. Chapter 6 discusses idiomatic vocal techniques associated with the old Italian school of singing, with the attendant expressive qualities of those techniques. Chapter 7 offers a new definition of *bel canto* and provides the historical context for the rise and development of this kind of singing, and in the process raises certain controversial matters.

The Appendix is a kind of 'Afterword' – a report on a series of experiments that I developed and carried out under the expert direction of Harm K. Schutte and Donald G. Miller at the Groningen Voice Research Lab in the Netherlands. These experiments represent a modest 'hands on' attempt to measure and compare some of the techniques discussed in the first five chapters.

The field of singing is alive with inquiry and controversy. As George Bernard Shaw wrote in 1886, 'Though there must by this time be in existence almost as many handbooks for singers and speakers as a fast reader could skip through in a lifetime or so, publishers still find them safe investments' (Shaw 1969, 127). (I and my publisher hope he is correct!) Authors on singing have ranged from geniuses to fools, and have included voice teachers, singers, critics, voice buffs, and musicologists. During the past few decades, the field of voice science as it relates to artistic singing has blossomed with the founding of new laboratories, scholarly journals, organizations, conferences, and new books and articles by distinguished researchers. Increasingly, voice teachers and performers have been drawn into this orb. We are now able to draw upon a wide and varied literature in which singers, voice teachers, musicologists, and voice scientists alike strive to unravel the mysteries of good singing.

This book is both premature and overdue. It is premature because voice science continues to reveal and quantify elements of singing which will doubtlessly render some of my observations naïve, or worse, wrong, in the years ahead. It is overdue because it is past time for a drawing together of opinion from the various fields of vocal inquiry in order to formulate an integrated view of singing. Like many others, I believe there is a paradigm of good singing that can serve as the reference point for discussions of voice, song, and expression. This model is most often associated with 'classical' singing styles, extending from the early Baroque period to the present, in which the singer performs remarkable feats that bear little resemblance to the way the voice is used in any other form of vocal communication. Voice scientists, too, recognize that classical singing techniques offer the most elegant and sophisticated use of the voice, and that these techniques provide the reference point for understanding other forms of vocal usage. The common name of this paradigm among singers and voice teachers is *bel canto*, a term that has gained general usage despite its shades of meaning.

In this work I have made no attempt at completeness or comprehensiveness; rather, I have tried to follow la Rochefoucauld's admonition to say all that *should* be, not all that *can* be, said. There are numerous places the reader can look to find greater detail; the extensive citations and bibliography will lead the reader to those works. The surveys of Fischer (1993), Martienssen-Lohmann (1993), Monahan (1978), and Fields (1947) are all more comprehensive than mine, but have a different perspective and a different method. I do not discuss the history of singing prior to the emergence of a professional class of virtuoso singers and a repertoire of solo vocal music in the late sixteenth century. I largely ignore the writings of idiosyncratic authors in favour of those whose ideas formed 'schools' of shared opinion and doctrine. I do not discuss diet, vocal hygiene, or lucky charms. I provide no vocal exercises – the literature is full of them. I provide few graphics, referring the reader instead to the standard works on vocal anatomy, physiology, and acoustics. I have not dwelt on biographical and anecdotal information regarding great singers; these can be found in numerous volumes already available, including the surveys of Pleasants (1966), Steane (1992, 1974, 1993), Kesting (1993), and the numerous biographies and autobiographies of individual singers. Also, I do not try to explain greatness in singing; there are too many imponderables to attempt such a task. Of course, experts in any one field may well wish for a more exhaustive consideration of some aspects of singing, while others may find some of my discussion too detailed. This is the price that one pays for steering a middle course.

The scholarly trappings of this book are not meant to suggest that I am presenting a dispassionate and objective analysis of good singing. On the contrary, my own biases and opinions are scarcely disguised. One cannot be engaged in a lifelong study of singing without forming a body of beliefs and preferences. I have tried not to cross the line between conviction and crusading; if I have failed in this, the reader is sure to find me out and to judge me accordingly.

A word about certain editorial matters is necessary here. In this book all pitch names are based upon their position on the piano keyboard, with the lowest C being *C1*; hence, middle C is *C4*, and the 'high C' of a tenor is *C5*. These pitch names are in italics. This is standard practice in acoustics, and avoids the conflicting systems found in musical textbooks. In order to avoid confusion, *formants* will be indicated by F_1, F_2, etc., using subscript for the number. *Harmonics* will be indicated by H_1, H_2, etc., again using subscript for the number. Fundamental frequency will be indicated by either F_0 or H_1 (they are synonymous). Phonetic sounds are indicated by symbols from the International Phonetic Alphabet (IPA), enclosed in square brackets (for example [a]). Whenever published English translations of non-English works were available, I have used them; in all other cases the translations are my own. I have used a two-tiered system for citations: short citations are embedded in the text between parentheses; longer citations are relegated to the notes at the end of the book so as to not interrupt the flow of the text. Citations in the text and the notes indicate the author, date, and page numbers; all other relevant information is provided in the bibliography, thus avoiding needless duplication. The date in a citation is the date of the specific text that is cited. Thus, a citation of an eighteenth-century treatise will have an eighteenth-century date, but a citation of a twentieth-century translation of that treatise will have a twentieth-century date. In cases where the date of the original work is not precisely known, I have enclosed the estimated date in square brackets in the bibliographical entry. Technical terms are limited as much as possible, but of course they are sometimes necessary and are defined in the text. Foreign words which have not been anglicized by usage appear in italics. I hope this is all in keeping with Albert Einstein's oft-quoted remark that 'everything should be as simple as possible – but not simpler.'

This book has been so many years in the making that it would be impossible to list all those who have influenced it in some way. They include voice teachers, musicology professors, voice science researchers, students, musical colleagues, audiences, and of course my voice pupils who have embraced so enthusiastically the vocal techniques discussed here. Financial support has come from the Social Sciences and Humanities Research Council of Canada, from Mount Allison University in Sackville, New Brunswick, and from the Bell Faculty Fund at Mount Allison, for which I am most grateful. My research in Groningen, first with the late Janwillem van den Berg in 1974, and more recently with Harm Schutte and Donald G. Miller, has helped me to articulate and demonstrate vocal matters in a more informed way than would have been possible otherwise. Harm Schutte's critical sense, his great skill in conducting experiments, and his expansive knowledge of the voice science literature is truly admirable. He has been most generous of both his time and his personal library of published materials. Don Miller has painstakingly read and reread the entire manuscript, making countless suggestions, many of which I have followed, and others which I have not. He has saved me from myself in numerous ways, especially by curbing my predilection for immoderate language, and by patiently explaining certain complex phenomena to me in terms I could understand. His help has been of inestimable value. Of course, any remaining gaffes or errors are mine alone. Thanks also to the anonymous peer reviewers whose suggestions and recommendations were most useful.

To the staff at the University of Toronto Press I could not be more grateful. Ron Schoeffel, Editor-in-Chief, encouraged me in this project over many years, waiting patiently for the manuscript. Ruth Pincoe edited the manuscript with extraordinary skill and understanding. Barbara Porter kept everything running smoothly. I must also extend a special thanks to the 'East Main Street Irregulars,' a hastily assembled team of colleagues, kith, and kin who helped me with the final proof-reading when I was unable to do it myself.

But of course my biggest debt is to my family, without whom this project might have been completed years ago. The diversions, stresses, and rewards of a large family kept me from becoming obsessed with a project that might otherwise have consumed me. Special thanks to my son Paul, whose computer wizardry was my frequent salvation. To my family, then, I dedicate this book.

JAMES STARK

Introduction
The Search for *Bel canto*

Bel canto is a term in search of a meaning, a label that is widely used but only vaguely understood. The English literal translation is 'beautiful singing,' but the connotations range over many aspects of vocal history and pedagogy, including several 'golden ages' of singing, a number of specific techniques of voice production, and a variety of stylistic vocal idioms. There is no consensus among music historians or voice teachers as to the precise application of the term. According to the *The New Grove Dictionary of Music and Musicians*, 'Few musical terms are so loosely used or open to as many interpretations as "bel canto"' (Jander 1980a). There are numerous reasons for this confusion, as a study of the circumstances which led to such varied concepts of *bel canto* will show.

The *bel canto* tradition is associated with the rise of a virtuoso class of singers and the emergence of a repertoire of solo song and opera that goes back as far as the late sixteenth and early seventeenth centuries. From these early days a general recognition that the human voice could be used in extraordinary ways set virtuoso singers apart from amateur and choral singers, and resulted in a new kind of vocal expression. But the specific vocal techniques that led to this kind of singing were not clearly spelled out. The early source material in vocal pedagogy is diffuse and imprecise. There is a paucity of works, and those that exist are scattered in time and provenance. Voice teaching has always been largely based upon oral tradition. Few of the best singers or teachers systematically described their methods in writing, and works by lesser authors earned a reputation that was sometimes well beyond their intrinsic value. Even the best works suffered from vague nomenclature, a problem that continues right up to the present day.

Historical remarks on vocal pedagogy and early singing styles can be found in many places: prefaces to song collections and operas; chapters on singing in comprehensive treatises on music; court chronicles and letters; didactic works on musical ornamentation and style; manuals of taste and manners; early books on the history of music; travel diaries; polemical tracts on musical style and national differences. Musical scores present their own record of what was required of singers, but not even the written notes bear witness to the music as it was actually performed, since singers delighted in embellishing, transposing, expanding, and otherwise varying the printed score.

Complete vocal method books, or 'tutors,' emerged in the eighteenth century, and became important sources on vocal technique from that point onward, but these works, too, often lacked specific instructions on how to use the voice. The language of vocal pedagogy took various twists and turns, often with obsure meanings. Critical accounts of singers occasionally gave fairly objective information about vocal ranges, registers, vocal strength, or long-breathedness in particular singers, but verbal descriptions of voice quality have always been inadequate. Sound recordings offer the only remedy, but even recordings cannot always be trusted; singers may have friends in the engineering booth whose production skills are at least equal to the vocal skills of the singer. Another source of documentation – historical reminiscences or critical reviews – often tells us more about the reporter than about the singer, and contradictions between critics are not uncommon.

The term *bel canto* did not come into general use until the late nineteenth century, when it arose from the 'sulfur of pro- and anti-Wagner invective.'[1] Philip Duey, in his book on *bel canto,* made the point that it was the reaction to Wagner's declamatory style that caused the Italians to rally round their banner of *bel canto,* 'and this was the struggle that made the term famous.' Duey suggested that Nicola Vaccai (1840) and Francesco Lamperti (1864) may have given the first impetus to the term as a designation for a traditional Italian style of singing, and he traced the subsequent use of the term through many late nineteenth-century publications (Duey 1951, 4–12). Owen Jander, the author of the article on *bel canto* in *The New Grove Dictionary of Music and Musicians,* agrees that the first references to *bel canto* appeared around the mid-nineteenth century 'when a weightier vocal tone came to be prized and less emphasis was placed on a light, florid delivery.' This heavier tone quality, which supposedly displaced *bel canto,* was also linked to larger orchestras, larger halls, and the 'darkly romantic subject matter' of some operas

(Jander 1980a). This matter of vocal weight and colour – terms that will be defined later – was certainly a major factor in arguments about *bel canto*, but it was not the only one.

For scholars of this century the term *bel canto* has taken on a number of different meanings. Giulio Silva found the beginnings of the art of *bel canto* in the late sixteenth- and early seventeenth-century practice of florid vocal ornamentation (Silva 1922; see also Kuhn 1902). Hugo Goldschmidt maintained that Giulio Caccini's *Le nuove musiche* (1602) marked the earliest school of good singing – a view echoed by others – while Goldschmidt's compatriate Friedrich Chrysander drew attention to Lodovico Zacconi's earlier treatise of 1592 as the harbinger of the new vocal style.[2] Robert Haas and Manfred Bukofzer shifted the ground by using the term *bel canto* in reference to the *cantabile* style of Venetian and Roman operas and cantatas of the 1630s and 1640s, a view that still exists in some quarters.[3]

Bel canto was associated not only with the seventeenth century but also with the eighteenth century (Duey 1951, 12). Andrea Della Corte's book on *bel canto* was based on the well-known eighteenth-century vocal tutors of Pierfrancesco Tosi (1723) and Giambattista Mancini (1777).[4] The 1969 edition of the *Harvard Dictionary of Music* equates *bel canto* with eighteenth-century opera in general and with Mozart in particular (Apel 1969, 88); the 1986 edition maintains that 'the period from the middle of the seventeenth century to the beginning of the nineteenth is thought of as the golden age of bel canto' (Randel 1986, 87). Italian music critic Rodolfo Celletti's book *A History of Bel Canto* (1991) focuses on the virtuosic style and aesthetic of Italian opera in the Baroque period of music history, from Monteverdi to Handel. Celletti passes by Mozart altogether and proceeds to Rossini as the last proponent of the *bel canto* style. He maintains that music of the Romantic period lay outside the framework of *bel canto*, and he has little regard for anything that is not Italian. Hermann Klein (1923), on the other hand, placed a particular emphasis on the music of Mozart. The *New Grove* nudged *bel canto* forward in time to include the early nineteenth century (Jander 1980a). Indeed, many listeners today associate *bel canto* primarily with Rossini, Donizetti, Bellini, and perhaps early Verdi. Erna Brand-Seltei (1972) carried the designation of *bel canto* to Manuel Garcia II and his pupils, thus extending the term to the threshhold of the twentieth century, and she even included Russian national opera under this label. It is apparent that the time frame for *bel canto* is highly malleable, and that the term is used for a variety of historical periods and styles.

Also malleable are the critical criteria used to identify *bel canto*. Some authors base their concept of *bel canto* on particular treatises, others on certain composers, and still others on a circumscribed compositional style or taste. Some consider *bel canto* to be synonymous with the flourishing of the castrato singer and highly florid styles. Duey, for instance, said that the castrato was the 'most important element' in the development of *bel canto*, a view shared by Edward Foreman.[5] Blanche Marchesi, on the other hand, thought that *bel canto* techniques were equally useful for all styles of opera, even the declamatory and powerful singing required for Wagner (B. Marchesi 1935, 155). Her view is shared by Pleasants (1966, 20).

Many individual voice teachers have laid claim to possessing a true understanding of *bel canto* vocal techniques. George Bernard Shaw described the 'bel cantists' with his usual acid wit in 1885, when he said, 'Every private teacher with whom I am or have ever been acquainted, has rediscovered Porpora's method, can explain it at considerable length, teaches exclusively on it, and is the only person in the world who can do so, all others being notorious quacks and voice destroyers' (Shaw 1960, 99). Pleasants echoed this remark when he said that the term could be appropriated 'by any teacher satisfied that he possesses the secret of beautiful singing or by any singer who thinks that he sings beautifully' (Pleasants 1966, 20). Many of the voice books issued by such teachers are, in fact, personal statements about their own preferences in vocal techniques. Such books are rich in colourful imagery and inventive descriptions of vocal function, but spare in facts about specific physiological, acoustical, or aerodynamic details of the singing voice. They often fail to draw important distinctions between male and female voices or between the different vocal requirements necessary for singing music of various stylistic eras. The implication is that there is only one kind of vocal instrument and one way to use it: this is too narrow a view of *bel canto*.

Despite the disagreements in the pedagogical literature, we cannot ignore the common theme that runs through so many works – namely, that there is something special, perhaps even 'secret,' involved in singing according to *bel canto* principles. In the broadest sense, *bel canto* represents the 'classically' trained voice of opera and concert singers, extending from Caccini at the dawn of the Baroque era to the best singers of today. Other terms for the classically trained voice include the 'cultivated' voice[6] and 'elite vocalism.'[7] Such singing requires a highly refined use of the laryngeal, respiratory, and articulatory muscles in order to produce special qualities of timbre, evenness of scale and register, breath control, flexibility, tremulousness, and expressiveness. This kind of singing requires a different vocal technique than 'natural' or untrained singing, and it also differs from both choral singing and the many forms of popular singing nowadays referred to as 'vernacular' styles. Few listeners would have any trouble making these distinctions.

Beyond this, however, even within the category of classically trained voices, there are distinct types of singing, ranging from the light, florid voices associated with the works of composers from Monteverdi to Rossini to the more sustained and robust voices associated with the music dramas of Wagner. There are many shades of meaning to *bel canto*, but whatever shade one chooses, the extraordinary use of the human voice remains a fairly constant theme in the description of this term.

A few scholars have argued that there were no extraordinary demands or secrets to *bel canto*. Duey, for instance, maintained that there was 'an amazingly direct and simple approach to the business of singing' (Duey 1951, 155). Edward Foreman said, 'The precepts set down are admittedly simple, but, given the prevailing conditions, are more than adequate to explain the results which they produced.'[8] Vocal author Edgar Herbert-Caesari maintained that the foundation of the old Italian school, from Caccini onward, is the 'completely natural voice ... that, without training, is able to articulate, enunciate, and sustain with perfect ease and freedom all vowels on all pitches in its particular compass' (Herbert-Caesari 1936, 4). These views are unrealistic. Why one may ask, if the techniques of *bel canto* are so simple and direct, has great singing always been the art of the few and not of the many? Or, if Herbert-Caesari thought *bel canto* was just natural, untrained singing, why did he bother to write a book about vocal technique?

The strategy of this book is to examine the physiological, acoustical, and aerodynamic properties of classically trained voices for qualities that resemble the historical descriptions of the old Italian method. Before the emergence of modern voice science, authors of voice manuals were unable to describe their singing methods in objective, quantifiable terms. The vocal instrument is hidden deep in the neck; it cannot be directly viewed and touched and examined as other musical instruments are. Hence, early descriptions of vocal function were bound to be vague or even incorrect. All this changed in 1855 when voice teacher and author Manuel Garcia II invented the laryngoscope, a small angled mirror, not unlike a dentist's mirror, that he used to view the vocal folds during singing. Garcia's translator Donald V. Paschke noted that 'the use of the laryngeal mirror in virtually every instance verified the theories which the author had formed earlier as a result of his knowledge of the anatomy of the vocal mechanism and his experience as a teacher' (Garcia 1975, iii). Garcia's observations of the larynx with the laryngoscope marked the beginning of a scientific approach to singing which affected the entire dynamic of vocal history.

Garcia's scientific approach to vocal pedagogy had many detractors. In his reviews of new voice books, G.B. Shaw was critical of Garcia and other writers who adopted the scientific approach (Shaw 1932, 2: 187–92). English voice teacher Franklyn Kelsey called Garcia 'the very greatest and last of the old school of teachers,' but added: 'It is an instance of the irony of things that we might have believed him if he himself had not invented the instrument which was to undermine our belief' (Kelsey 1950, 11). Duey, too, maintained that voice science, instead of being an aid to good singing, 'appears only to have broadened the field of controversy where the problem of correct singing is involved' (Duey 1951, 1). Cornelius L. Reid joined those who blamed the disappearance of *bel canto* techniques on the 'entry of the scientific investigator into the field of vocal endeavor' (Reid 1950, 156, also 169–92). Music psychologist Carl Seashore seemed resigned to the fact that musicians are 'very slow to accept' scientific terminology and points of view (Seashore 1932, 9).

Garcia polarized the whole field of vocal pedagogy with his introduction of the laryngoscope, with his theories of vocal onset, timbres, and registers, and with his original and largely misunderstood terminology. His theories became the focus of generations of disciples and detractors. Garcia's vocal pedagogy became the concern not only of traditional voice teachers, but also of scientists and medical doctors. His pioneering work with the laryngoscope opened the door to throat doctors, some of whom used the device to support their own theories of laryngeal function in singing. His theories of vocal timbres, together with Hermann Helmholtz's seminal work of 1862, paved the way for the modern study of vocal acoustics. In many ways Garcia can be considered the father of modern voice science whose legacy is no less present today than in his own time.

Modern voice scientists do not generally concern themselves with elaborate historical or pedagogical constructs like *bel canto*, nor do they put much stock in resonance imagery, 'placing the voice,' or other traditional techniques of voice teaching. Rather, they try to isolate specific physiological, acoustical, and aerodynamic aspects of the singing voice in the controlled environment of the voice research laboratory. Some experiments require invasive instrumentation, such as the placement of catheters in the esophagus or electrodes in the vocal folds. Some experiments use breath masks, rigid laryngoscopes, or other paraphernalia that can inhibit good tone production. Many procedures are based on short samples of single tones, rather than on artistically sung phrases or complete pieces. World-class professional singers rarely serve as subjects in the laboratory. Despite these limitations, there is a growing literature of useful studies on vocal folds, breath pressure and airflow, vocal resonance, vibrato, registers, and other aspects of the trained voice. Like voice teachers, voice scientists are trying to define and understand the parameters of good singing.

The difference between traditional voice teachers and voice scientists sometimes manifests itself in certain outlooks that influence their work. For instance, many voice teachers retain the methods and terminology of earlier periods, rejecting the more objective methods of voice science as unnecessary or even mischievous; demonstration, imitation, and trial-and-error are the tools of their trade. It cannot be denied that the older traditional methods often produced and continue to produce great singers. The long history of virtuoso singing demonstrates the fact that scientific understanding of the voice has never been a prerequisite for becoming a good singer. Happily, the last few decades have seen an increasing acceptance by traditional teachers of the value of voice science and its contribution to vocal pedagogy.

On the other hand, some medical doctors have had an *a priori* bias against vigorous and robust singing techniques, for fear that these techniques will lead to vocal abuse and damage. Controversial techniques such as Garcia's use of the *coup de la glotte* to achieve strong glottal closure and G.B. Lamperti's insistence on 'compressed breath' might well suggest vocal strain to some observers, and the heavy vocal demands of Wagner's music dramas is sometimes cited as the ruination of singers. But what appears to be strenuous to some may be the workaday technique of others. There are indeed too many cases of vocal abuse and faulty technique in the field of singing and the matter cannot be taken lightly. Nevertheless we cannot dismiss all robust singing out of hand as dangerous. Many such singers enjoy long and illustrious careers.

The bias against high effort singing has had a significant effect on vocal pedagogy. For instance, at the beginning of this century certain influential doctors-*cum*-voice teachers in the United States, Britain, and Germany subscribed to the notion that high physical effort caused the ruin of voices, and that the remedy was to sing with a 'relaxed' throat. George Bernard Shaw referred to this as the 'no-effort' school of singing. In Germany, there was a debate between those who advocated a vigorous type of singing using the principle of *Stauprinzip* (breath damming) and those who recommended a more relaxed technique using *Minimalluft* (minimum breath). Both sides claimed to be pursuing the techniques of *bel canto*. As we will see, such arguments continue today with new terminology such as 'flow' phonation versus 'pressed' phonation.

Another vocal phenomenon that has polarized thinking about *bel canto* is vibrato. Once again, the historical literature is vague and equivocal, with opinions clearly divided as to whether vibrato is a good or bad feature of the voice, or even whether it is a part of *bel canto* at all. Some early music specialists have argued, on flimsy evidence, that vibrato was simply an embellishment added to a vocal line at suitably expressive points, or that vibrato was a vocal fault which should be eliminated altogether from the singing voice. This view has been countered by modern voice scientists who regard vibrato as a normal and desirable feature of the artistic singing voice. They argue that vibrato is an integral part of the voice that develops as a natural consequence of voice training, and that the delicate balance of muscular tensions that leads to good singing also leads to a pleasing vocal tremulousness. This debate cannot be resolved on the basis of the historical record, but the idea that vibrato is idiomatic to the classically trained voice will be carefully explored.

The idea of 'idiomatic' singing is important when discussing *bel canto* techniques. The critical muscular balances of the old Italian method manifest themselves as particular vocal effects that are well suited to the highly trained voice. Giulio Caccini described good singing in terms of specific vocal *affetti* that expressed certain emotions, and he provided illustrations from his own songs to show how voice quality, articulation, dynamic gradations, and melodic and rhythmic ornaments could become the means of heightening the expressiveness of the song. Later authors, most notably Garcia, expanded upon this, showing how breathing, timbres, registers, *legato, portamento, messa di voce*, trills, and floridity could all play a role in expressive singing. Garcia distinguished between categories of singing and song, and provided detailed instructions on how to use certain vocal techniques for specific expressive purposes.

Musicologists have largely ignored the role of vocal idioms in their critical apparatus for analysing vocal music. They judge the value of songs and arias on the basis of a so-called word-tone relationship, an analytical technique that discusses only words and notes, not voice qualities. What they do not seem to recognize is that much of the expressive power of song lies in the voice itself, as Caccini, Garcia, and discerning listeners have always known. Expressive singing is based upon a word-note-*tone* relationship, in which the voice itself plays a significant role. This, too, is crucial for an understanding of *bel canto*.

In the end, after careful consideration of all these contradictions and controversies, I believe it *is* possible to defend the concept of *bel canto*, using as defining elements the specialized vocal techniques, idioms, and expressive qualities of the classically trained voice. *Bel canto* does not apply to just one stylistic era, nor is it a single way of using the voice or a specific set of stylistic conventions. Rather, it is based upon certain irreducible vocal techniques that set it apart from other kinds of singing. These techniques can be adapted to a wide variety of musical styles from several historical epochs without losing their integrity as fundamental vocal principles.

A recurring theme in vocal history is the decline of good singing and the loss of the secrets of the old Italian school. But this may only be a cyclical reaction to the mutations of *bel canto*, as singers met the challenges of new musical styles by modifying their technique rather than abandoning its essential components. These essential components are still the backbone of operatic singing, as many great singers continue the old traditions. Just as a prism breaks a single beam of light into many different colours, *bel canto* represents a way of singing in which a basic vocal technique accommodates itself to a wide spectrum of musical styles. If there are indeed secrets to *bel canto*, they remain secret only because people have not paid sufficient attention to the authors who tried to share them with us. Modern voice science will continue to reveal those secrets in a specific way as the search for *bel canto* enters its fifth century.

BEL CANTO

1

The *Coup de la glotte*: A Stroke of Genius

Manuel Garcia II

If there was a single point in music history when the tradition and science of singing met, it was in the life and work of Manuel Garcia II (1805–1906). Perhaps it would be more correct to say that with Garcia, tradition and science not only met, but collided with a force that is still felt today. Garcia was one of those seminal historical figures whose career marked a watershed between the past and the future. An heir of the old Italian school of singing, at the same time he belonged to a generation of scientific minds who wished to look beyond the mere appearance of things to their underlying causes. In the process he developed theoretical ideas that were based on close empirical observation and leavened with uncanny intuition. His work was touched by genius, but it was opposed by those who were less gifted and less prescient. He was a man ahead of his time – so far ahead that although more than 150 years have passed since his first treatise appeared, he remains a presence that must be reckoned with in any serious study of the history and technique of singing.

By any measure, Manuel Garcia was a remarkable man.[1] He was born in Madrid in 1805 to a musical family. His father, Manuel Garcia I, was a famous singer from Seville who became Rossini's favourite tenor; the role of Count Almaviva in *Il Barbiere di Siviglia* was only one of the roles created especially for him. The younger Manuel's mother, Maria Joaquina Sitches, was a singer and dancer, and two of his sisters (Maria Malibran and Pauline Viardot) became famous as mezzo-sopranos under their married names. Garcia studied voice with his father and harmony with François Joseph Fétis. He may also have had some 'informed lessons' with the Italian teacher Giovanni Ansani when he was only ten (Mackinlay 1908, 25–6). Ansani had been a student of the celebrated teacher and composer Niccolò Porpora, so it is possible that the younger Manuel received an early initiation into an old tradition of Italian singing.

In 1825 the Garcia family, along with several other singers, travelled to New York and Mexico as the first Italian opera troupe to visit the New World, performing operas of Rossini and Mozart. The stress of singing during the pubertal mutation of his voice and taking on leading roles at too young an age apparently damaged the young Manuel's voice, and he stopped performing in 1829 at the age of twenty-four. Subsequently, he worked in military hospitals where he had occasion to study the larynx in cases of neck wounds. This may well have stimulated his interest in vocal anatomy. When his father died in 1832, the young Manuel took over the vocal training of his sisters, who were still in their formative years. Their outstanding success as professional singers is at least partially attributed to this teaching. In 1835 he was appointed Professor of Singing at the Paris Conservatoire.

The Conservatoire was well known for its comprehensive method books in singing. Bernardo Mengozzi (1758–1800) compiled materials for a vocal method for the Conservatoire, but he died before he could complete this project. The work was edited by Honoré Langlé and published in 1803 as the *Méthode de chant du Conservatoire de musique*. Mengozzi claimed that his method, which was based on the Italian tradition and especially on the teachings of the celebrated castrato Antonio Bernacchi, was adaptable to the music of all epochs. Around 1830, Mengozzi's book was updated and expanded by Alexis de Garaudé (1779–1852), and renamed the *Méthode complète de chant*. Garaudé had been a pupil of the famous castrato Girolamo Crescentini in Paris, and he taught at the Conservatoire from 1816 to 1841. He added *solfèges* by Jommelli, Porpora, and others, and said his method developed as a result of his visits to major Italian centres and reflected the singing practices of the great singers of his time. It should be observed that from 1822 to 1842 the Paris Conservatoire was under the direction of Luigi Cherubini, who ensured that the Italian school of singing was the officially sanctioned method of that venerable institution.

When Garcia became a professor at the Paris Conservatoire, he entered an institutional environment in which the Italian method of singing was well established and the large, articulate, and well-organized instruction manuals of Mengozzi and Garaudé were firmly established. He had to make a strong impact in order to secure his place. In 1840, in an act that established his career, Garcia presented his *Mémoire sur la voix humaine* to the Académie des sciences de Paris, to widespread notice. This *Mémoire* was absorbed into the first part of his *École de Garcia: Traité complet de l'art du chant*, which appeared the following year, and which contained his main theories of vocal technique. This publication was reprinted with the addition of a second part in 1847. Part One of Garcia's *Traité* is largely concerned with vocal technique; Part Two is a digest of the stylistic practices of the day with some elaboration of earlier points. Garcia made it clear that he was well acquainted with earlier treatises on singing, which he frequently cited in his footnotes. In the preface to the 1841 edition of his *Traité*, he wrote, 'Unfortunately, that epoch has left to us only some vague and incomplete documents of its traditions. The works of Tosi, Mancini, Herbst, Agricola, some scattered passages in the histories of Bontempi, Burney, Hawkins, and Baini, give us only an approximate and confused idea of the methods then followed' (Garcia 1984, xvii). The *Traité* went through several editions; recent publications include a facsimile edition of the complete 1847 work (Garcia 1847), and a two-part English translation which compares the 1841 and the 1847 edition with the revised sixth edition of 1872 (Garcia 1984 and 1975).

Garcia remained in Paris until 1848, when he followed his wellheeled clients to England as they fled the rising political temperature in France. In 1854, while on holiday in Paris, Garcia is said to have noticed the sun's reflection off a windowpane of the Royal Palace. This supposedly inspired him to use mirrors and the sun's rays to look directly at his own larynx (autolaryngology) (von Leden 1983, 122). While it is widely believed that Garcia invented the laryngoscope in 1855, researcher Peak Woo maintains that Bozzini and M. Gagniard de la Tour had used dental mirrors to view the larynx in 1807 and 1829 respectively, and that in 1844 Mr Avery of London added a semispherical forehead reflector with a hole in the center. Woo concedes that Garcia may have been the first to use autolaryngoscopy (Woo 1996, 1–2). In his seminal presentation to the Royal Society, 'Observations on the Human Voice' (which was published in the 1855 *Proceedings of the Royal Society*), Garcia provided greater detail on the physiology of the larynx, based on his laryngeal observations and his close observation of laryngeal muscle fibres as revealed through dissection. He recognized that the laryngoscope was limited in that it did not always reveal the entire glottis (especially the anterior third) since the view was often obstructed by the epiglottis, especially when singing in chest voice (Garcia 1855, 408; Large 1980a, 130). Garcia's 1855 article led to the general use of the laryngoscope as the chief diagnostic tool in the medical practice of laryngology.

Garcia's final work, *Hints on Singing* (1894), was a response to some of the criticisms that had been leveled at his theories over the years. Garcia was true to his convictions, and did not back down from the vocal concepts he had held since his *Traité* of 1841. He taught at the Royal Academy of Music until 1895, and he continued to teach privately until shortly before his death in 1906 at 101 years of age – 36 years beyond today's mandatory retirement age.

Manuel Garcia was highly successful as a teacher. His pupils included (in addition to his sisters Maria Malibran and Pauline Viardot) Mathilde Marchesi, Charles Bataille, Julius Stockhausen, Sir Charles Santley, Henrietta Nissen, Antoinette Sterling, Johanna Wagner (Richard Wagner's niece), Catherine Hayes, and the most famous of them all, the 'Swedish Nightingale,' Jenny Lind. Garcia seems to have been most successful with sopranos and mezzo-sopranos. Mathilde Marchesi (who accepted only female pupils) established her own school, where she taught such famous singers as Emma Calvé, Emma Eames, Nellie Melba, and her own daughter Blanche Marchesi. Her influential vocal tutor, based on Garcia's teaching, went through several editions and is available in a modern reprint edition (M. Marchesi 1877, 1970). Charles Bataille, a medical doctor who studied with Garcia in Paris before entering the Paris Opéra as a bass, published a pamphlet on vocal physiology (Bataille 1861). Julius Stockhausen studied with Garcia in Paris and followed him to London. He returned to Germany where he became a celebrated lieder singer, and in 1856 gave the first public performance of Schubert's *Die schöne Müllerin* in Vienna. Brahms wrote the *Magelone Lieder* and the baritone part of the *Deutsches Requiem* especially for him. Stockhausen founded his own school in Frankfurt am Main in 1880, and his important vocal treatise, based upon Garcia's, was published in both German and English in 1884 (Stockhausen 1884). Hugo Goldschmidt, who studied with Stockhausen in Frankfurt am Main from 1887 to 1905, became an important musicologist and wrote several books on the history of Italian singing.[2] Another pupil of Stockhausen, Max Friedlaender, studied first with Garcia in Paris and London. Friedlaender became a Schubert scholar and edited the widely used Peters edition of Schubert's songs. Garcia's influence as both scholar and teacher is thus well represented in his students.

The Larynx

Before looking at Garcia's description of the *coup de la glotte*, it is necessary to make a few preliminary remarks about vocal physiology. Any discussion of the larynx is bound to be a gristly business, as it involves the cartilages, muscles, and ligaments of the vocal mechanism. Garcia's *Traité* was one of the first singing methods to look seriously at the physiology of singing. He admitted that the vocal apparatus is 'rather complex on the whole,' and he addressed his remarks 'not to physiologists, but to singers.' He borrowed from science 'only the details strictly necessary for the intelligence of our theories,' and admonished his readers to 'be not at all frightened by them; these few terms will easily become familiar to them and cannot be the occasion of a real difficulty' (Garcia 1847, 1:5; 1984, xxxv). Garcia's reasonable approach has been adopted in this book.

The larynx is located at the uppermost end of the trachea and is comprised of several cartilages that form the enclosure, or voice box, for the vocal folds (until recently called 'vocal cords' or even 'vocal chords'!). These cartilages are connected by synovial (movable) joints and ligaments, and they change position relative to each other primarily by means of the 'intrinsic' vocal muscles – the muscles within the laryngeal enclosure. As well, the entire laryngeal structure is positioned and moved vertically in the neck by means of extrinsic, or 'strap' muscles which attach to points outside the larynx.

The foundation of the larynx is the cricoid cartilage, a complete ring of gristle that forms the top ring of the trachea. Sitting on top of the rear portion of the cricoid are the paired arytenoid cartilages; these small, pyramid-shaped cartilages with triangular bases move upon the cricoid. Each arytenoid has three prongs: a forward-extending one, which inserts into the vocal fold itself, called the vocal process; an outward-extending one called the muscular process; and an upward and backward-extending one called the apex or 'corniculate.' The largest cartilage, the thyroid, also sits upon the cricoid; it is shield-shaped, and the portion (in men) that protrudes from the neck is called the 'Adam's apple.' The intrinsic muscles of the larynx are named after the cartilages to which they are attached; when these muscles contract, they move the cartilages relative to each other and in so doing affect the shape of the glottis (Sataloff 1991, 7–12; Zemlin 1968, 119–28).

The glottis is the variable opening between the vocal folds. These folds, comprised of the thyroarytenoid or vocalis muscle(s) and a mucosal cover layer, including the vocal ligament, extend from their fixed anterior ends at the angle of the thyroid cartilage to their posterior ends at the vocal processes of the arytenoid cartilages. The glottis can be measured in its entire length as well as in two discrete portions. The membranous, or ligamental portion comprises about three-fifths of the total length of the glottis, and extends from the insertion of the vocal folds at the thyroid angle to the forward tips of the vocal processes. The cartilagenous glottis makes up the remaining two-fifths of the total length of the glottis, and is comprised of the vocal processes and the medial surfaces of the arytenoids. The vocal processes project into the vocal folds themselves, and can either participate in the oscillations of phonation or remain fixed in an adductory (closed) position. Zemlin notes, 'The membranous portion of the vibrating vocal folds appears to be the most active, although the cartilagenous portion also enters into vibration' (Zemlin 1998, 119). The adult male larynx is about 20 per cent larger than the female larynx. The membranous portion of the male glottis is about 60 per cent longer than the female, and the vocal folds are also thicker.[3] The shape of the glottis for phonation is controlled by a 'subtle, delicate interplay of the various muscle actions.' Varying degrees of glottal constriction lead to various voice qualities, although 'the exact relationship between muscular contraction and laryngeal behavior is not known with absolute certainty, and is a subject for some speculation' (Zemlin 1968, 174, 173).

Various terms have been coined to describe the muscular forces that lead to these degrees of glottal closure, as illustrated below. Figure 1.1, a schematic drawing of the larynx seen from above, shows the effects of *adductive tension* on the shape of the glottis. In adductive tension the posterior ends of the arytenoid cartilages, called the muscular processes, are drawn together by the contraction of the interarytenoid muscles, which leads to a 'five-fifths' glottis that includes both the membranous and the cartilagenous glottis.

Figure 1.2 shows how the shape of the glottis is affected when *medial compression* is added to adductive tension. These combined adductive forces result in a powerful squeeze which clamps the arytenoid cartilages together along their midline, thereby allowing only the three-fifths, or membranous portion of the glottis to vibrate.

The shortened glottis that results from the combination of adductive tension and medial compression can be amplified by the action of *longitudinal tension*, as illustrated in Figure 1.3. As the cricothyroid muscle contracts, it causes the thyroid cartilage to rock forward and downward on the cricoid cartilage. The arytenoid cartilages, which are attached to

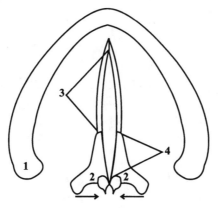

Figure 1.1 Adductive tension: the larynx as seen from above, surrounded by the thyroid cartilage (1). This figure illustrates the effect of adductive tension on the shape of the glottis. The contraction of the interarytenoid muscles (indicated by arrows) pulls the muscular processes (2) of the arytenoid cartilages together. The resulting five-fifths glottis includes both the membranous glottis (3) and the cartilagenous glottis (4).

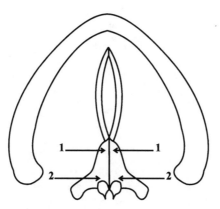

Figure 1.2 Medial compression: the shape of the glottis when medial compression (arrow 1) is added to adductive tension (arrow 2), resulting in a strong squeeze along the midline of the cartilagenous glottis. This confines the vibrating portion of the glottis to the three-fifths membranous portion.

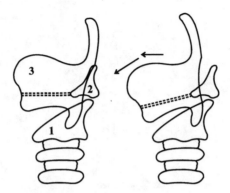

Figure 1.3 Longitudinal tension. A side view of the larynx. As the cricothyroid muscle contracts, it causes the thyroid cartilage (1) to rock forward and downward (indicated by arrows) on the cricoid cartilage (2). The arytenoid cartilages (3), which are attached to the posterior ends of the vocal folds, hardly move, causing the vocal folds (shown in broken lines) to stretch and stiffen.

the posterior ends of the vocal folds, scarcely move. This causes the vocal folds to stretch and stiffen as the thyroarytenoid muscles contract in antagonism to the cricothyroid muscles.[4] Van den Berg summarized these muscular actions as follows:

A contraction of the (powerful) interarytenoid muscles primarily adducts the apexes of the arytenoids and closes the back part of them so that no wild air can escape ... A contraction of the lateral cricoarytenoid muscles adducts the vocal processes of the arytenoids and therefore the body of the vocal folds. This adduction is augmented by a contraction of the lateral parts of the thyroarytenoid muscles (this contraction goes along with an adduction of the vocal folds). These adductional forces provide a medial compression of the vocal folds and reduce the length of the glottis which is effectively free to vibrate. (van den Berg 1968c, 294)

Zemlin notes that 'it is of utmost importance to realize that any changes brought about in the larynx are the result of the algebraic sum of the various forces in action' (Zemlin 1968, 191; 1938, 130–2). The combined action of these muscular contractions in glottal closure are sometimes referred to as *adductive force* (Leanderson and Sundberg 1988, 8).

Garcia's Theory of Glottal Closure

Manuel Garcia was the first to describe these different types of glottal closure. He maintained that the singer should have 'some exact scientific notions on the formation and the action of the vocal organ' (Mackenzie 1890, 75–7). His description of the vocal folds in the 1872 edition of the *Traité* clearly points out the difference between the cartilagenous and the membranous portions of the vocal folds: 'Let us notice henceforth that they are not homogeneous throughout their length; the posterior two fifths are formed by a cartilagenous prolongation, and the anterior three fifths by a tendon' (Garcia 1984, 205). In the 1847 edition of his *Traité*, even before his invention of the laryngoscope, he said: 'It is necessary to know that the lips of the glottis can vibrate equally, either when the posterior extremities are put into contact (by the bringing together of the internal processes of the arytenoids), or when these extremities remain separated. In the first case, the sounds are emitted with all the brilliance possible; in the second, the voice takes a dull character' (Garcia 1847, 2:54; 1975, 152). In a lengthy footnote, Garcia elaborates on this point:

This important idea merits some developments. When one very vigorously pinches the arytenoids together, the glottis is represented only by a narrow or elliptical slit, through which the air driven out by the lungs must escape. Here each molecule of air is subjected to the laws of vibration, and the voice takes on a very pronounced brilliance. If, on the contrary, the arytenoids are separated, the glottis assumes the shape of an isoceles triangle, the little side of which is formed between the arytenoids. One can then produce only extremely dull notes, and, in spite of the weakness of the resulting sounds, the air escapes in such abundance that the lungs are exhausted in a few moments. This enormous expenditure of air, which coincides with the production of veiled tones, indicates, according to us, that the glottis assumes the triangular form. One understands in fact that the air does not encounter any resistance toward the base of the triangle, and that it passes freely through the glottis almost without receiving any vibrations from it. It is only at the summit of the angle which parts from the thyroid cartilage that the condensations and rarefactions of the air are formed in a complete manner. Likewise, but in the opposite way, the brilliance of the sounds and the fourfold or fivefold duration of the breath indicates that the organ is offering no more than a linear or elliptical slit. (Garcia 1847, 2:54; 1975, 152–3)

When Garcia could actually see the vocal folds with the laryngoscope, he modified his description of glottal closure. He found that the triangular glottal shape that he had earlier associated with breathy voice did not in fact occur. Rather, when the glottis was 'agitated by large and loose vibrations throughout its entire extent,' including the cartilagenous portion, the tone emitted was 'veiled and feeble.' On the other hand, when the firm closure of the arytenoids brought the vocal processes into deep contact, a full and vibrant sound was created. This deep contact was critical to firm glottal closure. Said Garcia: 'This deep contact, which continues even after the apophoses [vocal processes] no longer partake in the vibrations, gives a deep tension to the membranes, increases the depth of their contact, and, as a necessary consequence, augments the resistance they present to the air' (Garcia 1855, 408; Large 1980a, 125).

Here Garcia was advocating a form of firm glottal closure in which there was strong adduction with deep contact of the vocal folds and a shortened glottis, producing a brilliant tone quality and requiring minimum airflow in order to sing efficiently. Firm closure was accompanied by a high degree of *tonicity* – that is, a state of partial contraction characteristic of normal muscle – in the surrounding pharyngeal musculature. He reiterated this when he said, 'it is necessary to conclude that the brilliance of the voice results from the firm closure of the glottis after each pulsation ... the glottis should close hermetically after each vibration; for, as we have just seen, if the air found a constant outlet, then the largest excursions of the glottis and the strongest expenditure of air would produce precisely the weakest tones' (Garcia 1984, 27).

Garcia's Theory of the *Coup de la glotte*

Of all Garcia's theories about singing, the most radical, influential, and controversial is his *coup de la glotte*, or 'stroke of the glottis.' The *coup de la glotte* is a technique of beginning a tone, including both the 'setting up' action of the vocal muscles prior to phonation (prephonatory set), and the actual initiation of phonation. Garcia's description of the *coup de la glotte* in his *Traité* begins with detailed instructions concerning the correct position of the body and the articulators and the long, slow inhalation. He goes on to say:

After you are thus prepared and when the lungs are full of air, without stiffening either the phonator [1872: throat] or any part of the body, but calmly and easily, attack the tones very distinctly with a light stroke of the glottis on a very clear [a] vowel. The [a] will be taken well at the bottom of the throat [1872: right at the glottis], in order that no obstacle may be opposed to the emission of the sound. In these conditions the tones should come out with ring and roundness ... It is necessary to prepare the stroke of the glottis by closing it, which stops and momentarily accumulates some air in the passage; then, much as a rupture operates as a means of relaxation, one opens it with an incisive and vigorous stroke, similar to the action of the lips in pronouncing the consonant [p]. This stroke of the throat also resembles the action of the palatal arch performing the movement necessary for the articulation of the consonant [k]. (Garcia 1847, 1:25; 1984, 41–2)

Here Garcia advocates a prephonatory setting in which the arytenoids are firmly closed, the pharyngeal tissues are firm, and there is a slight buildup of subglottal pressure. What is not so clear is the degree and force of the glottal opening at the onset of phonation. His comparison of the glottal opening to the facial lips when pronouncing [p] or [k] suggests a certain plosive effect, sometimes referred to as a glottal 'shock' – an explosion of the breath upon the onset of the tone. Indeed, many of Garcia's critics understood it that way. In response to those critics, Garcia added the following paragraph to his 1872 edition of the *Traité*:

One must guard against confusing the stroke of the glottis with a stroke of the chest [*coup de la poitrine*], which resembles a cough, or the effort of expelling something which is obstructing the throat. The stroke of the chest causes the loss of a large portion of the breath, and makes the voice sound aspirated, stifled, and uncertain in intonation. The chest has no other function than to nourish the tones with air, and it should not push them or shock them. (Garcia 1984, 42)

In *Hints on Singing* (1894), Garcia again tried to clarify his concept of the *coup de la glotte*. Here, he describes the *stroke of the glottis* as 'the neat articulation of the glottis that gives a precise and clean start to a sound ... The stroke of the glottis is somewhat similar to the cough, though differing essentially in that it needs only the delicate action of the lips and not the impulse of air ... The object of this is that at the start sounds should be free from the defect of slurring up to a note or the noise of breathing' (Garcia 1894, 13–14). This last remark certainly excludes the glottal plosive and other forms of breathiness. In practical terms, it may suggest the opposite of a plosive, namely, the continued squeezing together of the arytenoid cartilages upon the onset of phonation, which would result in a tone with 'ring and roundness.' Finally, as late as 1904 Garcia wrote to Charles Lunn, one of his critics, 'I do insist on the attack; but it must be the delicate, precise action of the glottis, not the brutal pushing of the breath that goes by that name, fit only to tear the glottis, not to rectify and regulate its movements ... (My merit or demerit consists in having noticed it and given it a name.) No one who starts the voice properly can eschew it' (Lunn 1904, 21).

Garcia was indeed at a disadvantage in that he was required to coin a name for this glottal phenomenon; his choice of *coup de la glotte* was unfortunate, since the word *coup* (blow) has a connotation of violence that he did not intend. However, 'attack' – another term that has been widely used – is no gentler than *coup*. Franklyn Kelsey wrote, 'if Manuel Garcia had only hit on the idea of calling the *coup de la glotte* the *caresse de la glotte*, a great deal of subsequent misunderstanding might have been averted' (Kelsey 1954, 56). Today the term 'vocal onset,' which includes both the prephonatory set and the initiation of the tone, is commonly used. To the best of my knowledge, no other vocal treatises up to Garcia's time had discussed vocal onset in any detail, nor had any other authors placed such importance on the method of beginning a tone. But the *coup de la glotte* was the very basis of Garcia's method, because it had such a great effect on glottal closure. 'One should insist on this first lesson, which is the basis of the teaching' (Garcia 1847, 1:26; 1984, 44). He found that the first instant of phonation was the key to the cultivated tone quality and vocal efficiency necessary for operatic and concert singing. The *coup de la glotte* was a stroke of genius in that it provided the practical means for achieving a bright and efficient tone quality.

The Great Controversy over the *Coup de la glotte*

To many voice teachers in Garcia's time, the *coup de la glotte* was not a stroke of genius, but of madness. While it was the cornerstone of Garcia's teaching, it was also the least understood element in his vocal method. Despite Garcia's repeated attempts to describe it as firm glottal closure leading to firm phonation, it was most commonly interpreted as a glottal plosive, an initial burst of tone in which the vocal folds smacked together violently and then rebounded to allow a breathy tone. Even Garcia's biographer M. Sterling Mackinlay missed the connection between the *coup de la glotte* and the ensuing tone: 'The famous *coup de la glotte*, or shock of the glottis, with which his name is associated, has often been misapplied from ignorance of its real object, which was to ensure that the vocal cords were closed at the commencement of the tone, and that there was consequently no preliminary escape of breath' (Mackinlay 1908, 285). Although Mackinlay missed Garcia's insistence that the singer *continue* to apply the glottal pinch in order to maintain firm phonation after the initiation of the tone, Mackinlay nevertheless defended the *coup de la glotte* as a form of onset. He noted, '[Garcia] was particularly annoyed at the way the *coup de la glotte* was misunderstood and exaggerated beyond all recognition by many musicians' (290). For instance, in 1892 Victor Maurel delivered a lecture in London on 'The Application of Science to the Arts of Speech and Song.' Said Mackinlay, 'This duly came off, and its main feature proved to be a virulent tirade against the *coup de la glotte*.' Garcia himself was present, and later wrote to *The Sunday Times*, saying that he had found Maurel's demonstrations 'extremely exaggerated' (256–7). Similar tales were told by Garcia's pupil and collaborator Hermann Klein: 'Possibly the practice of the act in question has been worked to excess by would-be imitators of Garcia's method; but certainly it was never so taught by him, and I have never come across one of his pupils who had suffered through its normal employment' (Klein 1903, 37).

Mathilde Marchesi, one of the chief advocates of the *coup de la glotte*, praised Garcia by saying that 'his ideas on the female voice and its development were a revelation to me, and they were the foundation of my own future career ... no Italian master could ever in any way approach Garcia in his method of teaching' (M. Marchesi 1887, 25, 29). She derided the methods that used aspirated or consonantal onsets as incorrect. In her own vocal manual, *Méthod de chant théorique et pratique* (*École Marchesi*), first published in Paris around 1885 with several later editions, Marchesi followed Garcia's instructions for the *coup de la glotte* closely. She described prephonatory set by saying that 'the glottis must be closed an instant before *Expiration* commences; in other words, it should be prepared' (Marchesi 1970, xii). Like Garcia, she also recognized the importance of the *coup de la glotte* to the continuation of the tone:

If the *Vocal Cords* are not firmly and evenly closed throughout their entire extent at the instant that the air commences to escape from the lungs, the lips of the glottis being unable to fully contract during *Expiration*, the sound will be weak and hoarse ... The firmer and more complete the approximation of the lips of the glottis, the more resistance they will offer to the air which escapes from the lungs, and the less air it will take to set the *Vocal Cords* vibrating ... The equal and continuous pressure of the air against the vibrating body produces *isochronous* (equal) vibrations, and maintains equality of sound throughout its entire duration. (xii)

This is the critical point that others missed: the quality of onset determines the quality of the ensuing phonation. What Marchesi was advocating here is firm onset and firm glottal closure for the duration of the tone.

Julius Stockhausen's description of the *coup de la glotte* also follows Garcia: 'The vocal attack is produced by the lips of the glottis being closed, and then a moderate explosion or expulsion of air taking place through the glottal chink. It must be distinct and decided, but free from harshness. The degree of firmness depends on the expression intended' (Stockhausen 1884, 9). Like Garcia, Stockhausen compared the *coup de la glotte* to the facial lips during the formation of a [p]. He also noted the connection between onset and the ensuing tone when he advocated the 'unchanged activity of the vocal chords [*sic*] once the sound begins,' and added that glottal onset should be accompanied by a lowering of the larynx to prevent making the notes 'poor and thin, and in the middle register often throaty and non-resonant' (xii, 119).

The drift away from Garcia's *coup de la glotte* seems to have followed two distinct paths. One path led to the description of a form of onset in which glottal closure and airflow are initiated simultaneously – a technique later called 'simultaneous attack.' Hermann Klein noted that the opposition to Garcia came mainly from Paris (Klein 1903, 37). He was probably referring to the prominent French doctor Louis Mandl, who was an influential consultant for the Paris Conservatoire. Mandl advocated the simultaneous attack in preference to the *coup de la glotte*, which he likened to a plosive (Mandl 1876, 35–6). Another influential book, *Voice, Song and Speech* (1883), written by voice teacher Lennox Browne and surgeon Emil Behnke, went through twenty-two editions and has been called 'perhaps the most widely circulated and oft-quoted vocal work of the nineteenth century' (Monahan 1978, 240). Browne and Behnke praised Garcia highly for his invention of the laryngoscope and for his clear description of the vocal folds, and they agreed with those who said the *coup de la glotte* was the 'central point' in his vocal method (Browne and Behnke 1904, 117, 153). Nevertheless, they failed to understand the fine nuances of Garcia's *coup de la glotte*. They provided what may be one of the earliest descriptions of the now orthodox three forms of onset: the aspirate attack, which they called the 'glide of the glottis';

the hard attack, which they called the 'check of the glottis'; and the *coup de glotte*, by which they meant the simultaneous attack. 'The vocal ligaments [folds] meet just at the very moment when the air strikes against them; they are, moreover, not pressed together more tightly than is necessary ... the attack is clear and decisive, and the tone consequently gets a proper start' (128). Clearly this is not what Garcia meant when he insisted upon pre-phonatory closure and 'pinching' of the glottis. In this, and many later descriptions of simultaneous attack, what is lacking – and what was crucial for Garcia – is a careful account of the role of the arytenoid cartilages and the glottal 'pinch' during phonation.

Sir Morrell Mackenzie was not a singer; he was a throat doctor and 'bedside baronet' to Queen Victoria, and was also one of the first private medical practitioners to set up shop in the famous Harley Street area of London. His widely read book, *The Hygiene of the Vocal Organs*, went through seven editions. Like Browne and Behnke, Mackenzie described the *coup de glotte* as 'the exact correspondence between the arrival of the air at the larynx and the adjustment of the cords to receive it.'[5] It is not surprising, then, that with the authority of Mandl, Browne and Behnke, and Mackenzie behind the simultaneous attack, the more specific meaning of Garcia's *coup de la glotte* was lost.

The second misapprehension about the *coup de la glotte*, one that did not endure, was put forward by Orlando Steed in 1879 and taken up by Charles Lunn and Edmund Myer in the last two decades of the century.[6] This was the theory that the ventricular bands, or 'false vocal cords,' are closed and inflated by the breath pressure before phonation, and opened with a false glottal plosive upon the onset of phonation. This, of course, had nothing to do with Garcia, but it served to further confuse the issue. Lunn, a prolific if outrageous writer, challenged Garcia and others in his several books on singing. His works were urbane, amusing, and quite eccentric. Yet his *Philosophy of Voice* (1878) went through nine editions. George Bernard Shaw, in a critique of Lunn's ideas, said in 1893, 'whilst Mr Lunn firmly believes himself a disciple of Garcia and an advocate of the *coup de glotte*, he has, as a matter of fact, spent his life in fighting against the practical results of Garcia's method of instruction, and is no more a *coup de glottist* than I am' (Shaw 1932, 2:126). Myer, quoting Lunn, said: 'The true point of resistance then is the approximation of the ventricular bands, the false vocal cords' (Myer 1891, 47–8). It is to the credit of Browne and Behnke that this theory, with its 'breath bands,' 'upper glottis,' and 'pocket ventricles,' was debunked.[7]

A far more serious enemy of the *coup de la glotte* was Henry Holbrook

Curtis, a New York physician who treated members of the Metropolitan Opera Company. His book, *Voice Building and Tone Placing*, first published in 1896, went through three editions. Blanche Marchesi, who was a staunch defender of the *coup de la glotte*, reported how a group of opera singers with failing voices, including Edouard and Jean de Reszke, met with Curtis and decided that the Garcia-Marchesi *coup de la glotte* was the source of many vocal problems. The group sometimes invited pupils of the Marchesi school, including Melba, Eames, and Calvé to their sessions, where they were shown 'the "bogey" of the "coup de glotte" and its terrifying consequences' (B. Marchesi 1932, 91–2). 'War was declared,' Blanche wrote:

> They could not distinguish between the hitting and closing of the glottis, and at once decided to condemn every method that allowed singers to make their vocal cords meet when emitting sounds ... At these meetings war was declared upon all followers of our method, and the artists' minds were worked upon passionately until they really believed that their way of using the voice was perilous. It was decided that vocal cords must be prevented from closing suddenly. This was the turning-point that brought about an error cultivated ever since ... This was the starting point of a new religion, but it did not stop there. It spread like a prairie fire, and all the ignoramuses, glad to find a new gospel at last, preached the pernicious discovery from the North Pole to the South. Dr. Curtis taught it to all his singing patients. He laid down in his book on voice a curse against all those who teach the 'coup de glotte.' This naturally meant Garcia and all his followers, including my mother and myself. (91–3)

While Marchesi was belligerent, she was nevertheless correct in her assessment of Curtis. Curtis complained of 'the singing teacher who commands her pupils to keep their palates up, sing in the back of their heads, and strike the glottis. Could ever villainy be more compounded!' (Curtis 1909, 149–50). This was a direct attack on Mathilde Marchesi. He added, 'The shock, or *coup de glotte*, is death to the voice; it is born of ignorance, and to teach or allow its continuance is a crime. We have no words strong enough to condemn it' (159). Curtis recommended the aspirate attack with a loose throat, and gave exercises 'for Acquisition of Relaxed Throat' (175–206). The battle lines were clearly drawn between the Garcia-Marchesi school, in which the *coup de la glotte*, with its firm glottal closure, was considered to be the key to good singing, and Curtis, Lunn, and others who advocated loose onset and a relaxed throat as a defense against the purported abuse of the *coup de la glotte*.

At the end of the nineteenth century the two camps became known as the 'local-effort' school and the 'no-effort' school respectively. In 1897 Edmund Myer, a New York voice teacher and author, wrote that nineteenth-century singing methods grew from scientists, not vocalists, and led to 'the *modern local-effort school* of singing' (Myer 1897, 20). He maintained that such local actions were 'relics of barbarism, so foreign are they to all true principles of voice use.' He said that a 'natural or automatic adjustment' of the vocal organs could be trusted to result in good singing, and that there should be 'non-interference or non-local control above the organ of sound' (11, 30–34). Shaw, who coined the term 'no-effort school,' was himself as anti-scientific and as anti-*coup de la glotte* as the others; he was also anti-Garcia and anti-Royal Academy (Shaw 1932, 2:209–14, 248–9). However, despite his apparent disdain for voice teachers, he seemed to relish getting into the fray with them. This may have had something to do with the fact that Shaw's mother was a voice teacher, and that Shaw himself had once aspired to become a singer.

The no-effort school continued to flourish after the turn of the century. David Alva Clippinger, a Chicago singer and choral conductor, said, 'The most important physical sensation is that of the absence of all effort' (Clippinger 1910, 4; Monahan 1978, 181). In *New Light on the Old Italian Method*, David C. Taylor spoke against all forms of local effort. 'Abandon the wrong action by relaxing the grip on the throat, then the tone will free itself of its own accord and come out clearly' (Taylor 1916, 84–5). He rejected voice science utterly, saying 'Scientific methods of voice culture are a complete failure. This fact is so well known to all who are actively interested in the subject that it need be supported by no proof' (70). Rather, he advocated 'natural' singing that required only a good physical and mental ear:

For the production of vocal tones of any kind, the mental ear is the guide to the voice. The desired tone is first conceived in the mind; the vocal organs then adjust themselves for the formation of the tone. A message is carried by the nerves, from the brain to the muscles of the vocal organs, bidding them to perform whatever movements are necessary for the tone demanded by the mental ear. The vocal organs instantly obey this command. Nature has endowed them with an instinct by which they know what adjustments to make in order to carry out the command of the mental ear. (8)

Vocal critic William J. Henderson wrote, 'All the muscles of the throat should be easy and reposeful in good tone formation ... Singers should never be conscious of effort in the throat ... The whole neighborhood of the throat should be kept quiet' (Henderson 1906, 39). In 1952 Norman Punt, a respected British laryngologist who specialized in treating singers and actors, echoed Henry Holbrook Curtis in his rejection of the *coup de la glotte*, believing that it caused vocal nodules, that is, small benign growths, usually bilateral, on the vocal folds. His remedy was relaxation: 'We would again emphasize that if you cannot sing a high note softly, you ought not to sing it at all – or at most only two or three such notes a week. Of course we realize that such advice if really strictly followed would lead to some gaps in operatic repertoires. We cannot help this. We are trying to help and advise singers. Heaven knows they need it!' (Punt 1952, 54). Punt's advice was both impractical and rather condescending to singers.

Modern Views of Vocal Onset

The debate regarding the *coup de la glotte* and other forms of vocal onset has continued right up to the present time. At issue is the larger question of relaxation versus the controlled balance between muscles. It was laryngologist Emil Froeschels, in 1943, who introduced the terms *hyperfunction* for excessive force of the muscles of the larynx and vocal tract, and *hypofunction* for muscular exhaustion and the condition of *paratetic hoarseness* (Froeschels 1943, 63). Friedrich S. Brodnitz, a well-known medical specialist in vocal disorders, linked vocal hyperfunction to tenseness in the vocal organs caused by the tensions of modern life. He especially condemned the *coup de la glotte*, which he mistakenly thought of as an abrasive glottal plosive as opposed to firm onset. He also cautioned against faulty respiration, the overextension of registers, poor posture, psychological factors, and many other aspects of vocal technique that can contribute to vocal damage. However, he did not subscribe to the no-effort school, or to the notion that relaxation is a panacea for all vocal ills. Rather, he said, '[Relaxation] is a popular concept, widely abused and based on mistaken notions of normal physiologic function. In our world of tensions, people have come to believe that all they have to do to overcome tenseness of mind and body is to "relax," and they usually mean by this the absence of activity.' He noted that in singing, vocal function is far too complex to be reduced to such a simple remedy. He said, 'Actually, alertness of mind and body and well-adjusted muscular tonus are characteristic for the normal functioning body. Every muscle, whether used or inactive, has tonus; it relaxes completely only in death' (Brodnitz 1965, 90). Another well-known voice doctor, Morton Cooper, held a similar view when he wrote, 'The traditional viewpoint is that relaxation must precede or accompany vocal rehabilitation.' He observed, however, that 'the process of locating and maintaining the correct pitch, tone focus, quality, volume, and breath support in and of itself is a tensing process' (Cooper 1973, 71). The message of Brodnitz and Cooper is that tensions are a normal part of our functioning as human beings, and tensions are also a normal part of singing. It follows that the *control* of tensions, the poise and counterpoise of muscles, results in good vocal function. This may mean relaxing some muscles, but it may also mean tensing other muscles in order to create muscular balance. Garcia's *coup de la glotte* and pinched glottis are based on this latter principle; the teachings of the no-effort school are based on the former.

At this point it may be useful to compare Garcia's description of the *coup de la glotte* with the orthodox views of our own time regarding vocal onset. As mentioned earlier, it is now customary to recognize at least three forms of onset: (1) 'soft' or 'aspirate' onset; (2) 'hard' or 'plosive' onset; (3) 'simultaneous' or 'instantaneous' onset.[8] In soft onset, the prephonatory setting of the glottis is open, that is, the vocal folds are unadducted or only partially adducted. The gesture of phonation begins with a short aspiration, sometimes heard as an [h], before the folds approximate sufficiently to create a tone. There is weak glottal closure, leading to loose phonation in the ensuing tone. Hard onset, in its prephonatory phase, requires strong adduction with a combination of adductive tension, medial compression, and a stiffening of the vocal folds themselves. Subglottal pressure is elevated as the expiratory muscles contract and the glottis remains closed against this pressure. At the moment of phonation, the glottis is suddenly blown open, resulting in a quick rush of air before phonation begins. This form of onset has long been disparaged by laryngologists and voice teachers alike for its abrasive effect on the vocal folds. Equally important, the quick release of air weakens the glottal closure, and this often leads to loose phonation.

The third type of onset, which is advocated by many, is the so-called simultaneous or instantaneous attack. Its exponents maintain that the expiratory muscles and the adductory muscles of the larynx should all be contracted at the precise moment of phonation, thereby eliminating glottal closure from the prephonatory phase of onset. If the breath begins in the same instant that the vocal folds adduct, so the theory goes, then there should be neither the breathiness of the soft attack nor the plosive quality of the hard attack. The trouble with this description is that it is seriously incomplete, since it does not specify the glottal setting *during* the ensuing phonation. Simultaneous attack could presumably be used to begin a tone which is produced with either firm or loose phonation, whereas Garcia's *coup de la glotte* admitted only firm phonation.

Garcia's *coup de la glotte* is significant precisely because it *does* describe a type of onset that promotes firm phonation. In its prephonatory phase, the arytenoid cartilages are firmly closed, however briefly, using both adductive tension and medial compression. Researchers Gould and Okamura asserted that the prephonatory setting of the arytenoids is 'the crucial period during which the entire character of phonation may be determined' (Gould and Okamura 1974, 359). Upon phonation, adductive tension and medial compression cause the arytenoids to remain firmly closed along their midline, so that only the membranous portion of the vocal folds participates in the vibration. This method of onset achieves firm phonation without a plosive, and is a clear alternative to the forms of onset usually described. Neurologist Barry Wyke has explained that the motor system that controls prephonatory set can be programmed to reduce the time interval between prephonatory tuning and phonation to as little as 50 milliseconds in trained singers (Wyke 1980, 46–7). Perhaps this is as close as one need get to a true simultaneous attack.

One further twist in the debate about the *coup de la glotte* represents yet another misunderstanding of Garcia's theory and is also related to the question of muscular balance versus relaxation. This twist grew out of an infatuation with the aerodynamic principle known as the 'Bernoulli effect.' It serves as a case history in how a theory can be shoehorned into a misbegotten shape in order to fit a new concept.

Daniel Bernoulli (1700–82) was a Swiss physicist who formulated a theory of fluids in motion. His theory states that along any particular line of fluid flow, called a 'streamline,' velocity and pressure are inversely proportional – that is, as velocity increases, pressure decreases, provided the total energy remains constant. The Bernoulli effect explains the lifting force on an airplane wing or the lifting of the fluid in an atomizer. In 1958, Janwillem van den Berg stated that the Bernoulli effect was also at work during phonation.[9] His theory stated that the air stream in the trachea has a constant velocity until it reaches the narrowed glottal restriction. As the air traverses the glottis, the velocity increases, thereby creating a negative pressure between the vocal folds, resulting in the 'snapping together of the vocal folds in the closing phase of the vibratory cycle in voice production' (Catford 1977, 33). Van den Berg proposed a 'myoelastic-aerodynamic' theory of voice production, in which vocal fold vibration is explained as a combination of muscular and aerodynamic forces (van den Berg 1958).

William Vennard, a well-known California voice teacher and researcher, was fascinated with van den Berg's explanation of the Bernoulli effect in singing. He wished to put it to good pedagogical use, and suggested that 'flooding the tone with breath,' and beginning the tone with an aspirate, an 'imaginary h,' or even a sigh, would draw the vocal folds together by means of the Bernoulli effect (Vennard 1961; 1967, 211–12). In their article 'Coup de Glotte: A Misunderstood Expression,' Vennard and Isshiki tried to explain Garcia's *coup de la glotte* with reference to the Bernoulli effect. After reviewing earlier misrepresentations of Garcia's technique, they said, 'Actually, an objective description of the crisp, but non-explosive attack had to wait for our understanding of the Bernoulli effect (van den Berg), which is a suction created when air is in motion, and which can draw the vocal cords together in a fraction of a second, provided they are *almost* approximated, *but not quite*, at the moment when breath flow begins' (Vennard and Isshiki 1964, 16). They reported that when they used the 'imaginary h' as a means of beginning the phonation with the breath, they came 'nearer meeting the condition described by Garcia for the *coup de glotte* than any other attack in this study. There is a flow of breath for a quarter of a second before the tone begins, but the ear does not detect the aspirate sound because the rate is lower and the flow is smooth. This momentary flow sucks together the vocal folds so smartly that there is a sensation of the breath striking them ... It is the belief of the authors that this is the attack that Garcia had in mind when he spoke of the *coup de glotte*' (17–18). Of course, this is not what Garcia described at all. He said, '*The vowels should always be attacked by the* coup de glotte, *and with the degree of force that is appropriate to the phrase*. One should scrupulously avoid having them preceded by the aspiration' (Garcia 1975, 11; the italics are his). Vennard's critical judgment was clouded by his misapprehension of Garcia's meaning and his zeal for the fashionable Bernoulli theory.

Not all researchers were persuaded about the relative significance of the Bernoulli effect in singing. One early objection maintained that there is no *continuous* streaming process during phonation, and that the frequent interruption of the air stream during the vibratory cycle may not allow enough time for significant negative pressure to be generated (Husson 1960, 31–2; Luchsinger and Arnold 1965, 26). It was also suggested that, given the relatively high subglottal pressures during singing and the presence of supraglottal pressure in some sounds, together with the strong elastic recoil of the vocal folds, the Bernoulli effect could play only a minor role in phonation (Scherer and Titze 1982, 79). It could also be argued that, since the wider glottal opening reduces the velocity differential between the trachea and the glottis, the Bernoulli force is actually reduced. Finally, in his recent analysis of self-sustained vibrations, Ingo Titze notes that the Bernoulli forces cannot distinguish between the inward and outward movements of the vocal folds, and that 'the mechanism for continued energy transfer from the airstream to the tissue involves more than the Bernoulli forces alone' (Titze 1994, 80–2). All these objections indicate that the Bernoulli effect in singing is probably less important than van den Berg, Vennard, and others thought.

Despite the many misrepresentations of Garcia's *coup de la glotte*, there were some voice teachers who continued to recognize its importance. Franklyn Kelsey, for instance, lamented that Garcia was so widely misunderstood, and said, 'The establishment and maintenance of a perfect approximation of the vocal cords is the key problem in singing ... he who cannot teach it cannot teach true singing, for it is the sole means which the singer has at his disposal *for launching a tone which has not an undesirable content of unphonated air*' (Kelsey 1950, 14; the italics are his). He asserted that 'since so many great singers have both practiced and recommended the *coup de la glotte*, the answer must surely be that all depends on how it is done' (48). Yet Kelsey, writing in 1950, seems to have been one of the last published defenders of Garcia's *coup de la glotte*.

Modern Views of Glottal Settings

It will be recalled that Manuel Garcia described two types of glottal closure in singing, which I have called firm and loose closure. He admonished the singer to 'pinch' the glottis in order to clamp the arytenoid cartilages firmly together, resulting in a three-fifths glottis that will produce a bright tone quality and low rates of airflow, as opposed to a five-fifths glottis that led to a veiled tone quality and high rates of airflow. Garcia based this neat theoretical construct on his knowledge of vocal anatomy, his examination of the glottis with a simple laryngeal mirror, and his instincts as a voice teacher. However, there seems to be a paucity of objective laboratory data to confirm this theory.

The shortened glottis described by Garcia was later called 'stop-closure' by Mackenzie, who said the phenomenon occurred only in high notes (Mackenzie 1890, 56–7, 257–77). The glottal squeeze was investigated by Joel Pressman in 1942, who found that in singing high notes, vocal fold vibration was restricted to the anterior two-thirds of the glottis. This is sometimes called 'Pressman's damping factor' (Pressman 1941, 1942). Zemlin described it as follows: 'When the folds have been tensed and lengthened as much as possible, further increases in pitch must be accomplished by a different mechanism, namely, damping. The posterior portions of the folds are very firmly approximated, and do not enter into vibration. As a result, the length of the vibrating glottis is shortened considerably' (Zemlin 1968, 195; see also Luchsinger and Arnold 1965, 80). Wilbur J. Gould, a prominent 'doctor to the Met' in New York and founder of the annual *Symposium: Care of the Professional Voice*, agreed that singers employ damping, using only the anterior portion of the vocal folds, to achieve high notes. He also speculated that this was related to high subglottal pressures and low larynx (Gould 1977). Gould did not go as far as Garcia, who maintained that the shortened glottis could be present not merely on the high notes but throughout the vocal range.

Phonetician J.C. Catford described two discrete glottal settings which produced different voice qualities. He called these 'anterior phonation' and 'full glottal phonation.' Regarding the shorter three-fifths glottis, he said, 'In anterior phonation the arytenoid cartilages are apparently clamped tightly together and only the front, ligamental part of the glottis participates in phonation.' In the five-fifths setting, 'the entire length of the glottis – both the anterior (ligamental) and the posterior (arytenoidal) parts – can be regarded as (potentially) functioning as a single unit' (Catford 1977, 102). This description resembles Garcia's, although Catford does not cite Garcia. John Laver, a follower of Catford, used the terms 'lax' voice and 'tense' voice for these two glottal settings, but recognized the pitfalls in these labels. He noted: 'A major difficulty in the discussion of tense and lax voices is that the adjectives "tense" and "lax" have been applied in such a variety of senses by different writers. It is extremely difficult to find alternative terms which would appropriately capture the underlying generality of differences in overall muscular tension between the two categories' (Laver 1980, 146).

Garcia's 'pinched glottis,' Mackenzie's 'stop-closure,' Pressman's 'damping factor,' Catford's 'anterior phonation' and Laver's 'tense' voice are all descriptions of a shortened glottis which results from strong glottal closure. While the shortened glottis seems to be a well-accepted theory among some researchers, more laboratory research into glottal closure is needed in order to produce the objective data that would better describe the exact nature of the shortened glottis. In the Appendix I will present data that supports the assertion that firm glottal closure can result in a shortened glottis throughout the singing range.

Not all modern voice teachers and researchers accept the concept of a tense, shortened glottis as a desirable glottal adjustment. As mentioned in the Introduction, there seems to be a bias against vigorous glottal closure, based on an assumption that such closure may be harmful to the voice. Voice teachers who emphasize relaxation are loath to use such words as 'pinch' or 'squeeze' in relation to singing. Some voice scientists have also veered away from advocating strong glottal closure. Catford and Laver, whose field is primarily the phonetics of speech rather than singing, both considered 'full glottal phonation' to be the 'normal' setting for speech as well as for the falsetto voice (Catford 1964, 32; Proctor 1980b, 55–6). They advised against 'anterior phonation,' maintaining that it results in a somewhat 'tight,' 'hard,' 'sharp,' 'metallic,' or 'tense' speaking voice, and is probably associated with a high laryngeal position. What they did not consider was the possibility that any tightness or hardness that might result from anterior phonation could be compensated for by controlling other factors, especially the vertical laryngeal position and the subglottal pressure.

Johan Sundberg, whose field is primarily acoustics, also cautions against firm glottal closure in singing. He discusses three types of phonation: 'breathy,' 'flow,' and 'pressed.'[10] He says, 'Pressed phonation is characterized by a high subglottic pressure combined with a strong adductive force, while flow phonation has a lower subglottic pressure and a lower degree of adductive force' (Sundberg 1987, 80). He uses the term 'adductive force' to refer to the ratio between subglottal pressure and transglottal airflow during phonation (Leanderson and Sundberg 1988, 9). Sundberg does not specifically describe 'adductive force' in terms of the position of the arytenoids or the length of the glottis. He says that pressed phonation seems to be 'affiliated with a raised larynx position,' and he maintains it is unhealthy (Sundberg 1987, 92; Leanderson and Sundberg 1988, 8–9). But, like Catford and Laver, he does not take into account the compensatory effect of laryngeal lowering on pressed phonation. His preference is for flow phonation, but again he does not provide specific data on glottal length, airflow rates, and subglottal pressures to help define this mode of vibration.

Recently, voice scientist Ingo Titze also came out in favour of flow phonation as opposed to pressed phonation. He defines pressed voice as 'tight adduction,' breathy voice as 'loose adduction,' and optimal voice as near the centre, but barely on the breathy side (Titze 1994, 227): 'A pressed voice is usually more efficient (aerodynamically and acoustically) than a slightly breathy voice ... But what price is paid for forceful adduction? An evaluation of contact stress and its resulting trauma to tissue is needed to get a more complete picture of what might be called efficient tone production' (245). However, even without such an evaluation of contact stress and tissue trauma, Titze goes on to call pressed voice *hyperadduction*, and breathy voice *hypoadduction*. He maintains 'pressed voice carries with it a higher risk of damage' and, like Sundberg, recommends the flow mode of vibration (249). He presents a theoretical model of several mechanisms of vocal fold oscillation in support of flow phonation, and he even seems to advocate Vennard's use of the 'silent [h]' as a means of weakening the adductory force (91–108).

It is interesting that in a study carried out by Ronald Scherer and Ingo Titze, a trained baritone was measured using 'breathy,' 'normal,' and 'pressed' phonation in both singing and speaking. It was discovered that the baritone pressed the vocal processes of the arytenoid cartilages firmly together during *all* the singing tasks. This was supported by evidence that the vocal folds had a large 'closed phase' during each vibration (Scherer and Titze 1987, 251). What is apparent is that, when measuring a real singer instead of discussing theoretical models, pressed phonation was discovered to be the preferred method of phonation. Voice scientist Thomas Shipp offered an argument against the notion that pressed phonation is equivalent to vocal hyperfunction. Unlike Sundberg and Titze, Shipp took into account the effect of a lowered larynx on pressed phonation. 'If laryngeal elevation does, indeed, facilitate vocal fold adduction such as during swallowing, a theory of opposites would argue that lowering of the larynx would decrease this adductory force. Such a gesture would inhibit the singer's hyperadducting the folds and producing "pressed" or "tight" phonation' (Shipp 1987, 219). It can be seen that arguments regarding glottal closure, which date all the way back to Garcia, are a matter of conjecture and disagreement even among today's voice scientists. This area of research needs more work, especially with observation of the glottal closure in classically trained singers.

Another factor may also play a role in the rejection of pressed phonation. If, under the term 'trained singer,' the researcher includes the choral singer who may have had some voice lessons, it is understandable that flow phonation would be the preferred sound, since flow phonation results in a tone which serves as the basis for 'choral blend.' Singers who use firm phonation and generate strong high-energy components in their tone will 'stick out' in a choral situation and ruin the blend. This is well known by opera students who are required to sing in choirs as part of their music degree programs, and who often sing with a different technique in choir than on the opera stage or the concert platform. Well-trained opera singers, on the other hand, should be able to sing with varying degrees of glottal closure, low larynx, and subglottal pressure, in order to meet the expressive needs of different styles and moods of music. In short, better controls are required in experiments where glottal closure is a factor. These are matters that will be resolved only when opera singers are used more widely as subjects in laboratory experiments. Theoretical constructs and computer models can be influenced by the vocal preferences of their designers. It is important to balance hypothetical assertions with experiments on real singers.

Closed Quotients and Patterns of Vibration

One of the most important consequences of different types of glottal settings is the way in which the open and closed phase of the vibratory cycle is affected. The 'closed quotient' is the percentage of time during each cycle of vibration that the glottis is closed, and the 'open quotient' is the percentage of time the glottis is open. The abruptness and length of closure in each vibratory cycle affects not only the quality of the voice at the voice source, but also the airflow rate, subglottal pressure, and intensity (sound pressure levels, or SPL). While Garcia was able to observe the glottis with the laryngeal mirror, he did not have the means to determine closed quotients.

The 'voice source' is the raw sound created by the vibrating vocal folds before this signal is modified by the vocal tract. Numerous studies have shown that strong glottal closure produces a large closed quotient and a quick rate of closure, accompanied by moderately high subglottal pressures and low rates of airflow. This results in a source spectrum that is rich in high-energy partials. 'A faster decrease in airflow toward zero at the end of the glottal closing phase [results] in a richer and stronger harmonic spectrum' (Rothenberg, Miller, and Molitor 1988, 246). On the other hand, weaker adduction produces a larger open quotient, higher airflow rates, and lower subglottal pressures, resulting in fewer and weaker harmonics.[11] A well-trained singer can control the adduction, closed quotient, and airflow rates to create a variety of tone qualities to meet the stylistic requirements of different musical styles. Depending on the musical circumstances, firm adduction and a brilliant tone quality may not always be desirable. Again, we can compare the differing ideals of tone quality between an opera singer and a chorister. Voice quality preferences play a role in determining degrees of glottal closure.

Another phenomenon that Garcia could not have seen with the simple laryngoscope is the patterns of vocal fold vibration. High speed motion pictures and videolaryngostroboscopy reveal that the vocal folds do not vibrate with a simple bilateral motion, but with a highly complex motion made up of several layers and phases. The viscosity of the vocal fold tissue is not well understood, but it is recognized that the moist tissue, or mucous membrane, has a high surface tension, and forms a loose covering over deeper and stiffer layers of muscle tissue. The different textures and contractile properties of the several layers of tissue can result in a complex undulatory wave motion of the folds.[12] This undulation does not affect the fundamental frequency of the tone being sung, but may have an effect on the quality of that tone. While the vibration of the folds is primarily horizontal – along the length of the folds – there is also a vertical displacement, in which the depth of the folds plays a role. This is known as the muco-undulatory phenomenon. Zemlin described it as follows:

From critical observations of high-speed motion pictures of the larynx, it seems that the vocal folds begin to be forced open from beneath, with an upward progression of the opening in an undulating fashion. Thus, the lower edges of the folds are the first, and the upper edges the last, to be blown apart. During the closing phase, however, the lower edges lead the upper edges. This mode of vibration produces what is known as a vertical phase difference ... The mode and rate of vocal fold vibration may vary with different conditions of pitch and intensity of phonation, as well as from person to person, to the extent that generalization may not always be well founded. (Zemlin 1968, 180)

Neuromuscular Control Systems

The critical relationship between vocal onset and the ensuing form of phonation is further explained by the neuromuscular systems that control them. Prephonatory set is largely controlled by the 'motor system,' in which the central nervous system sends signals to the laryngeal muscles, resulting in voluntary muscular contractions. The subsequent control of those muscles is sensory; it is achieved through a neuromuscular feedback system known as proprioception or kinaesthetic awareness, as well as through an auditory control system in which the ear monitors the sound and makes continuous corrections. Proprioception is sometimes called a 'sixth sense' or 'internal sensibility' (Kay 1963; Husson, 1962, 37). In the larynx there are special varieties of nerve-endings, called receptors: pressure-sensitive receptors in the mucous membrane of the subglottal region (which monitor subglottal pressure); stretch-sensitive receptors in the vocal muscles; mechanoreceptors in the joints (which monitor movement). Information from these receptors is fed back into the central nervous system, whereupon corrections can be made. Proprioception is thus a 'reflexogenic system' (Wyke 1974d; 1980; Gould 1971b; 1980). The auditory feedback system is sometimes referred to as the 'control loop' in singing. As soon as the singer hears the tone, control largely passes from proprioception to the auditory feedback system (Michel 1978). 'It is suggested that singing involves the sequential operation of three basic neurological control systems acting on the laryngeal musculature – namely, prephonatory tuning, reflex modulation, and acoustic monitoring' (Wyke 1974a, 261).

The coordination of these control systems is essential for good singing. In prephonatory set, the innervation of the adductory vocal muscles is very quick, second only to the eye; this is probably due to the protective function of the larynx in preventing foreign matter from entering the trachea.[13] Once phonation has begun and the vocal folds themselves must be monitored, the control passes to the reflexogenic systems of the larynx and to the auditory control loop. In effect, proprioception helps to maintain and stabilize the prephonatory glottal setting by preventing the vocal folds 'from being deflected from their pre-set posture during phonation' (Wyke 1980, 52). This is why Garcia's *coup de la glotte* is so important, and why a glottal plosive, which *does* dislodge the prephonatory posture, should be avoided. Once phonation begins, 'no neurological mechanisms exist to provide direct perceptual awareness of vocal fold status,' and 'the singer cannot exercise any conscious control whatsoever – which is in marked contrast to the control of the prephonatory activity of the laryngeal musculature' (48).

Conclusions

Manuel Garcia was the first to take the position that the preferred glottal setting for operatic singing is one in which there is strong adduction of the vocal folds, with the arytenoid cartilages firmly pressed together along the midline. This shortens and stiffens the vibrating portion of the glottis, and results in firm contact of the arytenoids and of the vocal folds themselves. This setting, which I call 'firm phonation,' is best achieved with what Garcia called the *coup de la glotte*, which I call 'firm onset.' In the instant before phonation begins, the arytenoid cartilages are drawn firmly together. During phonation, the combined muscular forces of adductive tension, medial compression, and longitudinal tension maintain strong glottal resistance to the breath. There is a large closed quotient of the folds, a vertical phase difference in the pattern of closure, and a muco-undulatory wave that may affect voice quality. Strong glottal resistance leads to raised breath pressures and low rates of airflow through the glottis. The resulting voice quality at the sound source is rich in high-frequency components. The prephonatory setting is under the voluntary control of the singer, since it is controlled by the motor system. The subsequent monitoring of the vocal folds during phonation is controlled by the reflexogenic system, as well as by the control loop of the auditory feedback system.

In contrast, the 'normal' glottal setting for conversational speech and some types of singing is loose glottal closure. The glottis is longer, the vocal folds are less stiff, and there is less vertical phase difference and depth of contact of the folds. This type of glottal setting is probably encouraged by either soft onset or a glottal plosive, both of which tend to lessen glottal resistance during phonation; the result is a relatively small closed quotient and higher airflow rates than with firm phonation. The voice quality produced by loose glottal closure is easily distinguished from firm phonation because it has weaker high-frequency components.

What all this suggests is that firm phonation is an 'unnatural' vocal adjustment not required for normal speech purposes or for some kinds of singing. I suspect it is rarely used outside of operatic and concert singing, and even there it is not used consistently; its use depends on vocal training and on the expressive demands of the music. Firm phonation is absent in most popular or vernacular forms of singing, especially those that depend on electronic amplification. Except for the opera chorus, it is probably also absent in most choral singing, since the brilliance associated with firm phonation may be inimical to choral blend (unless all the choristers can do it). Firm phonation is not 'user friendly.' The necessarily high level of effort and concentration on the mechanics of singing usually requires a special type of training that is specifically associated with classical singing styles. Garcia recognized that the first step in vocal training is strong glottal closure. His *coup de la glotte* was the key to achieving firm phonation, and was arguably the single most important pedagogical concept in the history of singing.

2

Chiaroscuro: The Tractable Tract

Chiaroscuro as an Ideal Voice Quality

During the eighteenth and nineteenth centuries, the ideal voice quality for classically trained singers was sometimes described as *chiaroscuro*, or, 'bright-dark' tone. Every sung note was supposed to have a bright edge as well as a dark or round quality in a complex texture of vocal resonances. The term was used as early as 1774 in Giambattista Mancini's *Pensieri e riflessioni pratiche sopra il canto figurato*, an influential vocal tutor that went through several editions, and was translated in whole or in part into French, German, and English.[1] In it, Mancini gave instructions in how to practise slow scales, saying 'this exercise will make [the singer] master of coloring at will any passage with that true expression which forms the cantilena colored with chiaroscuro, so necessary in every style for singing' (Mancini 1967, 42). *Chiaroscuro* was still the tonal ideal for Giovanni Battista Lamperti, one of the most famous teachers of the late nineteenth century. 'Although you may acquire a wide range of voice, you cannot modulate the sounds until the resonance of your tone becomes round and rich, *chiaroscuro* ... The "dark-light" tone should be always present' (W.E. Brown 1957, 38–9).

A modern description of *chiaroscuro* is offered by voice pedagogue Richard Miller, who considers it a necessary feature of 'the cultivated, artistic sound of the highly-trained professional singing voice.' He says:

An extensive terminology exists, in several languages, for the description of variations of vocal timbre found within the several [national] schools. One such term is *chiaroscuro*, which literally means the *bright/dark* tone, and which designates that basic timbre of the singing voice in which the laryngeal source and the resonating system appear to interact in such a way as to present a spectrum of harmonics perceived by the conditioned listener as that balanced vocal quality to be desired – the quality the singer calls 'resonant.' (*Transcripts* 1983, 2:135)

Chiaroscuro is a tone quality so distinctive that even a casual listener will quickly associate it with operatic singing; it can hardly be confused with vernacular styles of singing or with the choral voice. As we saw in chapter 1, the 'bright' element is associated with firm glottal closure, which produces a tone that is rich in high-frequency components – the 'laryngeal source' referred to above by Richard Miller. But this bright edge is only part of *chiaroscuro*. Simultaneously the voice must have a roundness and depth that gives it a dark quality. This dark quality is provided by the resonances of the vocal tract, that is, the air space, or 'resonance tube' between the glottis and the opening of the mouth and nose. *Chiaroscuro* is a voice quality that bears within itself a dynamic that is both complex and striking. It might be compared to the vivid contrast of silvery white and deep red on each petal of a 'fire-and-ice' rose, or to the taste of something sweet-and-sour. Even though there are many individual differences between the voices of trained singers, one quality which many singers have in common is the bright-dark tone of *chiaroscuro*.

The Early Treatises

The ideal of *chiaroscuro* did not spring fully formed from the head of any particular vocal theorist. Rather, it was developed by stages over a long period of time, as vocal theorists gradually turned their tonal preferences into a pedagogical concept. Throughout the history of singing, attempts have been made to describe voice quality in words. Such attempts have been understandably vague and subjective. From the rise of virtuoso solo singing in the late sixteenth century until Garcia's *Traité* in the mid-nineteenth century, vocal treatises and chronicles said little about vocal tone colour. Such works often admonished singers to sing with accurate pitch, good articulation, tasteful and flexible ornaments, accurate rhythm, and a tone which was stable, smooth, firm, clear, sweet, lovely, or sonorous. But none of these terms describes tone quality in any specific way.[2]

Some authors were more specific. For instance, Zacconi, writing in 1592, offered an unusually detailed account of different types of voice quality, and he made his preferences quite clear. Lodovico Zacconi

(1555–1627) was a singer and a *maestro di cappella* in Venice, as well as a composer, author, priest, and inventor – a true Renaissance man. His treatise *Prattica di musica* had limited circulation, but nevertheless his remarks on voice quality were later borrowed (one might say cribbed) by the Spanish theorist Domenico Pietro Cerone (1556–1625), who took over and translated into Spanish Zacconi's comments on singing almost verbatim.[3] Cerone apparently regarded Zacconi's remarks as authoritative, even twenty years after they were first written.

Zacconi lived at a time in music history when solo song was replacing polyphonic song as the art *à la mode*, and when virtuoso solo singers were emerging from the ranks of choristers and singers of part-songs. In a chapter titled 'On the types of voices which should be selected in order to make good music,' he differentiated between voices that were 'dull' (*obtuse, mute*), and those that were 'biting' or 'stinging' (*mordente*). He related these qualities to vocal registers – that is, the upper and lower registers common to all voices. The lower register was commonly known at that time as chest voice (*voce di petto*), while the upper register was called head voice (*voce di testa*) or falsetto. He expressed his preference for the bright and ringing chest voice, while discrediting both dull and shrill voices. 'Among all voices, one must always choose ... the chest voices, and particularly those which have the above-mentioned delightful biting quality which pierces a little, but does not offend; and one must leave aside the dull voices and those which are simply head voices, because the dull ones cannot be heard among the others, and the head ones are overbearing' (Zacconi 1592, fol. 77).

Zacconi's views were reinforced by the famous singer, voice teacher, and composer Giulio Caccini. His *Le nuove musiche* of 1602 includes an extended preface in which he discussed in considerable detail the techniques of singing to be used in the new solo vocal music (Caccini 1602, 1970). Caccini said that one should sing 'with a full and natural voice (*voce piena e naturale*), avoiding falsetto (*le voci finte*) ... without being constrained to accommodate himself to others' (Caccini 1970, 56). The 'full and natural' voice, at least in male singers, here refers to the 'chest voice,' which is the natural register of the male speaking voice; the *voce finta*, or 'feigned' voice, refers to the upper male register normally known today as falsetto. (This will be explored more fully in chapter 3.) The full quality and rich harmonic structure of chest voice contrasts with the thinner harmonic structure of the falsetto register. Caccini's remark about the singer not being 'constrained to accommodate himself to others' is a reference to solo singing, in which the singer does not have to worry about the choral blend associated with polyphonic song. It seems likely that the full voice of which he speaks had the quality of bite that was observed by Zacconi.

Caccini's remarks on voice quality and registers were echoed several years later by certain German authors who sought to establish the Italian style of singing in Germany. Music theorist and composer Michael Praetorius, in his comprehensive *Syntagma musicum* of 1619, took over large parts of Caccini's preface and translated them into German (Praetorius 1619, 2:231). Similarly, in 1642 Johannes Andreas Herbst wrote a description of the Italian manner of singing based largely on what he found in the works of Caccini and Praetorius. Herbst called for the singer to use a 'loud, bright sound without using falsetto' (Herbst 1642, 3; Sanford 1979, 7–8). As late as the first quarter of the nineteenth century, Garaudé's *Méthode complète de chant* (ca. 1830) described the preferred voice quality as chest voice with a 'round and sonorous' quality (Garaudé 1930, 20).

What we can modestly glean from these few scattered remarks is that the ideal voice should be clear and full, that chest voice is preferable to falsetto, especially because of its bright or biting sound, and that the tone should also be round and sonorous. These qualities, combined with a number of other techniques to be discussed later, marked the emergence of virtuoso solo singing in the late sixteenth and early seventeenth centuries. It is significant that from the outset of the new solo vocal styles, there was no pedagogical literature devoted to falsetto singing; rather, falsetto was discouraged and disparaged. Apparently the male falsettists who sang the upper parts in church choral music or sixteenth-century Italian madrigals were considered ill-suited to the new and expressive style of solo singing.

Garcia's Theory of Voice Source versus Vocal Tract

It was Manuel Garcia who first attempted to explain tone quality in a systematic way by making a clear distinction between the effects of glottal settings and the effects of the resonance tube in singing. As we have seen, his theory of the *coup de la glotte*, with its emphasis on establishing firm glottal closure, was intended to ensure a ringing quality (*voix éclatante*) in the voice. If there was loose glottal closure the tone would become 'veiled' (*voix sourde*). Garcia may have borrowed these terms from the castrato singer and teacher Crescentini (1762–1846), who referred to *voix éclatante* and *voix voilée* in a French version of his *Raccolta di esercisi per il canto* (1810, article 2). But this was only half the equation. Once that initial sound was made, there could be modifications of that sound caused by 'the changes in the tube which the sounds traverse.' The sound could be either 'clear' (*clair*) or 'dark' (*sombre*), depending on the position of the vocal tract (Garcia 1894, 11; 1847, 15).

Garcia's two-pronged approach to voice quality constituted a significant change from any previous discussion in the pedagogical literature. He first established this principle in his *Mémoire* (1840) when he said: '*Each modification introduced into the mode of producing the vibrations engenders a different timbre, and each modification which the tube of transmission undergoes modifies the original timbre*' (Garcia 1847, 1:16; 1984, 29; the italics are his). He reiterated this in part two of his *Traité* when he said, 'The timbre depends not only upon the modifications which the tube imparts to the sonorous waves, but also upon the place where these vibrations are born; that is to say that the voice receives its first character in the glottis, then from the numerous modifications of the pharyngeal and buccal cavities' (Garcia 1847, 2:54; 1975, 153). His most complete statement, perhaps, is found in *Hints on Singing*:

The student should thoroughly understand that the ring or dulness [*sic*] of sound is, in effect and mechanism, completely distinct from the open and closed *timbres*. The ringing and dulness are produced in the interior of the larynx, independently of the position, high or low, of this organ, while the open or closed qualities of the voice require the bodily movement of the larynx, and of its antagonist the soft palate. Hence, any *timbre* may be bright or dull. This observation is most important for the expressive qualities of the voice. (Garcia 1894, 12)

In the preface to the same book, he described how his observations with the laryngoscope confirmed these earlier statements. '[The laryngoscope] shows ... the manner in which the ringing and veiled qualities are communicated to the voices. These qualities – produced by the glottis – are distinct from the characteristics of the voice called *timbres*, and are originated in the pharynx by quite another mechanism' (iii).

In the dialogue passage that follows, he related these ringing and veiled qualities to glottal closure and to the rate of airflow:

Q. How do you obtain these bright and veiled sounds?
A. If after every explosion the glottis closes completely, each impinges sharply on the *tympanic membrane* [eardrum], and the sound heard is bright or ringing. But if the glottis is imperfectly closed, and a slight escape of air unites the explo-

sions, the impressions upon the tympanum are blunted, the sound being then veiled. The waste of air can be verified by placing a lighted match before the mouth. The brighter sound does not stir the flame, the veiled one will.

Q. Has this observation any importance?

A. Coupled with the theory of *timbres* and that of the breath, it puts the singer into possession of all the 'tints' of the voice, and indeed initiates him into all the secrets of voice production. (7)

The crux of Garcia's vocal method is found in the numerous ways the glottal source and the vocal tract interact in creating the 'tints' of the voice. In his *Traité*, he asserted that 'the dullness of the voice is corrected by pinching the glottis vigorously. The vowel [i] aids this movement of the organ' (Garcia 1984, 39). He reiterated this in 1894 when he wrote, 'The Italian [i] being the most ringing vowel, the same pinching of the glottis which gives it its brilliancy may be employed to give brilliancy to other vowels. Passing from a ringing to a dull vowel on the same note may also be recommended to improve the latter' (Garcia 1894, 15). Once a bright tone quality was created by the vocal source, it could then be acted upon by the vocal tract. The position of the vocal tract could be varied in a number of ways, including lowering the larynx, expanding the pharynx by raising the soft palate (velum) and by separating the pillars of the fauces (that is, expanding the sides of the pharynx laterally). As well, the singer could change the position of the tongue, lips, and jaw, which largely govern the formation of vowels.

Garcia noted that in an untrained voice the larynx rises as the pitch ascends (Garcia 1847, 1:9). A high larynx shortens the vocal tract and causes the vocal timbre known as *timbre clair*, while a lowered larynx creates a longer resonance tube and results in *timbre sombre* (Garcia 1984, 30–2). He also referred to the clear timbre as *aperto* (open), and the sombre timbre as *metallo oscuro* or *coperto* (dark or covered timbre) (Garcia 1975, 152). In the 1872 edition of the *Traité* he said that 'the most intolerable of all the timbres is the clear timbre deprived of brilliance' (Garcia 1984, 37). This tone quality, which he referred to as *voix blanche* [white voice], is produced with a high larynx and weak glottal closure. On the other hand, he said, 'The tone which [the pupil] should seek to adopt as preferable from the standpoint of instrumental beauty is that which is round, vibrant, and mellow [*moelleux*]; that is the important result which the teacher and student should seek together' (Garcia 1984, 37). The roundness and mellowness are created by the low larynx and expanded pharynx, while the 'vibrant' quality again issues from strong glottal closure.

Of all the possible adjustments of the vocal tract, the most important is the vertical laryngeal position, which significantly affects the colour of the voice. The 1840 report of the Académie des sciences confirmed the difference between the timbres after hearing a demonstration of Garcia's students, and noted that the changing position of the larynx could be easily followed with the eye (Garcia 1847, 1:4; 1984, xxxi). Garcia noted that as the larynx descends below the position of rest, the entire pharynx changes its conformation: the soft palate rises, the tongue flattens and becomes hollow along the mid-line toward the posterior part, the pillars of the fauces separate at their base, and the soft tissues of the pharynx gain greater tonus (Garcia 1847, 1:14–15, 25; 1984, lvi, lx; 1894, 11).

As we will see in greater detail in chapter 3, Garcia referred to the lower register as the chest register (*voix de poitrine*), and he described the upper register as comprised of two parts: the falsetto (*registre de fausset*) and the head register (*registre de tête*). Garcia maintained that either of the two primary registers can be altered by the vertical laryngeal position, although the difference is greater in the chest voice than in the falsetto, and becomes more distinctive above $D4$ (Garcia 1847, 1:10; 1984, lv, lix). Specifically, Garcia noted that when ascending the scale in chest register with *timbre clair* the larynx begins at a position 'a little lower than that of rest.' By the time the voice has reached the upper extreme of the chest register in *timbre clair*, the larynx has risen to approximate the jaw, and the tone is 'thin and strangled.' A similar phenomenon takes place as the voice rises through the falsetto and head registers in *timbre clair*. However, when singing in the chest register with *timbre sombre*, 'the larynx remains fixed a little below the position of rest. The lowering becomes especially apparent when the individual seeks, by a last effort, to exaggerate the timbre and to give to his voice all the *volume* of which it is capable. In this last hypothesis, the larynx remains immovably fixed in the lowest position for the entire compass of the register.' In falsetto register with *timbre sombre*, the larynx remains fixed below the position of rest, but to produce the head tones, the larynx almost always rises rapidly (Garcia 1847, 1:10; 1984, liv–lv).

Garcia reiterated that the clear and the dark timbres could borrow from each other, resulting in an infinite number of vocal colours (Garcia 1847, 1:24–5; 1984, 32, 36–8; 1894, 12). He devoted much of part two of his *Traité* to a discussion of the use of these vocal colours to express various emotions portrayed in music, and he provided lengthy instruction and numerous examples to illustrate where to use certain vocal colours in specific pieces of music, thereby relating vocal technique directly to musical styles (Garcia 1847, 2:49–105; 1975, 138–244). We will return to this subject in chapter 6.

Garcia mistakenly believed that the surfaces of the pharynx acted to 'reflect' and 'amplify' the tone, which is now known to be untrue (Garcia 1984, 37–8). Some later authors referred to these surfaces as 'sounding boards.' In fact, these soft tissues dampen or filter low frequencies in the tonal spectrum. Garcia correctly noted that a low larynx affects all vowels, making them darker, but that intelligibility is not lost if all vowels are modified in the same proportion (Garcia 1894, 45–6). He maintained that timbre modifications help to unite the falsetto and chest registers by means of the 'disposition of the pharynx' (Garcia 1894, 26; 1984, 46).

While Garcia's method allowed considerable latitude in the choice of voice colours, he considered the 'purest tone' to be that which was emitted with *éclat* and *rondeur*. This voice quality combined the brightness that he attributed to strong glottal closure and the darkness that he ascribed to a lowered larynx and widened pharynx (Garcia 1847, 1:16; 1984, 37, 46). While Garcia did not use the word *chiaroscuro* to describe this quality, his vocal ideal was nevertheless consistent with the definitions of *chiaroscuro* found in manuals by Mancini, G.B. Lamperti, and other advocates of the old Italian school of singing.

The effects of the vocal tract upon voice quality, and the role of vertical laryngeal positions in particular, have been widely discussed in the pedagogical literature dating back to well before Garcia or Helmholtz. In *L'art du chant* of 1755, singer and author Jean-Baptiste Bérard wrote (1710–72), 'All the art of singing, envisaged precisely with regard to the voice, consists of the correct raising and lowering of the larynx, and good inspiration and expiration' (Bérard 1969, 76). Much of his method book was a description of vertical laryngeal positions, which he felt should be constantly changing to suit pitch and vowel. After Garcia, other French authors, including Stéphan de la Madeleine (1852, 1864), Charles Battaille (1861), Jean-Baptiste Faure (1866), and Louis Mandl (1876) all remarked on the importance of the low larynx. Mandl in turn was quoted at length by Francesco Lamperti (1883). Emma Seiler, who was a protégé of Helmholtz and a piano student of Friedrich Wieck (Clara Schumann's father), wrote a book on singing (1881) in which she advocated low larynx. (In 1853 Wieck had published *Clavier und Gesang*, a short method book on piano and voice.) John Curwen (1875), influential English author and father of the tonic sol-fa method, drew upon Seiler, Garcia, Johann Müller, and others in advocating low larynx singing. Julius Stockhausen (1884) expanded upon Garcia in his espousal of low larynx singing. And, of course, the laryngologists-*cum*-voice teachers, such as Browne and Behnke (1883) and Mackenzie (1890) had to dip their oars into the water as well. The changing height of the Adam's apple was, after all, one of the only vocal manoeuvres that could be viewed directly with the eye, and was thus addressed by many authors.

Voix sombrée ou couverte

When Garcia first presented his theories to the Académie des Sciences on 16 November 1840, the subject of timbres and their relation to vertical laryngeal positions was a matter of considerable interest. Just seven months earlier, on 1 June 1840, two French biologists named Diday and Pétrequin had also made a presentation to the Academy. In their 'Mémoire sur une nouvelle espèce de voix chantée' (1840) Diday and Pétrequin reported on the radical technique of French operatic tenor Gilbert-Louis Duprez (1806–96), who was apparently the first tenor to gain celebrity for singing a high C_5 in chest voice in what was called *voix sombrée ou couverte* (dark or covered voice). This was the famous *ut de poitrine*, or *do di petto* (high C in chest voice) that set Paris on its ear in 1837 when Duprez sang the role of Arnold in Rossini's *Guillaume Tell*. Duprez earned a chapter in Berlioz's *Evenings in the Orchestra* (1852), as well as a chapter in music critic Henry F. Chorley's *Music and Manners in France and Germany* (1844), gaining both scorn and praise.[4]

Chorley told of pre-Duprez tenors who took passages of agility 'not merely to the heights – but to the pinnacles, as it were – of the extreme *falsetto*' (Chorley 1844, 1:148). One such singer was Domenico Donzelli (1790–1873), a Rossini tenor who reportedly sang up to F_5 (F above tenor high C) (Pleasants 1966, 160). Adolphe Nourrit (1802–39), who had been a student of the elder Garcia, and was a much admired tenor and a favourite of Rossini, apparently felt greatly challenged by Duprez's new manner of singing high notes in an extended chest voice. He went to Italy to learn the technique, and although he could apparently manage the feat, he belonged to the older style of singing that valued nuance and inflection over power (Pleasants 1995, 73). Chorley suggested that Nourrit may have wished for 'a chest voice in place of his own nasal and brilliant *falsetto di testa*,' as well as that 'honeyed and long-drawn *cantabile* which his countrymen were beginning to praise as an indispensible treasure' (Chorley 1844, 1:74). Chorley recounted the decline of Nourrit (who committed suicide in 1839 by jumping from a balcony)[5] calling it 'one of the saddest stories of compulsory retreat in the annals of the stage' (Chorley 1862, 317). Duprez himself praised Nourrit's singing, despite his *voix blanche* and his sometimes gutteral tones, and he felt somehow responsible for Nourrit's decline (Duprez 1880, 133–9). After Duprez, the *ut de poitrine* became a requirement for the Romantic tenor. It would be hard to overestimate the importance of the tenor high C, then or now, for the success or failure of tenors.

Apparently Garcia was quite 'acrimonious' about Diday and Pétrequin being given so much credit for describing *voix sombrée* (Mackinlay 1908, 131). He claimed that he had used this technique before their presentation to the Academy. In response to Garcia's complaint, the authors of the report from the Académie des sciences on Garcia's *Mémoire* added this footnote: 'In a letter which was read to the Academy of Sciences April 19, 1841, Mr. Garcia established that the lowered and fixed position of the larynx has been known to him since 1832, and that since that time he has not stopped propogating that fact by teaching it to all his students' (Garcia 1847, 1:4; 1984, xxxii). Garcia's proprietary interest in *voix sombrée* was perhaps an overreaction. Diday and Pétrequin focused their discussion of the covered voice on Duprez's high notes, and gave special attention to the volitional lowering of the larynx in order to extend the chest voice upward beyond its normal limit. Garcia, on the other hand, described the effects of the lowered larynx in all regions and registers of the voice, using both loose and firm glottal settings, as a means of achieving a dark timbre of the voice (1847, 1:4; 1984, xxxii). His treatment of *voix sombrée* was far broader in scope than that of Diday and Pétrequin, and was integral with many other aspects of his vocal theories.

Voce aperta and *Voce chiusa*

Garcia's approach to vocal pedagogy was by no means the prevailing outlook of the day. Far more prevalent was a 'traditional' school of voice teaching, based largely on oral tradition, and perhaps best represented in the writings of Francesco and Giovanni Battista Lamperti. Francesco Lamperti (1813–92), the son of a well-known Italian prima donna, had a long career as a teacher, largely at the Milan Conservatory. He wrote several vocal manuals, including *Guida teorica-practica-elementare per lo studio del canto* (1864), *A Treatise on the Art of Singing*, which appeared in English in 1871 and went through several editions (F. Lamperti 1916), and *L'arte del canto* (1883), which was translated as *The Art of Singing*

According to Ancient Tradition and Personal Experience in 1884 and also went through several editions (F. Lamperti 1884). Francesco Lamperti attracted students from all over the world, and produced an extraordinary number of first-rank singers (Stone 1980). Francesco's son Giovanni Battista Lamperti (1830–1910) was equally celebrated as a teacher. He studied with his father in Milan, and also served as piano accompanist for Francesco's pupils. He taught in Milan, Paris, Dresden, and Berlin, and, like his father, he produced a large number of illustrious singers. He wrote several works, including *The Technics of Bel Canto* (G.B. Lamperti 1905), but his teachings are best known today through *Vocal Wisdom: Maxims of Giovanni Battista Lamperti*, a book prepared by his pupil and assistant William Earl Brown and first published in 1931 (W.E. Brown 1957). While these 'maxims' come to us second-hand, there is no reason to believe that they do not represent Lamperti's views. The pedagogical approach of the Lampertis was based largely on timbres, resonance sensations, and breath control, often with no clear distinction between these separate functions.

The differences in pedagogical approach between the Garcia school and the Lamperti school were a topic of heated discussion in Europe. We can catch a glimpse of this, for instance, in the autobiography of Marjory Kennedy-Fraser (1857–1930), the Scottish accompanist and singer of classical art songs who became famous as a collector and arranger of folk songs. (Her *Songs of the Hebrides* published in 1909 are still perennial favourites of recitalists.) Her father, David Kennedy, was a well-known Scottish singer who saw to it that all his children received good voice training. Marjory considered her father to be a 'Lampertiite,' and her two brothers both studied with Francesco in Milan. She herself studied with both Mathilde Marchesi and with traditional Italian teachers. In her autobiography, Kennedy-Fraser discussed a number of details of vocal technique including the *coup de la glotte* of Garcia and Marchesi, the open tone of Francesco Lamperti, and voice placing. Her preference was for the traditional Italian method of the Lampertis, and she quite disliked Mathilde Marchesi as both a personality and as a teacher (Kennedy-Fraser 1929, 53–4, 64–7 passim). It is from such out-of-the-way sources as Kennedy-Fraser that one can get a taste of the contentiousness of voice pedagogy in the late nineteenth century.

The Lampertis, unlike Garcia, were quite content to leave the physiological aspect of singing to someone else. In fact, Francesco's introductory chapter on vocal anatomy and physiology in *The Art of Singing* (1884) was credited as an extract from Louis Mandl's *Hygiène de la voix*

(1879). Giovanni Batista Lamperti also cited Mandl in his book *The Technics of Bel Canto* (G.B. Lamperti 1905, 5). The Lampertis used traditional vocal terminology that lacked the specific physiological and acoustical reference points of Garcia and his school. Their comments on vocal pedagogy are often vague and difficult to interpret.

A case in point is their use of the terms *voce aperta* (open voice) and *voce chiusa* (closed voice). Francesco Lamperti quoted this statement by Mandl on *timbre*: 'Difference of *timbre* is entirely due to the small accessory sounds, and to the number and intensity of the harmonics produced by the form and nature of the resonance box, which in the vocal apparatus is represented ... by the pharynx and its neighbouring cavities ... It is the form given to the pharynx that determines the vowel ... In the close *timbre* the vowel *o* predominates, whilst *a* is the characteristic of the open *timbre*' (F. Lamperti 1884, 9). Francesco himself described *timbro aperto* as follows:

For the purposes of study, the pupil should make use only of the 'timbro aperto;' I would here warn him to be careful lest, by inattention to the rules of respiration, he should confound this with singing *bianco* [white tone] and *sguaiato* [coarse tone]. The open quality, as Duprez observes, should be produced by the vowel A, as in the word *anima*. It should be formed in the bottom of the throat, care, however, being taken that it does not change into O; since such an inflection, though it might give to the voice a more full and rounded character in a room, would render it smaller and without brilliancy in a theatre. (F. Lamperti, 1916)

This instruction implied that the singer should ensure a bright element in the tone for brilliancy, while ensuring a dark element as well by forming the tone 'in the bottom of the throat,' which may have meant lowering the larynx. This balancing of bright and dark elements is consistent with *chiaroscuro*. By saying that *bianco* is caused by 'inattention to the rules of respiration,' Lamperti may have been warning against too little glottal resistance to the breath, rather than referring to the manner of taking a breath. This interpretation is supported by another comment of Lamperti regarding the vowel [a]: 'This vowel must be absolutely founded upon the breath, and will become too open, or *white* as it is generally called, if the breath escapes before the vowel in emitting the sound. The same is true of other vowels' (F. Lamperti 1884, 13). This is apparently a warning against breathy onset.

Marjory Kennedy-Fraser commented on Lamperti's concept of timbres in a recollection of a session between her father and Francesco in Italy. 'His own "production" greatly pleased Lamperti, I remember – it was so "open" without being "white," and thus adapted itself to whatsoever "colour" he wished to use on it. He was a very high tenor ... but he could colour his voice so easily and articulate with it so perfectly, no matter what the pitch, that the public, if they thought of the matter at all, regarded him as a baritone' (Kennedy-Fraser 1929, 65).

Giovanni Battista Lamperti also discussed his preferred tone colour. Like Francesco, he indicated that the tone should start out with a dark timbre, and that the singer must be careful to avoid a quality which is too open or white. 'All tones are "closed" until "opened." When a tone "opens," the "focus" of vibration does not change. Return to "closed" quality is impossible if the tone becomes too "white." To bring word and tone to the lips, without losing the darker resonance is an absolute necessity' (W.E. Brown 1957, 53). At another point Giovanni said, 'In their inception all tones are dark to be opened or closed at will. This muted beginning evolves into the "dark-light tone" which is the ideal quality of the human voice' (37). Giovanni said that he preferred the term 'closed tone' to 'covered tone,' believing that the term covered tone was misleading (37). It seems then, that for tone production, both Francesco and Giovanni advocated a dark tone associated with an expanded pharynx as a starting point to be brightened sufficiently to create *chiaroscuro*.

Further light has been thrown on this terminology by Richard Miller, who visited many present-day Italian voice studios. He writes, '*La voce chiusa*, the closed voice, is a desirable condition in the Italian School, standing in opposition to *la voce aperta*' (R. Miller 1977, 82). Miller, like G.B. Lamperti, associates *voce chiusa* with covered singing. 'There can be little doubt that in desirable "closed voice" (*voce chiuso*), a timbre that should prevail throughout the singing voice regardless of the range, as opposed to "open voice" (*voce aperto*), there is a stabilized laryngeal position – relatively low – and a somewhat widened pharynx. These conditions together with proper vowel modifications (*aggiustamento*) produce the so-called "covered" sound of the upper range' (R. Miller 1986a, 151).

Helmholtz's Acoustical Theory

In many respects, Garcia's theory of resonance was simple, correct, and sufficient for his pedagogical purposes, but by today's standards it is incomplete. A fuller explanation of the particulars of vocal resonance had to wait for the development of modern acoustical theory. The foundation of this theory was laid by Hermann Helmholtz in his monumental book, *On the Sensations of Tone*, first published in German in 1862, and translated into English by Alexander J. Ellis in 1885. Acoustics was only one of Helmholtz's areas of expertise, but it is the one for which he is best remembered.

Helmholtz explained that the tones consist of a fundamental pitch as well as upper *partials*, or *overtones*, whose frequencies are in multiples of the fundamental frequency. From his studies with Johann Müller, a physiologist who had dissected human larynges from cadavers for experimental purposes (J. Müller 1837), Helmholtz understood that the glottis is the primary source of vocal sound, as it chops the breath stream into small puffs of air. He recognized that a strong voice requires 'perfect tightness' in the closure of the glottis. He remarked that music theorist Jean Phillipe Rameau had already described the upper partials of the voice in the early eighteenth century. Helmholtz especially noted that in the male voice there is an energy peak that corresponds to the highest octave of the piano, which he described as sounding like 'a clear tinkling of little bells.' He said: 'This kind of tinkling is peculiar to human voices; orchestral instruments do not produce it in the same way either so sensibly or so powerfully. I have never heard it from any other musical instruments so clearly as from human voices ... It is certainly remarkable that it should be precisely the human voice which is so rich in those upper partials for which the human ear is so sensitive' (Helmholtz 1885, 116, 103).

Helmholtz also established the framework for what would later become known as formant theory. Using tuning forks and resonators, he observed that there are resonances that are determined by the posture (today sometimes referred to as the 'articulation') of the vocal tract. These resonances, called *formants*, enhance the sound of any partials falling near them. Helmholtz noted that vowels are determined by the two lowest formants, and he also found that formants vary slightly between men, women, and children. He observed that vowel modification must take place on high female pitches: 'In singing ... especially at higher pitches, conditions are less favourable for the characterization of vowels. Every one knows that it is generally much more difficult to understand words when sung than when spoken, and that the difficulty is less with male than with female voices, each having been equally well cultivated. Were it otherwise, "books of the words" at operas and concerts would be unnecessary' (114). He said vowel modification is especially necessary in soprano voices above *F5*. Further, Helmholtz recognized the important relationship between the voice source and the vocal tract when he said that a 'ringing, keen and powerfully pentrating' quality of tone implies 'many and powerful upper partials, and the stronger they are, of course the more marked are the differences of the vowels which their own differences condition' (115).

Alexander J. Ellis, who was a disciple and translator of Helmholtz, wrote several important books, including the influential *Pronunciation for Singers* (1877). In this work he acknowledged Helmholtz's description of vocal resonance as an acoustical phenomenon caused by the interaction of the voice source and the vocal tract: '*All musical notes and all sung vowels have qualities of tone depending upon the relative loudness of the simple partial tones of the notes to which they are sung*. And this relative loudness is determined partly by the mode in which the air is excited by the vibrating body directly, and partly by the resonance of the air in a cavity through which the vibration of the air excited by the vibrating body is conducted before it reaches the outer air' (Ellis 1877, 9). But with Ellis, the study of *acoustic phonetics* gave way to the study of *articulatory phonetics*, which concentrated on the manipulation of the 'articulators' (tongue, jaw, lips, velum) in forming the sounds of speech. Ellis created *Glottic*, a system of phonetic spelling that antedated the modern International Phonetic Alphabet. At about the same time that he was working this out, A. Melville Bell (father of Alexander Graham Bell) published *Visible Speech* (1867), showing the position of the articulators during the formation of speech sounds. Ellis and Bell changed the emphasis from acoustical theory to a practical study of speech articulation.

Modern Formant Theory

It was the modern Bell Telephone Laboratories that returned to acoustic phonetics by demonstrating that vowels are created by formants. In 1952, Peterson and Barney published a seminal article in which they identified these formant frequencies in adult males and females, as well as in children, with the lowest voices generally having the lowest formants. Then, in 1960, Gunnar Fant crystallized the theory in *Acoustic Theory of Speech Production*, a major study in which he presented a 'source-filter' theory of vowels. According to this theory, the voice source – the glottis – produces a *harmonic series*, consisting of the fundamental frequency (F_0) and a large number of partials or *harmonics*. It has been theoretically posited that, if the sound source could be measured without the modifications of the vocal tract, the amplitude of the partials would decrease uniformly with frequency at the rate of about twelve decibels (dB) per octave (Sundberg 1977a, 82). The filter is the vocal tract which amplifies certain frequencies and dampens or reduces others.[6] The vocal tract has four or five important formants, designated as F_1, F_2, etc., in order of ascending frequency. While F_1 and F_2 largely determine the vowel, it is the relative strength of all the formants which determine tone colour. Of course there are individual differences between voices that are due to the physical makeup of each singer's larynx and vocal tract. This unique vocal 'fingerprint' is often an indispensable element in the success of the singer.

Since formants are resonances of the vocal tract, it follows that these formants can be altered by changing the posture of the vocal tract. This is important in vocal pedagogy, since it explains how singers produce different voice qualities. Adjusting the vocal tract in order to align formants with harmonics, thereby amplifying certain portions of the vocal spectrum, is known as *formant tuning*. The singer might think of this as colouring the voice, modifying the vowels, finding the resonance, placing the voice, or even projecting the voice. It is 'an intuitive act that has been practiced at least as long as skillful singers have striven to be heard against the background of other musical instruments.'[7]

An understanding of formant tuning in singers only developed gradually. Wilmer T. Bartholomew, Fritz Winckel, and William Vennard all maintained that the ideal voice quality has both a low formant and a high formant.[8] Their idea of both a low and a high formant, though incomplete, was consistent with the historical concept of *chiaroscuro*, with the high formant constituting the bright element, and the low formant the dark element. Johan Sundberg later refined these observations (Sundberg 1977a), and in 1987 he wrote, 'A long-time-average spectrum of the human voice normally exhibits at least one or more pronounced peaks. [The first] appears around 500Hz and is related to the first formant frequency ... In singing of both sexes, a second peak also appears in the vicinity of 2 or 3 kHz; it corresponds to the singer's formant' (Sundberg 1987, 130).

Formant tuning is highly dependent upon the vertical position of the larynx. Vertical laryngeal positions have been widely discussed in the voice science literature. The larynx can be made to move up by the contraction of elevator muscles, and down by means of depressor muscles, especially the sternothyroid muscle. The larynx rises when swallowing and descends at the beginning of a yawn. The larynx also descends during inhalation. 'The reason may be an increased tracheal pull on the larynx when the diaphragm is lowered during inhalation' (Sundberg, Leanderson, and von Euler 1989, 225). Trained singers may well take advantage of this lowering by causing the larynx to remain at its low position during phonation. There is general agreement that untrained singers sing with a higher larynx than trained singers.[9] Said Thomas Shipp, 'The most consistent finding across our studies was that singers trained in the traditional Western opera style principally sang with laryngeal positions at or below the resting level regardless of the vocal frequency or intensity produced. Nonsingers (those with no training) showed a strong tendency for laryngeal elevation with increased frequency. Further, nonsingers almost always had laryngeal positions above their resting level particularly at the higher frequencies in their range' (Shipp 1987, 218). In general, it has been shown that a low larynx darkens voice quality by lowering all formant frequencies, especially F_1. Tuning F_1 to H_1 only requires larynx lowering at frequencies that are below the F_1 for the natural larynx position. Lip rounding can also be used to lengthen the tube and lower the formants, but it affects F_2 most directly.

While lowered formants are certainly an important characteristic of trained voices, they sometimes have a negative impact on the intelligibility of the sung vowels. When the vowel formants are lowered well beyond their normal position for speech, the identification of the vowel can be obscured. This, as we have seen, was already recognized by Helmholtz, and it is a complaint that is still frequently directed at classically-trained singers. While Garcia advised singers to darken the vowels uniformly and only to an extent that their intelligibility would not be lost (Garcia 1894, 45–6), many opera and concert singers go well beyond this to the point that they cannot be understood. Acoustician Arthur Benade wrote, 'Most singers, throughout their musical range, constantly (though usually unconsciously) manipulate the vocal tract formants to place their frequencies at musically useful spots. These modifications in formant frequencies provide the major explanation for the difficulty we often have in understanding the words of a song' (Benade 1976, 386).

The so-called *singer's formant* (in Britain it is sometimes called the 'singing formant') is a band of high-frequency resonance that occurs at about 2500 to 3500 Hz. It can occur on most notes in the singer's range, although it is generally more apparent in male voices than in female, and is often stronger on loud notes than on soft. It is largely independent of the vowel being sung. This is what Helmholtz had described as the 'clear tinkling of little bells' in 1862. Bartholomew referred to it as the 'ring' of the voice, and suggested it was due to a lowering of the larynx which lengthens the larynx tube (Bartholomew 1985, 145–6; see also 1934). It can be explained acoustically as a clustering of F_3 and F_4, or F_4 and F_5, or in some cases F_3, F_4, and F_5, in which the distance separating these formants is narrowed.

The intensity of the singer's formant is dependent upon the presence in the source spectrum of high-energy partials that are created by abrupt and complete glottal closure in each glottal cycle (Sundberg 1987, 119; Miller and Schutte 1990, 231–2). Sundberg pointed out that the singer's formant enables a singer to be heard over an orchestra, since the orchestra's maximum energy is at around 450 Hz, and there is little competition from the orchestra in the critical range of the singer's formant (Sundberg 1997a, 89). This also echoes Helmholtz's observation of 1862. Equally reminiscent of Helmholtz is Fritz Winkel's observation that 'the ear has a particularly high sensitivity between 2000 and 3000 cps' (Winckel 1967, 98–9). The singer's formant is an acoustical phenomenon that does not require high vocal effort. According to Sundberg, 'The singer's formant serves as a means to survive as a singer. In other words, vocal economy seems to be the main principle behind this acoustic feature in male singing' (Sundberg 1985b, 208). It can be argued, however, that the aesthetic appeal of this tone colour is an equally important principle.

In the tenor voice there is another resonance strategy that has received little attention in the voice science literature, but that may be as important as the singer's formant. This is a type of formant tuning in which F_2 is tuned to H_3 or H_4. In the Groningen Voice Research Lab, spectral analyses of recorded performances by famous tenors revealed that on high covered notes some tenors use F_2 tuning instead of the singer's formant (Schutte and Miller 1996). The brilliance that comes from a strong F_2 has a different character from the singer's formant, and is perceived by this writer as more 'visceral' and 'dangerous.'

Formant tuning is also important in high soprano notes (Sundberg, 1977a, b). For these, the singer tunes the first formant to the level of the first harmonic (F_1 to H_1). This occurs on open vowels (vowels with a high F_1) from the pitch $F5$ and upwards, where F_1 would normally fall below H_1. Varying the vocal tract – for example shortening the vocal tract through opening the jaw, retracting the corners of the mouth, and raising the larynx slightly – the singer raises F_1 close to H_1 so that they reinforce each other. This strengthens the tone with little extra effort on the part of the singer. Sopranos often find this effect by trial-and-error, by imitation, or with the help of the keen ear of the teacher (Sundberg 1987, 132), and voice teachers sometimes refer to it as the 'bloom' of the voice. A second kind of formant tuning in the soprano voice takes place when F_1 and F_2 are brought close together and align themselves with H_1. This clustering of formants gives a single resonance to open vowels. D.G. Miller calls this the 'back-vowel strategy,' since it modifies the vowel [a] in the direction of [o]. It can be used in the middle of the female range as well as the upper, giving a somewhat throaty quality to the whole voice (D.G. Miller 1994, 13).

Resonance Imagery

Traditional vocal pedagogy, as opposed to the approach of Garcia and his followers, has been largely based upon indirect methods of achieving good tone quality, and this practice continues right up to the present day. Chief among these methods is the use of 'resonance imagery,' in which sensations of localized vibration are used as an indicator of good vocal function. There is an elaborate nomenclature that goes with resonance imagery, which includes such expressions as 'placing' the voice, 'focusing' the voice, or singing *dans le masque* (in the mask). All these terms refer to the notion of directing the tone to the bridge of the nose, the nasal pharynx, the sinuses or cheekbones, the back of the teeth, against the palate, and so on. In these cases the breath is imagined to be a malleable column or stream that can be aimed, rather like a garden hose with a nozzle. In other instances the image is of the stream being directed at some point outside the body.

Pedagogical methods based primarily upon resonance imagery were quite at odds with the theories of Garcia and his successors. In an interview published in the *Musical Herald* in 1894, Garcia discussed resonance imagery with Chicago voice teacher Frederic W. Root.

[Garcia's] great experience and his scientific habit of mind give unusual weight to everything he says. He was very emphatic in his recommendation to avoid all these modern theories, and stick clearly to nature. He also does not believe in teaching by means of sensations of tone. The actual things to do in producing tone are to breathe, to use the vocal cords, and to form the tone in the mouth. The singer has nothing to do with anything else. Garcia said that he began with other things; he used to direct the tone into the head, and do peculiar things with breathing, and so on; but as the years passed by he discarded these things as useless, and now speaks only of actual things, and not mere appearances. He condemned what is so much spoken of nowadays, the directing of the voice forward or back or up. Vibrations come in puffs of air. All control of the breath is lost the moment it is turned into vibrations, and the idea is absurd, he said, that a current of air can be thrown against the hard palate for one kind of tone, the soft palate for another, and reflected hither and thither. (Root 1894, 229)

Despite Garcia's protestations, resonance imagery has played an important role in voice teaching since at least the sixteenth century. Some of the basic terminology of singing, sometimes adopted by voice scientists as well as singers, is based upon resonance imagery. For instance, the terms 'chest voice' and 'head voice' refer to where the tone is felt, not where it is formed. Girolamo Maffei was one of the first authors to use resonance imagery. In *Letter 1*, addressed to Signor Conte d'Alta Villa, he discussed many aspects of vocal style in the emerging world of virtuoso singing, and he described vocal resonance as follows: 'Thus the voice resonates on the palate; by means of the air which is pressed from the chest to the throat and vibrates there, and is focused by the glottis and the nerves and engorged muscles, and is able to reinforce the voice which is emitted' (Maffei 1562, 16–17).

Although there are only scattered references to voice placing in the early pedagogical literature, by the late nineteenth and early twentieth centuries there was, in contradistinction to Garcia's theories, a whole school of teachers who based their approach on resonance imagery. The emergence of this school was sarcastically described by Blanche Marchesi, a Garcia devotée, as 'the foundation of a new religion.' Once again she placed the blame for this approach, which she called the 'nasal method of singing,' squarely on Henry Holbrook Curtis. 'Who has not detected within the last twenty years a tendency to more or less pronounced nasal singing? ... This was a mania for a system – a new system that was being preached and taught. Nasal voice-production was not the joke it had seemed to be; it was spreading all over the world, and not a day passed without bringing me one of its wrecked victims' (B. Marchesi 1932, 91, 95).

Curtis, the enemy of the *coup de la glotte* and the champion of the 'relaxed throat,' became a chief spokesman for the new method. His book, which he dedicated to Jean de Reszke, was based on the theory 'that the overtones introduced by the proper method of placing tone in the facial resonators induce a new plan of vibration of the vocal cords'

(Curtis 1909, vi). He said that 'to sing *dans le masque* ... requires the soft palate and uvula to be lowered' (154). This, of course, would result in a nasal quality, and is the opposite of Garcia's high palate and expanded pharynx. Curtis maintained that the sinuses 'have much to do with vocal resonance' (73). With pride, he quoted Jean de Reszke's remark to him: 'I find that the great question of the singer's art becomes narrower and narrower all the time, until I can truly say that the great question of singing becomes a question of the nose – *la grande question du chant devient une question du nez*' (159–60).

While Blanche Marchesi ridiculed Curtis for his fixation on nasal resonance, she herself associated the production of vowels with 'sounding boards,' thus creating her own brand of band-shell imagery (B. Marchesi 1932, 10, 11, 111–13). Mackenzie also recommended directing a 'column of sound' to the hard palate 'from which it rebounds sharply and *cleanly* to the outside' (Mackenzie 1890, 112). However, he added a warning that 'sensation is always an untrustworthy interpreter' of vocal function. 'Sensation, however, is a useful witness in confirming the results arrived at in other ways, and it can always be relied on when it tells whether an action causes strain or not' (63–4).

The Lampertis exercised similar caution. They often used resonance imagery, but they recognized full well that such imagery was illusory. Said Francesco, 'Strictly speaking there are no such things as nasal voice, head voice, chest voice, &c.; and, though we commonly speak of these, the terms are incorrect: all voice is generated in the throat, but the breath striking in various ways causes various sensations' (F. Lamperti 1884, 17). Giovanni said that 'what "goes on" above the throat are illusions no matter how real they may feel or sound. At the same time, observe that these illustrations of the senses of touch and hearing are the only proofs that the throat is functioning normally and efficiently' (W.E. Brown 1957, 39). He noted that such resonance sensations depended upon 'the initial tone in the throat, and not on your efforts to "place" the voice' (72–3). Nevertheless, Giovanni fell back on imagery from time to time. For instance, he wrote, 'The point of aim for the tone of the Medium Register is the front of the hard palate' (G.B. Lamperti 1905, 10), and he frequently said that the singer should feel the tone in the head, in the middle of the skull, or in other resonating cavities.

Resonance imagery was propelled on its course by Lilli Lehmann, whose celebrated book *Meine Gesangskunst* first appeared in 1902 and was translated into English as *How to Sing* (Lehmann 1916). As a singer, Lehmann could shift from Mozart to Wagner with no difficulty. In her book, she provided a bewildering array of diagrams and descriptions of how to direct the tone to particular resonators. She discussed resonance as 'whirling currents' of breath that fill the cavities and the 'elastic form' surrounding them. She insisted that 'the sensations must coincide with mine as here described, if they are to be considered correct; for mine are based logically on physiological causes and correspond precisely with the operation of these causes' (35). One rumour had it that Lehmann regretted this statement, and in fact tried to buy back all the copies of her book shortly after its release, but to no avail. Instead, it went through seven editions. As George Bernard Shaw said, voice books were a safe investment.

Numerous other authors also relied on imagery as a part of their vocal methods. Emma Seiler, who as a student of Helmholtz should have known better, described the voice as vibrating columns of air which would 'rebound from immediately above the front teeth' (Seiler 1881, 117–18). John Curwen also maintained the breath column could be aimed, 'and that this stream of air may be *caught* on different parts as the head itself is raised or lowered.' He suggested that tenors should 'throw the tone forward' by throwing the head back (Curwen 1875, 183–4). English voice teacher William Shakespeare rejected the idea of directing the voice to the forehead or nose, but instead described an elaborate sense of vibration at certain teeth (Shakespeare 1910, 31, 35–6). Even closer to the twilight zone was Edgar Herbert-Caesari, who said that the voice creates a 'focus ball.' He maintained that 'on the high notes we consider this focus, or *base* of the focus ball, as the reflected image of the laryngeal mechanism, or, in other words, the reflected image of the particular adjustment of the vocal cords for the emission of certain notes' (Herbert-Caesare 1936, 33–4 ff.). Earnest G. White wrote several volumes explaining what he called sinus tone production, in which he took the idea of aiming a column of air a step further. He maintained that it was not the glottis, but little eddies of air in the sinus cavities, that actually constituted the voice source (White 1938). Like Lunn, who compared the human larynx with the avian syrinx, White was urbane, witty, and dead wrong.

These excerpts are but a small sample from the many works which advocate resonance imagery as an important method for teaching singing.[10] Its exponents probably far outnumber scientifically oriented voice teachers. As well, many famous professional singers have learned to sing by using this method.[11] While some theories of resonance imagery are far-fetched, there are nevertheless positive aspects of this method.

Some authors acknowledge that local sensations can be an important feedback mechanism (Large 1972, 33). Vennard wrote, 'There is good evidence that when we are learning the shaping of the cavities above the larynx, we are training the vocal cords unconsciously at the same time' (Vennard 1967, 80). Ingo Titze recently defended some aspects of resonance imagery, saying:

A vocalist's sensation of where the vowel is localized (focused) is quite possibly related to the localization of pressure maxima of the standing waves in the vocal tract ... It is conceivable that some vocalists rely on these pressure sensations to modify their vowels as needed. Other sensations like 'singing into the mask,' 'resonating the cheekbones,' or 'aiming the tone toward the hard palate just behind the upper incisors' may also be related to achieving acoustic pressure maxima at specific locations in the vocal tract. (Titze 1994, 167)

Regarding 'nasal' resonance, Vennard conducted experiments that demonstrated that the nasal cavity was unimportant in singing (Vennard 1964), while more recently Sundberg discounted the importance of both the nasal cavity and head and chest resonances as 'not relevant to the major acoustic properties of the vowels produced in professional operatic singing' (Sundberg 1977a, 91). Nevertheless, from a practical point of view, it is often more effective to suggest to the voice pupil, 'Get the voice forward,' than to say 'Try to get more second-formant resonance in your tone.'

Among the many examples of colourful and highly imaginative accounts of resonance imagery in the pedagogical literature there is one in particular that bears repeating here. It is Blanche Marchesi's most delightful story about the composer Charles Gounod, who apparently dabbled in voice instruction. 'He never taught singing, but was often approached to do so. His only daughter one day implored him to give lessons to a young girl friend of hers ... Gounod put the girl in front of him, looked straight in her eyes and said: "Place your bow, let the urn of your voice pour out its contents, and give me a mauve sound, in which I may wash my hands."' Marchesi called this a 'poetical, but wholly unpractical, way of asking a pupil to make a sound' (B. Marchesi 1923, 287).

Conclusions

The vocal tract is indeed tractable. Adjustments to the vertical laryngeal position, the pharynx, the tongue, the jaw, and the lips can be coordinated with degrees of glottal closure to produce what Garcia called 'all the tints of the voice.' In the pedagogical literature, Garcia was the first to distinguish between the glottal source and the modifications of that sound by the vocal tract. Garcia's contemporary, Hermann Helmholtz, established the principles of acoustical theory in what is now known as the source-filter theory of tone production. Firm glottal closure creates a sound source which is rich in high-frequency components. The vocal tract can be adjusted to produce a strong F_2 or a 'singer's formant,' thus ensuring the brightness of the tone. The vocal tract can also be adjusted to enhance F_1, or to tune F_1 to H_1 to ensure the darkness or roundness of the tone. And, what is more, both the brightness and the darkness can be produced simultaneously in a single, complex tone.

For opera and concert singing, *chiaroscuro* has long been considered an ideal voice quality, with its combination of both bright and dark components. Singers have learned to achieve this tone colour through various means, including the age-old methods of demonstration and imitation, the suggestive use of descriptive adjectives, resonance imagery, and finally formant tuning. As well, male singers, especially tenors, have learned to 'cover' the voice so as to extend the chest register upward beyond its normal limits. This, too, relies on adjustments to the vocal tract, especially the lowering of the larynx. *Chiaroscuro* and the subtleties of formant tuning and covering are qualities associated primarily with the classical singing style. They are a trademark of the old Italian school of singing, and are as important to opera singers today as in past centuries.

3

Registers: Some Tough Breaks

The Problem of Registers

The human voice is often regarded as the perfect musical instrument – a model for other instruments to emulate. But, in fact, the human voice is not perfect at all, and like any other instrument, it must strive to give the illusion of perfection in the face of certain inevitable limitations. The most obvious of these imperfections, and the most difficult one to disguise, is the presence of discrete vocal *registers*, that is, the physiological and acoustical discontinuities that occur as the voice ascends the scale from the lowest notes to the highest.

Throughout the history of singing, singers, teachers, and voice scientists alike have asked how many registers there are, what causes them, how they differ from one another, how to join them, and how they differ between the sexes. The old Italian school held that there were only two registers – the chest voice and the head voice. In the eighteenth century this orthodoxy was disturbed by new theories that included other registers. By the beginning of the nineteenth century a three-register theory competed with the older two-register theory. Then, in his 1841 *Traité*, Manuel Garcia proposed his classic definition of registers, which has remained the reference point ever since. In this definition, he tried to create a *rapprochement* between the two-register and the three-register theories, but as with the *coup de la glotte*, his terminology was confusing and he was widely misunderstood. His disciples carried the controversy forward, adding their own twists, while a new breed of laryngologists-*cum*-voice teachers proposed novel and elaborate multi-register theories.

The transition points between the registers are often called 'breaks.' Teachers from the old Italian school advocated uniting or equalizing the registers to avoid a noticeable shift in voice quality from one register to another, but they offered little practical advice in how to achieve this. These are tough breaks to overcome. Not all singers are successful, and music critics were quick to ridicule singers, especially tenors, who shifted back and forth between chest and head registers. Gilbert-Louis Duprez's new manner of singing the upper tenor notes by 'covering' the voice rather than by making a switch to falsetto irrevocably changed the history of singing. However, some authors advocated a so-called mixed register that was associated with the older style.

Vocal pedagogues of the twentieth century have also addressed the problems of voice registers. Some elegant theories that appeared to be logical nevertheless turned out to be wrong, but the growth and sophistication of modern voice science now offers new insights into voice registers. Distinctions can be made between 'laryngeal' and 'acoustic' register phenomena, and these clarifications have helped to reconcile some of the pedagogical theories of the past. Through all these twists and turns of register theory, Garcia's definition of registers has proved to be flexible enough to absorb new ideas without becoming obsolete.

The historical, pedagogical, and scientific literature on registers is sizeable, and this chapter can do no more that point to the main developments in register theory.[1] Despite the progress that has been made in explaining registers, the answers are not all in, and researchers must continue to seize this problem by the throat as we enter the next century.

The Two-Register Theory of the Old Italian School

The two-register theory of vocal registers is associated with the old Italian school which dates from the beginning of the virtuoso era in the late sixteenth century. The most detailed early description of registers is found in Lodovico Zacconi's *Prattica di musica* (1592). As a *maestro di cappella*, Zacconi faced the problem of creating choral ensembles using ordinary untrained choristers as well as singers who had cultivated new soloistic qualities in their voices. He maintained that his observations represented the general understanding of his colleagues at the time, and were not simply his own personal views.

In describing the various kinds of singing at that time, Zacconi used the terms *voce di petto* (chest voice) and *voce di testa* (head voice). As pointed out in chapter 2, he preferred the chest voices to falsetto voices.

He did not like 'dull' voices, nor did he like pure head voices 'which issue with a shrill and penetrating quality.' He said that chest voices gave more delight than head voices, which 'are not only boring and annoying, but in a short time one comes to hate and abhor them.' The dull voices, he said, can never be heard and 'might as well not be there.' He observed that some singers switched back and forth between the registers, but the more they kept to chest voice, the better. He also found that the chest voices had more power and better intonation (Zacconi 1592, fol. 77). Cerone's *El melopeo y maestro* (1613) faithfully reiterated Zacconi's remarks in Spanish (Cerone 1613, ch. 73).

Of course, when Zacconi spoke of singers, he was referring primarily to male singers, since females were not admitted to chapel choirs. At that time the upper parts of choral music were sung by boys or male falsettists.[2] The difficulty that the male singer encountered in using the chest voice exclusively was that he could not reach higher notes without either yelling or switching to falsetto. Zacconi recognized this difficulty when he admonished singers not to force the high notes. 'For the forced voice, being defective, always offends; and if by chance the melody goes so high that the singer cannot sing it comfortably, he should not shout as madmen or those bedeviled. It is better to omit those tones than offer the ear something strange and unpleasant. Similarly when singing *piano* on high notes, if one cannot reach them comfortably, they should be sung in falsetto rather than sung badly' (Zacconi 1592, opp. fol. 56).

This same defect of shouting to achieve the upper notes had been observed earlier by Biagio Rossetti (1529) and Hermann Finck (1556). In 1580, Giovanni de' Bardi, patron of the Florentine Camerata, criticized basses who sang the upper notes in such a way that that they seemed 'like criers auctioning off the pledges of the unfortunate, like little snarling dogs stealing silently through the streets of others and imagining that they are making no end of noise.'[3] In 1581, Vincenzo Galilei, another member of the Camerata, likened the yelled upper notes to 'shrieking from excessive pain, internal or external.'[4] Other authors who commented on this were Giovanni Battista Doni (1763, 2:99–100) and Pierfrancesco Tosi (1986, 11–12).

Giulio Caccini, whose *Le nuove musiche* (1602) was a manifesto of the new style of solo singing, referred to the two registers as the *voce piena e naturale* (full and natural voice) and the *voce finta* (feigned voice, or falsetto). He made it clear that he disliked falsetto for its lack of nobility, its breathiness, and its inability to create strong contrasts between loud and soft (Caccini 1970, 56). Caccini's own compositions fell within a modest vocal range in which the tenor was rarely stretched beyond the normal limits of chest voice. Caccini also advocated transposition as a means of keeping the voice within the comfortable range of chest voice. He was apparently a one-register singer who eschewed falsetto and knew nothing of covered singing. His views were echoed by Praetorius, who urged the singer to sing *mit ganzer und voller Stimme* (with a complete and full voice) (Praetorius 1619, 2:29), and by Herbst, who considered falsetto to be 'a half and forced voice' (Herbst 1642, 3).

One of the most important vocal treatises in the eighteenth century was the *Opinioni de' cantori antichi, e moderni, o sieno osservazioni sopra il canto figurato* by Pierfrancesco Tosi. First published in 1723, it went through numerous editions and translations into English, French, and German. The English translation, *Observations on the Florid Song* (1743), was by J.E. Galliard, a German oboist and composer.[5] The 1757 German version, *Anleitung zur Singekunst*, was by Johann Friedrich Agricola, a composition student of J.S. Bach and J.J. Quantz who became a court composer in Prussia.[6] Tosi was himself a castrato singer and teacher as well as a composer. His career as a singer seems to have been rather limited, and he spent most of his later years in England where he apparently sang chamber music but never opera.[7]

Tosi addressed his book primarily to sopranos, by which he meant castrato singers. By Tosi's time, of course, castrati had become the reigning stars of Italian opera and the exemplars of good singing practices. While the castrato phenomenon will be discussed further in chapter 7, it should be noted here that the eunuch's voice, though higher than the normal male voice (there were both contralto and soprano castrati), nevertheless had two primary registers that required uniting; from a pedagogical point of view, the castrato singer was taught the same techniques as the normal singer.[8] What is not quite clear is whether the register breaks in a castrato voice occurred in the same places as those in normal singers. Tosi used the terms *voce di petto* and *voce di testa* to describe the primary registers, and said that the singer must learn to use both registers. He urged the voice teacher to cultivate the pupil's head register for the high notes or risk losing the voice. He noted that the head voice was best for singing florid music and for singing trills, but also that it was weaker than the chest voice (Tosi 1986, 14–15). Since this weakness of the head voice made the register change too noticeable, he advised equalizing the two registers: 'A diligent instructor, knowing that a soprano without the falsetto must sing within the narrowness of a few notes, should not only attempt to acquire it, but should leave no means untried so that he unites it to the chest voice, in such a way that one cannot distinguish the one from the other, since if the union of the registers is not perfect the voice will be of many registers, and consequently will lose its beauty' (14). Regarding the transition point between registers, he wrote, 'The jurisdiction of the natural voice, or chest voice, ordinarily ends on the fourth space or the fifth line, and here begins the domain of the falsetto, both in ascending to the high notes and in returning to the natural voice, wherein consists the difficulty of the union' (14). Tosi was probably referring to the soprano clef (which was commonly used at that time) in which middle C ($C4$) is on the first line. This places the transition point for the castrato voice at $A4$ or $B4$, about a sixth higher than $C4$ or $D4$, the usual transition point for female sopranos. Alessandro Moreschi (1858–1922) was the only castrato to make sound recordings. In his 1904 recording of the Bach-Gounod 'Ave Maria,' made in Rome, the break between chest voice and falsetto occurs between $B4$ and $C\#5$.[9] This is consistent with Tosi's description. Tosi noted that few sopranos knew how to unite the registers, but he gave no advice on how this very difficult task might be accomplished.

After Tosi, there was a long succession of authors who subscribed to the two-register theory. The most influential was Giambattista Mancini, whose *Pensieri e riflessioni pratiche sopra il canto figurato* was first published in 1774. It went through several editions, including a French translation in 1776, a second Italian edition in 1777, and later editions in French, Italian, and English. The most recent English translation compares the Italian editions of 1774 and 1777.[10] This work, like Tosi's, was well known to Garcia, who cited it in his *Traité* (Garcia 1847, 1:25; 1984, 40).

Like Tosi, Mancini was a castrato. Also like Tosi, he divided the voice into two registers, the chest and the head: 'The voice in its natural state is ordinarily divided into two registers, one of which is called the chest, the other the head or falsetto. I say ordinarily, because there are rare examples in which one has received from nature the most unusual gift of being able to execute everything in the chest voice' (Mancini 1967, 20). Edward Foreman considers the last sentence to be the 'single most famous statement of the eighteenth century' (Foreman 1969, 53). Certainly the statement is ambiguous in its meaning. It could refer to singers whose upper register sounded equal to the chest register, or to singers who skillfully extended the chest register upward by some unspecified means, or to something else altogether. In any case, Mancini returned to the subject, and said with equal ambiguity, 'It is a rare case when the two registers are both united into a chest register in one person. This total union is generally produced only by study and the help of art' (Mancini, 1967, 39).

Mancini emphasized repeatedly how difficult it was to join the registers. 'Have no doubt that of all the difficulties that one encounters in the art of singing, the greatest by far is the union of the two registers: but to overcome this is not impossible to him who will seriously study how it is to be done' (20). He later elaborated on this:

The great art of the singer is to render imperceptible to the listener or watcher, the greater or lesser degree of difficulty with which he brings forth the two different registers of chest and head. This can be obtained only through endless refinement: but it is not easy to master this in a simple and natural method. One must use study, effort and industry to correct the defects provided by the greater or lesser strength of the organs, and one reaps a management and economy which render the voice equally sonorous and pleasing, which few scholars reach, and of which few masters understand the practical rules, or how to execute them. (101–2)

Mancini noted that the *voce di testa* is weaker than the *voce di petto*, and he offered advice for uniting the registers: 'The head voice being in need of help, since it is separated from the chest, the most certain method to help unite them is for the scholar, without losing time, to undertake to establish in his daily studies the manner of holding back the chest voice and of strengthening little by little the unfriendly notes of the head, in order to render the latter equal to the former in the best possible way.' In the unlikely event that the head voice should be stronger than the chest, the process should be reversed. In either case, Mancini tried to remain optimistic in the face of doubt when he said, 'It may happen that the union of the two registers has not arrived at the desired point; nevertheless I beseech the master and the scholar not to lose courage thereby; because I am sure that, continuing the same way, they must have a happy success' (40). He did not specify how to strengthen the weaker register.

Another Italian who followed the orthodox two-register theory was Vincenzo Manfredini (1737–99). His *Regole armoniche* (1775) was a general work on music that included a discussion of singing techniques. A second edition was printed in 1797. Regarding voice registers, Manfredini did not go beyond what Mancini had said. He noted that the *voce di testa* was commonly called falsetto, and that it should be united with the chest voice by strengthening the weaker register (Manfredini 1797, 61).

German authors once again followed the Italians in matters of singing, even when they were not singers themselves. In his manual on flute playing (1752), Johann Joachim Quantz (1697–1773) discussed the singing voice, which he recommended be emulated by flautists. He repeated the two-register theory, noting that the falsetto was produced with a 'contracted' throat, and that it was weaker and used more breath than the chest register. 'The Italians and several other nations unite this falsetto to the chest voice, and make use of it to great advantage in singing' (Quantz 1966, 55–6). Other German authors who shared the common view were Georg Joseph (Abbé) Vogler, Johann Baptist Lasser, and Nina d'Aubigny von Engelbrunner.[11]

The difficulty of uniting the registers was illustrated by Johann Samuel Petri (1738–1808) in his *Anleitung zur practischen Musik* (Primer in Practical Music) of 1767. In his discussion of registers he described a performance of a soprano falsettist, whose highest notes were magnificent, but when he tried to take the falsetto too low, 'his falsetto did not reach there, and all at once he fell into his piercing and robust tenor voice. I was shocked, and my entire pleasure in his lovely soprano voice was utterly destroyed.'[12]

Other accounts of singers with prominent register breaks were written by Leigh Hunt, English opera critic for *The Examiner* from 1808 to 1821. In one review of 1817, he described the singing of two tenors named Pearman and Incledon: '[Pearman's] transition [to falsetto] however from the natural voice is not happy. It is not indeed so violent as Incledon's, who in his leap from one to the other slammed the larynx in his throat, like a harlequin jumping through a window shutter; but it is poor and unskilful; neither does he seem to care upon what sort of words or expression he does it, so as the note is such as he can jump up to' (Fenner 1972, 95). In 1819 Hunt described the singing of tenor Thomas Phillips: 'The passage between his natural voice and falsetto, has that unpleasant gurgle to jump over, which is common enough, but which in Mr. Phillips is more than usually prominent to the ear. He has to slip over it, like a bump on the ice' (95).

On the other hand, in 1824 Rossini's biographer Stendhal spoke glowingly about the young Giuditta Pasta for her 'two voices' which he found 'charming and thrilling.' He quoted one connoisseur of music as saying, '*Thus with Madame Pasta: her voice, changing from register to register, inspires in me the same sensation as this memory of moonlight, veiled an instant, darker, softer, more entrancing ... then shining forth anew, a silver shower a thousandfold increased.*'[13] From this it appears that female singers fared better with discontinuous registers than did tenors.

Countercurrents to the Two-Register Theory

The two-register theory that had descended from Zacconi and Caccini to Tosi, Mancini, and the others, was thrown into disarray in the eighteenth century. The confusion seems to have begun with Tosi's English and German translators, who appended their own views to Tosi's. Galliard, in his English translation, used his footnotes as a gloss, and he added this remark regarding registers: '*Voce di Petto* is a full Voice, which comes from the Breast by Strength, and is the most sonorous and expressive. *Voce di testa* comes more from the Throat, than from the Breast, and is capable of more Volubility. *Falsetto* is a feigned Voice, which is entirely formed in the Throat, has more Volubility than any, but [is] of no Substance' (Tosi 1743, 22 n. 18). Galliard thus advanced a three-register theory in which he considered the head voice and the falsetto to be two separate registers.

Like Galliard, Johann Agricola (1757) added numerous interpretive remarks on registers, with what musicologist Franz Häbock (1927) called 'sense-disturbing inexactness' (Häbock 1927, 87). In a long and rambling section on registers, Agricola identified chest and head registers as properties of the windpipe and glottis, saying that both the windpipe and the glottis are wider in chest voice than in head voice. 'In the head voice the opening of the windpipe is softer and thus less elastic; the windpipe is itself more narrow; and the lungs are not as expandable.' He complained that Tosi and other Italians confused head voice with the falsetto (*Fistelstimme*), which he considered to be a different mechanism (Agricola 1995, 75). For Agricola, the falsetto occurred on both the highest and the lowest notes in the voice, and were considered to be 'forced tones.' For the high falsetto notes, he said that 'the whole head of the windpipe becomes further stretched and pulled up higher and further into the deepest cavity of the palate under the hyoid bone.' He seems to be suggesting that the high falsetto notes are sung with a high larynx, which gives them a forced quality. As the falsetto descends into the lower register, the larynx resumes its previous position, but the transition between registers is problematic. 'It is of great advantage in uniting the natural with the falsetto note in the upper register if one can produce the intermediate note, the highest of the one and the lowest of the other, with both kinds of voice' (77).

Agricola's comments on the presence of falsetto notes in the lower reaches of the chest voice are bizarre. He said that these few notes, which are always weaker than the normal chest notes, are not produced by raising or lowering the larynx, but by 'the lowering of the lower jaw, accompanied by an inclination of the head,' which creates 'obstacles in the path of the free passage of air from the mouth. Consequently, these forced low notes can never maintain the same power and beauty as the natural notes.' He noted, 'The Germans call those baritones (high basses) who try too hard to force out notes lower than are natural for them [by the name of] straw basses. However, singers with high voices who wish to sing too low (besides the fact that their low notes are not heard well) are in danger of ruining the entire voice by forcibly stretch-ing the windpipe' (77). The German word *Strohbass* refers to the lowest tones in the voice, which crackle like the sound of straw underfoot. This voice quality had been observed since at least the seventeenth century, when the music theorist Marin Mersenne spoke of the 'rattle in the throat which basses sometimes use in order to supplement the natural voice when it is not low enough' (Mersenne 1636, 1:9).

It seems then, that Agricola distinguished the high falsetto notes from the head voice by the high position of the larynx, and that his low fal-setto was not falsetto at all, but an auxiliary register known today as the 'pulse' register (to be discussed below). Agricola sought to justify his register theory with reference to the writings of physiologists Denis Dodart (1700) and Antoine Ferrein (1741), but in the end he was a mere dabbler whose faulty understanding of vocal physiology failed to clarify the remarks of Tosi, but rather obfuscated the whole matter of registers.

Agricola's description of registers was widely read and influenced other German authors, none of whom completely agreed with his views. Friedrich Wilhelm Marpurg (1718–95) drew heavily on Agricola, but embraced the two-register theory of Tosi, calling Agricola's *Fistelstimme* a vulgar name for falsetto (Marpurg 1763, 19–20). Johann Adam Hiller (1728–1804), in a 1774 book on singing, seemed thoroughly confused by the new register terminology. He regarded Agricola's account of chest, head, and fistel-voice to represent a three-register theory, and tried to distinguish between 'natural' and 'artificial' registers. He called the upper register in males the fistel-voice, but he called the upper register in females and boys the falsetto (Hiller 1774, 6–10). Then, in a second book on singing (1780), he abandoned Agricola altogether for Mancini's tidier two-register theory.[14]

Johann Samuel Petri considered falsetto and *Fistelstimme* to be synon-ymous: 'One should learn to use the falsetto, the so-called fistel-voice, and equalize it with the natural or chest voice, which he may then use to sing an aria which is otherwise too high, but without transposing it down or altering the melody' (Petri 1767, 61–2). Later he added, 'But I must admit that only a few learn to use a good falsetto which is not differentiated appreciably from the chest voice' (205–6).

Another author who added grist to the mill of register theory was Isaac Nathan (1790–1864), a wild character who was born in England and became a composer of light opera. He was a student of Domenico Corri in 1809. The first edition of *Essay on the History and Theory of Music* (1823) was followed by an enlarged second edition in 1836 under the title *Musurgia Vocalis*. This large, rambling, and seemingly erudite book covered a wide variety of musical subjects ranging from music history to the fondness of camels for hearing singing! Chapter 6 is titled 'Of the Human Voice, and its General Qualities.' While it is engagingly written and laced with quotations from Greek and Roman writers, it is nevertheless the work of a dilettante. His chapter on the singing voice is no exception. In it, Nathan described four separate registers: the *voce di petto*, or chest voice; the falsetto, or throat voice; the *voce di testa*, or head voice; and the *feigned* voice, which was neither falsetto nor *voce di testa*. His concept of the feigned voice was novel: 'It is a species of ventriloquism, a soft and distant sound produced apparently in the chest, and chiefly in the back of the throat and head – an inward and suppressed quality of tone, that conveys the illusion of being heard at a distance: – It is as a sweet and soft melodious sound, wafted from afar, like unto the magic spell of an echo' (Nathan 1836, 117). He maintained that the chest voice and the falsetto must be joined by *il ponticello* (a little bridge), and that the blending of the registers 'cannot be accomplished without the aid of the *feigned voice*, which may be justly considered the only medium or vehicle by which the *falsetto* can be carried into the *Voce di petto*.' He added that the falsetto was entirely governed by the contracted aperture of the mouth, its intonation being chiefly produced in a small cell or cavity above the arch of the mouth (what we now call the naso-pharynx) which he called 'the internal nose' (144–5). He considered the male falsetto acceptable for tender, but not for masculine, words.

Nathan's remarks are difficult to interpret, but his description of the feigned voice seems to suggest a light vocal emission that is especially useful for passing back and forth between the chest and head voice. Cornelius Reid, in his book *Bel Canto: Principles and Practices* (1950), described Nathan's 'feigned' voice as a 'combination of the lyric quality of falsetto with the "bite" of the chest voice' (Reid 1950, 52, 69). A more recent description of *voce finta* is offered by Richard Miller (1977), who says it is a 'clearly identifiable quality' produced with a slightly elevated larynx, weak glottal adduction, a high rate of 'breath mixture,' and weak support of the torso. 'Voce finta is permitted in the male voice in the Italian School only as an occasional vocal coloration. At best it sounds sweetly ethereal, at worst somewhat emasculated' (R. Miller 1977, 117–18).

In the closing years of the eighteenth century, several authors proposed a three-register theory especially for female voices. In *Mélopée moderne* of 1792, Jean Paul Egide Martini (1741–1816) described three female registers: the *voix de poitrine* for the low tones, the *voix du gozier* (throat voice) for the middle, and the *voix de tête* for the high.[15] Bernardo Mengozzi (1758–1800), in a treatise published posthumously in 1803, described a two-register theory (chest register and head or falsetto) for male singers. He maintained that contraltos and mezzo-sopranos also have two registers, but that sopranos have three registers, namely, chest, middle, and head (Mengozzi 1803, 4–5). He offered tasty advice on uniting the registers, advising the singer to 'sweeten' (*adoucir*) the last note of the chest register, and to reinforce and 'nourish' (*nourrir*) the first note of the head register.[16]

In 1818 Giacomo Gotifredo Ferrari (1763–1842) published a short treatise on voice in both Italian and English. Ferrari was ambiguous regarding registers. At one point he identified three registers – the grave, the medium, and the acute. But he then aligned himself with Tosi and the two-register theory: 'Two of [the voice's] qualities are distinguished by the appelations, *voce di petto, voce di testa*, chest and head voice, although both are generated in the throat by the impulsions of the lungs ... if [the pupil] feels a difficulty in uniting the chest and head voice, he must, by art, strengthen the extremity of that which happens to be weakest' (Ferrari 1818, 2–4). Adolphe Müller, in a bilingual vocal tutor of 1844 (German and French), also described two male registers and three female registers (Müller 1844). He noted that the singer should slip back and forth between the registers, and that the unification of the registers was more difficult in the male voice. But by this time Manuel Garcia had published his *Traité*, and the debate over registers took on new dimensions.

Garcia's Theory of the Main Registers

When Garcia entered the debate about registers, things were in a state of flux. The old Italian concept of two registers was still widely accepted, and Garcia was well acquainted with the works of Tosi, Mancini,

Herbst, and Agricola, all of which he cited in his *Traité* (Garcia 1847, 1:25; 1984, 40). He was also familiar with the treatise of J.P.E. Martini (Garcia 1847, 1:29, 71), as well as the tutors by Mengozzi and Garaudé, his mentors at the Paris Conservatoire (71, 73). All these authors supported a three-register theory for female voices and a two-register theory for male voices. The nomenclature for registers was expanding; the terms *falsetto, voce di testa, voce finta, voce di mezzo petto, voix mixte, voix du gozier,* and *voix sombrée ou couverte* all referred to registers above the normal *voce di petto.* He stated in the 'Préface' to his *Traité* that he wanted to make some kind of sense out of all this, and that his *Traité* was an attempt to reduce past practices to a new theoretical form with specific reference to the physiological causes of registers, timbres, and other vocal phenomena (Garcia 1947, pref. 1; 1984, xvii). In his theory of registers Garcia created a *rapprochement* between the two-register and three-register theories which were so much an issue of the day.

Garcia's now famous definition of vocal registers, offered in his *Mémoire* (1840), and again in his *Traité* (1841), is still the reference point in modern studies of registers:

By the word register we mean a series of consecutive and homogeneous tones going from low to high, produced by the development of the same mechanical principle, and whose nature differs essentially from another series of tones equally consecutive and homogeneous produced by another mechanical principle. All the tones belonging to the same register are consequently of the same nature, whatever may be the modifications of timbre or of force to which one subjects them. (Garcia 1847, 1:6; 1984, xli)

Much of the confusion regarding Garcia's theory of registers came about because of a lack of understanding of what he meant by 'mechanical principles' and his use of the term 'falsetto.'

In his *Mémoire,* Garcia recognized two main registers. The lower register he called the chest register (*registre de poitrine*), and the upper register he called the falsetto-head register (*registre de fausset-tête*). He described the falsetto-head register as a single register consisting of two parts, 'of which the lowest takes the name of *falsetto,* or *medium,* and the highest takes the name of *head*' (1847, 1:6; 1984, xl n.8). In other words, he considered the head register to be an upward extension of the falsetto register, but with certain differences that justified a separate name (1847, 1:8; 1984, liii).

When Garcia presented his *Mémoire* to the Académie des sciences on

12 April 1841, he brought some pupils to demonstrate his explanation of the different registers. Using a metronome as a time-measuring device, he showed that the singer could maintain a chest tone longer than a falsetto tone (26 oscillations for chest voice, and only 16 to 18 oscillations for falsetto). He also demonstrated the range of notes in both male and female voices that could be sung with either chest voice or falsetto, with clearly perceptible differences. However, between falsetto and head notes there was no such overlap but rather a continuous quality of voice. This demonstration persuaded members of the Académie of the validity of Garcia's theory (1847, rapport 3–4; 1984 xxvii–xxix).

While Garcia's practical demonstration was simple and effective, his theoretical explanation of registers was more complex. He described the two main registers as being produced by two distinct modes of vibration of the vocal folds. In the chest voice, the vocal folds vibrate throughout their length and depth; in the falsetto-head register only the inner margins of the vocal folds vibrate, so that the vibrating mass is smaller. This was the 'mechanical principle' that distinguished the two main registers. Garcia's second mechanical principle – strong versus weak glottal closure, as described in chapter 1 – distinguished the falsetto from the head voice.

In addressing the first principle, Garcia cited Johann Müller's *Physiologie du système nerveux*, which stated that 'the essential difference between the two registers consists in the fact that in falsetto only the edges of the cords vibrate, whereas in chest voice the entire cord is involved in broad excursions' (Garcia 1847, 1:12). While Garcia said this difference did indeed require serious consideration, he was not persuaded that Müller's theory could explain all the differences between the two registers. He was especially doubtful that the edges alone could account for the considerable power of the falsetto register in some singers. With his later laryngoscopic investigations he was able to see that the mode of vibration of the vocal folds was indeed different in the two primary registers. But equally important, he also observed how the position of the arytenoid cartilages during glottal closure affected these registers. His most succinct description of the action of these separate mechanical principles in the untrained voice is found in *Hints on Singing*:

When preparing to emit a sound the two sides of the glottis, which are separated for breathing, shut the passage, and if the sound be a deep *chest* note, they become slightly tense. The whole length and breadth of the lips (comprising the anterior prolongation, or process of the arytenoid cartilage and the vocal cord) are engaged in the vibrations. As the sounds rise in the register the tension of the lips increases, and the thickness diminishes. Meanwhile the contact of the inner surfaces of the arytenoids will progress and extend to the end of the vocal processes, thereby shortening the vibratory length of the lips. The *medium* or *falsetto* is the result of similar actions, save that the lips come into contact, not through their depth but merely at their edges. In both registers the glottis has its length diminished from the back, by the arytenoids, which advance their contact till their adhesion is complete. As soon as this takes place, the *falsetto* ceases, and the glottis, consisting of the vocal cords alone, produces the *head* register. The resistance opposed to the air by the large surfaces generates the *chest* register, and the feebler opposition presented by the edges produces the *falsetto*. (Garcia 1894, 8; see also 1984, 25)

He also noted that this 'feebler opposition' in the falsetto resulted in a tone that was 'frequently weak and veiled' and used much more breath. 'Requiring a less vigorous contraction of the glottic lips than the chest notes, a relative relaxation of the vocal cord is felt when the voice passes from the chest to the medium on the same note' (Garcia 1894, 9). In his 'Observations on the Human Voice' Garcia noted: 'The moment in which the action of the apophyses [vocal processes] ceases, exhibits in the female voice a very sensible difference at once to the ear and in the organ itself' (Garcia 1855, 403). In other words, as the singer passed from the falsetto or medium register to the head register, there is a shortened glottis and stronger adduction of the folds.

It was apparently this difference between firm and loose phonation in the upper register that caused Garcia to vacillate as to whether the head register was a true register or just a continuation of the falsetto. He observed a similar phenomenon in the chest voice, but he did not give it two names:

If we compare the two registers in these movements, we shall find some analogies between them; the sides of the glottis, formed at first by the apophyses and the ligaments [vocal folds] become shorter by degrees, and end by consisting only of the ligaments. The chest-register is divided into two parts, corresponding to these two states of the glottis. The register of falsetto head presents a complete similarity, and in a still more striking manner. (1855, 127)

Garcia has been accused of propagating a 'classic misunderstanding' by referring to the female middle voice as 'falsetto' (*Transcripts* 1980, 1:104). However, Mackworth Young (1953) pointed out that physiologists had placed the falsetto between chest and head registers since around 1800; hence, Garcia was not the first to use the term falsetto for the middle portion of the voice. Garcia may have called this region of the voice falsetto because of its weak and breathy emission and its dull and veiled tone quality. He wrote, 'The falsetto belongs particularly to women and children. This register is weak (*faible*), covered (*couvert*), and rather resembles the low notes of the flute, principally in the lower part.' He said the female falsetto extended from about $A3$ or $B\flat3$ to $C4$ or $C\sharp4$, and added, 'The more the tones descend below the [$D4$] the more they fade; below the [$A3$], they cease to exist.' As soon as the female singer reached about $E5$, the voice became 'distinctive and brilliant.' This was the point at which he maintained that the vocal processes became fully adducted, resulting in what he called head voice (Garcia 1847, 1:4, 1984, xliv).

More confusing was Garcia's description of the same range, from $A3$ to $C\sharp4$, as constituting the male falsetto. 'The falsetto, with men, is of the same nature, and placed on the same lines as that of women. But the low tones are difficult to utter and elude the masculine larynx, much better suited to produce the same tones in the chest voice' (1847, 1:8; 1984, xlvi–xlvii). Louis Mandl referred to the weak middle register as a 'hole' in the uncultivated voice (Mandl 1876, 42). Even today, one often hears criticism of singers who have a 'hole in the middle of the voice.' The key to understanding Garcia's meaning here is to realize that, for him, falsetto was the weak and veiled tone quality that resulted from weak glottal closure, and that it was found in middle portion of both female and male voices. The more brilliant voice above the range of the falsetto in the female voice was called by Garcia the *fausset-tête*, and it extended to $F6$ in the highest voices. In the male voice, the *voix de tête* corresponds to what we normally think of as falsetto in the old Italian sense of the word. Garcia said, 'Men lose the head voice as a result of mutation; however, some individuals keep the major third of it' [about $C\sharp5$ to $F\sharp5$] (1847, 1:8; 1984, xlvii). There is a consistency to Garcia's theory, but his two-pronged approach to registers, which included both glottal closure and mode of vibration, was lost on most readers, while his use of the term falsetto for the middle part of the voice led to widespread misunderstanding.

Garcia was sensitive to this misunderstanding, and he later capitulated and adopted a three-register model that abandoned the term falsetto for the middle portion of the voice and was thus more easily accepted. In *Hints on Singing* he wrote, 'Every voice is formed of three distinct portions, or registers, namely, *chest, medium*, and *head*. The chest holds the lowest place, the medium the middle, the head the highest. These names are incorrect, but accepted' (Garcia 1894, 7). Paschke remarked that Garcia's change of mind may also have been influenced by his observations with the laryngoscope after 1855 (Garcia 1984, 207).

Like his predecessors, Garcia sought to equalize the registers, but he went further by providing specific instructions on how to do this. For Garcia, the key to uniting the registers was found in the mechanical principle of firm glottal closure. He noted that it was the so-called falsetto voice – that is, the octave above the break – which used loose glottal closure, and was therefore weak, veiled, unstable, and inefficient. 'The very pronounced *pinching* of the glottis will be the remedy for the weakness which we have just pointed out' (1984, 26). He described the dull voice, with its weak glottal closure, but he did not generally condone it. 'By teaching how to produce the veiled, cottony, dull timbre, we have learned how to recognize it and avoid it' (1984, 39). Garcia warned the female pupil not to 'give in to the tendency to aspirate the falsetto tones at the moment when she leaves the chest register' (1847, 1:28; 1984, 51). He said that in order to equalize the registers, 'one will practice by primarily passing alternately from one register to the other on the tones [D4, E♭4, E4, F4] without interruption and without aspirating in that passage between registers.' The same advice applied to males (1847, 1:28; 1984, 50–2). In *Hints on Singing* Garcia reiterated this advice:

Q. What is to be done when the medium [or falsetto register] is veiled, and lets the air escape by a continuous leakage?
A. The leakage is caused by the lips of the glottis being imperfectly closed. The ring can be obtained by attacking with a sharp stroke of the glottis every sound of the interval [E4–C5]. (1894, 15)

Here then, Garcia equated his *coup de la glotte* with 'pinching the glottis' in order to achieve brilliance of tone, breath efficiency, and register equalization. The mechanical principle of strong glottal closure was the common denominator in his theories. His advice was to avoid the weakness of falsetto by using the same firm glottal setting as for chest register.

Regarding the transition from the falsetto (middle) register to the head register, Garcia's advice was similar to his comments on the transition between chest and falsetto. He again noted the weakness of the falsetto, and encouraged the use of the *coup de la glotte*, as well as the use of the *sombre timbre*:

Rather often the extreme notes of the falsetto [$C\#5$ and $D5$] are weak, while the tones [$Eb5$, $E5$, $F5$], which are the first in the head register are round and pure. Since this roundness and this purity proceed only from the position of the pharynx and the contraction of the glottis, one will impart them to the preceding notes by arching the velum and by avoiding all loss of unused air. It is thus by the position which the pharynx adopts in the sombre timbre and by the pinching of the glottis that these registers are equalized. (1984, 45–6)

This was a recognition that both the glottal source and the vocal tract play a role in uniting the registers.

Voix mixte and Mezza voce

Prior to the famous *ut de poitrine* of Gilbert-Louis Duprez, tenors apparently sang their highest notes with a light vocal emission – either the *voce di testa* (which we now call falsetto), or a technique that was called *voix mixte* (mixed voice), or *voce di mezzo petto* (half-chest voice) (Pleasants 1966, 158–65). In 1830 Garaudé wrote, 'In the tenor voice, the head tones regularly employed have an infinite charm. One must attack them with strength and purity, and must unite them imperceptibly with the chest voice.' His musical examples show these transition notes to be from $E4$ to $F\#4$, that is, the notes of the *passaggio*. He said that in order to extend the chest voice upward a few notes, or to unite the chest and head registers, tenors employed the *voix mixte*, in which 'the one [register] participates a little with the other.' An intelligent tenor could make good use of this technique in order to sing certain phrases 'without changing the register' or to remove the 'hard' type of transition (by which he presumably meant the undisguised break between the registers). His musical example shows the mixed voice ascending to $Bb4$ (Garaude 1830, 22). This may be the technique that Rossini intended for his tenor high notes. When Rossini heard Duprez's high C in chest voice, he very much disliked it, saying it sounded 'like the squalk of a capon whose throat is being cut.'[17]

The idea that some sort of mixed voice could be produced differently from the main registers is a recurring theme in the history of vocal pedagogy. As we have seen, several authors, including Galliard, Agricola, Nathan, and Garaudé, described ways of using a light vocal emission variously called feigned voice (*voce finta*), fistula-voice (*Fistelstimme*), half-chest voice (*voce di mezzo petto*), and mixed voice (*voix mixte*). While the precise meaning of any of these terms is not clear, the cumulative impression is that there was indeed a vocal technique that was different from chest voice, falsetto, or covered voice.

It was again Manuel Garcia who tried to describe in more specific terms ways to sing notes above the *passaggio*. His discussion of how and where to employ the clear versus the dark timbres includes a lengthy and somewhat arcane footnote in which he discussed tenor high notes in detail. He rejected the terms *voix mixte* and *voce di mezzo petto*, 'for they make us suppose that these clear and high pitched tones are produced by the two mechanisms of the chest and falsetto registers at the same time.' This idea he considered unacceptable. 'In fact, the production of any one sound places the organ into entirely different and irreconcilable conditions, according as it is formed by the mechanism of the chest voice or that of falsetto.' Instead, Garcia described two ways of singing high notes each of which depended upon a distinct relationship between the glottis and the pharynx.

In the first of these, tones were sung 'without the cooperation of the pharynx to reinforce them. One knows in fact that the intensity of a tone depends in general upon the number of partials which vibrate concurrently to form it, and upon the amplitude of the vibrations which these partials execute; as a consequence, by reducing the number of vibrating partials, one decreases the sound.' This could be achieved if the singer 'completely relaxes all the muscles of the pharynx' and 'narrows more and more the column of air.' It seems that what Garcia is suggesting here is weak glottal closure, a low larynx, and a relaxed pharynx with as little muscular engagement as possible. By adopting this particular configuration of the voice source and the vocal tract, the singer would produce a tone with few high-frequency components. This sound would strike the ear as soft as opposed to loud singing, even if the sound pressure levels were not much different. Garcia continued:

If, while the glottis alone vibrates and all other parts of the instrument are relaxed, one moderately increases the pressure of the air, one obtains an increase of brilliance and intensity, but never an increase of volume. One can conceive the immense advantage which the male voice can draw from these observations, completely new in theory, and too rarely applied instinctively by some artists. They serve to clarify the relatively high notes ordinarily so thick in basses, baritones, and tenors. They indicate to these latter the mechanism to practise to increase the range of the chest register; they permit the *piano* and *mezza voce* use of this register in the high tones and thus the dispensation of the excessive use of the falsetto tones; finally, they facilitate the union of the registers, etc. (Garcia 1847, 2:58; 1975, 161–2)

It seems that what Garcia is here describing is not a *mixed register*, which he considers a physiological impossibility, but *mezza voce*, which extends the chest register upward using loose phonation and a relaxed pharynx. The ensuing tone is weak in high-frequency components, and is perceived as being a quiet 'half-voice.' If this interpretation is correct, then Garcia was probably the first author to offer a detailed description of *mezza voce* in the male voice.

Garcia described a second method of singing male high notes in which 'the contraction of the pharyngeal muscles is added to that of the glottis. The instrument then forms a single whole which the excessively held column can no longer make vibrate, but which was sufficient to set the glottis alone into action. A vigorous thrust here becomes indispensable to put the entire mass into action.' Garcia went on to describe a much more muscular approach to the high notes, which required high subglottal pressure, as well as the strong contraction of both the glottal muscles and the muscles of the vocal tract, and which resulted in strong high-frequency components in the tone. He recognized that 'the [$Bb4$, $B4$], and the [$C5$] require energetic efforts which in the preceding hypothesis would not be appropriate.' When this is done with 'clear timbre' (which implies a high larynx) it may well correspond to what Francesco Lamperti called *sguaiato*, or even to what we call 'belting.' When it is done with *sombre timbre* and a low larynx, Garcia described it as 'especially striking' (*surtout frappante*). This sound is, of course, the high covered notes of the *ut de poitrine*. In any case, Garcia made it clear that he did not recommend this kind of singing, since 'exhaustion and paralysis of the organ are the inevitable and unfortunately too frequent result of this procedure' (1847, 2:58; 1975, 162–3). Garcia's last comment is often echoed today by those who worry that such vigorous singing is damaging to the voice. We cannot know exactly what Garcia had in mind here, and whether he was opposed to all covered high notes or only to those that were produced with too much force or too high a larynx. But, given his affinity for the traditional way of singing Mozart and Rossini, it would not be surprising if he preferred a *mezza voce* approach to the high notes in preference to the novel *ut de poitrine* of Duprez.

Garcia's Auxiliary Registers

In addition to the principal registers, covered singing, and mixed registers, Garcia also made some brief remarks about the *registre de contrebass* (contra-bass register), *voix inspiratoire* (inspiratory voice), and a type of singing now known as 'overtone singing.' Garcia made it clear that he did not understand the mechanisms involved in these kinds of singing, and that, in any case, such sound did not play a role in artistic solo singing. The contra-bass register, which includes the lowest notes of a deep bass, is heard primarily in Russian choral basses, and the rough, growly quality of those notes is different from those of the low chest register. These may be the same notes that Agricola mistakenly described as low falsetto notes. Garcia speculated that the epiglottis might be involved, and he maintained that the larynx was higher for the contrabass notes than for the low chest tones. He found two weaknesses with this register. The first was that there was a lacuna between the lowest chest tones and the highest contrabass tones, and the second was that the use of the contrabass tones would weaken the rest of the voice, leaving only contrabass tones and weak chest tones (Garcia 1847, 1:4, 15; 1984, xlviii). Garcia was cautious in his remarks, since his understanding was indeed limited.

Garcia also commented on the inspiratory voice, in which the vocal folds are set into vibration by the ingress of air. He noted that both male and female singers could achieve higher pitches with this tone than with the head voice, but that such tones should only be used for dramatic declamation, such as a stage sigh (1847, 1:15).

Finally, Garcia discussed a type of singing that we know as 'overtone singing,' but for which he did not have a label. He associated this kind of singing with certain peasant horsemen who sang while riding through the streets of Saint Petersburg. The technique, he said, was cultivated from childhood, and consisted of singing a low drone while at the same time manipulating the resonance cavities in order to create a melody by selectively resonating upper partials above the drone. It required great physical effort and involved puffing out the cheeks and other facial contortions. This kind of singing can still be heard today.[18] In any case, to Garcia, this technique was just a curiosity and was not important for artistic singing (1985, 13–14). However, it does indicate Garcia's awareness of and fascination with what are today called extended vocal techniques.

The Aftermath of Garcia's Register Theory

Garcia's register theory became a model for his disciples and a springboard for later, more elaborate theories based on laryngoscopic observations. For Mathilde Marchesi, the existence of an independant middle register in female voices was a fact beyond dispute. She rejected Garcia's early two-register model in favour of his later three-register model which recognized the problems faced by female singers. 'I most emphatically maintain that the female voice possesses *three* registers, and not *two*, and I strongly impress upon my pupils this undeniable fact, which, moreover, their own experience teaches them, after a few lessons' (M. Marchesi 1970, xiv). Marchesi's advice for uniting the registers also showed Garcia's influence:

To equalize and blend the *Chest* with the *Medium* register, the pupil must slightly close the two last notes of the former in ascending, and open them in descending. Every effort expended upon the highest notes of a register increases the difficulty of developing the power of the lower notes in the next register, and therefore of blending the two registers, until eventually it becomes impossible ... The same instructions that we have given for the change and blending of the *Chest* and *Medium* registers also apply to the *Medium* and *Head*. (xv)

Marchesi's instruction to 'close' certain notes resembles Garcia's advice to 'pinch the glottis.' This, at least, was the position taken in 1978 by researchers John Large and Thomas Murray in their article 'Studies of the Marchesi Model for Female Registration.' They wrote, 'Our results suggest the laryngeal mechanism of medial compression as the agent for register blending, at least for the chest-medium registers' (Large and Murray 1978, 11). However, there is also a possibility that Marchesi's instruction regarding 'closing' certain notes refers to the darkening of the vowel.

Julius Stockhausen also followed Garcia's concept of registers by recognizing two modes of vocal fold vibration (associated with chest voice and falsetto) as well as three registers (chest-voice, falsetto or middle-voice, and head-voice): 'Male voices use two registers only, the chest and falsetto. Quite exceptionally tenors may use head-voice. Generally female voices use three registers, the only exception being very high sopranos, which use only falsetto and head-voice, and not the chest-register. The principal register of female voices is the falsetto, of male voices the chest-register.' In his discussion of uniting the registers, he spoke only of the role of the vocal tract and not of the glottal setting. He advocated a fixed position for the larynx on the transitional notes, and said that 'the blending of the chest and falsetto register can be achieved in ascending by using the sombre quality, in descending by using a clear quality of tone. In this instance the working of the epiglottis is unmistakable' (Stockhausen 1844, 13, see also 44).

One of the first singer-scientists to follow Garcia in the use of the laryngoscope as a means of identifying registers was Emma Seiler, a music student of Friedrich Wieck and a science student of Hermann Helmholtz. Her observations were first published in German in 1861; the English translation, *The Voice in Singing* (1868), went through several editions and was quoted by Curwen (1875), Lunn (1878), Mackenzie (1890), and Curtis (1909). Seiler praised Garcia lavishly for his work, calling him 'the most eminent singing master now living' (Seiler 1881, 40). However, she noted that his findings 'were received with distrust, scarcely noticed, and in many instances entirely rejected, by teachers of vocal music' (88). She spoke harshly of those whose 'superficial treatment of science, and the unfortunate results of its application, have injured the art of singing more than benefited it' (32). She also acknowledged, as had Garcia, that the laryngoscope was an imperfect instrument for observation, rarely revealing the entire glottis (52).

Emma Seiler is credited with first proposing a five-register theory (Monohan 1978, 285). She described these 'five different actions' of the vocal organ as follows:

1. *The first series of tones of the chest register*, in which the whole glottis is moved by large, loose vibrations, and the arytenoid cartilages with the vocal ligaments [folds] in action.
2. *The second series of the chest register*, where the vocal lips alone act, and are likewise moved by large, loose vibrations.
3. *The first series of the falsetto register*, where again the whole glottis, consisting of the arytenoid cartilages and the ligaments, is in action, the very fine interior edges of the ligaments, however, being alone in the vibrating motion.
4. *The second series of the falsetto register*, the tones of which are generated by the vibrations of the edges alone of the vocal ligaments.
5. *The head register*, in the same manner and by the same vibrations, and with a partial closing of the vocal ligaments. (Seiler 1872, 65–6)

Seiler's explanation of registers was largely a recasting of Garcia's two-pronged approach to registers, in which one mechanical principle was the mode of vibration of the vocal folds, and the other was the glottal setting. The chest register was divided into firm and loose glottal closure, as was the falsetto-head register. This accounts for the four laryngeal actions described earlier by Garcia. The fifth seems to be a variant of the 'deep contact' described by Garcia, in which the membranous folds close beyond the point at which the tips of the vocal processes meet. Seiler offered no advice on uniting the registers; rather, she simply said that 'the most natural and the simplest way of singing, as in all things, is the best' (Seiler 1881, 82). She did criticize the practice of carrying registers up beyond their 'natural limits' as being 'a chief cause of the decline of the art of singing' (82), and like Garcia, she objected to the covered high notes of tenors (73).

In his widely used *Teacher's Manual of the Tonic Sol-Fa Method*, John Curwen adopted Seiler's register theory as authoritative (Curwen 1875, 17–18, 172–4). Lennox Browne and Emil Behnke were also influenced by Seiler. Based on their own laryngoscopic findings, they renamed Seiler's five registers the *lower thick; upper thick; lower thin; upper thin*; and *small*.[19] Like Seiler, they seemed rather nonchalant regarding the discontinuities caused by registers, saying only, 'The change from one register to another should always be made a couple of tones *below* the extreme limit, so that there will be, at the juncture of the two registers, a few "optional" tones which it will be possible to take with both mechanisms' (Browne and Behnke 1904, 183). This statement is hardly sufficient to explain to students the maneuvers necessary to unite the registers.

In the waning years of the nineteenth century the influential Morrell Mackenzie, who was a Garcia detractor, presented his own definition of registers: 'By a register I mean the series of tones of like quality producible by a particular adjustment of the vocal cords' (Mackenzie 1890, 40). He said that in the lower register, which he called the 'long reed,' the vocal folds vibrate over their full length, and change pitch by stretching. The upper register, or 'short reed,' uses only part of the fold, and raises the pitch by 'stop-closure,' or damping (40–1). Mackenzie thus oversimplified registers by regarding vocal fold length as the only factor. Unlike Seiler, he rejected the use of the laryngoscope, and did not personally observe the vocal folds during registration events. He also rejected Seiler's five-register theory, and said that 'the immediate effect of the invention of the laryngoscope was to throw the whole subject into almost hopeless confusion by the introduction of all sorts of errors of observation, each claiming to be founded on ocular proof, and believed in with corresponding obstinacy' (245). Regarding the equalization of the registers, Mackenzie was vague and unhelpful. He wrote that the uniting of the registers was achieved by 'dovetailing the one into the other and as it were *planing* the surface of the sound till the voice was smooth and uniform throughout the entire compass and no "break" or difference of timbre could be detected. In the proper management of the registers lies the secret of fine singing' (99). He said this training should be controlled by the physician, but he gave no advice on how to 'dove-tail' or 'plane' the tone.

Among the traditional Italian teachers of singing, the Lampertis were again pre-eminent. Francesco Lamperti subscribed to a three-register model in females (chest, mixed, and head), and a two-register model in males (chest and mixed). He apparently preferred the term 'mixed' for both female and male voices to Garcia's 'falsetto,' and he considered the weakness of the middle notes in women to be a natural flaw (F. Lamperti 1916, 9, 12). He was reluctant to target specific transition points between the registers because of individual differences, but gave a range of notes where the shift could occur (F. Lamperti 1884, 9, 18–19). He did not always make clear distinctions between timbres and registers. Unlike Garcia, he wrote 'It is impossible to give precise rules as to the employment of different timbres' (18).

Like Francesco, Giovanni also treated registers, timbres, and breathing as parts of a whole, rather than as separate techniques. 'The vocal registers are determined by the different points of resonance of the tones; the mode of breathing always remains the same' (G. Lamperti 1905, 10). Giovanni subscribed to a three-register theory for females, namely, chest, medium, and head. Regarding male voices he said, 'Besides the registers already enumerated (chest, medium, and head), the male voice possesses a fourth, which renders it essentially different from the female voice, namely the 'mixed' voice (*voix mixte*), wrongly called "falsetto." And the very fact that the training of this register has been neglected, may be the chief reason that we have so few eminent tenors, and that artists endowed with great vocal powers often mistake *quantity* of tone for quality' (25). This is in agreement with Garcia's description of *voce di mezzo petto* or *voix mixte*, and is a further indication that the robust *ut de poitrine* of Duprez was not easily accepted by those acculturated to the earlier vocal style of Rossini. He further said that tenors should learn to 'mingle' head resonance with chest voice, and to 'blend' the medium register with the *voix mixte*. All this was stated in the language of resonance imagery. 'The point of resonance for the medium voice is the hard palate; for the head-tones, the top of the head, in front' (25–6).

One of Francesco Lamperti's pupils was the English voice teacher William Shakespeare, who brought Italian vocal techniques to an English readership during the first decades of the twentieth century. His famous treatise *The Art of Singing* was first published in 1899, and went through several editions in both England and the United States. In *Plain*

Words on Singing (1924), he added a chapter entitled 'Teachings of the Old Masters,' which demonstrated his clear grasp of vocal history, with extracts from Giulio Caccini, Bénigne de Bacilly, Pierfrancesco Tosi, Giovanni Bontempi, Daniele Friderici, Johann Mattheson, Johann Agricola, Johann Adam Hiller, and others (Shakespeare 1924, 71–114). In his earlier writings he followed Garcia's three-register theory, including the use of the term falsetto for the middle register, and said the three registers could 'dovetail, as it were, one into the other, as to form one long even voice.' He coupled this with elaborate resonance imagery focusing on the teeth (Shakespeare 1910, 32–40). Later he replaced the term 'falsetto' with 'medium' register, and discussed 'stop-closure' (damping) in the female head register (Shakespeare 1924, 11–12). He said, 'Some teachers have found that there are five registers. [Francesco] Lamperti felt that a change in the action of the vocal cords occurs every few notes. Indeed, one may say with equal truth that for every note and every degree of force pertaining to the note, there is a mechanism suitable to it alone. It may even be asserted that when a note is rightly sung, it is sometimes difficult to discover what register really produces it.'[20] By extension, this idea of every note requiring its own special adjustment of the vocal folds led away from a theory of discrete vocal registers to a 'no register' concept, which was espoused by several turn-of-the-century authors (see Monahan 1978, 143–4). It is apparent that the late nineteenth century was awash with register theories, some of which were based on a mixture of traditional methods and fashionable but dimly understood scientific methods – they were, like the proverbial curate's egg, 'good in parts.'

Register Theory and Modern Voice Science

The whole matter of voice registers continues to engage voice scientists today, with close attention being paid to physiological, acoustical, and aerodynamic aspects of registration. Modern laboratory equipment and techniques have made it possible to observe and measure register phenomena in finer detail than ever before. Even with these advantages, however, there is no single accepted theory of registers, although there are many points of agreement among the numerous studies.

The most widely accepted view of registers supports the old Italian theory of two primary registers separated by a break; these primary registers are considered to be particular modes of vocal fold vibration. In addition, there are so-called secondary, or acoustic, registers that are distinguished by certain resonance phenomena in the voice. Together, primary and secondary registers constitute a two-level concept of vocal registers.[21] Finally, there are auxiliary registers at the extreme high end of the soprano voice and the extreme low end of the bass voice, which also play a role in singing.

The Primary Registers

The theory of two primary registers was reaffirmed by Janwillem van den Berg in an oft-quoted article of 1960, where he proposed 'a new and simple concept of the origins of the main registers.' These registers are achieved 'with extreme and mutually exclusive adjustments of the larynx' (van den Berg 1960, 19). Like Johann Müller in 1840, van den Berg carried out experiments with excised human larynges. He discovered that the longitudinal tension of the vocal folds takes two forms which correspond to the two main registers.[22] In the lower part of the voice, the main body of the vocal folds are thrown into vibration. As the pitch ascends, the folds are stretched by the increased pull of the cricothyroid against the active resistance of the vocalis muscles, and stiffened by the internal tensors. This is called 'active longitudinal tension.' The maximum pitch that can normally be achieved while preserving this configuration is about $E\flat4$ (311 Hz), at which point the vocalis muscles are fully contracted. Beyond $E\flat4$ a completely different adjustment of the vocal folds is required. At this point there is a quick shift of muscular function as the active tension of the vocalis muscles is completely released. This is the so-called register break. Now the cricothyroid stretches the folds until resisted by the fully distended vocal ligaments, which are within the inner margins of the vocal folds. In this configuration only those inner margins vibrate. The passive resistance of the vocal ligaments to the active pull of the cricothyroid is called 'passive longitudinal tension.' When singing down the scale, this configuration can be extended to about $E\flat3$ (155 Hz), at which point the voice jumps into the lower register. This means that there is about an octave, from $E\flat3$ to $E\flat4$, which can be sung in either register. Van den Berg noted that the position of the arytenoid cartilages, together with subglottal pressure variations, can affect the two main registers (van den Berg 1960).

Van den Berg's theory was reinforced by another well-known article from 1960, in which Henry Rubin and Charles Hirt reported on their high-speed motion pictures of vocal fold behaviour in the two primary registers and in the break between them. By viewing the film at greatly reduced speed, they were able to observe that in chest voice the entire length and depth of the vocal folds participated in the vibrations. At the break the folds were thrown into momentary chaos, after which the falsetto mode of vibration took over. The folds continued to vibrate at about the same rate, but they hardly touched; their margins became quite thin, and the main body of the vocal folds did not appear to participate in the vibratory activity. They remained in a state of 'tonic contraction sufficient to withstand the air-stream yet not enough to bring them together or at best only lightly in the midline. Only the margins now vibrate' (Rubin and Hirt 1960, 1311). This resulted in the weakness observed by so many earlier authors. Both van den Berg's observations with excised larynges and Rubin and Hirt's direct observations of the human larynx with high-speed motion pictures are consistent with the observations Garcia made with his simple laryngeal mirror.

There is general agreement among modern researchers that the lower register creates a source spectrum that is richer in high frequency components than is the upper register.[23] As well, the lower register is often considered more efficient than the upper, using less airflow and higher subglottal pressure to create greater intensity.[24] Here again, however, it must be noted that firm glottal closure in either register increases the richness of the spectrum and the efficiency factor.[25] In other words, both the register and the glottal setting affect quality and efficiency. Again, all of these findings are consistent with Garcia's theories.

There are disagreements about the transitional point, or *passaggio*, between registers. Some authors have said that there is an octave phenomenon between male and female voices, with the register transition points being separated by an octave between genders.[26] But the more widely accepted view, going back to Garcia, is that the primary register break in both male and female singers is at about $Eb4$ (311 Hz) (Large 1973b, 13–15). The *passaggio* can take place over a range of several pitches where the registers overlap, and various studies have shown that listeners can perceive the difference between the primary registers with a high degree of accuracy.[27] Richard Miller, who visited numerous Italian voice studios, describes male voices as having a *primo passaggio* and a *secondo passaggio*, with a *zona di passaggio* between them (R. Miller 1977, 104, 117, 123, *seq.*). However, he cites no published literature regarding this theory, and most written sources discuss only one *passaggio* in male voices (between the chest and the falsetto registers) and two *passaggi* in females (one between chest and middle, and one between middle and head registers).

Covered Singing

It will be recalled that Garcia used the term *voix sombrée* to apply to the darkening of any tone in either register, while Diday and Pétrequin used the term *voix sombrée ou couverte* more specifically to describe covered high notes in tenors. Nowadays, the voice science literature uses the term 'covering singing' largely in the latter sense, and focuses on the role of the vocal tract in covered singing, while paying relatively little attention to the role of glottal closure.[28]

Aatto Sonninen described the muscular manoeuvre in covering as the 'external frame function' in singing (Sonninen 1956, 1961, 1968). The raising or lowering of the larynx is controlled by the strap muscles, which suspend the larynx in the neck by attaching to the hyoid bone above, the sternum below, and the pharyngeal musculature behind. The depressor muscles not only increase the supraglottal space, but also influence the cricoid-thyroid articulation in altering the length and tension of the vocal folds. When the strap muscles raise the larynx, a passive force called 'tracheal pull' tends to tip the cricoid arch upward, thus limiting the range of the cricoid muscle, and inhibiting the upward extension of the chest register. However, according to Sonninen, when the larynx is lowered to a position at or below its position of rest by the contraction of the sternothyroid muscle, the thyroid cartilage is tilted back and upward, thus leaving the cricothyroid muscle free to contract through its whole range. This reduces the length of the vocal folds, thereby delaying the register shift and permitting the chest register to function beyond its normal limits. The pitch can now be raised by an increase of the internal tension of the vocal folds, which reduces the effective vibrating mass while avoiding the maximal length and tension of the chest register.[29] Shipp agreed that a low laryngeal position allows more slack in the vocal folds than a high vertical laryngeal position, and results in more energy in the higher harmonics (Shipp 1987, 219).

The covering manoeuvre in male voices is employed for the notes above the *passaggio*. The precise location where covering begins varies with each voice category. For tenors, it usually occurs at around F♯4 (370 Hz); for baritones it is closer to E♭4 (311 Hz), and for basses it is somewhat lower again. However, the location can vary somewhat from singer to singer, and even within an individual voice it can vary with intensity, vowel, time of day, metabolism, and musical context. Operatic tenors carry covered voice up to C5 (523 Hz), the *do di petto*, while operatic baritones take it up to about A4 (440 Hz). The covering manoeuvre involves lowering of larynx and expanding of pharynx, which results in a darkening of the vowel (hence the association of *voix couverte* with *voix sombrée*). In the upper portion of the male chest register, F_1 is normally tuned to H_2 until the *passaggio* is reached. At that point the singer lets F_1 fall below H_2 and there is a shift of the dominant resonance to either the singer's formant, namely, a clustering of F_3, F_4, and sometimes F_5, or to an alignment of F_2 with H_3 or H_4 (Miller and Schutte 1990, 1994).

Covered singing has taken on a number of labels since Diday and Pétrequin first called it *voix sombrée ou couverte*. The Italians widely refer to it today as *voce piena in testa* (full head voice), while the Germans call it *Vollton der Kopfstimme* (full tone of the head voice), (Luchsinger and Arnold 1965, 95). Richard Miller calls it the 'legitimate head voice' (R. Miller 1977, 113; 1986a, 118). It has also been called the 'male operatic head register' (Large, Iwata, and van Leden 1972). Despite this proliferation of names, the term 'covering' seems to prevail in the parlance of most singers.

Belting

At this point I will digress, in order to discuss the vocal technique known as 'belting.' Even though it is not thought of as a part of classical singing styles, it is nevertheless closely related to the covering manoeuvre. Belting is widely used in some popular forms of singing, especially Broadway musicals, which increasingly employ classically trained singers to fill leading roles.[30] Belting is thus a necessary technique for 'crossover' singers, who move between classical and vernacular repertoire.

Belting takes place in both male and female singers when the chest voice is carried beyond the point where it would ordinarily switch registers, at about $E4$ (330 Hz). At this point the singer allows the larynx to rise, thereby raising F_1 to follow H_2. The vowels are not darkened as they would be in covered singing. Belting requires a large closed quotient and increased subglottal pressure. All this requires high effort and muscle rigidity which often results in a tone without vibrato, or one in which vibrato only begins toward the end of the duration of the note in what is sometimes called a 'vibrato crescendo.' Schutte and D.G. Miller offer this definition of belting: 'Belting is a manner of loud singing that is characterized by consistent use of "chest" register (>50% closed phase of glottis) in a range in which larynx elevation is necessary to match the first formant with the second harmonic on open (high F_1) vowels' (Schutte and D.G. Miller 1993, 142). In the male voice, belting is distinguished from covering primarily by the high position of the larynx. If the singer were to belt a high note, and then lower the larynx and expand the pharynx, he would achieve a covered tone. In either covering or belting, the chest register is extended upwards beyond its normal limits. In the female voice, belting takes place if the chest voice is carried up into the range usually referred to as the middle register. Many belters would be surprised to know how close they come to an operatic technique. Like covered singing, belting is often considered hazardous, and for those singers who do not execute it skillfully it probably is. However, as with covered singing, there are famous belters who have enjoyed long careers without vocal injury. More research is needed to determine precisely what is hazardous and what is not. There are probably some important differences between 'good' and 'bad' belting. As well, there may be individual differences in singers regarding vocal hardiness. It would be useful if these factors could be identified and measured before making wholesale condemnations of vigorous singing techniques.

Mixed Registers

As we have seen, the theory of mixed or blended registers has been around at least since Mengozzi's treatise of 1803. A century later, Browne and Behnke wrote:

The 'voce mista' is 'mixed' in the sense that it combines the *vibrating mechanism* of the 'lower thin' with the position of the larynx of the 'lower thick'; that is to say, while the vibrations are confined to the thin inner edges of the vocal ligaments, the larynx itself takes a much lower position in the throat than for the 'lower thin,' and the result is a remarkable increase of volume without any corresponding additional effort in the production of the tone. (Browne and Behnke 1904, 184)

More recent researchers have also maintained that registers can be 'blended.' Rubin and Hirt, after studying frames of their high-speed motion pictures, noted that some skilled singers could blend the transitional notes between registers. 'The movements are so well controlled that there is no real "break" and a true blending of the registers is achieved' (Rubin and Hirt 1960, 1320). Janwillem van den Berg theorized that the registers could be blended by a graduated change between active and passive longitudinal tension. 'This mixture between chest and falsetto may be called mid-voice.'[31] He said that 'the mid-voice is not really an "independent" register but a "mixture" of chest and falsetto register' (van den Berg 1960, 26–7). Some voice teachers also maintain that the two modes of vibration associated with the primary registers can be blended.[32] However, it is difficult to reconcile van den Berg's own assertion that the registers are caused by 'mutually exclusive adjustments of the larynx,' with his parallel theory that 'mid-voice' is a blending of those same exclusive adjustments. D.G. Miller writes:

Simultaneous activation of 'chest' and 'falsetto' modes of vibration of the vocal folds, while experimentally feasible, is not applicable in singing, and even the ability to pass imperceptibly from one to the other is considered more an exceptional gift than a pedagogical goal. The skilful blending of registers remains an important characteristic of the well-trained voice, but it is effected by other means than a percentagewise blending of the 'chest' and 'falsetto' voice source. (D.G. Miller 1994, 27)

Those 'other means' may include the role played by strong glottal closure during register transition. Researchers have noted that there is normally weak adduction immediately above the register break, corresponding to what Garcia had called the beginning of the falsetto.[33] Rubin and Hirt observed that in well-trained voices, especially female voices, strong glottal adduction at this point allowed the vocal fold action in the upper register to more closely resemble the lower register (Rubin and Hirt 1960, 1312–13). John Large, in a critique of van den Berg's work, suggested that the true basis for register blending was the firm closure of the arytenoids:

If the mechanism of equalization is related to the mechanism of medial compression ... the appearance of similar energy in the higher partials of the two registers can be explained on the assumption that the singer somehow learns to make the glottal pulses in the two registers similar. In other words, the pedagogical notion of 'mixing' some chest sound with the middle register to make it sound like chest – and therefore, blended or equalized – may mean that the singer prevents a glottal 'chink' from appearing in the middle register, thus maintaining the explosiveness of the glottal pulse characteristics of chest register adjustment. (Large 1974, 27)

The idea of keeping the arytenoids firmly pressed together, especially in the weak notes of the lower middle register, is precisely what Garcia had in mind when he recommended the glottal 'pinch' at the register transition points.

Acoustic Registers

The discussion of 'secondary' registers is a fairly recent idea which takes account of certain discontinuities in the voice that are related to the shifting of the dominant resonance. These are sometimes referred to as 'resonance registers' (as opposed to 'laryngeal registers') although the word 'registers' may be too strong, since they are not of the same order as laryngeal registers. Paul B. Oncley was among the first to point out this distinction. After describing the two primary registers, he went on to discuss 'a series of changes in voice quality, sometimes designated as "lifts," which are purely acoustic in origin' (Oncley 1973, 35). These lifts are described as shifts in the tuning of formants to lower harmonics as the fundamental frequency rises, thereby resulting in a quick change from one dominant resonance of the vocal tract to another.[34]

From a pedagogical point of view, the most important lift in the female voice takes place at the juncture of the so-called middle and head registers (about D_5, 597 Hz). In her middle register, a soprano may produce a full, dark sound by approximating F_1 and F_2 and tuning them to H_2. If she tries to carry this dominant resonance beyond its normal limit of about D_5, the voice quality may be described as too 'heavy,' and there is a risk of an abrupt and unwelcome change to an F_1–H_1 tuning. The singer may perceive this as a 'lift,' a 'flip,' or even a 'break.' A skillful singer will thus prepare for the formant shift to F_1–H_1 before the pitch D_5. This may be perceived as a 'lightening' of the tone, or as singing in 'head voice.' The shift of the dominant resonance at D_5 is consistent with the three-register theory of the female voice.

An equally important phenomenon that takes place in the high female voice, as well as in the male falsetto voice, is the increased glottal resistance that results from acoustic backpressure during F_1–H_1 formant tuning, thereby reinforcing the vocal fold oscillation. In a 1986 study, H.K. Schutte and D.G. Miller reported that in the female 'head' register, beginning at about F_5–G_5 (700–800 Hz), there is a second source of glottal resistance (in addition to an adjustment in the intrinsic laryngeal muscles) that is caused by a kind of momentary acoustic backpressure during each vibratory cycle. This supraglottal pressure wave derives from the phase relationships between the glottal cycle and the standing wave in the pharynx, and occurs when F_1 is tuned to H_1.[35] This backpressure reduces (and even momentarily reverses) the airflow at the glottis. The phenomenon is also present in male falsetto, and is a factor in the ability of countertenors to sing long phrases on a single breath.

Subjectively, it may be experienced as a form of ease, or of 'letting go,' as the singer no longer has to consciously pinch the glottis in order to achieve a lower rate of airflow.

One might safely conclude, then, that there are several phenomena which converge to distinguish the female head register from the middle register. As discussed by Garcia and others, the arytenoid cartilages come firmly together for head voice, thus shortening the glottis. In addition, there is a shift to F_1–H_1 formant tuning in the head register. Finally, glottal resistance is increased by acoustic backpressure, which reduces airflow. If Garcia had known about these phenomena, he might well have agreed that they constitute different 'mechanical principles' from the other registers, and that they reinforce the three-register theory.

Auxiliary Registers

In addition to the registers already discussed, there remain two further registers that must be considered – one at the extreme lower end of the male voice, and the other at the extreme upper end of the female voice. The low auxiliary register, which is sometimes employed by basses, has already been referred to as *Strohbass*. It has also been called 'vocal fry,' or 'pulse register,' owing to its crackling quality,[36] and as we saw earlier, Garcia called it the *contre-bass* register. It is often heard in Russian choral music. Mackenzie compared this voice to the growling of animals, and said it must, 'as a rule, end in destroying it' (Mackenzie 1890, 101). The *Strohbass* sound is produced by a combination of adductive tension of the transverse interarytenoid muscles and inactive lateral interarytenoids. This causes 'the posterior parts of the arytenoids at the apex to contact each other, but the vocal processes do not contact each other, or the contact is very slight.' The airflow and subglottal pressures are low, there are large amplitudes of the vocal folds, a small closed quotient, and a small number of partials (van den Berg 1960, 25). Subharmonics, which sound an octave below the original tone may also be present (Švec, Schutte, and Miller 1996).

The high soprano voice also has an auxiliary register, which is known by various names such as 'flageolet,' 'whistle,' 'bird-tone,' or 'flute.' Until recently, this register was mistakenly described as being caused by 'posterior phonation,' in which the sound source was not the vibrating vocal folds at all, but rather, eddies of air that formed in a posterior chink between the arytenoid cartilages called the 'short triangle.'[37] However, a recent pilot study by D.G. Miller and H.K. Schutte (1993) has shown that this register is characterized by its resonance, not by a change in the sound source.

The *flageolet* register typically begins between $B4$ and $Eb5$. Below this, the first formant is still tuned to the first harmonic (F_1–H_1). In the flageolet register the first harmonic passes the first formant and moves to a resonance formed by the approximation of F_1 and F_2. Physiologically, *flageolet* is characterized by 'minimal/reduced vocal fold oscillation and no apparent phase of complete closure,' perhaps influenced by the reduced driving force in the vocal folds when F_1 falls below F_0 (Miller and Schutte 1993, 210). The singer may experience this as a sense of disengagement of the vocal muscles, due to the reduction in the effort to raise F_1. There can still be a strong intensity in such notes, even though F_1 does not align with F_0, but vowel identification is lost. From a pedagogical point of view, sopranos need not know about the particulars of formants or vocal fold oscillation in order to make the minute adjustments necessary for the *flageolet* register. Resonance imagery may play an important role in making these adjustments.

Conclusions

This brief review of registers has tried to address several important matters. The human voice is not a perfect instrument from the standpoint of evenness of quality from the lowest notes to the highest. Rather, the history of solo singing is bound up with a recognition of the natural discontinuities in the voice, which cause it to be segmented in its strength, colour, mobility, and vowel intelligibility. Singers have long attempted to find ways of unifying the voice so as to give at least the *impression* of evenness throughout its range.

Garcia was correct in ascribing registers to different 'mechanical principles.' We now know that there are several different mechanical principles involved. The mode of vibration of the vocal folds is different for chest voice, falsetto, *Strohbass*, and *flageolet*. As well, different glottal settings can affect the strength and brilliance of both primary registers, and can play an important role in 'equalizing' the registers. Vocal tract adjustments can lead to shifts in the dominant resonance, or 'lifts' in the voice, as well as to the 'covered' quality in male voices. Garcia's definition of registers was a good starting point for a fuller understanding of this subject. Modern voice science has now provided more specific information regarding registers, but the matter requires more research.

4

Appoggio: The Breath Be Dammed!

The Concept of *Appoggio*

Chi sa ben respirare e sillibare saprà ben cantare (He who knows how to breathe and pronounce well, knows how to sing well). The actual source of this quotation is not clear, but it is most often ascribed to the famous late eighteenth-century castrato and teacher Gasparo Pacchierotti (1740–1821).[1] Another quote from about the same time, 'It is one thing to *breathe*, and another to *vocalise* that breath,' was ascribed to a Dr Holder by the celebrated eighteenth-century English music historian Charles Burney (1935, 2:501). Taken together, these two statements frame the range of opinion on breath control which seems as familiar today as it was then. Pacchierotti implied that there was a special manner of taking a breath that was the key to good singing; Holder maintained it was the way that the breath was turned into tone that was most important. Today, as then, there are teachers who concentrate on methods of inhalation, as opposed to those who concentrate on phonation itself. According to a joke in the singing profession, some teachers produce good singers, others produce good breathers.

Of course this is oversimplified. It is certainly possible that when Pacchierotti used the word *respirare*, he was referring not just to inhalation but to the complex dynamics of breath control in singing. It goes without saying that singers must take in more breath than is necessary for ordinary life functions. Numerous views and countless pages in the pedagogical literature are devoted to the relative merits of diaphragmatic (belly) breathing, clavicular (shoulder) breathing, raised-rib (intercostal) breathing, and back (dorsal) breathing.[2] There are descriptions of breathing practices in national 'schools' of singing, suggesting that German, Italian, and English singers tend to use different breathing techniques (R. Miller 1977, 7–44). Experience shows that voice pupils's eyes tend to glaze over when the subject of breathing comes up, especially when breathing exercises are isolated from singing itself. I have seen some professional singers with heaving chests, some with protruding bellies, some with raised shoulders, and some with bouncing epigastriums, all of whom sang beautifully, regardless of their breathing methods. I have also seen awkward postures that have not adversely affected good singing (for example, a famous soprano at the Metropolitan Opera, eight months pregnant and stuffed into a gunnysack, who sang Gilda's final scene from *Rigoletto* beautifully). While good posture and good breathing methods are certainly important, especially in a singer's early training, it is ultimately the way in which the breath is turned into a singing tone that is crucial. On this issue, I lean toward the view of Burney's friend Dr Holder.

In singing, exhalation becomes synonymous with phonation, and phonation must be controlled by the careful management of the breath in such a manner as to produce the optimum tone quality and flexibility. The critical parameters of breath management are subglottal pressures and airflow rates, which are affected both by the respiratory muscles and by glottal resistance to the breath. A full explanation of breathing for singing must include details of the physiology of respiration, as well as the mechanics of glottal resistance. Other matters, such as vocal onset, registers, proprioceptive feedback systems, carbon dioxide tolerance, vertical laryngeal positions, tone quality, vibrato, and expression, are all related to breath control.

From a pedagogical point of view, the complexity involved in breathing and breath management might well confound, rather than help, the voice pupil. As an antidote to this, voice teachers of the past turned to figurative language as a means of reducing complex functions into simple images that fall easily within the mental grasp. We have already seen that the term *chiaroscuro* provided just such an image for achieving a bright-dark voice quality, in place of more laborious but specific descriptions of physiology and acoustics. The history of vocal pedagogy has also produced helpful terms when discussing breath control. Chief among them is *appoggio*.

The Italian word *appoggiare* means 'to lean.' I believe that in singing, this term has two specific applications. The first refers to the muscular antagonism between the inspiratory and expiratory breathing muscles during singing. This is often described by singers as a feeling of 'bearing down' with the diaphragm. The second refers to the role of the larynx in 'holding back,' or 'damming' the breath by means of glottal resistance, and by the intentional lowering of the larynx against the upward-bearing pressure of the breath. Hence *appoggio*, in its fullest sense, refers to a complex equilibrium between several sets of muscles at both the respiratory and the laryngeal level, in which an image of leaning on the voice is an effective metaphor in breath control. This concept of *appoggio* developed slowly in the history of vocal pedagogy, and was fully formed only in the nineteenth century. Subsequently, other terms that served a similar purpose were coined. They will be discussed in due course, but first it is necessary to see how breathing and breath control were described in the earlier periods.

The Early Treatises

The early treatises on singing did not offer any elaborate theories of inhalation or breath control. The few remarks that were offered were highly pragmatic, advocating quiet inhalation and the economical use of the breath for the effective rendering of the musical phrase. Girolamo Maffei's eighth rule of singing was 'to gradually press the breath with the voice, and pay great attention that it does not go out through the nose or by the palate, for the one or the other would be a very great error' (Maffei 1562, 35; MacClintock 1979, 45).' This seems to be a description of glottal resistance to the breath. Maffei also noted that the falsetto register used more breath than chest voice (26; 42) In 1592 Zacconi discussed breath control in relation to musical phrasing, and instructed the singer to 'undertake only as many figures [ornaments] as he can comfortably accommodate on one breath.' He also said that a singer should have good lung capacity and throat agility so that the long florid passages would be neither too weak nor interrupted for the sake of taking a breath (Zacconi 1592, fol. 59).

In his manual on vocal ornamentation published in 1594, Giovanni Battista Bovicelli also cautioned the singer to be discreet in the use of the breath. He said the singer should 'breathe in time, and with judgement; and especially one should not breathe between those notes which serve for accents.' The word *accenti* here referred to those vocal flourishes or ornaments that were an important part of the emerging virtuoso singing style; Bovicelli, like Zacconi, admonished the singer to not breathe in the middle of an ornamental passage. He poked fun at singers who stopped to breathe too often, 'like a horse who is afraid of his own shadow,' and he complained of 'those who make more stir with their breathing than with their voice' (Bovicelli 1594, 16). (Our little joke about breathers versus singers is obviously not a new one.) Bovicelli was one of the first authors to advocate silent inhalation, a point that was repeated in many later manuals.

In 1602 Giulio Caccini expressed some of the same concerns as his predecessors, but he also raised some new issues. He noted that 'a good voice [is] very essential, especially as regards breath control [*la respirare del fiato*],' and he advocated breath economy, advising singers to avoid falsetto and the wasting of breath. But the aspect of breathing which most concerned him was the swelling and diminishing of the voice, which required the greatest control of the breath:

Rather must one use [the breath] to give more spirit to vocal crescendos-and-decrescendos, *esclamazioni*, and all the other effects we have demonstrated: let one make sure not to fall short in a pinch. From the falsetto no nobility of good singing can arise; that comes from a natural voice, comfortable through the whole range, able to be controlled at will, [and] with the breath used only to demonstrate mastery of all the best affects necessary for this most noble manner of singing. (Caccini 1970, 56).

Caccini stressed the importance of breath control in making all the gradations between soft and loud, and he described several variations of these gradations. (Today's musical terminology refers to intensity levels as 'dynamic levels,' or simply 'dynamics.' This is an unfortunate use of the word *dynamics*, which normally has far broader implications, but we are stuck with it.)

In 1638 the late-blooming madrigalist Domenico Mazzocchi (1592–1665) published a book of five-part madrigals, and in his preface, gave a colourful description of the vocal crescendo-decrescendo. He said that, to perform his compositions, one must gradually increase both breath and tone, or 'sweetly increase his voice in liveliness but not in tone; then he should gradually quieten it and make it smooth until it can scarcely be heard and seems to be coming from the depths of a cavern.'[3] His admonition to increase the voice in 'liveliness but not in tone' is a tantalizing one, but eludes a clear interpretation.

In 1668 Bénigne de Bacilly (ca. 1625–90) repeated the advice of earlier authors when he said that good breathing is essential to good vocal performance. He said the singer should avoid 'cutting a word short or cleaving a syllable in two. Many singers commit these faults and the resulting effect is very bad. Although good breathing would seem to be entirely dependent upon good lungs, it has been established that it is acquired and aided by training in addition to other particulars of singing' (Bacilly 1968, 25).

Other brief references to breathing and breath control in early treatises, are limited to common-sense issues: when (or when not) to take a breath, taking enough air, using it economically, and controlling the breath well for affective passages and dynamic gradations.[4] More detailed descriptions of breathing and breath management had to wait for a later time.

The Eighteenth-century Tutors

The main vocal tutors of the eighteenth century did not go much beyond the earlier treatises in their advice about breathing. Like his precursors, Pierfrancesco Tosi cautioned against breathing in the middle of a word, discouraged breathing during long florid passages, urged the student to make good use of breath, and advised the pupil to take breath quietly and be sure that he has enough (Tosi 1986, 36–7; 1743, 60–1). Tosi referred to the *crescendo-decrescendo* as the *messa di voce*, and complained that the art of singing the *messa di voce* was in a state of decline:

[The *messa di voce*] consists in letting [the voice] come out softly from the least piano, so that it goes little by little to the greatest forte, and then returns by the same artifice from the forte to the piano. A beautiful *messa di voce* in the mouth of a professor who is not stingy with it, and does not use it except on the open vowels, will never fail to make the greatest effect. There are now very few singers who esteem it as worthy of their taste, whether because they love instability in the voice, or because they wish to remove themselves from the despised past. (1986, 17; 1743, 27–8)

In 1774, Giambattista Mancini (1714–1800) also touched on the subjects of breath economy and the *messa di voce*. He said that 'the most necessary thing for success, is the art of knowing how to conserve the breath, and manage it' (Mancini 1967, 62). He maintained that the *messa di voce* required advanced training in breath management: 'I repeat that the scholar should not presume to be able to execute the *messa di voce* if he has not first acquired, in the manner described above, the art of conserving, reinforcing and taking back the breath: since on this alone depends the gift of the just and necessary gradation of the voice' (45). Mancini reiterated the importance of the *messa di voce*, saying that it 'lends great excellence to singing,' and enables the singer to 'sustain and graduate without any defect.' In it lies 'the secret no less than the art' of beautiful singing (44). He rebuked those who did not know how to sing the *messa di voce* properly, while praising the castrato Farinelli (Carlo Broschi, 1705–82) for his mastery of the breath, saying, 'The art of knowing how to conserve and take in breath with reserve and neatness, without ever becoming noticeable to anyone, began and ended with him.' Mancini made a stronger case for breath management and for the *messa di voce* than any of his predecessors, saying, 'I have gone far beyond the call of duty, reasoning so much on the *messa di voce*, but I tell you, studious youths, that it is so close to my heart that I could speak of it forever' (46).

In 1792 Jean Paul Egide Martini (1741–1816) also discussed the importance of conserving the breath: 'When, upon respiration, the lungs are filled with air, it is necessary to hold back the air with greatest care and not let anything be expelled other than the portion required to make the vocal chords [*sic*] vibrate. This manner of breathing gives the strength to swell and diminish the tones at will; it increases the volume of the voice on low and high notes; it provides facility and lightness in difficult passages' (Sanford 1979, 90). Martini's notion of 'holding back' the breath, like Mancini's 'taking back the breath,' was repeated by many later authors, and was a precursor to the concept of *appoggio*.

In his *Raccolta di esercizi* the castrato Girolemo Crescentini discussed the *messa di voce* under the heading 'Flexibility' (Crescentini 1810, article 3). He defined it as the effortless 'attack, strengthening, and diminishing' of the tone. He continued by saying that this should be done not only over an entire musical phrase, but also for the period, and even the individual note. This concept is in contradistinction to what Garcia called 'tones held with equal force' (*les sons tenus de force égale*) (Garcia 1847, 1:63; 1984, 132). Singers who continuously vary the intensity of each note by means of the *messa di voce* are seldom heard today; instead singers who produce tones with equal force seem to be far more common.

The Garcia School

As discussed earlier, the practices of the old Italian school were absorbed into the method books of Mengozzi (1803) and Garaudé (1830) at the Paris Conservatoire, even before Garcia's *Traité* (1841). Garaudé claimed that these treatises reflected the singing practices of the major Italian centres and the most famous singers from the previous several decades (Garaudé 1830, 11). Like the Italians, Garaudé said that there should be quiet inhalation, and that the breath must be economized in order to sustain long phrases. He described both full breaths for long phrases and half breaths for short ones (25–8), and he described the *messa di voce* as follows: 'Each tone of the scale is made on the vowel [a], and it must be *filé*; it is said that it must begin very sweetly, and be gradually increased until halfway through the note (where it reaches its greatest force), then diminished insensibly to the end of the note. This manner of spinning the tone [*filer les sons*] is called *mise de voix* or *messa di voce*.' He continued by saying that the *messa di voce* must be done 'with purity and without effort. In reinforcing the weak tones, it must be done without altering the organ or disfiguring its sound. The quality of the timbre (*metallo*) of the voice must be natural.' He maintained that 'one must not change the timbre. The registers should remain the same regardless of the force of the voice, and one should not use the *voce di testa*' (28–9).

Garcia devoted only about half a page to respiration in the 1841 edition of his *Traité*, and this dealt largely with inhalation; he added a few further remarks in the 1847 edition, and in *Hints on Singing* (1894). The brevity of his remarks demonstrates that the manner of taking a breath was not the focus of his method; rather, singing itself was the pressing matter. Garcia advocated taking a quiet breath by combining a raised chest with a lowered diaphragm: 'This double procedure, on which I insist, enlarges the lungs, first at the base, then by the circumference, and allows the lungs to complete all their expansion and to receive all the air which they can contain. To advise the abdominal breathing exclusively would be to voluntarily reduce by one half the element of strength most indispensible to the singer, the breath' (Garcia 1847, 1:24; 1984, 33). He described both the full breath (*respiro*) and the half-breath (*mezzo-respiro*), and cautioned against taking too much breath which then tends to escape too quickly. During singing itself, he required a continuous and well-managed pressure of the diaphragm, and he spoke of the necessity for 'steady,' 'moderate,' and 'prolonged' pressure (Garcia 1894, 13, 22).

Garcia recognized that the *messa di voce* (which he also called the *sons filés* and *spianata di voce*) was the best test of breath support. He said this exercise is not meant for beginners, since it 'requires a singer to be expert in the control of the breath and of the *timbres*.' After describing the *messa di voce* as a crescendo-decrescendo on a single tone, he proceeded to give a detailed description of the exercise:

The student *will begin the tone softly in the falsetto and in sombre timbre*. As we have seen, this procedure makes the larynx firm and contracts the pharynx. Then, *without varying the position, and, as a result, the timbre, one will pass into the chest register*, fixing the larynx more and more firmly in order to prevent making the abrupt movement which produces the hiccough at the moment of the separation of the two registers. Once established in the chest register, one will raise the larynx again and will dilate the pharynx to clarify the timbre in such a way that toward the middle of the duration of the tone it will have all its brilliance and all its force. In order to soften the tone, the student will do the reverse; that-is-to-say, that before passing into the falsetto register, *at the moment the voice is diminished he will darken the chest tone*, again fastening the larynx low and contracting the pharynx in order to support it and to avoid the jerk of the change of registers. Then he will pass slowly from the chest register to the falsetto; after which he will relax the pharynx and extinguish the tone. I deduce this rule from the physiological fact that the larynx, being held low by the sombre timbre, can produce the two registers without being displaced. Now, the displacement produces the hiccough which so disagreeably separates the one register from the other. (Garcia 1847, 1:60; 1984, 135–6)

Garcia's *messa di voce* thus involved a finely controlled coordination between glottal settings, vertical laryngeal position, and the contraction of the pharyngeal muscles. His *messa di voce* begins softly with the loose glottal closure associated with *falsetto* (middle register), and with a low larynx that darkens the timbre; the crescendo requires a 'pinching' of the glottis, which is associated with the chest voice, as well as a raising of the larynx and an adjustment of the pharynx to create a brilliant quality. Presumably the 'force' is gained by increasing the breath pressure. For the decrescendo, glottal closure is relaxed, and the larynx descends to again darken the voice quality. The *messa di voce* thus requires fine control of glottal closure, breath pressure, and the posture of the vocal tract. It is easy to see why the *messa di voce* is often considered to be the most difficult of all vocal manoeuvres.

It is apparent that there was an important difference of opinion between Garaudé and Garcia regarding the best manner of performing the *messa di voce*. Whereas Garaudé advocated an even tone quality throughout the exercise, with no change of register or timbre, and no use of the *voce di testa*, Garcia required both a change of register and a change of timbre. This indicates that there were two ways of performing the *messa di voce*, and, as we will see, both methods continue to be taught up to the present time.

Garcia's student Julius Stockhausen devoted only one short paragraph to breath inhalation in his treatise of 1884. In it he echoed Garcia in saying that diaphragmatic breathing alone is sufficient only for the quick *mezzo-respiro*, and that a combination of diaphragmatic and rib breathing is necessary for a full breath (*respiro pieno*). He quoted Garcia's statement on *the messa di voce* in full, apparently considering it to be definitive. However, he expressed surprise that Garcia delayed discussion of the *messa di voce* until page sixty of his treatise, since he considered this technique to be 'the basis of voice culture' (Stockhausen 1884, 13–17). Apparently, Stockhausen regarded the *messa di voce* as a beginning exercise rather than an advanced one. Some pre-Garcia authors had indeed placed the *messa di voce* at the beginning of their manuals as the most elementary vocal manoeuvre in a singer's training.[5] On this matter, too, there was a difference of opinion among voice teachers.

Garcia's teachings were carried into the twentieth century by Hermann Klein (1856–1934), an English writer and student of Garcia who helped him in the writing of *Hints on Singing* (1894). Klein also published his own book, *The Bel Canto, with Particular Reference to the Singing of Mozart* (1923), as well as several books of musical criticism. He maintained that silent breathing brought the larynx to a favourably low position for singing, whereas a noisy breath indicated a high laryngeal position. He advocated a high chest, abdominal breathing, and 'compressed breath' (Klein 1923, 21–4). He regarded the *messa di voce* as 'the central characteristic of the old Italian school,' both on individual notes and in phrases, and he said the singer 'must be guided by ease and economy of breath-pressure' (31–2). He said that Garcia's first rule was 'to repress the breathing power and bring it into proper proportion with the resisting force of the throat and larynx' (Klein 1903, 36).

The Mandl-Lamperti School

In *Hygiène de la Voix* (1876) Dr Louis Mandl offered a new term for good breath control in singing. Mandl was the Paris physiologist whose work was absorbed and cited by the Lampertis in their manuals of singing. He coined the term *lutte vocale* to describe the 'vocal struggle' between the inspiratory and expiratory muscles. Francesco Lamperti quoted him as follows:

To sustain a given note the air should be expelled slowly; to attain this end, the respiratory muscles, by continuing their action, strive to retain the air in the lungs, and oppose their action to that of the expiratory muscles, which, at the same time, drive it out for the production of the note. There is thus established a balance of power between these two agents, which is called the *lutte vocale*, or vocal struggle. On the retention of this equilibrium depends the just emission of the voice, and by means of it alone can true expression be given to the sound produced. (F. Lamperti 1916, 25)

Mandl maintained that the *lutte vocale* is primarily the struggle between the abdominal muscles and the diaphragm, and that this struggle is reflected in the contractions of the larynx as well (Mandl 1876, 16–17). When the mechanism of breathing and the movements of the larynx and pharynx are all favourable to the singing voice, there results a balance which he called *bien posée*. He added that the prephonatory set of the glottis is one of the most important aspects of the *pose de la voix* (71–2). His 'pose of the voice' is thus a complex balance of respiratory and laryngeal muscles.

Francesco Lamperti embraced these remarks, since his own opinions 'coincide with those expressed by the celebrated Dr. Mandl of Paris' (F. Lamperti 1916, 24). In his treatise, Lamperti gave the orthodox description of three methods of inhalation – diaphragmatic, lateral, and clavicular. He admonished the singer to avoid noisy breathing (F. Lamperti 1884, 14). 'Diaphragmatic respiration is the sole kind that should be comployed [sic] by the singer, for it is the only one of the three that allows the larynx to remain in a natural and unstrained condition' (11). He elaborated on this point with the statement, 'Let him take the deepest inspiration he can, making use of the diaphragm and muscles of the belly. Any effort about the chest-ribs in breathing must be absolutely and entirely avoided. It is here that the evil lies' (56). What Lamperti may have been implying here is that the elastic recoil forces of chest-rib breathing could cause the singer to unwittingly close the glottis and raise the larynx against the breath pressure that can result from such recoil forces. On the other hand, since belly breathing is accomplished largely through relaxation of the abdominal wall, such unwelcome recoil forces are absent, and the singer has greater control over both glottal closure and laryngeal height. Whether or not this interpretation is correct, it is clear that with these remarks, Lamperti unequivocally established his preference for what is now called 'deep' breathing or 'belly out' breathing.

Another aspect of breath control discussed by Lamperti is the rate of airflow during singing. He advised the singer to 'hold a lighted taper close to his mouth; if the flame does not flicker during the emission of the sound, it shows that the air is gently emitted, and proves him to be a master of the art of respiration' (14). In addition to advocating low air-flow rates, Lamperti also made comments which seem to advocate elevated subglottal pressures. He said, 'Throughout its extension, the voice must be less vigorous than the breath' (49–50). He noted that the same 'internal effort,' that is, the 'energy of vocal emission' should be employed whether singing *piano* or *forte*, and that the tension of the abdominal muscles must not relax in soft tones, but must be maintained in order to 'colour and enliven' the voice (52).

It was probably Francesco Lamperti who was most responsible for entrenching the concept of *appoggio* in the pedagogical literature. Jekyll translated the term as 'fixing the voice' (vii, 2, 8), and Lamperti defined it as follows: 'By singing *appoggiata*, is meant that all notes, from the lowest to the highest, are produced by a column of air over which the singer has perfect command, by holding back the breath, and not permitting more air than is absolutely necessary for the formation of the note to escape from the lungs' (F. Lamperti 1916, 22). This could be accomplished by a particular form of vocal onset, in which 'the sound is to be attacked with a slight back-stroke of the glottis, almost as if one continued to take breath.' He admonished the singer to 'take care to hold the breath during the act of *portamento*,' thus implying the continued contraction of inspiratory muscles during singing. The same breath control applied to *legato* singing (F. Lamperti 1884, 13, 21; 1916, 17). Lamperti further elaborated on breath retention when he said: 'Here I warn the scholar, when attacking the sound, to sustain the breath by supposing that he is still taking in more (after a full breath taken), so that the voice may lean upon the breath, or, to express it more clearly, be sustained by the column of air' (F. Lamperti 1884, 13). G.B. Lamperti expressed it this way: 'When one sings well, one has the sensation of drinking' (W.E. Brown 1957, 129). The metaphor 'drinking the tone' remains in use today. Francesco Lamperti also employed resonance imagery under his rubric of 'fixing the voice' when he said that 'the sounds must appear to the singer to be reflected in the back part of the head; he must feel them there, rising as the note rises, and falling as it falls' (F. Lamperti 1884, 14). In short, Lamperti credited *appoggio* with many of the attributes of good singing. He concluded: 'It is by singing with the voice well *appoggiata*, that the pupil, under careful supervision, will learn what is the true character and the capabilities of his own voice; he will know what music to sing, how to render his singing elegant, and remedy defects of intonation. In this, in my idea, lies the great secret of the art of singing' (F. Lamperti 1916, 14).

Lamperti gave only a brief description of the *messa di voce*, and like Garcia, he reserved it for the advanced student: 'The last, the most important, and most difficult method should only be practised when the pupil is well advanced in vocalization, and consists in a note *pianissimo*, reinforcing it to the full extent of the voice, and then gradually diminishing it, so as to end *pianissimo*, retaining the same quality of sound in all the gradations of crescendo and diminuendo' (F. Lamperti 1916, 13). He reiterated this in his discussion of vocal intensity: '*Piano* should in all respects, with the exception of intensity, resemble the *forte*; it should possess the same depth, character, and feeling; it should be supported by an equal quantity of breath, and should have the same quality of tone, so that even when reduced to *pianissimo* it may be heard at as great a distance as the *forte*' (19). In *The Art of Singing* (1884) he offered yet another description of the relationship between loud and soft singing:

Given a phrase, it is indispensable that the same energy of vocal emission should be employed in singing it *piano*, as in singing it *forte*, or, to express it better, the same intensity of *internal effort*. The volume and sonorousness of the voice are qualities entirely independent of what I call *internal effort*. If, in emitting a small quantity of voice, the tension of the diaphragm be diminished, the result will be that the *piano* will have less life, less colour than the *forte*, whereas it often requires more. There must therefore be no relaxation of tension in the abdominal muscles ... (F. Lamperti 1884, 52)

By saying that soft and loud tones should be similar in all respects except loudness, Lamperti subscribed to Garaudé's (rather than Garcia's) description of performing the *messa di voce*.

Francesco Lamperti considered breath control to be the most important aspect of singing, and he used the concept of *appoggio* as a means of achieving that control. For him, *appoggio* was a broad term that referred not only to the balance of inspiratory and expiratory muscles, but also to vocal onset and glottal closure, position of the vocal tract, airflow and breath pressure, legato, the *messa di voce*, and even good intonation. Thus, *appoggio* became an inclusive term for breathing dynamics, and a useful catch-word in vocal pedagogy.

Francesco's son Giovanni carried on his father's tradition while adding his own stamp to it. Like his father, he followed Mandl in advocating abdominal (diaphragmatic) breathing as the chief means of inhalation, but he also accepted the action of so-called auxiliary muscles, such as the intercostal muscles, in order to ensure 'compressed' breath.

He coupled this to his own brand of vocal imagery: 'When the top and bottom of the lungs are equally full of compressed air, the voice will focus in the head, and awake all the resonance in the head, mouth, and chest.'[6] He also encouraged 'silent breathing' (W.E. Brown 1957, 106), and in reference to glottal resistance to the breath he stated, 'Finally the voice controls the breath – not the reverse.'[7] He said, 'Breath is "held back" by two fundamentals, vibration (pulsating of the vocal lips) opposing the exit of compressed air from the lungs, and concerted action of [the] entire muscular covering of the body restraining the energy of the escaping air, the diaphragm acting as a "stop-cock"' (W.E. Brown 1957, 23–4). Giovanni placed great emphasis on the control of a steady, elevated subglottal breath pressure. 'With insufficient pressure, the tone lacks in steadiness (*appoggio*; that is, the steady air-pressure on the vocal cords during tone production). Higher breath-pressure presupposes deeper inspiration. Each and every tone must have steady support!' (G.B. Lamperti 1905, 9). The function of the glottis was to 'release' compressed breath. In his fullest statement, he said:

Loose, pushed out breath is useless even injurious, though you have lungs full, for it causes local effects, irregular vibration and disrupted energies. Compressed breath comes through co-ordination. It has only to be guided, and restrained. Its inherent power feeds all the effects made by the vocal-cords. It does not upset the pose of the voice. It permits the throat to act naturally, 'open' as in talking. It does away with both breathy and pinched tones. It does not demand one quality of resonance only but commands all colors, from the darkest to the lightest and all pitches, from highest to lowest. Compressed breath permits all effects made in declamation, provided same effects do not become a 'method.' In fact, stereotyped singing is impossible, when breath is compressed. There is no 'attack,' no 'mouth position,' no 'tongue control,' no 'voice placing,' no 'fixed chest,' no relaxing this or that muscle, no stiffening any part of the body, in fact, nothing that would not spring from instinctive utterance. (W.E. Brown 1957, 64–5)

Lamperti noted that aspirates (such as those that occur on the letter 'h') required in some languages were detrimental to compressed breath and to the steadiness of the legato. 'The language best suited for the study of singing is the Italian, because it is the only one without aspirates' (7). Regarding muscular effort, Giovanni said, 'It takes more muscle to hold the breath energy back, than it does to let it go. Therefore, soft singing is more difficult than loud singing, and should be studied last' (51). Like Francesco, he rejected relaxing the glottal resistance for soft tones.

Giovanni's concept of *appoggio*, then, was that it required a steady and elevated subglottal pressure, on soft notes as well as on loud, and a holding back of the airflow both by glottal resistance and by the balance between inspiratory and expiratory breathing muscles. He called the point of resistance to the breath 'the point of support' (G.B. Lamperti 1905, 10). He said, 'Escaping breath will turn into tone only when the inherent energy in the compressed air feeds the pulsations in the throat' (W.E. Brown 1957, 64). He also recognized the role of proprioception in controlling breath pressure when he referred to the sensitivity of the 'inside skin' – the mucous membrane with its network of nerves. 'They keep the singer informed as to what is taking place in these cavities, and finally anticipate and control the vocal process. Also, through the sense of touch in the tissues of the body does the mind control the power of the breath' (35).

The younger Lamperti described the *messa di voce* as 'the most difficult problem in singing' (W.E. Brown 1957, 13), and he agreed with Francesco in saying that it was for advanced students. 'The *messa di voce* is produced solely by breath-control. The spinning-out technique (*filare la voce*) is very difficult; it must be managed with the utmost circumspection' (G.B. Lamperti 1905, 20–1). 'Singing loudly is releasing; singing softly is restraining the pent-up energy in compressed air filling the lungs, co-ordinately gauged in doing so' (W.E. Brown 1957, 61). There was no suggestion here of changing registers or timbres in the execution of the *messa di voce*. There was no room for loose glottal closure in the Lamperti school, not even in the *messa di voce*.

It is apparent that the Mandl-Lamperti school placed more emphasis on elevated subglottal pressure levels than did Garcia. The teachings of Garcia met the demands of the music of Mozart and Rossini. The Lampertis, however, taught a later generation of singers who performed the repertoire of Meyerbeer, Verdi, and Wagner. As the orchestra grew and the demands of the music required more powerful voices, adjustments to vocal technique had to be made.[8] This may be the reason for the increasing discussion of compressed breath and strong glottal adduction in the teaching of the Lampertis. But despite the increased power and effort associated with late-nineteenth-century singing, the principle of *appoggio* remained the same. Garcia wrote, 'It is necessary to pinch the glottis in proportion to the amount of pressure one gives the air' (Garcia 1984, 27). This principle lent itself to the demands of changing musical styles, including the powerful voices required by late-nineteenth-century composers.

Francesco Lamperti's pupil William Shakespeare recognized that breathing for singing was '*a considerable amplification of the ordinary breath-taking*,' but that it should *appear* natural (Shakespeare 1910, 9). Unlike his teacher, he combined diaphragmatic breathing with rib-breathing, but his description of *appoggio* followed Mandl and Lamperti closely. He spoke of 'powerful breath pressure' which could be regulated 'by balancing the *upward and downward* action of the muscles of the ribs, while balancing the downward movement of the diaphragm against the contraction of the abdominal muscles' (13–14). He found that this dynamic balance was necessary for expressive singing: 'With the great singer a never-ceasing pressure of breath is maintained, alike when he is singing his softest notes and when he is making his most dramatic effects; but through his natural production the effect reaches the audience as intensity of emotion, and so touches the soul, without the hearer being reminded of the force of breath and effort employed. Should this become apparent, the artistic effect is destroyed' (42). This, I believe, is a most significant statement. Shakespeare rejected loose glottal closure in favour of vocal efficiency, in which '*less breath produces more sound.*' Like Lamperti, he advised the singer to practise before a candle in order to avoid puffs of breath that would make the candle flicker (24–5). However, his statements on the *messa di voce* seemed to follow Garcia more than Lamperti. He reserved the technique for advanced students, and said that it involved 'an undefined change of register' which science had not yet been able to show clearly (41, 126).

Closer to our own time, the principles of *appoggio* have continued to play an important role in vocal pedagogy. In his 1954 article 'Voice-Training,' Franklyn Kelsey reiterated the importance of *appoggio*, which he described as 'leaning upon the breath.' He wrote, 'There is only one place where the voice can be felt to be leaning against the column of air below it. That place is at the top of the windpipe, where the breath ceases to be "breath" and becomes "voice"' (Kelsey 1954, 48). He considered the 'controlled pressing up of the diaphragm by the respiratory muscles' to be the chief mechanism for raising the breath pressure for singing, and maintained that this 'constituted the respiratory basis of *bel canto*.' He referred to the steady control of the breath pressure at the glottis as the 'respiratory squeeze':

It causes a complete transformation of the singer's voice. Those who are instructed in its use can detect in a moment, from the mere sound of the voice, whether it is being employed or not, so that the term 'singing' has a special significance for those who have been taught to use it ... Up to the time of Manuel Garcia the physical cause of this vocal transformation remained undiscovered; all that the old teachers could say about it was that it occurred when the breath was correctly managed and was absent when it was not. (54)

Franziska Martienssen-Lohmann, writing in 1956, stressed the idea that *appoggio* was a total system (*Ganzheit*) in singing, in that it involved glottal resistance to breath, balance between respiratory muscles, and vocal resonance. 'The idea of a totality in singing is unthinkable without *appoggio*, yes: both could almost be considered synonymous' (Martienssen-Lohmann 1993, 31–2). Richard Miller advanced a similar position in his book about national singing styles. 'Appoggio embraces a total system in singing which includes not only support factors but resonance factors as well.' Miller cites Francesco Lamperti and gives a detailed physiological interpretation of how he believes the respiratory muscles should function during singing (R. Miller 1977, 41–4). As well, there exist many anecdotal accounts of opera singers, from Enrico Caruso to Luciano Pavarotti, who employed the techniques of *appoggio* in their own singing. These accounts stress the need to bear down with the diaphragm, to lower the larynx, to resist the breath with strong glottal closure, and to use as little breath as possible.[9]

Stauprinzip and *Minimalluft*

During the late nineteenth and early twentieth centuries, certain German voice teachers developed a special theory of breath control known as *Stütze*, or *Stauprinzip* (stemming principle), a concept that has been somewhat problematical and controversial. Some authors considered *Stauprinzip* to be synonymous with *appoggio*. Georg Armin, one of the earliest published spokesmen for *Stauprinzip*, traced it back to the teachings of Friedrich Schmitt in the 1850s, and to Müller-Brunow and Lauritz Christian Törsleff in the 1890s (Armin 1946, 5). Armin's book *Das Stauprinzip und die Lehre von Dualismus der menschlichen Stimme*, published in Leipzig in 1909, was a highly polemical account of this technique, which revolved around the 'dualism' of the human voice. By dualism he meant the antagonistic tug-of-war between the inspiratory and expiratory muscles of respiration during singing. Rudolf Schilling (1925) was less agitated and more scientific in his defense of *Stauprinzip*. He conducted a number of experiments measuring the activity of the diaphragm and intercostal muscles during singing as well as airflow rates during different kinds of glottal closure. He, too, emphasized the necessity to balance inspiratory and expiratory muscles and coordinate them with glottal resistance. Luchsinger and Arnold, in their summary of the work of Armin and Schilling, argued, 'It is obvious that the slightest degrees of the stemming principle are identical with the classical method of breath support, the appoggio of bel canto' (Luchsinger and Arnold 1965, 13–14).

In a 1937 article, Richard Maatz offered a 'physical clarification' of *appoggio*, which he equated with *Stütze*. His physical hypothesis was based on the theory that during singing there should be a synchronous oscillation of the subglottal airstream with the fundamental frequency. He said, '"Appoggio" is obtained by adjusting the respiratory apparatus in such a way that the larynx is most conducive to the production of vibrations of tonal pitch in the vibratory system below the vocal chords [*sic*]. And "singing on the breath" is singing with the air currents below the vocal chords already in vibration. Appoggio makes it possible to "sing on the breath"' (Maatz 1937). Regarding the coupling of a subglottal formant to the fundamental frequency of the sung note, later researchers have maintained that the first subglottal formant has a fixed frequency of 500 to 600 Hz, which may either reinforce vocal fold vibration or impede it, depending on glottal waveforms and fundamental frequencies. This may affect the breaks between registers, but it does not constitute the kind of continuous support, or *appoggio*, suggested by Maatz.[10] Maatz also advocated keeping the larynx low and the supraglottal spaces wide in an attempt to produce a tone with a strong fundamental and strong lower harmonics. He maintained that the subglottal pressure should be regulated by the simultaneous innervation of the inspiratory and expiratory muscles, and matched to glottal resistance in such a manner as to ensure complete glottal closure during each vibratory cycle.

In a 1952 article, Fritz Winckel also tried to define *Stütze*. He called attention to the balanced tension between the inspiratory and expiratory muscles, as well as glottal closure (*Griffe*) and 'cover' (*Decken*) as defining characteristics of artistic singing, and he noted their relative absence in amateur singing. He called this vocal configuration *Stützfunktion* (support function), a term he borrowed from Armin and his followers. Winckel's use of the term *Paradoxen Atmung* (paradoxical breath) to describe this use of the respiratory muscles probably derives from Armin's 'dualism.' Winckel believed that it could serve to reduce the subglottal pressure to its optimal value for singing (Winckel 1952, 105). Like

Maatz, Winckel maintained that singing with *Stütze* had a significant effect on voice quality. He coupled *Stütze* with the lowered larynx and increased supraglottal space associated with *Decken* (covering), which he said occurred naturally in a tone with *Stütze*, and which darkened the tone and limited the number of upper partials in the tone. He wrote, 'The beauty of the tone depends on the limitation of the partials' (104).

Later German authors continued to grapple with the concept of *Stauprinzip*. Luchsinger and Arnold recounted how, during the first part of the twentieth century, 'singers and their teachers became excited and confused by a special technique of breath support known as the stemming principle, or damming up of the breath stream.' However, they completely neglected the role of glottal closure in this principle, thus adding to the confusion (Luchsinger and Arnold 1965, 13). Franziska Martienssen-Lohmann (1993, 31–2, 384–5) and Peter-Michael Fischer (1993, 177–80), in their commentaries on breath control, discussed the shades of meaning among German authors regarding *appoggio* and *Stütze*. In general, they regarded the two terms as roughly equivalent. Both concepts address the function of the inspiratory-expiratory balance of the respiratory muscles as well as glottal resistance to the breath by the laryngeal muscles. As well, both concepts consider the effects of this support on the tone. Martienssen-Lohmann noted that *Stütze* is clearly associated with a robust and athletic use of the voice suitable for Wagner. She pointed to the great Italian tenor Enrico Caruso as a master of this technique. More recently still, Wolfram Seidner and Jürgen Wendler (1997, 62–5) have again equated *appoggio* with *Atemstütze*.

Richard Miller's description of *Stauprinzip* also points to its extreme use of breath pressure and glottal resistance: 'breath damming is a technique of breath retention through marked sub-glottal muscular pressures. The flow of breath is stemmed by the glottis as a result of muscular tension similar to that experienced in a painful groan or grunt.' He maintained that this groaning utterance, called *Stönlaut*, is the primitive power of the vocal instrument, and that 'a long list of successful German singers in this century have given allegiance to it,' including a number of Wagnerian *Heldentenöre* (R. Miller 1977, 28).

The view that *Stauprinzip* is a robust use of the voice, requiring high subglottal pressures, is an important one. Some authors, including Luchsinger and Arnold, perhaps overstated their case when they said that *Stauprinzip* was 'identical' to *appoggio*. While *Stauprinzip* partakes of some of the same principles as *appoggio*, it does so in a more extreme form: higher subglottal pressures, stronger glottal resistance to the breath, and a lower larynx. The difference between *appoggio* and *Stau-prinzip* is thus one of degree, not of kind. During the late nineteenth century, the ability to sing in a declamatory style with sufficient power to be heard over a large orchestra took precedence over the grace and flexibility of earlier operatic singing. While *appoggio* is the preferred technique for the more florid styles, *Stauprinzip* is more applicable to Wagner.

Although *Stauprinzip* certainly had supporters, it also had detractors – most notably Paul Bruns, who wrote a strident response to Armin and Schilling in his book *Minimalluft und Stütze* (1929). Bruns took issue with the claim that *Stütze* was equivalent to *appoggio*. He claimed that *Stütze* was created by 'pumped-full lungs' (*vollgepumpten Lungen*) in order to achieve a full, powerful tone, and that it could not be associated with *bel canto*. Rather, he maintained, the singer should only partially fill the lungs, and then use the 'residual air' (*Residualluft*) in order to capture the *Freilauf* of the voice. *Freilauf* or *Freilauf-Phänomen* is an abstract idea, somewhat akin to 'free voice' (a fuzzy concept sometimes encountered in English-language works) or to the 'no-effort' school of Henry Curtis. Bruns suggested that *Freilauf* was largely intuitive, that it was based upon relaxation, that it preferred the fluty resonance of the upper partials to the deeper resonance of the lower partials, that it used 'lofty' resonance imagery, and that it was antithetical to the strong, muscular approach of *Stütze*. He said the residual air was sufficient for 17 to 20 seconds of singing, and resulted in a light, lyrical, disembodied tone quality which he considered typical of the 'old Italian method' as opposed to the 'new German dramatic style.' For him, the secret of good singing was not in strong lungs (which resulted in a lack of flexibility and a reliance on the chest voice) but rather in a mobile diaphragm (which resulted in elasticity, an emphasis on falsetto tones and upper partials) and the inscrutable *Freilauf-Phänomen*. While Bruns did not explain his theory in specific physiological terms, it seems likely from his discussion that he was advocating a light production with low subglottal pressure, and limited airflow that relied on the inspiratory-expiratory balance of the respiratory muscles more than on glottal resistance. His instructions for singing 'whisper-words' (*Flüsterwörter*) encouraged this light vocal production (Bruns 1929, 1–25, 38–9).

Throughout the main body of his book Bruns was careful not to utter the name of Wagner in association with *Stütze*, but in his 'Afterword' (*Schlusswort*, 104 *seq.*) he took off the gloves. There he decried the war (*Kampf*) between the human voice and the contrapuntally animated opera orchestra, as well as the emphasis on large stage sets and production values over the human voice. He put the blame squarely on Wagner for the 'twilight of opera' (*Operndämmerung*, a parody of Wagner's own opera title) and he berated both 'hypermodern trends' in opera and Wagner's new dogma of the 'future opera.' He blamed 'autocratic' conductors such as Artur Nikisch for their insensitivity toward singers, and also found fault with critics and audiences as well. Finally, he scorned Verdi for his glorification of tenor high Cs in roles such as Manrico (*Il Trovatore*). Bruns certainly got a few things off his chest in this 'Afterword'!

More recent authors have also attacked *Stauprinzip* as ruinous to the voice, while nevertheless acknowledging its place in contemporary operatic singing. For instance, Frederick Husler and Yvonne Rodd-Marling referred to *Stauprinzip* as the 'congested method.' They said, 'The pupil is taught to congest the air under the throat ("damming it up") and then to press with it against the vocal folds ... Although this method has ruined innumerable voices, it has lasted through the years and continues to find new and enthusiastic disciples' (Husler and Rodd-Marling 1965, 44–6).

One further manifestation of the debate between *Minimalluft* and *Stütze* was the eagerness of both sides to justify their theories by appropriating Enrico Caruso to their cause. Caruso, who died in 1921, was widely regarded as the finest tenor of his, or perhaps any other, time. In his 1922 book *Carusos Technik*, Bruns tried to align Caruso with *Minimalluft*. Husler and Rodd-Marling, who opposed *Stauprinzip*, also praised Caruso's singing. Salvatore Fucito's *Caruso and the Art of Singing* also appeared in 1922. Fucito was Caruso's long-time accompanist and coach. In describing Caruso's breath control, he wrote, 'His manner of inhalation, to be sure, supplied him with ample motive power; but this reservoire of power would have been of indifferent effect had he failed to make use of every particle of the outgoing column of air. It was this perfect control over the emission of breath, so that no air should be exhaled unproductively, that enabled Caruso to attain his unique mastery of tone production' (Fucito and Beyer 1922, 127). While Caruso may well have used minimal airflow to produce his tone, he clearly did not sing with either the 'residual air' described by Bruns or the fluty quality of *Freilauf*. Rather, he sang with great power and stentorian high notes. It is symptomatic of the greatness of Caruso, as well as the virulence of the debate, that he was made an exemplar by advocates on both sides of the debate.

Modern Views of Breath Mechanics

Having examined the pedagogical literature on breath control, we now turn to the voice science literature for a modern perspective on breath mechanics, only to discover that it, too, is full of contradictions and controversy. This is partly due to the different requirements for normal breathing (sometimes called vegetative breathing), breathing for speech purposes (sometimes called phonic breathing), and breathing for singing (usually called breath control by singers, although voice scientists usually avoid this term as being too inexact). Since the dynamics of the inspiratory and expiratory phases of respiration are so complicated and difficult to measure in their totality, and individual breathing strategies are so complex and varied, the prospect of a consensus on 'proper' breath control for singing is perhaps an illusory goal. Breathing for singing makes much greater demands on the respiratory system than vegetative breathing or speech. Singers usually take in large amounts of breath in order to sustain prolonged phonation. Through training, singers can develop an enlarged ventilatory capacity, and can increase the availability of usable air by reducing the residual volume of air in the lungs (Proctor 1980a, 34–42). As well, singers must be able to maintain fine control over subglottal pressures and airflow rates during singing. This requires the controlled valving action of the glottis, which, in turn, affects the actions of the respiratory muscles. The following review presents some of the basic breathing mechanics for singing, and also points out areas of disagreement between different schools of thought.

The respiratory system is the power source in singing. The energy for singing is created by the movements of the respiratory bellows (often referred to as the 'chest wall') which includes the rib cage, the diaphragm, and the abdomen. During inhalation, the intrathoracic space must be increased by the expansion of the chest wall. This expansion can include both the lowering of the diaphragm and the raising of the ribcage in various proportions. The diaphragm is a thin tendon midplate, surrounded by muscles; it is dome-shaped when relaxed, but it flattens out when it contracts for inhalation. The diaphragm is the floor of the thorax as well as the roof of the abdomen, and its downward movement requires the displacement of the abdominal contents by a bulging of the anterior abdominal wall – referred to by singers as the 'belly-out' position. Researcher Ronald Baken points out that 'the floor of the thorax is a single, functionally indivisible structure, consisting of the diaphragm, the abdominal mass, and the anterior abdominal wall'

(Baken 1980, 9–10). The second part of the system is the ribcage, which can be raised and lowered by the contraction of the external (inspiratory) and internal (expiratory) intercostal muscles, respectively. The raising of the rib cage, like the descending diaphragm, increases the intrathoracic space and draws in air during inhalation. Inhalation accomplished by the raising rib cage alone (with no descent of the diaphragm or bulging of the anterior abdominal wall) is referred to by singers as the 'belly in' position.[11] It is clear that there are quite different breathing strategies among singers. Baken maintains that the best inspiratory effort requires the action of the entire chest wall, including the raised rib cage, the lowered diaphragm, and the yielding abdominal wall. 'When both parts of the chest wall are functioning, each contributes to the total change in lung volume ... both parts of the system are necessary for meaningful statements to be made. Many a foolish interpretation has resulted from a failure to do so' (Baken 1980, 10). The actions of the two parts of the system can function in a variety of ways and still be effective for breathing (Leanderson and Sundberg 1988; Proctor 1980a, 41). It is this variability that has led to diverse opinions on methods of inhalation for singing.

During singing, the expiratory phase of breathing is more complex than the inspiratory phase because phonation is superimposed on the simple act of exhalation. Expiration is caused by the contraction of the abdominal muscles and the contraction of the internal intercostal muscles, which together reduce the intrathoracic space and force the expiration of air from the lungs. The simultaneous contraction of the inspiratory and expiratory muscles leads to a necessary stabilization of the breathing mechanism. Donald G. Miller (1994, 22) uses the clever analogy of applying the brakes and the accelerator simultaneously while driving a car. Subglottal pressure levels and rates of airflow during singing require further adductive force, in which glottal resistance to the breath is manifested both in raised levels of subglottal pressure and in reduced rates of airflow (Leanderson and Sundberg 1988).

The main bone of contention regarding breath support in singing is the relative role played by passive recoil forces as opposed to active muscular forces during phonation. Some researchers maintain that, during the production of a single long tone, the expiratory force is initially caused by the relaxation of inspiratory muscles, as the raised chest-wall recoils toward its position of rest. This is followed by the smooth transition to contractile forces of the abdomen and perhaps the internal intercostals. According to this view, elastic recoil and muscular contraction occur in sequence, and form a continuum of expiratory action.[12] Leanderson and Sundberg point out the importance of maintaining a fairly constant subglottal pressure during singing:

Thus, subglottal pressure is decisive to phonation and controlled by a rather complex system of passive and active recoil forces supplemented by active muscular forces. As the recoil forces change with the air volume in the lungs, or the lung volume, the need for muscular forces to maintain a constant air pressure during phonation continuously changes with lung volume. To sustain soft or loud tones, constant subglottal pressures are required ... To generate such constant pressures, different degrees of muscular force are needed, depending on the lung volume. (Leanderson and Sundberg 1988, 4)

This theory has come to be particularly associated with a group of researchers collectively called the 'Edinburgh group,' but the Edinburgh theory has been seriously challenged. Thomas Hixon and Gary Weismer (1995) question the validity of the research that led to the formulation of this theory and the whole matter of phonic breathing, challenging the Edinburgh group's experimental methods and interpretation of the results including the activity of the various breathing muscles and the sequence of their engagement. Hixon's point is that the Edinburgh group exaggerated the role of the passive forces, even in the early stages of expiration, and overlooked active abdominal effort, at least in speech. In singing, one can assume that this matter is even more critical, since the extraordinary volume and pressure of the breath required for singing suggest that the entire expiratory function is governed by active muscular forces.

A related problem is the disagreement regarding the role of the diaphragm during singing. Some researchers maintain that the diaphragm itself has little to do with phonic expiration. Donald F. Proctor went so far as to state, 'The idea, deeply seated in the minds of many voice teachers, that the diaphragm is a key muscle during singing is wrong.'[13] Proctor's statement oversteps the available objective data on this matter. Other researchers maintain that 'the diaphragm is relaxed during the whole of the phonatory process associated with singing, except during each interphase inspiration, and therefore makes no contribution to the so-called "support of the voice."'[14] According to this view, expiration is controlled largely by the balance between expiratory and inspiratory intercostal muscles, with help from the abdominal muscles, as well as by the passive elastic recoil of the inspiratory muscles.[15] A different view is that the diaphragm, together with the external intercostals, does play a role in balancing the expiratory force and regulating subglottal pressure, and that the diaphragm is sometimes active and sometimes passive, with considerable individual differences between singers.[16] One study has shown that 'the diaphragm may act synergistically with the external intercostals to counteract the strong elastic recoil forces during the first part of the phrase,' and that this action is especially evident during rapid phonatory changes.[17] Voice teacher and researcher William Vennard (1967, 28–30) maintained, as did Francesco Lamperti before him, that the diaphragm is the chief antagonist of the inspiratory muscles. He said that its action could be indirectly determined by observing the bulging of the epigastrium, that is, the uppermost ventral part of the abdominal wall just below the sternum. Leanderson and Sundberg (1988, 4) state that 'this bulging is caused by the simultaneous contraction of the abdominal wall musculature and the diaphragm.' Some celebrated present-day singers still argue that, during singing, the bulging epigastrium indicates that the diaphragm is indeed active as it bears down against the inward-and-upward contraction of the abdominal muscles (Hines 1994, 136, 104).

The assertion of the Edinburgh group, Donald Proctor, and others, that active recoil forces play an important role in singing is incompatible with the history of vocal pedagogy. It would be difficult to name any prominent voice teachers, past or present, who accept this assertion. A singer cannot achieve a smooth transition from passive to active expirational forces that satisfies the precise demands of subglottal pressure and airflow rates in singing. In this respect, passive recoil lies outside the concept of breath *control*, which is considered to be entirely an active, not a passive, process. Thus, singers usually opt for the 'simultaneous use of brakes and gas pedal' from the moment of prephonatory set to the end of the phrase. This means that inspiratory and expiratory muscles are in a constant state of antagonism during singing. The question regarding the active use of the diaphragm as a component of the 'brakes' remains open and scientific opinion is mixed on this matter. Among voice teachers, however, the prevailing wisdom is that the diaphragm plays a major role in breath control.

Subglottal Pressure, Intensity, and Airflow

The control of subglottal pressure and airflow rates are essential elements in vocal technique. T.A. Sears (1977, 84) maintained that the critical element in breath control is the regulation of subglottal pressure. Proctor (1980a, 67) agreed, saying 'It is indeed the control of subglottic pressure which is the key to the major problem of breathing in phonation, especially in artistic singing.' A wide range of subglottal pressure measurements indicate that there are significant individual differences between singers as well as variations within a single singer. Subglottal pressure can be generated with a variety of abdominal and intercostal configurations (Leanderson and Sundberg 1988). For sustained notes, as well as for a smooth *legato*, a relatively constant subglottal pressure is desirable. Subglottal pressure is typically measured in centimetres of water (cmH_2O).[18] Researchers differ in their views of optimal subglottal pressure levels. In general, the minimum subglottal pressure necessary for threshold phonation is about 2 cmH_2O; for ordinary speech it ranges from 7 to 10 cmH_2O, depending on accentuation, reaching around 10–12 cmH_2O for loud speech and about 40 cmH_2O for shouting.[19]

Subglottal pressure is the primary control mechanism for intensity as measured in decibels (dB).[20] Subglottal pressures during singing are generally higher than in speech. Proctor says that most singing generates between 5 and 20 cmH_2O; certain tones may go as high as 40 to 70 cmH_2O, but the upper limit is rarely above 60 cmH_2O.[21] Sears (1977, 84) put the upper limit at 50 cmH_2O for a 'maximally loud crescendo,' but Schutte (1980, 167) found higher levels, especially for tenors, who might reach 100 cmH_2O or more on high, loud tones. Husson (1962, 21–8) claimed even higher levels for members of the Paris Opéra, and his figures are consistent with his estimates of intensity. Male singers, especially tenors singing above the *passaggio*, typically generate higher subglottal pressures than females. Lower subglottal pressures are characteristic of untrained singers, and of some popular singers who rely on amplification to be heard. Belting, on the other hand, requires high subglottal pressures. From such a broad range of measurements it is difficult to draw any firm conclusions regarding 'correct' levels of subglottal pressure. As a general guideline, it might be proposed that singers who generate up to 100 cmH_2O in loud singing be referred to as 'high-pressure singers,' those who generate up to 60 cmH_2O be considered 'moderate pressure singers,' and those who produce maximal pressures of about 40 cmH_2O or less be called 'low-pressure singers.' What is clear is that singing admits a broad range of subglottal pressures, depending on the training of the singer and the requirements of different styles of music.

Closely related to subglottal pressure, and equally variable, is the rate of airflow through the glottis during phonation, measured in millilitres of air per second (ml/s). The rate of airflow can depend on many vocal and musical variables and here, too, there are no clear guidelines as to optimal rates.[22] It has already been shown that falsetto singing often uses higher airflow rates than chest voice, and that airflow rates decrease with strong glottal closure and a large closed quotient.[23] Covered singing may require more breath volume per second than pitches below the *passaggio* (Luchsinger and Arnold 1965, 107). Schutte has shown that, in order to produce a tone that meets the aesthetic demands of artistic singing, a singer may have to sacrifice vocal efficiency to a degree, and he concludes that the efficiency factor is 'of secondary importance to the aesthetic demands' (Schutte 1980, 167). One such demand in most artistic singing is the presence of vocal vibrato. Researchers have shown that the oscillation of vibrato results in some breath loss at the weakest point of adduction during the vibrato cycle, and that a tone with vibrato may use about ten percent more breath.[24] Other aesthetic demands may well require a variety of tone qualities, ranging from breathy to strident, or from lax to taut, depending on the expressive intent of the text, the emotion being portrayed, or the particular demands of the music.

The *Messa di voce*

As noted earlier, voice teachers have traditionally maintained that the *messa di voce* is the ultimate test of vocal coordination, since it requires critical control and balance of glottal closure, subglottal pressure, registration, and timbre. This view is echoed by some voice scientists.[25] We have already noted two different ways of executing the *messa di voce*: Garaudé and Francesco Lamperti called for an even timbre with no register break, while Garcia advocated a change of both timbre and register. The argument continues today. One purported effect of the *messa di voce*, according to some researchers, is that 'it involves a change of register along with the dynamic change' (Vennard, Hirano, and Ohala 1970b, 33). Vennard (1967, 213–14) maintained that, when properly executed, the *messa di voce* is achieved by the 'transition from one mode of laryngeal vibration to another,' starting in head voice, which he called 'quasi-falsetto,' shifting to chest voice, and returning to head voice. Numerous other authors have also described register transition as an element in the *messa di voce* (see Monahan 1978, 169–72). These authors echo the views of Garcia. Ingo Titze, in a recent article, also recognized that 'singers do it [the *messa di voce*] in two rather different ways.'

In one way, the vocal folds are initially adducted (brought together) to their optimum state and kept there for the entire exercise. The sound quality remains 'legitimate' throughout, without 'airy' or 'breathy' initiation and release. This offers the respiratory system a firm and steady resistance for maintenance of air-flow and subglottal pressure. In the second way of producing the exercise, there is a progressive adductory gesture during crescendo and a regressive abductory gesture during the decrescendo. The voice first sounds breathy (falsetto-like) but finally attains full timbre. (Titze 1996, 31)

This is consistent with the view of Garaudé and Lamperti rather than Garcia's view. I will return to this matter in chapter 8, where I will pro-vide laboratory data on these two methods of singing the *messa di voce*.

Neuromuscular Control Systems

The control of respiration involves both voluntary and reflexive con-trols. Although breathing for 'life purposes' takes place at an involun-tary level, respiration can also be controlled at the conscious level. It is a common misconception that the breathing impulse is triggered by the need for oxygen. Rather, the impulse to take a breath is caused by chemoreceptors that respond to the accumulation of carbon dioxide in the lungs and blood (Widdicombe 1974). Inhalation uses the motor sys-tem to innervate the diaphragm and intercostals. When the lungs are inflated, stretch receptors trigger inhibitory impulses to the brain, and inhalation ceases. Long-held notes result in a concentration of carbon dioxide in the lungs and airways, which stimulates the urge to breathe. Hence, singers must increase their tolerance for accumulated carbon dioxide through practise in resisting this impulse.[26] Singers also learn to match the depth of inhalation to the needs of the musical phrase. If the singer repeatedly inhales a volume of air that is significantly greater than needed to execute the next breath-phrase, and then 'tops up' at the end of each phrase, the accumulation of carbon dioxide makes the urge to breathe almost impossible to resist, thereby giving the impression of short-windedness, when in fact the lungs are full. It is this phenomenon which led to the practice of 'half-breaths.' Matching breath volume to phonatory needs is an essential skill which can be cultivated in the singer to a high degree (Wyke 1980, 45).

Proprioceptive control contributes to all aspects of respiration, includ-ing posture, prephonatory chest-wall set, and the maintenance of an ele-vated subglottal pressure. The abdominal and intercostal muscles are liberally endowed with proprioceptive nerve-endings called spindles, which are 'continually mediating and adjusting the autonomic mechanisms governing the interplay between voice, posture, and breathing' (Gould 1971b, 8). The diaphragm has very few spindles, and this has led some researchers to assert that it plays a passive role in controlled expiration (Lieberman 1977, 77). Even before phonation begins it is necessary to raise the subglottal pressure to the threshold needed for proper vocalization (Gould and Okamura 1974a, 356). The abdominal muscles, which contract to cause a rise in subglottal pressure, are held in check by the contraction of the diaphragm, even as the inspiratory intercostal muscles are opposed and balanced by the expiratory intercostals.[27] The intercostal muscles are considered especially important for the fine tuning of subglottal pressure (see Proctor 1980b, 16). Once phonation begins, the maintenance of the appropriate subglottal pressure is controlled by mucosal reflexes in the subglottal area and by the abdominal-intercostal balance. Highly sensitive pressure receptors located in the laryngeal mucosa monitor the subglottal pressure levels and are 'important in maintaining appropriate laryngeal tension.'[28] These neuromuscular control systems are complemented during phonation by laryngeal reflex mechanisms and by the auditory feedback system.

Conclusions

This examination of breath control in singing, both historical and scientific, shows that classical singing styles have special respiratory requirements, both for inhalation and for controlled phonic expiration. The early treatises admonished singers to breathe quietly, to get enough breath to sustain long phrases, to avoid breathing in the middle of florid passages, and to avoid falsetto which expended more breath than chest voice. Caccini's *esclamazione* and his *crescere e scemare della voce* required fine respiratory control. The *messa di voce* was often regarded as the most difficult vocal exercise, requiring a high degree of control of the breath. It was also considered an important stylistic and expressive device in vocal music.

Certain eighteenth-century authors urged singers to 'hold back' the breath while singing, that is, to create a balance between inspiratory and expiratory forces. In the nineteenth century, this idea was referred to as *lutte vocale*, or 'vocal struggle,' leading directly to the concept of *appoggio*. *Appoggio* referred not only to the balance between inspiratory and expiratory breathing muscles, but also to glottal resistance to breath pressure, airflow rates, and voice quality. It has been described as a 'total system' (*Ganzheit*), since it subsumes so many elements of vocal technique into a single pedagogical concept.

A late nineteenth- and early twentieth-century German reformulation and extension of the same principles, called *Stauprinzip* or *Stütze*, was associated with the more powerful singing required for the operas of Verdi, and especially with the music dramas of Richard Wagner. In reaction to this, an opposing theory called *Minimalluft* prescribed singing with 'residual air' and with less breath pressure. Its advocates maintained that *Minimalluft* was a truer approximation of the historical *appoggio* than was the more robust *Stauprinzip*, and that it was the technique used by singers for the earlier forms of *bel canto* opera, such as the operas of Rossini.

Modern voice science has made some progress in objectifying matters of phonic breath control, with specific measurements of subglottal pressure, rates of airflow, percentages of open and closed quotients, laryngeal height, voice quality, registration factors, and neurophysiological control systems. Such measurements have demonstrated that singers can vary these parameters in numerous ways, both according to their training, and according to the physical and musical demands of diverse kinds of music. But the pedagogical concept of *appoggio* does not lend itself well to the methods of basic research and objective description, since it includes so many parameters and so many variables. Hence, the term is better suited to the subjective insights of singers and voice teachers, who interpret it in a more holistic fashion. In ending this chapter, then, I will add my own interpretation of *appoggio* to those which have already been recounted above.

Like Martienssen-Lohmann, I agree that *appoggio* is a *Ganzheit*, that is, a total system of coordinated physical adjustments that leads to a very special kind of singing. It is a form of vocal coordination that can be both felt and heard by the singer in an unmistakable way. Subjectively, I would describe the feeling of *appoggio* as an elastic 'cushion' of pressurized breath just below the glottis; this cushion is established with prephonatory set and maintained throughout the ensuing phonation. The effect of *appoggio* on voice quality goes beyond *chiaroscuro* by adding a finely wrought buoyancy and malleability of colour and intensity to the voice, and by giving the voice 'projection.'

In order to achieve this unique quality, the singer must ensure that certain conditions are met, beginning with inhalation and extending to the sustained tone itself. Regarding inhalation, I agree with Francesco

Lamperti's preference for a 'low' breath achieved primarily by the relaxation of the abdominal muscles, which coaxes the diaphragm into a low position, and also causes the larynx to descend to a comfortably low vertical position. This low breath tends to prevent a 'clutching' at the larynx that is sometimes caused by the elastic recoil forces of chest and rib breathing. At the end of the inhalation, the glottis should be quickly and firmly closed and the larynx should be at the same low position it assumed during inhalation. Then the expiratory muscles contract to elevate the subglottal pressure to a level commensurate with the intensity desired. Care must be taken that this upward-bearing pressure does not cause the larynx to rise. Garcia compared this kind of prephonatory set, with the buildup of breath pressure, to the conditions in the throat just before a cough. Other singers have compared it to the intrathoracic pressures necessary for a grunt or a painful groan (*Stönlaut*), and even to childbirth or evacuative functions.[29]

At the onset of phonation, care must be taken to avoid a glottal plosive, but rather, to sing with a firmly adducted glottis and large closed quotient while maintaining the subglottal pressure. This pressure is felt as 'pent-up' breath energy, and is sometimes described as held-back breath, compressed breath, or breath damming. The constant interplay between breath pressure, glottal resistance, and vocal tract adjustments (especially the vertical laryngeal position) gives the singer the tools to vary the intensity and voice quality, and to sing with a seamless *legato* and without apparent register transitions. The type of *messa di voce* described by Garaudé and Francesco Lamperti, on both long and short notes, depends on this *appoggio*. As well, the equipoise of the *appoggio* permits a controlled undulation of subglottal pressure that may give the singer a small measure of respiratory control of the vibrato (see chapters 5 and 8).

Appoggio, then, is a complex coordination of all the muscles of singing, and it is rooted in the equilibrium between breath pressure and controlled phonation. While its quantification in scientific terms remains to be fully determined, its usefulness as a pedagogical concept has long been an important factor in the history of vocal pedagogy.

5

Vocal Tremulousness:
The Pulse of Singing

The Problem of Vocal Tremulousness

One of the most controversial aspects of singing is the role played by vocal tremulousness. There are many questions regarding this matter. Should the artistic voice be steady and unwavering, or should it exhibit some form of tremulousness – either continuously as an integral part of the vocal tone, or occasionally for purposes of embellishment? What is the physical cause of such tremulousness? Is it a natural vocal phenomenon which occurs spontaneously in the voice, or is there something that the singer purposely *does* to make the voice tremble? What are the physiological and acoustical parameters of vocal tremulousness? How is it perceived by the listener? Does the pulse of the tremulous voice propel florid singing? How does it affect the expressiveness of the singing voice?

Throughout the history of vocal pedagogy there have been arguments about these matters – arguments that continue today, especially in the field of early music where authenticity and historically informed performance are the goals. But those goals are elusive, due to the relative paucity of historical references to vocal tremulousness, the vague descriptions and confused labels used for it, the apparent difficulties in perceiving it, and of course the varying musical tastes of each historical epoch. Authenticity is often based more on opinion and current biases than on fact. In order to mediate this situation, it is helpful to turn to modern voice science, which provides a known body of objective data about vocal tremulousness that can serve as the critical platform for interpreting the historical documents. Even this, however, will not resolve the disagreements regarding vocal tremulousness. The historical record itself is simply not sufficient to provide unequivocal answers to the questions posed above.

The word 'tremulousness' is used advisedly, since it refers to several different vocal mechanisms. The most familiar form of tremulousness is today known as *vibrato*. Researcher Carl Seashore defined a good vibrato as 'a pulsation of pitch, usually accompanied with synchronous pulsations of loudness and timbre, of such extent and rate as to give a pleasing flexibility, tenderness, and richness to the tone' (Seashore 1932, 7). This continuous *legato* undulation of the voice is what I will refer to as 'normal' vibrato. Seashore defined a bad vibrato as 'any periodic pulsation of pitch, loudness, or timbre which singly or in combination, fails to produce a pleasing flexibility, tenderness, and richness of tone' (Seashore 1947, 56).

An important vocal ornament that may be related to the vibrato is the *trill*. A trill is a rapid alternation between two adjacent notes, in which the voice oscillates between separate pitches, perhaps using the same impulse that drives the vibrato. Another possible extension of the vibrato is the rapid singing of florid passages, as the voice rides on the impulse of the vibrato in scalar patterns.

A second main kind of vocal tremulousness – today referred to as 'glottal articulation' or 'laryngeal trill' – is characterized by a quick reiteration of a single pitch, in which a steady stream of tone is partially interrupted by the rapid opening and closing of the arytenoid cartilages, resulting in a quasi-*staccato* effect. It is often used by children to mimic the sound of a machine gun or a horse's whinney. It is also heard in the word 'whoa!' when reining in a horse, or in a giggle (Hamlet and Palmer 1974, 362). Some researchers have shown that this mechanism can also be used to sing rapid passages, thus offering an alternative method to the one based on the vibrato.

Yet another kind of tremulousness is created by a respiratory impulse, in which the respiratory muscles are consciously used to rapidly raise and lower the subglottal pressure on either a single pitch or in florid passages. In general, it is safe to say that of the three mechanisms of tremulousness glottal articulation is the fastest form, vibrato the second fastest, and the respiratory impulse the slowest. There are important differences among these fundamentally different techniques, but these distinctions are not usually clear in the historical treatises.

The vibrato may have always been a normal part of artistic singing, but this is not reflected in the historical sources. Major authors such as Caccini, Tosi, and Mancini did not even mention vibrato; others, such as Manuel Garcia and Francesco Lamperti, seemed to reject it. But the absence of discussion of vibrato cannot be construed as proof that it was not an ordinary part of cultivated singing. This absence could equally well imply that vibrato was so ubiquitous and so natural as to not merit comment. Even when vibrato is rejected by historical authors, it is not always clear whether this rejection applies to both good and bad vibrato, or only to bad vibrato. Ambiguity of terminology and uncertainty about perception of vibrato complicate the matter even further.

This chapter cannot resolve the disagreements about vocal tremulousness. Rather, it will attempt to present the available data, both historical and scientific, in a fair manner, followed by a number of reasonable arguments regarding the use of vocal tremulousness in historical singing styles. There are no unequivocal answers. At best, all that can be offered is a range of possibilities.

The Early Treatises

Glottal articulation is a technique that can be traced back to at least the sixteenth century, and perhaps further (Sanford 1979, 56). It was often associated with the singing of florid passages (called *coloraturae, passaggi* or *gorgie*), and it was also used to perform the rapid reiteration of a single note (called a *tremolo* or *trillo*). The *trillo* was not universally admired, and it seems to have faded from use by about the 1640s. Some authors claimed that glottal articulation was also used for the *groppetto* or *gruppo* (early names for the vocal trill) but this idea can be challenged on physiological grounds.

An early description of glottal articulation is found in Nicolà Vicentino's *L'antica musica* (1555). His remarks were intended for chapel choristers who apparently used the technique in a coarse manner: 'How hard it is to listen to the singing of many notes over one vowel if the vowel is always repeated in a manner as if to say, a, a, a, a, a, a, e, e, e, etc., and the same with i, o, and u, thus moving the listener more to laughter than devotion' (Vicentino 1555, ch. 18, fol. 80). Hermann Finck, in his *Practica musica* (1556), also criticized this practice: 'The *coloraturae* of the throat are employed when the text is sung. Presently, however, several who make the *coloratura* of the throat not dissimilar to the bleating of a she-goat, make a serious mistake; for no pleasure, nor distinction, nor suitability of the embellishment is heard, but only rumbling and a confused and ugly racket is heard' (MacClintock 1979, 64).

In his *Prattica di musica* (1592), Lodovico Zacconi described the *tremolo* as a mechanism for propelling florid passages. His remarks were probably meant for solo singers as well as choristers:

The *tremolo*, that is, the tremulous voice, is the true portal by which to enter into *passaggi* and the learning of *gorgie*; for the boat moves with greater ease when it is already in motion; and the dancer who wishes to leap, does better if he is in motion before making the leap. This *tremolo* should be narrow and attractive; for if it is coarse and forced, it tires and annoys. It is by nature such that, when used, it should be used continuously, since use converts it into habit; for this continuous movement in the voice helps and spontaneously carries the movement of the *gorgie*, and miraculously facilitates the emission of *passaggi*; this movement of which I speak should not occur without the proper speed, but with vigour and vehemence.[1]

This sounds more like a description of a normal vibrato than of glottal articulation, since it is hard to conceive of 'continuous' glottal articulation as desirable in any musical style. On the other hand, Zacconi's reference to 'vigour and vehemence' seems more appropriate to the quasistaccato quality of glottal articulation. Zacconi admonished the singer to avoid the use of head and torso motions since the *tremolo* 'has nothing to do with the head.' He added that 'the tremolo in music may be necessary for expressing sincerity and ardor; it embellishes the vocal melody' (Zacconi 1592, fol. 55, 59). This statement indicates that the *tremolo* had an expressive purpose. In calling it an 'embellishment,' Zacconi may have been implying that the *tremolo* was not indicated in the score by musical notation, but was added by the performer. His statement that the *tremolo* was the 'true portal' for making other kinds of *passaggi* suggests that the mechanism used for the reiterated single note was also used for florid passages. This point was later repeated by Caccini and others.

In about 1593 (the date is not entirely legible on extant copies) Giovanni Luca Conforto, a singer who flourished in the 1580s, illustrated a rapidly reiterated single note (which he called the *trillo*) and a quick alternation of two adjacent tones (which he called the *groppo*). These ornaments were intended primarily for cadences (Conforto 1593, 25). In 1594, Giovanni Battista Bovicelli, a Milanese singer, described an ornament called the *groppetto* (apparently similar to the modern trill) as a rapid alternation of two adjacent notes. He said the *groppetto* was most suitable for ornamenting long notes, and was best used on accented syllables and in cadences. He also described the *tremolo* as 'nothing other than the trembling of the voice over a single note.' Like Zacconi and Conforto, he did not specify how this was to be done; rather, he stated, 'That which has been said of *groppetti* should also be observed in the *tremolo*' (Bovicelli 1594, 8, 11–13). This implies that the same mechanism should be used for both the *groppetto* and the *tremolo*. Bovicelli's last remark is problematical, since, as we will see, it may not be physiologically possible to use glottal articulation to oscillate quickly and repeatedly between two adjacent pitches. However, Bovicelli seemed to take this into account when he said that notes 'which are of extreme velocity, cannot be performed except in one manner, (even if one is able to make a shake on them), and that is, rapidly and not shaped (*formato*)' (Bovicelli 1594, 13; trans. MacClintock 1976, 38). Musicologist Carol MacClintock noted that Bovicelli made a distinction between slower passages, which could be performed *formato*, and faster passages at the thirty-second-note rate, which had to be performed *non formato*. Perhaps *formato* referred to a *legato* form of articulation, while *non formato* referred to glottal articulation, which was less easily controlled by the singer (see MacClintock 1979).

In *Le nuove musiche* (1602), Giulio Caccini used the terms *trillo* and *gruppo* in place of the earlier *tremolo* and *groppetto*. Like Zacconi, Caccini maintained that 'the *trillo* and the *gruppo* are necessary steps for many things here written out, effects with that grace most sought after in good singing' (Caccini 1602, v; 1970, 51). And, like Bovicelli, Caccini considered these two devices to be related. He illustrated the *trillo* and *gruppo* as starting slowly with quarter-notes and accelerating to thirty-second notes. He claimed to have taught the *trillo* to members of his household in the following way:

I observed no other rule than that which is written out for both, that is, to begin with the first quarter-note, then restrike each note with the throat (*ribattere ciascuna nota con la gola*) on the vowel à, up to the final double-whole-note; and likewise the trill ... If it is true that experience is the best teacher, I can state with some assurance that no better way to teach them can be found, than is given here for both. (1602, iv–v; 1970, 51)

Alas, Caccini's description is not as clear as he thought. The problem is that the *trillo* and *gruppo* are produced by two different mechanisms. In brief, the *trillo* is created by the rapid opening and closing of the arytenoid cartilages. Caccini described this as 'restriking each note with the throat.' This technique can work on a reiterated note or on *passaggi* moving in one direction, such as a falling scale (*cascata*) or a rising scale (*tirata*). But there is no evidence that it can be used for the *gruppo*, where the pitches reverse direction. The pitch-changing mechanism – the antagonistic actions of the cricothyroid and the thyroarytenoid muscles – apparently requires a longer time to reverse direction than the articulation of separate tones either on a single pitch or in an ascending or descending scale. While this assertion requires further research in the voice laboratory, I do not know of any present-day singers of early vocal styles who use glottal articulation for the *gruppo*. Bovicelli's and Caccini's claim that both the *trillo* and the *gruppo* use the same technique is open to question.

In his renowned *Harmonie universelle* of 1636, French music theorist Marin Mersenne (1588–1648) drew heavily on Caccini's treatise for his discussion of the singing voice. Like Caccini, he referred to embellishments which required the singer 'to beat the air of the throat.' He also stated that a similar technique was used to make trills (translated by MacClintock as 'shakes'), which he seemed to prefer to the *trillo*: 'One should also remark that the aforementioned shakes are not on a single note or string, like those produced by strings, for they would be faulty, unless one wished to imitate the *Trillo* of the Italians; rather they descend and rise a semitone or a tone' (MacClintock 1979, 171–2). Mersenne returned to the comparison of vocal and instrumental tremulousness when he wrote: 'It is certain that if the instruments are taken in proportion that they imitate the voice, and if of all the artifices one esteems most that which best represents the natural, it seems that one must not refuse the prize to the viol, which imitates the voice in all its modulations ... just as the tremblings and caresses of the left hand, which is called the fingering hand, naïvely represent its manner and charms' (Mersenne 1957, 254). At another point he said, 'The tone of the violin is most ravishing [when the players] sweeten it ... by certain tremblings which delight the mind' (24). Mersenne appreciated the tremulousness of the human voice, especially among Italian singers, and used that tremulousness as a model for other instruments.

Another important author who contributed to the discussion of vibrato was Giovanni Battista Doni (1594–1647), a friend of Pietro de' Bardi (the son of Giovanni, the patron of the Florentine Camerata). Through his correspondence with Pietro, Doni became familiar with the vocal practices in Florence (see Strunk 1950, 363–6). Doni's remarks, probably written in the 1630s, remained unpublished until 1763 and are sometimes overlooked in discussions about vibrato. In *Lyra Barberina*

Doni distinguished between the *trillo*, which he called a 'ripple' (*increspamente*) or vibration (*vibratio*) of the voice, and the *tremolamento*, which he described as an imperfect *trillo*. He said that the *trillo* was better for cheerful material, while the *tremolamento* had a feminine quality and was best avoided in sad or heroic subjects. Doni turned the tables on his predecessors by suggesting that the vocal vibrato was an imitation of the string vibrato rather than vice-versa. 'Likewise, the constant raising and lowering of the voice, which imitates the sound of a string of a violin which is played with a bow, with the finger swinging up and down in approximately the same manner, has too much of the feminine, and is only suitable to the female ... Likewise, in the castrato it is more tolerable' (Doni 1763, 2:71–2).

English author John Playford (1623–86) provided an English translation of Caccini's preface in his *Introduction to the Skill of Music* (1693). In it, he inserted a lengthy footnote in which he tried to improve upon Caccini's description of the *trillo*:

Some observe that it is rather the shaking of the uvula or palate on the throat in one sound upon a note. For the attaining of this, the most surest [*sic*] and ready way is by imitation of those who are perfect in the same. Yet I have heard of some that have attained it after this manner: In the singing a plain song of six notes up and six down, they have in the midst of every note beat or shaked with their finger upon their throat, which by often practice came to do the same notes exactly without. (Strunk 1950, 391 note a)

He also suggested imitating that 'breaking of a sound in the throat which men use when they lure their hawks, as in *he-he-he-he-he*' (391 note a). This could be a reference to glottal articulation. Playford seemed to treat the *trillo* as a novelty, and it is unlikely that it played any significant role in English singing of the late seventeenth century.

Although a number of treatises described *tremolo* or *trillo* as a beating of the throat, there were also works that described what seems to be a normal vibrato. Some of these latter descriptions are found, not in vocal manuals, but in instrumental tutors where vocal and instrumental tremulousness are compared. For instance, in *Opera intitulata Fontegara* (1555), a book on recorder playing, Sylvestro di Ganassi dal Fontego wrote:

Be it known that all musical instruments, in comparison to the human voice, are inferior to it; for this reason we should endeavor to learn from it and to imitate it

... Just as a gifted painter can reproduce all the creations of nature by varying his colours, you can imitate the expression of the human voice on a wind or stringed instrument ... And just as a painter imitates natural effects by using various colours, an instrument can imitate the expression of the human voice by varying the pressure of the breath.[2]

Ganassi's advice to recorder players to vary the pressure of the breath in order to imitate the voice implies a *legato* form of vibrato as opposed to articulation through tonguing. In his later book on playing the viol he advocated a 'trembling' of the fingers on the strings, which accomplished the same purpose as the undulating breath in wind instruments. This trembling would likely produce the sound of a modern string vibrato (Ganassi 1542, ch. 2). Another author of the same period, Martin Agricola (1483–1556), wrote of string players in 1545, 'If one trembles the finger [on the string], the melody is sweeter than when one does it another way' (M. Agricola 1545, fol. 42 r).

Jean Rousseau (1644–? ca. 1700), another French author who compared the voice and stringed instruments, wrote manuals for the viol (1687) and for the voice (1678). In his book on singing he said, 'The *tremblement* is a beating or agitation of the voice on certain tones which lends itself naturally to vocal ornamentation, particularly at the cadences where it is almost mandatory' (Rousseau 1691, 54). In his *Traité de la viole* he noted that this tremulousness, which was natural to the voice, had to be added artificially to the viol. He distinguished between an extreme form of vibrato, called the *batement*, made by two fingers, and the *langeuer*, or normal vibrato, made by swinging one finger on the fret. In either case, he said the technique should be used during the entire duration of long notes, thus implying a continuous vibrato (Rousseau 1687, 100–2).

Bénigne de Bacilly devoted a section of his *Remarques curieuses sur l'art de bien chanter* of 1668 to vocal *cadence* and its application in ornamentation. Austin B. Caswell, the editor of a modern edition of Bacilly's book, translates *cadence* as vibrato. In describing the tremulousness of a single note, Bacilly wrote:

First, I make a great differentiation between the *pretty* voice and the *good* voice. A single tone of a *pretty* voice is very pleasing to the ear because of its clearness and sweetness and above all because of the nice vibrato (*cadence*) which usually accompanies it. The *good* voice, on the other hand, may not have all this sweetness and natural vibrato, but nevertheless is effective because of its vigor, strength, and its capacity to sing with expression, which is the soul of the vocal art. (Bacilly 1968, 20)

Bacilly maintained that not all voices had the *cadence*, and that some singers did quite well without it. He also noted that strong voices often had an erratic *cadence* that needed correction. He maintained that the singer's vibrato was a gift of nature, but that it could be refined through training (83).

Several seventeenth-century German treatises included descriptions of Italian singing techniques, often based on Caccini's *Le nuove musiche*. In 1614, Daniele Friderici (1584–1638) published *Musica figuralis oder newe Singekunst* (Figured music, or the new art of singing). In it he gave the following rule: 'The students should, from the beginning, become accustomed to singing with a refined naturalness, and, where possible, with the voice trembling (*zitternd*), floating (*schwebend*), or pulsating (*bebend*) in the throat, and formed in the larynx or neck' (Friderici 1614, 41; 1901, 17). This passage is usually regarded as a description of the vibrato. Just five years later, in *Syntagma musicum*, Michael Praetorius (1571–1621) provided advice for those who wished to sing in the Italian style, apparently drawing on the writings of Friderici. He described one type of singer who was 'endowed by God and Nature with an especially beautiful, vibrant, and floating or quivering voice (*liebliche zitterten und schwebenden oder bebenden Stimm*) as well as a round neck and throat suitable for diminutions [passages]' (Praetorius 1619, 3:229–30; see also MacClintock 1979, 163).

A similar description, written by Johann Andreas Herbst (1588–1666) in *Musica practica* (1642) uses much the same language as Friderici and Praetorius, thereby demonstrating how authors borrowed from each other. Herbst stipulated the first requirement in a good singer: 'That he have a beautiful, lovely, trembling and shaking voice (*eine schöne liebliche zittern und bebende Stimme*) (though not like what many out of ignorance have become accustomed to in school, but with a particular moderation) and a smooth, round throat for diminutions' (Herbst 1642, 3; trans. Sanford 1979, 10). Musicologist and singer Sally Sanford interprets Herbst's remarks as advocating the presence of a vibrato, albeit one with a relatively narrow amplitude, or one used only selectively (Sanford 1979, 9). It is unlikely that Friderici, Praetorius, and Herbst were describing glottal articulation rather than vibrato. Herbst's description was later paraphrased by two other German writers, Wolfgang Mylius (1686) and Georg Falck (1688), again using much the same vocabulary (Sanford 1979, 10). Falck made a distinction between a pleasant, rustling tremulousness and the harshness of the *trillo*. He cautioned that the notes should 'flow from the throat and must not be thrust out in the manner of a female goat,' thus echoing the earlier allusion of Finck (Falck 1688, 102; Sanford 1979, 179). Later authors referred to this articulated sound as the *chevrotement* or *Bokstriller* (bleating of a goat) (J. Agricola 1995, 135).

Another German theorist, Christoph Bernhard (1628–92), addressed this subject in his treatise *Von der Singe-Kunst oder Maniere* (ca. 1650). It is apparent that he was familiar with the writings of Praetorius and others, as well as with Italian vocal practices. He noted that Italian singing styles varied from region to region, and that these styles ranged from the *cantar sodo* (plain singing) to the *cantar passaggiato* (florid singing). The plain style employed a steady voice (*fermo*) and no *passaggi*, except for the occasional *trillo*. Vocal tremulousness could be used in passionate phrases, where it was called *ardire*. Otherwise, Bernhard considered the *tremulo* to be a defect associated with the elderly (Bernhard 1650, 31–2; 1973, 14; Sanford 1979, 71–2).

Eighteenth-century Sources

The scattered references to vocal tremulousness in the eighteenth century are not significantly different from those of earlier authors. In 1757, Johann Agricola (1720–74) joined Sylvestro Ganassi (1542), Martin Agricola (1545), and Jean Rousseau (1687) in comparing the vocal vibrato to the string vibrato: 'The vibrato (*Bebung*) on one note – which is achieved on stringed instruments by rocking the fingertip back and forth on the same note, making the pitch neither higher nor lower, but gently beating it – is also an ornament that in singing is especially effective on long sustained notes, particularly when applied toward the end of such notes' (J. Agricola 1995, 149). His remarks were copied by Giuseppe Tartini (1782). Sally Sanford, in her survey of this literature, cited further instances of authors she believes were speaking of vibrato. French author Michel Pignolet de Montéclair (1736) said that vocal tremulousness (*flaté*) should be used sparingly and be almost imperceptible (Sanford 1979, 73–4). Jean-Baptiste Bérard (1755) also asked for a narrow *flatté* [his spelling] of no more than a quarter-tone in extent (Bérard 1969, 108; Sanford 1979, 73). Johann Mattheson (1739) remarked that the *tremolo* should be 'the slightest possible oscillation on a fixed tone' (Sanford 1979, 77).

Two of the best known castrati were Nicolini (1673–1732) and Crescentini (1762–1846). Nicolini sang Italian operas in England, where English author Roger North (ca. 1651–1734) made the following comment on his performance of an aria from Mancini's opera *Hydaspos*: 'And the swelling and dying of musicall notes, with *tremolo* not impeaching the tone, wonderfully represents the waiving of air, and pleasant gales moving, and sinking away' (North 1959, 128). When Crescentini sang in Vienna in 1804, the critic for the *Allgemeine Musikalische Zeitung* said, 'Especially beautiful is the pure, even, ever stronger pulsation of his heavenly voice ...' (Pleasants 1966, 90). Both these remarks may indeed refer to a normal vibrato.

The distinction between vibrato and glottal articulation was still a subject for Johann Mattheson (1631–1764) in *Der vollkommene Capellmeister* (1739). In his discussion of *tremolo* he said it was not a figure consisting of two tones, but rather 'the slightest possible oscillation on a single fixed tone, which in my opinion must be accomplished for the most part by the upper tonguelet of the throat (*epiglottis*) through a very soft movement or restriction of the breath: just as on instruments merely bending the finger tips without yielding the positioning accomplishes the same thing to some degree, especially on lutes, violins, and clavichords, which sufficiently illustrates that nothing more is required for it than a single pitch' (Mattheson 1981, 270). He cautioned that this 'trembling of the voice' must not be confused with the *trillo* and *trilletto*, which consist in a sharp and clear striking of two adjacent notes, nor with the goat or sheep trill' (271). While Mattheson was wrong in ascribing the vibrato to the action of the epiglottis, he was nevertheless clear in his distinction between vibrato and other forms of vocal tremulancy.

Pierfrancesco Tosi did not make reference to the vocal vibrato, although he did mention the *trillo*, which he called the *caprino* (goatbleat): 'The goat-bleat causes laughter, for it is born in the mouth like a laugh, and the best [trill is born] in the throat' (Tosi 1986, 29). He also discussed the importance of the vocal trill and the *passaggi*. Regarding the trill, he said that 'he who lacks it (or possesses a defective trill) will never be a great singer, even though he knows much' (25). He also maintained nature only bestowed the trill on a few students and that there was no good way to teach it. Above all, he wrote, the trill must be 'equal, solid, facile, and moderately fast.' Tosi described two sorts of *passaggi*: beaten (*battuto*) and gliding (*scivolato*). It is possible that the beaten form was produced by glottal articulation, while the gliding form was *legato*. Tosi's preference was for the beaten type, which could be sung faster than the slurred, but he preferred the smoothness of the *scivolato* and the *strascino* (the modern *portamento*) for sicilianas (songs with a pastoral character and a characteristic dotted rhythm in 6/8 or 12/8 meter). Unlike seventeenth-century authors, Tosi allowed the singer to breathe in the middle of long *passaggi* (30–7). Finally, Tosi decried the singing of a reiterated single tone (the old *trillo*), which he called the *mordente fresco* and compared to 'the prodigious artifice of singing like crickets,' or 'laughing singing, or singing like hens when they have laid an egg' (106). Apparently the *trillo* still invited bestial comparisons.

Giambattista Mancini, unlike Tosi, believed that anyone could learn to sing a trill: 'This is not a grace denied by nature.' But when asked how to teach it, he said, 'I confess that this certain rule cannot be formed at this moment in the author.' He spoke of the 'indispensible necessity of the trill,' and exclaimed, 'O trill! sustenance, decoration, and life of singing' (Mancini 1967, 48–9). He also criticized glottal trills, again with reference to livestock. 'Among trills the most defective are: the goat bleat, and the horse whinney ... I wish to say that it is because the singer does not avail himself of the motion of the fauces, but only of the motion of the mouth, and that in the manner and guise which he uses when he laughs, so that consequently he makes a natural sound like the bleating of a goat or the whinneying of a horse' (51–2).

In his *Regole armoniche* (1775), Vincenzo Manfredini (1737–99) disagreed with Mancini on many points, including the importance of the trill. Manfredini said that 'the trill must be natural, natural and then natural. To say that the trill is the most interesting quality of music is to increase its merit beyond its worth ... the trill is only an ornament.'[3] Mancini fought back in the 1777 revision of his *Pensieri*, belittling Manfredini for being a mere theorist and not a singer. He said that in addition to the trill, the voice must 'be united to brio, agility of the voice, vibrato [*vibrare*], detached notes [*distaccare*], the drawing back [*ritirare*], strength, and appropriateness of expression' (Mancini 1967, 121). Here, the vibrato is listed as a necessary part of the cultivated voice.

Charles Burney gave an account of his 1772 meeting with Mancini in Vienna, during which they discussed trills and *passaggi*. Burney reported of Mancini: 'For the shake [trill], he thinks it ruined ninety-nine times out of a hundred, by too much impatience and precipitation, both in the master and scholar; and many who can execute passages, which require the same motion of the larynx as the shake, have notwithstanding never acquired one. There is no accounting for this, but from the neglect of the master to study nature, and avail himself of these passages, which, by continuity would become real shakes' (Burney 1775, 115). This extraordinary comment seems to link both the trill and *passaggi* to the natural motion of the larynx, which may also be related to the natural tremulousness of the vibrato.

Burney's flautist friend Johann Joachim Quantz (1697–1793) also discussed the trill, and in his flute tutor, published in 1752, he criticized French singers for their erratic forms of tremulousness:

Slowness or quickness, however, must not be excessive. The very slow shake is customary only in French singing, and is of as little use as the very quick, trembling one, which the French call *chevroté* (bleating). You must not be misled even if some of the greatest and most celebrated singers execute the shake chiefly in the latter fashion. Although many, from ignorance, indeed consider this bleating shake a special merit, they do not know that a moderately quick and even shake is much more difficult to learn than the very fast trembling one, and that the latter must therefore be considered a defect ... In the case of the human voice, I might further conclude that the soprano could execute the shake more quickly than the alto, and, in the proper proportion, the tenor and bass could execute it more slowly than the soprano and alto. (Quantz 1966, 101–3)

In 1774 Wolfgang Amadeus Mozart wrote a revealing letter to his father, Leopold, in which he made a distinction between a good and a bad vibrato. In describing the singing of a man named Meisner, Mozart wrote:

Meisner, as you know, has the bad habit of making the voice tremble at times, turning a note that should be sustained into distinct crotchets, or even quavers – and this I never could endure in him. And really, it is a detestable habit and one which is quite contrary to nature. The human voice trembles naturally – but in its own way – and only to such a degree that the effect is beautiful. Such is the nature of the voice; and people imitate it not only on wind-instruments, but on stringed instruments too and even on the clavier [clavichord]. But the moment the proper limit is overstepped, it is no longer beautiful – because it is contrary to nature. It reminds me thus of the organ when the bellows are puffing. (Anderson 1985, 552)

Meisner's voice apparently had a slow wobble that attracted attention to itself in a negative way. Leopold Mozart, himself a violinist, described vibrato (which he called *tremolo*), in his 1756 *Violinschule*: 'The Tremolo is an ornament that originates in Nature herself, and can be applied elegantly on a long note not only by good instrumentalists but also by skill-ful singers. Nature is the preceptress hereof' (MacClintock 1979, 329). There can be little doubt that both Leopold and Wolfgang Mozart con-sidered vocal vibrato to be a natural and desirable quality unless it took a faulty form.

Nineteenth-century Sources

Among nineteenth-century vocal treatises, those of Manuel Garcia are again central. His view of vibrato was largely negative. In *Hints on Sing-ing* (1894), he advocated 'steadiness of sound,' that is, 'a firm and contin-uous flow of sound, free from every sort of tremor or quavering' (Garcia 1894, 49). Hermann Klein said of Garcia's singing, 'Though his own voice might tremble with sheer weight of years, he never, to my knowl-edge, brought out a pupil whose tones were marred by the slightest shade of vibrato' (Klein 1903, 36). Garcia, in fact, did acknowledge that the tremolo could be used for highly emotional passages, but he cau-tioned against its consistent use, such as was common among violinists:

When the same agitation is produced by a grief so vivid that it completely dom-inates us, the organ experiences a kind of vacillation which is imparted to the voice. This vacillation is called *tremolo*. The tremolo, motivated by the situation and managed with art, has a certain moving effect ... The tremolo should be used only to portray the feelings which, in real life, move us profoundly ... Even in these circumstances, the use of it should be regulated with taste and modera-tion. (Garcia 1975, 149–50; 1984, 60)

It is difficult to reconcile Garcia's apparent dislike of a continuous vibrato with his insistence upon firm glottal closure, lowered larynx, and elevated subglottal pressure. As we will see, these are the same muscular antagonisms which tend to result in vibrato. Perhaps Garcia did indeed prefer a straight tone, free of vibrato. But perhaps, like other authors, he was speaking about excessive tremulousness and made no comment on what might be considered a normal vibrato. Unfortunately, Garcia's own star pupils flourished before the invention of sound recordings. However, pupils of his protégé Mathilde Marchesi – Nellie Melba, Emma Eames, Emma Calvé, and Blanche Marchesi, among oth-ers – made recordings, and all sang with vibrato.[4] In 1922, Max Schoen measured the vibrato of Nellie Melba and Emma Eames, and noted that in Melba's voice 'the vibrato is constantly present,' while with Eames 'the vibrato is intermittent,' with tones often beginning without vibrato and ending with a vibrato (Schoen 1922, 252–3). These singers represented the Garcia-Marchesi school, and their use of vibrato raises reasonable questions regarding Garcia's apparent rejection of it.

Garcia also discussed trills and florid passages at great length. In keeping with the requirements for a Conservatoire method book, he treated these topics comprehensively. He described the trill as a 'very loose and swift oscillation of the larynx,' and a 'spontaneous trembling of the throat.' He disagreed with those who said it was a gift of nature, maintaining that it could be learned by anyone (Garcia 1894, 42; 1984, 163). He described in detail a number of variants of the trill: 'Let us observe that the doubled trill, the trill mordent, the *battuta* and the *ribattuta di gola*, the mordent [*tour de gosier*], the *acciaccatura*, the *martellement* (also called the *ribattuta di gola*), are only the different effects presented by the modifications of the *pulsating* or the *trembling* of the throat' (Garcia 1975, 129).

After Garcia, opinions continued to vary regarding vibrato, *passaggi*, and glottal articulation. Emma Seiler advocated glottal articulation for florid passages, but preferred the legato form of the vocal trill (Seiler 1881, 130–1). Stockhausen described Caccini's *trillo* as an 'aspirated attack,' and he also described *legato*, as well as several degrees of glottal articulation including *spiritus asper* (a form of *staccato*, but without an audible 'h') and *spiritus lenis* (also called *martellato*), in which there was a respiratory impulse rather than an interruption of the tone. He maintained that *staccato* was better for females and *martellato* better for males (Stockhausen 1884, 46–7, 129). He did not mention vibrato. Morrell Mackenzie, however, did discuss vibrato, and he rejected it, saying, 'Tremolo is injurious … as tending to beget a depraved habit of singing. The voice, like the hands, may tremble from emotion, and art should of course imitate this as well as other natural effects, but continual quavering is as disagreeable as the tremulous fingers of the drunkard' (Mackenzie 1890, 133).

Francesco Lamperti distinguished between a good and a bad vibrato. He remarked that the voice becomes tremulous with vocal strain, forced upper notes, or an unduly extended chest register. But then he added, 'I should remark that tremulousness must not be confounded with oscillation, which is a good effect produced by a strong, vibrating, sonorous voice' (F. Lamperti 1884, 18). He reiterated this in a later edition of *The Art of Singing*: 'I would put the pupil on his guard once more against the trembling of the voice, a defect which in the beginning of this century was sufficient to exclude any singer from the stage. I would not have him confound this, however, with the oscillation produced by expressing an impassioned sentiment' (F. Lamperti 1916, 19).

Emil Behnke, the nineteenth-century laryngologist and voice teacher, ascribed *tremolo* to a weakness of the muscles of the midriff or diaphragm, or to a weakness of the laryngeal muscles. He noted that this *tremolo* was 'one of the greatest vices besetting modern singing.' But then he added, 'I need scarcely add that there is yet another kind of tremolo, which, being absolutely under the control of the performer, is one of the chief ornaments of song, and to which the observations just made in no way apply' (Behnke 1880, 21–2).

In an interesting quirk of history, some authors held that a single singer, Giovanni-Battista Rubini, was responsible for introducing the vibrato to the operatic stage. Rubini, a celebrated singer of Donizetti and Bellini operas, was a tenor whose career flourished from about 1830 to 1845. In *Thirty Years' Musical Recollections*, first published in 1862, English music critic Henry Chorley described Rubini as 'the only man of his class who deserves to be named in these pages as an artist of genius' (Pleasants 1966, 132). Chorley wrote, 'Before ... Rubini came to England [1831] his voice had contracted that sort of thrilling or trembling habit, then new here, which of late has been abused *ad nauseam*. It was no longer in its prime – hardly capable, perhaps, of being produced mezzo forte or piano; for which reason he adopted a style of extreme contrast betwixt soft and loud, which many ears were unable, for a long period, to relish' (Chorley 1926, 21).

According to Garcia's biographer Sterling Mackinlay, even Garcia blamed poor Rubini. Garcia is quoted as saying, 'The tremolo is an abomination – it is execrable. Never allow it to appear, even for a moment, in your voice. It blurs the tone and gives a false effect.' Then, Garcia supposedly related how an 'eminent vocalist [Rubini] could not eliminate tremolo from his aging voice, and turned it to his advantage as a mannerism to display intense emotion, and the Paris audience loved it, and others imitated it' (Mackinlay 1908, 281–2). Curiously, Rubini was only 35 years old in 1831 when Chorley first criticized his vibrato, which hardly qualifies as an 'aging voice' (Pleasants 1966, 132). However, the reference to the aging voice may provide a clue as to the nature of the vibrato that Garcia rejected, since an overly slow and wide vibrato – a 'wobble' – is most common in aging singers. Hermann Klein said the vibrato was common in Italy, but disagreeable to English ears. Since he maintained that the 'sin' started in the mid-nineteenth-century at the Paris Opéra, presumably he meant that the sinner was Rubini (Klein 1923, 25–6). Music critic William J. Henderson happily perpetuated the condemnation of Rubini with an air of finality: 'It is said that the vibrato was introduced by Rubini. At any rate, it was new to the singers of his day, and had not at that time been heard in the memory of man' (Henderson 1906, 215). In 1932, Milton Metfessel suggested that Rubini's vibrato was actually an exaggerated one, used for emotional, tremulous expression, and that it thus called attention to itself. He maintained that when the vibrato was used in such a manner, it could be regarded as an embellishment (Rothman and Timberlake 1985, 111).

Modern Views of the *Trillo*

There has been little research on the form of glottal articulation associated with Caccini's *trillo*, which is sometimes referred to as a 'laryngeal trill.' It has been described as a quick opening and closing of the arytenoid cartilages, probably aided by aerodynamic forces and elastic recoil.[5] One study referred to this type of glottal articulation as 'flow' vibrato (as opposed to 'pitch' vibrato) since it is produced almost entirely by a tremor of the abductory (opening) and adductory (closing) laryngeal muscles. The *trillo* uses different muscles and has a different neural origin from vibrato, and this is probably why the rate of glottal articulation is faster than the rate of vibrato (Rothenberg, Miller, and Molitor 1988, 259). Glottal articulation also differs from repeated glottal stops; glottal stops are limited to a frequency of about 3.0 to 5.0 per second, whereas glottal articulation has been measured at up to 12 pulses per second, although the rate is not completely regular (Hamlet and Palmer 1974, 369). One study says, 'The subjective impression when hearing a laryngeal trill is of distinct bursts of voice, separated by minute periods of silence. The data never showed silent periods, however, laryngeal trills are continuously voiced' (Hamlet and Palmer 1974, 367). It is likely that glottal articulation is often managed better by those who sing with low subglottal pressures than by those who sing with high ones, and better by females, falsettists, and tenors than by the deeper voices. While glottal articulation can be faster than vibrato or vibrato-generated trills and florid passages, it can also lead to pitch, rhythm, and resonance irregularities. While the modern data on the *trillo* is meager compared with the data on vibrato, it nevertheless serves to corroborate the observations found in the historical treatises.

Modern Views of Vibrato

The vibrato came under intensive investigation by Carl Seashore and his associates at the University of Iowa in the 1920s and 1930s. Max Schoen, one of the Seashore group, had already mapped the parameters of vibrato in 1922. The Seashore studies were a notable achievement, a team effort of significant proportions devoted to the study of vibrato, both vocal and instrumental. There is probably no other collective study in any area of singing that can rank with the depth and breadth of this undertaking. It examined many aspects of vibrato including the physiological origins, properties of rate, extent (compass), and timbre, 'good' and 'bad' forms, degree of presence or absence in artistic voices, aesthetic implications, and the ability of listeners to perceive it. In addition to Seashore and Schoen, authors of articles in the Iowa Studies include Milton Metfessel, Joseph Tiffin, Jacob Kwalwasser, and others.[6] In one study alone, Metfessel measured the vibrato from sound recordings of a number of great singers including Caruso, Galli-Curci, Gigli, Jeritza, Martinelli, Ponselle, Schumann-Heink, and Tetrazzini, often using hundreds of samples of each voice (Metfessel 1929, 1932). Despite this concentrated effort, the information is partial at best, and leaves many questions unanswered. Since the publication of the Seashore group's work, there have been numerous individual studies by a variety of scholars; in general these studies have tended to confirm and refine Seashore's findings, rather than contradict them.[6]

Seashore regarded the vibrato as a vocal 'ornament' – that is, a feature 'not indicated by the regular score or demanded by the melodic, harmonic, qualitative, or temporal constitution of the song' (Seashore 1932, 108; see also 1938, 33). He did not think of vibrato as an ornament in the 'add on' sense, but rather as something that 'occurs in practically all the tones of artistic singing,' thus enhancing the cultivated voice as a normal occurrence. Seashore said that an artistic vibrato has a pitch oscillation of approximately a semitone, a rate of approximately six or seven cycles per second, and synchronous intensity and timbre oscillations which play a secondary role (Seashore 1932, 349). His description of vibrato has been reaffirmed by many later authors, with only small deviations from his observations.[8]

Neuromuscular Origins of Vibrato

The physiological and neurological origins of the vocal vibrato are not yet fully understood.[9] Nevertheless, there is general agreement that the vibrato is related to the larger phenomenon of neuromuscular tremor which affects all the musculatures of the body. Tremor can be described as a work-rest cycle in which muscles alternately contract and relax as a means of protecting against fatigue. With the use of sensitive instruments, this tremor can be measured in muscles that show no outward signs of trembling, and can easily be seen during certain kinds of strenuous physical effort (such as push-ups or arm-wrestling); as the muscles approach the point of fatigue, there is a visible and palpable trembling. Among most musculatures such tremor generally becomes apparent only at the point where fatigue is imminent, or when certain pathologies exist. However, the delicate balance of vocal muscles during singing causes a periodic oscillation of the voice which is considered normal, and which helps prevent vocal fatigue.

In 1922 Max Schoen, one of the first researchers to link vocal vibrato to neuromuscular tremor, wrote, 'The vibrato is a manifestation of the general neuro-muscular condition that characterizes the singing organism.' He described this general neuromuscular tremor in precise terms, and concluded, 'It is evident that the vibrato is a phenomenon in every respect similar to the tremor here described. The tremor is a constant rate but varies in amplitude, so is the vibrato; the tremor is beyond the control of the patient, so is the vibrato; it only occurs when the muscle is slightly under strain, so does the vibrato; it is about half the rate of normal muscular discharge, so is the vibrato.' He also pointed out the fact that what is natural in the vocal vibrato would be considered pathological in other musculatures.[10] Schoen went on to relate this tremor to human emotional behaviour. 'The psychological effect of the vibrato is probably due to the fact that the human ear has, because of the behavior of muscle under emotional stress, come to associate a trembling with emotional expression' (Schoen 1922, 253).

Seashore and Tiffin also related vibrato to neuro-muscular tremor, and acknowledged that both the specific muscle groups involved and the neurological timing device which regulates vibrato were imperfectly understood. Seashore said, 'It seems probable that the vibrato is but one of the normal periodicities which occur in all the large musculatures in animal life. It also seems probable that a certain type of tension or instability favors the emergence of the periodicity in the voice analogous to tremor.'[11] He later elaborated on this: 'It is a basic phenomenon of nature, both in man and in higher animals. It rests fundamentally upon the periodic innervation of paired muscles under emotional tension ...

We are born with the neuromuscular organism which has a number of natural periodicities. One of these is at the rate of from five to ten pulsations per second, and it is probably a phenomenon related to the refractory phase, which means the time after one nervous discharge into a muscle before the next discharge can become effective' (Seashore 1947, 59–60). Later researchers have agreed with Seashore's conclusions.[12]

There are five or six muscle groups which could be involved in producing the vibrato, including the abdominal, diaphragmatic, and thoracic muscles of the respiratory system, the extrinsic and intrinsic muscles of the larynx, and possibly the articulatory muscles (Rothenberg, Miller and Molitor 1988, 244). Prominent among these muscles is the cricothyroid, which is the principal pitch-regulating muscle of the larynx, and which is opposed during phonation by the vocal folds themselves, namely, the thyroarytenoid muscles. In a study using electromyography to measure muscular activity, Mason and Zemlin noted that the cricothyroid muscle was 'seen to be active in phase with increases in pitch and intensity,' and that 'the crests of cricothyroid activity occurred 82 per cent of the time in phase with the crests of the pitch and intensity modulations' (Mason and Zemlin 1966). Similar conclusions were reached in later studies (Vennard, Hirano, and Ohala 1970a; Mason 1971).

While the cricothyroid is often regarded as the chief muscle of vibrato, its contractions scatter to the neighbouring muscles of articulation. This was already noted by Schoen in 1922, and confirmed in later studies.[13] The tangential muscles that sometimes participate in vibrato include the velum, tongue, side walls of the pharynx, and jaw. When the tremor of these muscles can be clearly seen, it is sometimes regarded as a vocal defect. It has been suggested that other muscles should be inhibited from joining the oscillation, since 'the more the activity is confined to the CT [cricothyroid], probably the cleaner the signal.'[14] However, Sundberg notes that a physical tremor is sometimes seen even among world-class singers, especially females, without any apparent negative effect (Sundberg 1987, 1966). Martin Rothenberg speculates that the tremor of the articulatory muscles could be a reaction to a strong vibrato rather than a causal factor in its production (Rothenberg, Miller, and Molitor 1988, 244).

Rate, Extent, Intensity, and Timbre

According to the Iowa Studies, the normal or acceptable vibrato rate is between five and eight pulsations per second, and the singer has some flexibility in this rate (for example operatic arias sometimes have a faster rate than art songs) (Seashore 1932, 110). Numerous later studies have agreed with this acceptable rate, finding only minor differences.[15] Some researchers maintain that the singer can make modest adjustments in the rate.[16] The normal rate of vibrato has generally slowed down since the early twentieth century, perhaps because of 'a shift in our aesthetic value system' (Rothman and Timberlake 1985, 114). For instance, Enrico Caruso's vibrato rate was near 7.0, whereas Luciano Pavarotti's is near 5.5. Ingo Titze says, 'audiences and singers today seem to prefer a more "settled" sound,' implying that the slower rate is a cultural phenomenon.[17] Early sound recordings confirm the faster rate of late nineteenth- and early twentieth-century singers. (It also seems likely that there is a cultural factor present in, say, the fast, fluttery vibrato of the French *chanteuse*.) In any case, Seashore's judgment that the normal rate is 5.0 to 8.0 has stood up well.

Seashore noted that bad vibratos – those that deviated from the norms outlined above – were 'very abundant, even among well-trained musicians' (Seashore 1932, 9). The terminology used for bad vibrato has become a source of confusion. The twentieth-century use of the term *tremolo* often refers to a faulty vibrato, usually one that is too fast.[18] This is a completely different definition of *tremolo* than the historical one, which was itself ambiguous. Seashore suggested scrapping the term *tremolo* altogether, but it seems to be too late for that. In a 1985 article, Marian McLane provided a detailed survey of the confusion in the literature regarding artistic vibrato and *tremolo*; in the end, she seemed resigned to the use of the term *tremolo* for a bad form of vibrato (McLane 1985a, b). A second faulty form of vibrato is one in which the rate is slower than the norm and the compass is overly wide. A vibrato with a pitch fluctuation greater than 1.5 tones and a rate of 4.0 or slower is generally referred to as 'wobble' (Rothman and Arroyo 1987; Titze 1994, 291).

The pitch oscillation in vibrato is referred to as the extent or the compass. Seashore wrote:

Each singer tends to have a characteristic average, but may vary from this selection to selection and from tone to tone. The variation of individual vibrato cycles from this average in acceptable vibrato may be from 0.1 to 1.5 of a tone in a given singer. There are no marked and consistent variations with the sex of the singer, the vowel quality, the musical mode, the pitch level, or the loudness of the tone. For short tones, it is slightly wider than for long tones. (Seashore 1938, 44)

In general, the pitch fluctuation ranged from 0.5 of a tone to 1.0 or more. Seashore found that, for up to three out of four singers, the extent was between 0.45 and 0.55 of a tone (44). This finding is again confirmed by early sound recordings, but today's slower vibratos are often wider as well. Sundberg says that anything wider than two semitones sounds bad, and is usually associated with the advanced age of the singer (Sundberg 1982, 3; 1987, 163). Richard Miller (1977, 96) speculates that the slower rate of today's singers may be due to the cultivation of a darker voice quality associated with *chiaroscuro* and *appoggio*. The implication is that the muscular antagonisms necessary for these techniques causes the slowing of the vibrato.

In the vocal vibrato, pitch undulations are accompanied by variations in the intensity and the timbre of the voice. Kwalwasser considered the intensity vibrato and the frequency vibrato to be equally necessary for a beautiful tone. Seashore measured synchronous intensity fluctuations of 2 to 3 dB in each cycle of the vibrato. He found that this fluctuation was present in singers about one-third of the time, and that it was ordinarily less frequent, less regular, less conspicuous, and less prominant perceptually than the pitch fluctuations of vibrato, but that, like the pitch vibrato, 'it is underestimated in hearing.' He referred to intensity vibrato as a 'secondary' phenomenon which was modified by room acoustics. He also recognized that the intensity vibrato cannot be separated from the timbre vibrato. As the fundamental frequency fluctuates, so too do the partials, which move toward and away from formants; whenever a partial approaches a formant there is a boost of intensity (Seashore 1938, 44–5). Later researchers have concurred with Seashore's theory, and have further noted that the sweeping of the vibrato will intermittently activate the singer's formant.[19] The complex undulation of pitch, amplitude, and formant tuning 'is significant in the perceptual "richness" ascribed to vibrato by investigators such as Seashore' (Schutte and Miller 1991, 223). Vibrato may aid in the intelligibility of the vowels by sweeping the vowel formants, and may also give the voice greater audibility, due to the independence of vibrato from rhythmic patterns of the music (Benade 1976, 381).

Respiratory Control of Vibrato

One of the unresolved questions about vibrato is the degree to which the singer can control it. While the initial oscillation of the vibrato takes place at the laryngeal level, some researchers maintain that vibrato can, to some extent, be controlled by the respiratory system through the periodic variation of the subglottal pressure.[20] Rothenberg has suggested that there is likely 'a small respiratory-induced component to the vibrato,' in which a singer can affect the pressure, flow, and intensity fluctuations by some degree of respiratory muscle involvement (Rothenberg, Miller and Molitor 1988, 256). William Vennard maintained the fluctuations of breath pressure caused by the breathing apparatus could alter the vibrato rate by up to two oscillations per second (Vennard, Hirano and Ohala 1970a, 19). Shipp, Sundberg, and Haglund (1985, 117) disagreed, saying that 'the singer has no conscious control over vibrato rate, but can control a wide range of vibrato frequency extent.' Nevertheless, Sundberg suggests that subglottal pressure cannot be discounted as a 'vibrato-generating force' caused by pumping the chest apparatus.[21] D. Ralph Appelman (1967, 17–23) considered this respiratory pumping to be the preferred method of achieving coordination between phonation and respiration. He advised singers to use this pumping action on single notes as an exercise, and also in scale passages (see also Smith 1970). It may be that the singer can use respiratory control of the vibrato to help achieve the desired qualities of evenness and regularity of pulsation.[22] Pumping of the chest apparatus can also be used to create an exaggerated form of vibrato. Fischer has cited several German authors who also maintain that the respiratory musculature can have an effect on the rate, amplitude, intensity, and expressive qualities of vibrato (Fischer 1993, 175–7). If the respiratory muscles can indeed offer a measure of control over the vibrato, this control would likely be exercised only on notes of a certain duration (and perhaps especially on high notes) rather than continuously.

Trills and Floridity

Some researchers have theorized that the same mechanism that produces the vibrato can be used to produce the trill. The vocal trill is defined by Seashore as 'no more than a very wide vibrato' in which the pitch fluctuation 'covers a recognizable tonal pitch interval' (Seashore 1932, 63, 114, 365). Other authors agree with this view.[23] Metfessel measured 137 trills, and found that the average rate of the trill proved to be much the same as vibrato (Seashore 1932, 368–9). Vennard (1971) measured and compared the trill and the vibrato in the singing of a soprano, and found that both had a rate of 6.25 oscillations per second. Titze (1994, 293) wrote, 'The basic difference between a vocal trill and vibrato is that the *average* pitch is raised in trill, but not in vibrato.' This is because the trill alternates the target pitch with the upper neighbouring tone. Titze found the trill to be about 1 Hz faster than vibrato. Vennard and von Leden maintained that there are two intensity peaks in each cycle of the trill, which 'call the attention of the listener to the top and bottom of the pitch fluctuation,' thus giving the impression of the trill doubling the rate of the vibrato.[24] Despite these general agreements regarding the trill, there are still some researchers who are not persuaded that the trill and the vibrato are related.[25]

There is also a lack of agreement on whether the impulse of the vibrato can be used as the vehicle for singing rapid runs and passages. In 1945 Douglas Stanley (1945, 178–9) suggested, 'A properly executed run moves on the vibrato. When the vibrato is in proper control, all runs can be made legitimately and without difficulty.' William Vennard maintained that the singer simply changes pitches on each cycle of the vibrato, thus making the passages ride on the impulse of the vibrato (Vennard 1967, 198–9; 1971). He also suggested that 'a good singer sets the tempo in multiples of the vibrato.'[26] Myers and Michel, however, found that 'in the majority of cases, the singers could alter their vibrato in order to adhere to the timing of the musical line' (Myers and Michel 1987, 157). When Sundberg tested Vennard's theory, he found that singers 'switched off' the vibrato during florid passages. He did not discount Vennard's theory, but said that 'the system may be programmed in quite different ways' (*Transcripts* 1985, 1:127) Titze (1994, 292) also holds that the vibrato frequency cannot usually be synchronized with the rate of pitch change. Richard Miller does not agree that the rate of the vibrato must be adjusted to the rate of pitch change in fast passages. He says, 'This is a misconception of the role of vibrancy in velocity; although temporally dictated, vibrato frequency *need not* exactly coincide with the written note change.' He remarks that this would be too limiting to accommodate many passages in the *bel canto* repertoire (R. Miller 1986a, 194). This question obviously requires further research.

Vibrato and Expressiveness

As a professional psychologist, Carl Seashore was interested in the 'nature of beauty in the vibrato.' He wrote, 'We shall find that musical beauty in the vibrato consists primarily of three elements: (1) enrichment of tone, (2) flexibility of tone, and (3) the expression of tender feeling through instability.' He was opposed to 'the thinness, the rigidity, and the coldness' of straight tone (Seashore 1932, 108; 1947, 61). Some voice scientists are troubled by the speculative nature of beauty. For instance, W. Dixon Ward (1970, 422) states, 'Until some intrepid soul finally scales flexibility, tenderness, and richness of tones, this definition leaves much to be desired. The implication is, though, that the presence of vibrato increases these attributes.' With this caveat in mind, let us examine Seashore's arguments.

Seashore claimed that the 'enrichment' of the tone is due to two aspects of 'fusion': *timbre* and *sonance*. In timbre there is a simultaneous fusion of the fundamental frequency with the overtones at any single moment during singing. In *sonance* there is the fusion of a succession of timbres, caused by periodic changes in timbre, loudness, and pitch. 'The beauty of the vibrato lies in the field of sonance.'[27] The beauty which arises from the 'flexibility' of tone is due to the pulsating quality itself and the 'indefiniteness of outline' that is created by the fluctuations of pitch, loudness, and timbre within the parameters of 5.0 to 8.0 pulsations per second. 'This characteristic of the tone presents a relief from the rigidity and coldness of a non-vibrato tone and is in itself a specific source of beauty, when used in moderation.' The third element of beauty in the vibrato is 'tenderness of tone,' which Seashore defined as the expression of feeling conveyed by 'the impression of instability as a symbol of emotion.' He maintained that the vibrato was a musical manifestation of the physical trembling associated with intense emotion, which arises out of 'heightened tension, conflict, and struggle' (Seashore 1932, 110–17). He said that beauty is an 'esthetic deviation from the regular,' and that 'beauty in the vibrato is found in artistic deviation from the precise and uniform in all the attributes of tone' (Seashore 1936, 9, 46–7). His fervor for the vibrato is apparent in his statement, 'The genuine vibrato is automatic and expresses the truth – like the spontaneous smile or the frown (Seashore 1947, 62).' A number of later authors held views similar to Seashore's.[28] For example, Damsté, Reinders, and Tempelaars maintained that the vibrato is, 'without any doubt, intended to convey emotional tension to the audience. A stable tone is experienced as dead; an oscillating tone, in the right proportion, radiates life and warmth.' They related a well-controlled vibrato to 'warm human expression of feeling, dynamic equilibrium, readiness for change, reaching out for contact' (Damsté, Reinders, and Tempelaars 1983, 17, 20). In summarizing his view of vibrato, Damsté went so far as to say, 'If a singer cannot appeal to his audience with his vibrato, then he might as well sing with a closed curtain' ('Discussion of Vibrato' 1987, 170).

The term *dynamic equilibrium* occurs frequently in discussions of vocal technique, and in general it seems to refer to the balance of antagonistic muscular forces which are reversible in both directions. In vibrato, dynamic equilibrium can be interpreted as including both a physiological and an expressive dimension. Physiologically, it is caused by the work-rest cycle of muscular contraction, involving both laryngeal and respiratory muscles. Its expressive quality may be related to the balance between fragility (suggested by the wavering of the voice) and stability (suggested by the regular periodicity of the vibrato).

The Presence and Perception of Vibrato

The presence of vibrato in modern voices is pervasive. In 1921 Thomas Edison purported to have found only twenty-two singers out of 3,800 who did not have the vocal tremulancy which he called *tremolo* (McLane 1985, 2:11–12). Seashore, in his measurements of sound recordings of singers from the first two decades or so of this century, found that 'the vibrato was present in the voices of all great *artists* in about 95 per cent of their phonated time including transitional tones, attacks and release, and rapid passages as well as sustained tones.' Vibrato was also present in the voices of adult voice students, children, and even in primitive peoples (Seashore 1932, 351). Kwalwasser found vibrato in 93 per cent of trained singers, 87 per cent of untrained singers, and 41 percent of children (Kwalwasser 1926, 212). More recently, Sundberg said, 'Almost all professional opera singers develop vibrato without thinking about it and without trying to actually acquire it. Thus, vibrato develops more or less by itself as voice training proceeds successfully' (Sundberg 1987, 163).

In trained singers, a straight tone does not constitute a 'purer' or more natural use of the voice than a tone that exhibits vibrato; rather, the straight tone requires the *inhibition* of the natural vibrato by preventing certain muscles from engaging in the work-rest cycle. The fact that the muscles that generate the vibrato must be 'held' implies muscle rigidity. In his experiments, Schoen noted that it was difficult for a trained singer to eliminate the vibrato for more than a fraction of a second (Schoen 1922, 252). Thomas Shipp maintained that straight tone is the 'maximum inhibition ... once the constrictions are removed, the vibrato will emerge.'[29]

Another element in this argument was provided by Fritz Winckel, who maintained that both the acoustical nerve of the ear and other organs associated with the ear might be overloaded by straight tone.

Tone with movement, such as vibrato or rapid passage-work, can be considered 'a physiological necessity' (Winckel 1959, 190). Early music specialist Robert Donington held a similar view, saying that auditory fatigue ensues with any undifferentiated tone after only 1/20th to 1/18th of a second, at which point 'the ear goes a little dead on us ... The vibrato just mitigates that deadening persistence' (Donington 1982, 35).

Seashore maintained that 'a fundamental cause for the prevailing confusion' regarding the vibrato is that it is 'never heard as it really is in the actual tone. It is modified by a number of illusions which result in our hearing something entirely different from that which is performed' (Seashore 1932, 8). He also stated that the vibrato 'is the factor on which artistic singing and playing are more frequently judged, whether the factor is consciously recognized as vibrato or not' (Seashore 1936, 7). In other words, the ability to perceive vibrato differs widely from one individual to another, and some listeners are unable to discern it at all. Seashore also maintained that 'the repulsiveness of the bad vibrato has put many a musician on edge against all vibratos ... Thus the good is often thrown out with the bad; the good vibrato is ignored through the offense of the bad' (9).

There are two aspects of vibrato perception: (1) detecting its presence, and (2) distinguishing between different kinds of vibrato. The chief 'illusions' as described by Seashore are due to the fact that the ear and brain of the listener cannot detect the short sound of individual sound waves; instead the listener perceives a blend of successive sound waves over a period of time, from about a twentieth of a second or more. The same fusion that enriches the voice is an example of an illusion. 'This tone quality, which results from a series of changes in a tonal flux, we call successive fusion or sonance. It is another grand illusion, because if we should hear all the successive changes, the result would be chaos in tone, but the fusion results in a pleasing blend which we call musical quality' (Seashore 1932, 106). More recently, Sundberg said that the ear takes about 200 milliseconds in order to interpret the oscillation of pitch into the perception of a single pitch. This would require a vibrato of 5.0 cycles per second. Sundberg also refers to this as 'fusion time,' or 'gluing the partials together.'[30] Rothman and Arroyo (1987, 138) found that the important parameters for the perception of vibrato are the frequency and amplitude variations around their respective means. 'Sometimes it is both of them and sometimes it is one or the other.'

As an example of perception problems, Kwalwasser described a 'bitter controversy' over Amelita Galli-Curci's début in London. One critic described her concert as 'a sorry, sordid, and ridiculous business.' He especially attacked her vibrato, saying, 'steadiness of tone [is] one of the most elementary requisites without which good singing does not even begin to exist.' However, a second critic commended her for the beauty of her 'steady, clean vocal tone.' Said Kwalwasser, 'Both critics heard the same voice and, yet, are unable to ascertain whether the vibrato was employed; and whether the effect was good or bad because of omission or commission. This episode shows something of the status of the vibrato and also that of musical criticism' (Kwalwasser 1926, 225). Kwalwasser maintained that the proponents of straight tone misapprehended the facts, and that he had measured vibrato even in their favourite voices. The statistics on Galli-Curci's vibrato are in fact documented in the Seashore studies (Seashore 1936, 63, 69).

The ambiguity surrounding the perception of vibrato is well illustrated in the writings of voice teacher Franklyn Kelsey. In his article on voice training for the 1954 edition of *Grove's Dictionary of Music and Musicians*, he thoroughly rejected the vibrato, considering it a vocal defect. He said it was 'the infallible hallmark of a faulty method of using the voice,' and that it was caused by 'uncontrollable nervousness or the physical deterioration due to age' (Kelsey 1954, 64). He maintained that any unsteadiness of tone was unacceptable (44). Nowhere in this article did he mention any redeeming features of vibrato. Yet, in his book *The Foundations of Singing* (1950), he wrote, 'Every voice has a natural vibrato which renders it pleasing to the ear, and without which it would soon sound hard and expressionless.' When he turned to criticizing a faulty vibrato, he said, 'The vibrato with which we are now dealing is not like this natural pulse of the voice, but a perverse and unpleasing oscillation of the pitch which has now become endemic throughout the whole body of international song' (Kelsey 1950, 96–7). Kelsey's ambivalence and lack of clarity serves as a case study of the confusion regarding vibrato. Even today one occasionally reads or hears reviews of singers who supposedly sang with no vibrato, but whose recordings and performances prove otherwise.

There is some disagreement over whether the vibrato has a good or bad effect upon the perception of pitch accuracy. Some choral directors and early music specialists maintain that accurate singing requires a straight tone directly on the 'target pitch' (the printed note). However, Sundberg's experimentation revealed that 'the pitch perceived from a vibrato tone appears to correspond approximately to the average fundamental frequency. Moreover, the vibrato does not appear to affect the certainty with which the pitch is perceived.' He concludes, 'Consequently, the vibrato can hardly reduce the demands on intonation accuracy in singing' (Sundberg 1982, 15; see also 1987, 170–1). This explains why most professional singers and orchestral players use vibrato without sounding out of tune.

Titze (1994, 292) cites studies that show that choristers adjust both the vibrato and the timbre of the voice in order to achieve both a better definition of pitch and an ensemble blend. Sundberg (1987, 143) suggests that, whereas blend is important for choral singing, individual timbre is important for the soloist. Hence, individual voice characteristics such as the singer's formant or vibrato are often rejected in favour of a more neutral sound in choral music. This is a sticking point in the conflict between choral and solo singing.

Pitch accuracy is sometimes tied to the production of acoustical 'beats' – the periodic intensification of the sound due to two sound waves of slightly different frequencies (Helmholtz 1885). Beats can occur between the fundamental frequencies of two tones as well as between partials. When beats are produced at a frequency of 6.0 to about 30.0 per second, the effect on the ear is increasingly disagreeable. Sundberg noted that voices and instruments with a harmonic spectrum generate beats when their fundamentals are slightly mistuned. Vibrato can mitigate acoustical beats, since 'there is no partial which has a constant frequency, and therefore no beats can occur. The elimination of beats allows the singer to deviate slightly from the expected pitches' (Sundberg 1985a, 99–100). He observed that beats among the partials are hard to avoid when singing with a straight tone, and says, 'Singing without vibrato must be a very tricky thing indeed!' (Sundberg 1987, 177). He found that when a singer is accompanied by instruments or other voices, 'it is likely that a vibrato is capable of hiding beats between mistuned sounds under these conditions.' He considered this a good acoustical argument for using vibrato in music and particularly in singing. The musician's increased freedom regarding the choice of fundamental frequency can be used artistically for expressive purposes (Sundberg 1982, 15).

Despite the weight of evidence that points to normal vibrato as a natural and desirable part of the singing voice, there are still detractors, especially among devotees of early vocal styles. As early as 1912, vocal historian Bernhard Ulrich was at a loss to understand why so many sixteenth- and seventeenth-century authors considered vibrato to be a desirable quality. Ulrich asserted that every case of vibrato was due to a weakness in breath control, and he rejected every kind of tremulousness out of hand (Ulrich 1973, 66–76). More recently, early music enthusiast Irving Godt continued to plump for 'the crystalline perfection of tone and intonation' associated with straight-tone singing, while deriding modern 'athletic voices' for their 'fog of meaningless vibrato.' Godt even considered the fact that the vibrato avoids acoustical beats to be a defect, calling it a poor substitute for accurate pitch. He maintained that only a straight tone can be perfectly in tune, and he valued accurate intonation above every other consideration. Significantly, recordings of some of the singers he admires reveal clearly discernible vibratos on sustained notes without ornaments; this throws doubt on the acuity of Godt's perception of vibrato (Godt 1984, 317–18).

Conclusions

Vocal tremulousness has been an important component in good singing since at least the early Baroque period. It has also been a contentious issue, since tremulousness can take several forms, some of which gained greater acceptance than others as styles and tastes changed from age to age. Modern voice science has been able to define and describe certain features of tremulousness in an objective way. Using this information, it is possible to come to some guarded conclusions regarding vocal tremulousness which bear upon authenticity and historically informed performance of vocal music.

There is little doubt that the terms *trillo* and *tremolo* in a number of late sixteenth- and early seventeenth-century treatises refer to a form of glottal articulation whereby the tone was partially interrupted by the rapid opening and closing of the arytenoid cartilages. The same kind of glottal articulation could be used with other vocal ornaments and florid passages. While this technique was sometimes praised for its artifice and delicacy, it was also ridiculed for its coarseness, and was compared to the bleating of a goat, the cry of a hawker, the whinneying of a horse, or laughing. These descriptions suggest that, except in exceptionally skilled singers, it was not a particularly lovely or musical sound, and this may be the reason that the technique soon fell out of fashion. Today the use of glottal articulation still elicits a divided response. Early music enthusiasts may regard it as a delightful example of an early virtuoso technique, while more general audiences may find it humourous because of the resemblance to bestial bleating. Said one critic: 'In modern performances it usually is heard as an ornament which is entirely different from any other: no matter what its mode of execution, it does not sound consistent with the general musical line, either because of a striking change of timbre, a cessation of the "vocal legato," or some other vocal aberration' (Greenlee 1983, 5). Glottal articulation seems to be most successful in singers who use low subglottal breath pressures, and in singers with high voices, including falsettists. It is still used in highly florid styles found in compositions ranging from Monteverdi to Rossini.

Early treatises also referred to a pleasant and continuous wavering of the tone, which was probably what we now commonly refer to as a normal vibrato. It seems likely that vibrato has always been a part of cultivated singing, since it is a natural periodicity or tremor of the vocal muscles under stress. The critical question here is whether the vibrato is a vocal embellishment which the singer enlists at will, more or less independently of other elements of voice production, or whether it is integral with the finely balanced muscular forces which constitute the cultivated singing voice. Said Robert Mason, 'the functional synergism of opposing muscles is responsible for vibrato, and is a rather basic physiological phenomenon' (Mason 1971). If vibrato is a natural periodicity of the vocal muscles under heightened muscular effort, it seems reasonable to assume that vibrato was present in historical singing styles proportional to the presence of such effort. Vibrato should not be regarded as a secondary element in an otherwise straight tone, but rather as a primary element in the sophisticated vocal matrix of the cultivated voice.

The vocal manoeuvres which result in heightened muscular effort include glottal closure, the 'pose' of the vocal tract – namely, a lowered larynx and expanded pharynx – the building of subglottal pressure through the contraction of antagonistic respiratory muscles, and glottal resistance to that pressure. These manoeuvres have been identified by such labels as *coup de la glotte*, the glottal pinch, *voix sombrée ou voix couverte, lutte vocale, appoggio, Stauprinzip,* and the *messa di voce.* All of these require the skillful contraction of opposing muscle groups, and will likely result in vocal tremor unless such tremor is inhibited, either by design or by rigidity. There are no instructions in the historical treatises for a method of inhibiting tremor. As opera composers increased the size and strength of orchestras, and as opera houses grew in size, voices required more strength. The necessary strength was presumably gained through an increase in breath pressure, which also necessitated an increase in glottal resistance and a concomitant lowering of the larynx, putting all the singing muscles under greater stress and leading to a more pronounced vibrato. It is no accident that arguments about vibrato increased in fervor in the late nineteenth and early twentieth centuries, as the operas of Verdi, Wagner, and the *verismo* composers made greater demands on singers for vocal power. As power was gained, floridity was often sacrificed, and vibrato became more pronounced.

Considering the ambiguities surrounding the use of various forms of vocal tremulousness, it would be unwise to be doctrinaire regarding historical authenticity. There is sufficient evidence to suggest that there has always been a plurality of styles of vocal tremulousness, and this allows for generosity toward and a tolerance of diverse interpretations. As with many other issues, it is not only historical and scientific knowledge, but also intuition and good musical sense, that determine what is desirable in musical performance.

6

Idiom and Expression: The Soul of Singing

Problems of Idiom and Expression

The inherent ability of the singer to be expressive and to touch the soul of the listener lies at the heart of the vocal art. Yet, the analysis of expressivity in music is fraught with difficulties. Such analysis has long been unfashionable for many scholars, because it relies more on speculation than on objective data. For them, subjectivity, insight, and aesthetics are all suspect. As Richard Taruskin has often pointed out, traditional musicology has tended to focus on the style and structure of music, while the subject of musical meaning has been considered 'off-limits to properly musicological investigation' (Taruskin 1995, 42). On a second front, it is not uncommon to hear listeners say that vocal expressiveness is self-evident or perhaps even transcendental, and that to submit it to methodical anaysis is to deny its very nature. It is true that we can never fully describe or explain expressivity in singing; it involves intuitive matters that do not yield to rational analysis. But we can at least look more closely at the techniques and idioms that provide the tools for expressive singing in the classical style. This means that our musical analyses must reach beyond the words and the notes to include purely vocal matters as a part of the expressive resources of the artistic singer.

This added dimension has been generally unrecognized or avoided by musicologists, whose interests are based largely on the printed musical score rather than on performance elements. These scholars have created an analytical model known as the 'word-tone relationship' (*Wort-Ton Verhältniss*), which posits that, while the text of a song has its own structure, symbolism, imagery, and logic, the musical elements in that song follow their own intrinsic laws that may, to some degree, be at odds with the words. Critics often base their judgment of the value and success of songs upon the balance between textual and musical elements, with some kind of musico-poetic synthesis as the ideal (Ivey 1970). But something important is missing from this equation: the role of the singer and the use of the voice in bringing a song to life. The term word-tone relationship might more accurately be called the 'word-*note* relationship,' since its subject includes the printed word and the printed note but excludes the ways in which the singer's performance can affect the expressiveness of the song. There are good analytical tools that can be applied both to poetic structure and imagery and to melodic, harmonic, rhythmic, textural, and formal aspects of music, but the role of the cultivated singing voice as a crucial element in the expression has been largely avoided in the musicological literature.

It is in the pedagogical literature that this matter is directly addressed. Expressivity in singing can be strongly linked not only to the structure of the music or the meanings of the texts, but also to the manner in which the voice itself is used. Opera and concert singers, from Caccini onward, have cultivated certain characteristic combinations of vocal techniques, or *vocal idioms*, that are unique to the classically trained voice, and that distinguish it from other forms of vocal usage, such as choral singing or singing in the popular or vernacular styles so common in today's culture. Treatises by Caccini, Tosi, Garaudé, Garcia, and others have linked vocal techniques to the musical styles of the day and discussed how the singing voice could be made expressive. These treatises included both vocal and musical advice. Vocal technique was considered to be inseparable from matters of musical style. These authors considered idiomatic singing to be not just a peripheral element, but an integral part of the value and success of a song. By including the vocal element in musical analysis we can arrive at a 'word-note-*tone* relationship,' which offers a better (although still incomplete) measure of musical expressivity.

The Art of Diminutions

The waning years of the sixteenth century witnessed a radical change in musical style and sensibility that is usually regarded as the dawn of the Baroque era. Many historians maintain that the wellspring for this epochal change was found in the emergence of solo vocal music from the polyphonic part-music tradition of the late Renaissance. The Italian madrigal, which had grown out of the homogeneous contrapuntal style of the Low Countries, strained for more dramatic expression than could be contained within its conventional forms. Composers such as Cipriano de Rore, Luca Marenzio, Carlo Gesualdo, and especially Claudio Monteverdi transformed the madrigal by including declamation, daring harmonies, and virtuosic voice parts in many of their compositions. As well, Italian court singers had a penchant for arranging part-songs as accompanied solos, and by the end of the century the practice of embellishing the vocal lines with florid ornamentation was considered *de rigueur* (Einstein 1949, 2:836–49). But even these developments were insufficient to satisfy the Italian predilection for solo vocal music with its capacity for dramatic expression.

The florid vocal patterns used for ornamenting polyphonic song were known as 'diminutions' (from *diminuire*), in which long notes were broken up into passages of smaller notes.[1] The main patterns of diminution were scale passages which moved by step around or between pitches. An ascending scale pattern used to fill an interval was called a *tirata* (tirade), while a descending passage was known as a *cascata* (cascade). A pattern that departed from and returned to the same pitch in an arc of notes was known as a *circolo mezzo* (half-circle). The singer could vary these simple patterns in numerous ways and add dotted rhythms for greater interest. Cadential ornaments included the *gruppo* and the *trillo*, as previously discussed. Diminutions were also known as *coloraturae*, *gorgie* and *passaggi*, and in England, *divisions*.

It was generally recognized that, in order to perform these ornaments well, the singer required a good *disposizione della gorga* (disposition of the throat) or *disposizione della voce* (disposition of the voice) which indicated a particularly supple throat for singing *gorgie*. This was often regarded more as a gift of nature than a trainable skill. As the manuals show, embellishments in part-songs were restricted to long notes, and could be added to only one voice at a time. Such embellishments were not indicated in the printed score, but at that time the embellishment of a melody was a normal practice, and was seen as a means of allowing singers a creative element in the performance. In addition to arrangements of part-songs for solo voice – called 'pseudo-monodies' by Alfred Einstein (1949, 2:836 ff.) – the repertoire of the day included newly composed songs with simple accompaniment and ornate vocal lines written into the score by Luzzasco Luzzaschi (1545?–1607), composer at the court of Alfonso II d'Este of Ferrara. During the 1580s Luzzaschi wrote virtuosic solos, duets, and trios for the famous 'three ladies' of Ferrara who were known as the *concerto delle donne*. These were published in Rome under the title *Madrigali per cantare e sonare* (1601).[2]

The earliest manuals of diminution were written for instruments. Sylvestro di Ganassi's manual for recorder, written in 1534, was followed by Diego Ortiz's violin manual of 1553. The manuals for singers came later: Giovanni Camillo Maffei (1562), Girolamo dalla Casa (1584), Giovanni Battista Bassani (1585), Giovanni Luca Conforto (1593), and Giovanni Battista Bovicelli (1594). As well, many published collections of late sixteenth-century secular part-music were in fact designated *per cantare o sonare* (for singing or playing).[3] These collections bear witness to the age-old art of getting by, in which performers made do with whatever voices or instruments were at hand. Diminutions could be added, especially on long notes, to one voice at a time. The melodic motion of diminutions was mostly stepwise, and the ranges were limited to about an octave or a ninth. It is easy to imagine an especially gifted singer or player turning her or his part into a florid display while the other musicians took on the role of accompaniment – quite in contrast to the principle of equal part-writing of Renaissance polyphony. This arrangement would make for a most felicitous way to spend an evening, but such music could hardly be regarded as an ideal vehicle for passionate or dramatic musical expression. Giovanni Camillo Maffei caught the essence of this singing style when he wrote, 'In the end the true method of singing in a courtly style is to please the ear and to sing in the ornamental style' (Maffei 1562; trans. MacClintock 1979, 60).

The addition of diminutions to music by performers was not entirely a form of extemporaneous musical improvisation. From the earliest manuals of diminution to Benedetto Marcello's satirical essay *Il Teatro alla moda* (ca. 1720), we are told that singers carried little books of ornaments from which they could select passages for inclusion in their performances (Marcello 1720; 1948–9, 394).This practice could hardly be described as extemporaneous, nor could it be called improvisation. Singers probably learned a certain number of diminution patterns that could be added to any score that would admit such accretions; it was as much a matter of selecting ornaments as inventing them. While authors of the day insisted on good judgement (*giudizio*) in the use of diminutions, there was also a litany of complaints about the indiscriminate use of florid ornaments that served no purpose other than empty virtuosity.

Caccini's Affective Vocal Devices

It was in protest against the practice of indiscriminate and vacuous florid ornamentation that Giulio Caccini wrote *Le nuove musiche*, in which he rejected the 'old style of *passaggi* formerly in common use (one more suited to wind and stringed instruments than to the voice).' He found that *passaggi* were often 'ill used,' and that they 'were not devised because they are essential to good singing style but rather, I believe, as a kind of tickling of the ears of those who hardly understand what affective singing really is. If they did understand, *passaggi* would doubtless be loathed, there being nothing more inimical to affective expression' (Caccini 1970, 47). He claimed that his new solo songs had 'more power to delight and move [the listener] than several voices together,' and he maintained that his songs, when sung with a good singing style, 'will make a better impression and will give greater delight than another full of contrapuntal art.' Counterpoint, he said, prevented any 'clear understanding of the words, shatter[ing] both their form and content, now lengthening and now shortening syllables to accommodate the counterpoint (a laceration of the poetry!).' He said that expressing the poetry through affective music and singing was 'much more useful than counterpoint' (Caccini 1970, 43–6; see also Hitchcock 1970).

Le nuove musiche is a collection of his arias and madrigals for solo voice with simple accompaniment. This music grew out of his activities in the Camerata of Giovanni de' Bardi in Florence during the last two decades of the sixteenth century. This group included some of the most celebrated singers, poets, and theorists of his age.[4] Caccini's extensive preface contains the clearest statement of the day concerning the essential elements of the new affective style of singing. He used the word *affetto* to suggest the ability of certain vocal techniques to arouse a strong emotional response in the listener. In his musical examples he demonstrated how certain *effetti* (ornaments) could be affectively rendered to increase the expression of the text, and he emphasized the need for good judgment in adding such *effetti* to the printed score. While some modern scholars have rightly pointed out that Caccini was vain and arrogant, and that he ran roughshod over other members of the Camerata, this does not alter the fact that he was a seminal figure in the establishment of what is now called the 'old Italian school of singing' (Pirrotta 1954; Kirkendale 1993, 119–73).

It is worth examining Caccini's preface in detail. Caccini said the chief requirements for expressive singing were a good voice and good breath control, which together enabled the singer to produce all the devices of affective singing. A 'good voice' excluded the falsetto (*voce finta*), which he said was wasteful of breath and 'often [became] harsh and unbearable to the ear' when singing a crescendo (Caccini 1970, 56, 49). He advocated a full, natural voice (*voce piena e naturale*), and transposition to keys where this kind of singing was best accomplished. He also considered the tenor voice to be more expressive than the bass voice (Caccini 1978, xxxi). This is consistent with the preference for high voices in the late sixteenth century (Einstein 2:822–5). High voices were considered more expressive than low ones, but in addition, different expressive qualities were assigned to the low, middle, and high portions of individual voices, probably due to the increased effort necessary for the higher portions. Vincenzo Galilei, a member of the Camerata, described the lower portion of the voice as 'lazy and somnolent,' the middle as 'tranquil,' and the high portion as 'querulous' (Palisca 1960, 347). The 'falseness' of the *voce finta* apparently prevented it from being affective in the same way as the tenor or soprano voice, despite its high range.

Caccini illustrated a number of specific vocal devices necessary for affective singing. One of these was the *intonazione della voce*, in which the first note of the phrase was begun about a third below the written note. The device was also known as the *clamatione* (H.M. Brown 1976, 10). He cautioned against staying too long on this lower note, saying that 'it should be scarcely suggested' lest it become 'unpleasant.' He also cautioned against using the device too frequently. Despite Caccini's reservations, it is apparent that the *intonazione* was widely used. A similar device was described by Zacconi, Bovicelli, Praetorius, and Bernhard.[5] Johann Agricola referred to it as a *Schleifer* (slide), and Montéclair called it a *son glissé* (Stanford 1979, 204, 228). Perhaps the *intonazione* was favoured because of its resemblance to expressive speech, where the voice is in a constant state of pitch modulation and does not settle on target pitches. Caccini's preferred method of beginning a musical phrase was to sing the first note directly on the target pitch, but to immediately add a crescendo or decrescendo, animating the note by a change in intensity rather than a change in pitch. This should be done 'to give delight and to move the affect of the soul' (Caccini 1970, 48–9). Mersenne advocated hitting the target pitch directly, the same as other instruments (Mersenne 1636, 353; Sanford 1979, 4–5).

Another important affective vocal device was the *esclamazione*, which Caccini described in this way:

Now, an *esclamazione* is really nothing but a certain strengthening of the relaxed voice; and the vocal crescendo in the soprano range, especially with falsetto, often becomes harsh and unbearable to the ear, as I myself have heard on many occasions. Without a doubt, therefore, as an affect more apt to move [the listener], a better result will be had from a decrescendo on the attack than from a crescendo; for in the first manner – the [attack with a] crescendo – to make an *esclamazione* one must after relaxing the voice crescendo even more, and thus, I say, does it seem strained and coarse. But a wholly different result is obtained by [an initial] decrescendo, since at the point of relaxation giving it just a bit more spirit will make it ever more affective. Aside from this, by using sometimes now one, now the other, variety may also be achieved. (Caccini 1970, 49)

The *esclamazione* was clearly different from the gliding pitch of the *intonazione*. It was apparently also different from the vocal crescendo-and-decrescendo (*il crescere e scemare della voce*), since Caccini advised the singer to use the *esclamazione* on half-notes but not on whole-notes 'which offer more room for a crescendo-and-decrescendo without using *esclamazioni*' (50).

Caccini's explanation of the *esclamazione* is obscure and has long puzzled scholars. Hitchcock noted that while the *crescendo-decrescendo* was an intensity change (one that was harsh in the falsetto voice), the *esclamazione* was more than just graduated vocal dynamics. It 'also seems to involve matters of vocal relaxation *vs.* intensity (having little to do with dynamics) which cannot be represented graphically (and with some difficulty verbally!)' (50). Hitchcock was probably correct. If the *esclamazione* was not a gliding pitch (like the *intonazione*), and was not just graduated dynamics (like the *crescendo-decrescendo*), then it seems likely that it was a particular voice quality.

Perhaps the key to understanding Caccini's *esclamazione* is provided by Garcia's description of the *messa di voce*. It will be recalled (see chapter 4) that Garcia's method of executing the *messa di voce* involved both a change in intensity (soft-loud-soft), and a change in voice quality (veiled-bright-veiled). The intensity was governed by breath pressure, while the voice quality was governed by the degree of glottal closure and the posture of the vocal tract. Caccini's *esclamazione* required both 'strengthening the relaxed voice,' and adding 'more spirit' to the voice. In the absence of any clear interpretation of this, I suggest that, like Garcia, Caccini was referring to both an intensity change and a change in voice quality in his description of the *esclamazione*.

Yet another affective device, for which Caccini coined no distinctive term but provided several musical examples, consisted of rhythmically prolonging a note, then following it with a quick rush of notes that released pent-up vocal energy. Caccini illustrated this by paired musical examples (Caccini 1970, 51–3). In order to increase the affective quality of a phrase, he lengthened certain notes beyond their written value, and often tied them to the next note, as a method of building vocal and musical tension. This lengthened tone was followed by an urgent vocal release – a *tirata*, a *cascata*, a *gruppo*, a *trillo*, or a *ribattuta di gola* (a strongly dotted rhythm redolent of a sob). I suggest that this pent-up energy of breath and tone followed by the voice breaking out into a vocal flourish made this style of singing affective. This pattern of restraint and release is implied in almost every musical phrase of Caccini's affective songs, and can be regarded as a hallmark of his style.

Meraviglia, Sprezzatura, and *Grazia*

Contemporary accounts of Caccini and other singers of the early Baroque period describe a performance aesthetic known as *meraviglia* (the marvellous), which was characterized by wonder, surprise, the unexpected, the extraordinary, the supernatural. This is a central theme in Celletti's *History of Bel Canto* (1991). The term *meraviglia* was used in reference to the conceits and artifices of Giambattista Marino's poetry (see Mirollo 1962, 117–18). It was also used to describe the *effetti meravigliosi* of virtuoso singers. For example, Victoria Archilei, a singer in Caccini's circle, was praised by Alessandro Guidotti in 1590 for moving her audience marvellously to tears (*mosse meravigliosamente a lacrime*) (Solerti 1903, 5). She was also admired by Caterina Guidiccioni, who praised Archilei's ability to stupefy everyone (*fa stupir tutti*) (Solerti 1902, 813). In 1608 Marco da Gagliano lauded both Antonio Brandi for 'the grace of his marvelous singing' (*la grazia del cantare maravigliosa*), and Caterina Martinelli, who 'filled with delight and wonder everyone at the theatre' (*ch'empiè di diletto e di meraviglia tutto il teatro*) (Solerti 1903, 87, 79). In 1634 Pietro de' Bardi (the son of Giovanni) wrote a letter to G.B. Doni in which he described the singing he had heard in his father's Camerata. He recalled that the young Caccini sang *'con meraviglia di chi lo sentiva'* (to the wonder of his listeners), and that the singing of Jacopo Peri left him *'stupido per la meraviglia'* (speechless with wonder) (Solerti 1903, 145–6; Strunk 1950, 365). Similar remarks are found in numerous other works of this period.[6]

Caccini's affective singing style was further characterized by *sprezzatura*, a rhythmic flexibility that allowed for the natural accentuation of the words, and a departure from Renaissance rules of part-writing so as to create dissonances that enhanced the expression of the words. The term *sprezzatura* had earlier been used by Baldassare Castiglione in *Il libro del cortegiano* (Book of the Courtier, 1528), where it was defined as 'that virtue opposite to affectation ... whence springs grace' (Caccini 1970, 44). *Sprezzatura* is sometimes translated as 'nonchalance' or 'negligence.' Said Caccini:

Having thus seen, as I say, that such music and musicians offered no pleasure beyond that which pleasant sounds could give – solely to the sense of hearing, since they could not move the mind without the words being understood – it occurred to me to introduce a kind of music in which one could almost speak in tones, employing in it (as I have said elsewhere) a certain noble negligence of song [*una certa nobile sprezzatura di canto*], sometimes transgressing by [allowing] several dissonances while still maintaining the bass note (save when I wished to do it the ordinary way and play the inner parts on the instruments to express some affect – for which, however, they are of little value). (44–5)

Caccini described this negligence in the preface to his opera *Euridice* (1600), where he wrote, 'in this manner of singing I have used a certain neglect [*sprezzatura*] which I deem to have an element of nobility, believing that with it I have approached that much nearer to ordinary speech.'[7] Similarly, Marco da Gagliano, another member of the Camerata, in the preface to his opera *Dafne* (1608), discussed the use of *sprezzatura* with reference to the expressive performance of the prologue to this opera.[8]

Caccini and Gagliano were referring, of course, to the new *stile recitativo*, in which the singer altered the rhythm of the notes to fit the natural accentuation of the words, even to the point of singing without a beat (*senza battuta*) or without strict measure (*senza misura*) (Caccini 1602, vii–viii; 1970, 54–5). It is likely that tempo changes, accelerandos, and ritardandos have always been a part of solo vocal music, from troubadour songs to jazz. After all, language consists of syllables of varying duration – even in metrical poetry – and cannot easily be shoehorned into the confines of strict metrical units without becoming rigid in the process. If singing is meant to be an extension of the expressive use of language, it too must engage in this kind of rhythmic articulation. The 'errors' of dissonance against the bass line were a feature of the *seconda prattica*, in which affective harmonies took precedence over the *prima prattica* rules of Renaissance part-writing.[9] It is apparent that *sprezzatura* was an important element in the new monodic style.

Modern scholars have offered their own views of *sprezzatura*. In 1968 musicologist Nino Pirrotta praised Caccini's use of *sprezzatura*, saying, 'The goal of the singer is to attain whatever spirit there is beyond the letter of music – that is, of Caccini's music – which goal can be reached through the *sprezzatura*, that is, through the intangible elements of rhythmic buoyancy and dynamic flexibility of the performance' (Pirrotta 1968, 54). More recently, musicologist Warren Kirkendale, who does not hesitate to speak his mind, noted the significance of *sprezzatura* in the singing of Caccini and his contemporaries. He described *sprezzatura* as 'a most important concept for eloquent performance of music, unfortunately not recognized by many specialists of "early music" in the age of computers: they play like robots, aiming at a deadly mechanical precision contrary to all musicality and historical practice. One is reminded of the brutally precise, electronically generated rhythms of rock "music," or the sound of a machine gun' (Kirkendale 1993, 156 n.245).

The quality of *grazia* in singing was closely related to the rhythmic subleties of *sprezzatura*. As Hitchcock pointed out, 'for the sixteenth-century artist, *grazia* had rather more subtle and significant connotations than does "grace" for us.' He again referred to Castiglione, and also to Giorgio Visari, a Renaissance artist and art historian who considered *grazia* to be an artistic ideal that went beyond mere beauty by including technical effortlessness (*facilità*), sweetness (*dolcezza*), and softness (*morbidezza*). It was a natural gift that could only spring from 'an effortless, unforced manner,' not unlike *sprezzatura* (Caccini 1970, 43–4). Sometime between 1640 and 1650, Severo Bonini (1582–1663) wrote *Discorsi e regoli*, an important Florentine source on monody and early opera. Like Caccini, Bonini used the term *grazia* to refer to the nonchalant subtleties of the artful singer. He noted that 'music has the power to induce various passions in man' through the four elements of harmony, rhythm, narrative, and a subject well disposed. To these he added a fifth element, 'namely, the *grazia* with which the singer must present the above four elements in a beautiful way in order to cause the effect toward which music is directed.' He said this was particularly true in *stile recitativo*, as sung by Jacopo Peri of the Camerata. 'He so moved the spectators to tears that truly it was something to wonder at' (Bonini 1979, xxi, 122). It is apparent that the qualities of *meraviglia*, *sprezzatura*, and *grazia* were defining characteristics in the new manner of expressive singing associated with the Camerata.

The Development of Idiomatic Singing

Caccini's 'new and noble manner of singing,' refers to the vocal style of early Baroque opera and monody. His affective vocal techniques can be considered idiomatic in that they use the voice in a manner that is distinct both from speech and from the vocal usage of choral singers and falsettists. The affective vocal devices that he described laid the foundations for similar and related techniques that developed over the centuries. Later authors amplified Caccini's remarks, and absorbed his vocal devices into their own vocal method books. Today, these techniques continue to play a role in classical singing styles.

Voice Quality

The chief distinguishing characteristic in classical singing is, of course, the quality of the voice, with its special powers of expression. Even the casual or non-expert listener can tell in an instant if a voice sounds 'classically trained' by the tone alone. This was the quality that Caccini referred to as 'the noble manner of singing,' with its *voce piena e naturale*. As we have seen, later authors maintained this quality was characterized by *chiaroscuro*, register equalization, *appoggio*, and vibrato. Garcia said that timbres and breathing 'form an inarticulate language, composed of tears, interjections, cries, sighs, etc., which one could properly name the language of the soul,' and he devoted numerous pages to instructions on the use of these colours and vocal devices in works by Gluck, Mozart, and Rossini (Garcia 1975, 138–65). Francesco Lamperti maintained that 'expression is wholly wanting in a voice not appoggiata.' He considered *appoggio* absolutely essential in order to 'convey the emotions of the soul or express the various feelings of the human passions (F. Lamperti 1216, 14). Regarding vibrato, even Garcia, who seemed to largely reject it, nevertheless noted that 'the tremolo, motivated by the situation and managed with art, has a certain moving effect,' and he gave illustrations showing how to employ the tremolo in specific arias from well-known operas. He said, 'The tremolo should be used only to portray the feelings which, in real life, move us profoundly' (Garcia 1975, 149–50).

Vocal Articulation

While voice quality is central to artistic singing, there are also devices of articulation and rhythmic freedom that further define the classical vocal idiom. The term articulation here refers to the ways in which tones are begun, joined, separated, and ended. One technique of articulation is a form of low pitch onset that developed from Caccini's *intonazione della voce*. We can only speculate as to why this device became a part of idiomatic solo singing when it did. Obviously, choral singing did not permit vocal glides at the beginning of tones, and Renaissance treatises are full of admonitions to sing with dead on pitch in polyphonic music. Yet, discrete tones with dead on pitch are totally removed from what happens in expressive speech, where pitch is in a constant state of modulation. When Caccini advocated 'negligence' in singing, 'speaking in tones,' and committing certain 'errors' of harmony, he was apparently trying to integrate certain speech-related qualities into the singing voice. Low pitch onset is still practiced by singers today, and there are fine singers who sometimes approach a target pitch from an interval of more than a third or fourth below. If this approach is done very quickly, as Caccini suggested, the listener may not even be aware that it is taking place. However, if it is done too slowly, it sounds like sloppy singing. Francesco Lamperti called this error *strisciato* – 'slurring up to his notes in mistake for legato' (F. Lamperti 1916, 17). Today it is called 'scooping' (Michel 1983).

When done with skill and good taste, low pitch onset can enhance both the expression and the intelligibility of a text, and provide a link to the pitch modulation of the spoken word. Modern researchers have shown that the vocal 'sweeping' action associated with low pitch onset helps to convey more linguistic information than is possible with a dead on pitch. This is because the perceived sound envelope is filled in by the quick ascent of the fundamental frequency and its attendant partials, thereby increasing the possibility of touching vowel formants. In 1985, Johan Sundberg reported using low pitch onset (which he playfully called 'Bull's roaring onsets') in synthesized singing, where he maintained it played an expressive role (Sundbery 1985a, 102–3). There may be a further advantage to low pitch onset, namely, its effect on vertical laryngeal position. It is generally agreed that good classical singing uses a low laryngeal position. It is also recognized that as the pitch rises, there is a tendency for the larynx to rise as well, unless the singer purposely maintains a low laryngeal position. In practical terms, starting a tone below the target pitch enables the singer to establish a low laryngeal position, and then to maintain that position as the pitch rises. This can be an effective way of ensuring that a high note does not begin with a high larynx.

The most important form of vocal articulation in classical singing is the *legato*. Franceso Lamperti stated categorically, 'Without *legato* there is no singing (*chi non lega non canta*); and, the two things that render the human voice superior to every other instrument are the power of *legato*, and the variation in colour' (F. Lamperti 1884, 21). G.B. Lamperti said the pupil must 'observe a strict *legato*, a smooth and unbroken passage from one tone to the other. The breathing must not be interrupted between the tones, but flow evenly as if a single tone were sung' (G.B. Lamperti 1905, 12; W.E. Brown 1957, 6). But a good *legato* depends on more than just unbroken breath. It also requires register equalization, carefully controlled subglottal breath pressure, stability of vertical laryngeal position, and source-tract compensations such as the singer's formant, that give some form of acoustical continuity to the tone. It can be said that the only musical instrument (excluding electronic instruments) capable of a true *legato* is the human voice. Pitches, intensity levels, voice colours, and vowels can all be changed without discrete breaks in the tone, due to the elastic properties of the singing muscles. Of course, pure *legato* is necessarily disrupted by words, but the singer can minimize this disruption by maintaining a stable low larynx and uniform breath pressure. Garcia called this the 'breadth or holding of the voice on the words' (*largeur ou tennue de la voix sur les paroles*), and maintained that the singer must be able to separate the functions of various organs in order to create *legato* with words (Garcia 1847, 2:7).

Portamento is closely related to *legato*. In a *portamento* the voice glides from one pitch to another, passing through all intervening pitches, in a slower manner than in a vocal onset or a legato. Like *legato*, *portamento* is ideally suited to the continuous and elastic capabilities of the human voice. While it can occur between any two pitches, *portamento* should be used sparingly for expressive purposes (Garcia 1975, 85; F. Lamperti 1916, 16–17). It is heard more frequently descending from a higher note to a lower one than vice-versa. The Italian word *portamento* suggests a 'carrying' of the voice from one pitch to another, as opposed to an abrupt shift of pitch. Perhaps the best historical description of *portamento* was given by Mancini (1774), who considered it necessary 'in every style of singing.' He wrote, 'By this *portamento* is meant nothing but a passing, tying the voice, from one note to the next with perfect proportion and union, as much in ascending as descending. It will then become more and more beautiful and perfected the less it is interrupted by taking breath, because it ought to be a just and limpid gradation, which should be maintained and tied in the passage from one note to another.' He also noted that the *portamento* 'cannot be acquired by any scholar who has not already united the two registers, which are in everyone separated' (Marcini 1967, 40–1). Manfredini echoed Mancini in the second edition of his *Regale armoniche*, adding that *portamento* was not to be used in recitative or parlando pieces (Manfredini 1797, 22). Numerous later authors also described *portamento* as a necessary part of good singing, and some also provided vocal exercises.[10] G.B. Lamperti added one further piece of advice when he said that, as the voice curves upward or downward, 'the *appoggio* remains unmoved,' thereby linking *appoggio* to *portamento* (W.E. Brown 1957, 21).

The antithesis of *legato* and *portamento* is glottal articulation, in which the arytenoid cartilages rapidly open and close, causing loss of breath and resonance. We have seen that Caccini's *trillo* and *passaggi* were early examples of this. Howard Mayer Brown considered the *trillo* to be a true idiomatic device: 'The *trillo*, apparently one of the glories of late Renaissance and early Baroque singers, may be the earliest example of an idiomatically conceived ornament; it is specifically intended for the human voice alone and, indeed, it can scarcely be imitated satisfactorily on any instrument, although some Baroque instrumentalists did attempt it (H.M. Brown 1956, 10–11). However, as we have seen, its resemblance to the bleating of a goat or lamb weakens Brown's argument that it is unique to the human voice, and instances of ridicule or rejection of the *trillo* indicate that it was never fully accepted as a desirable idiomatic vocal device.

Several degrees of non-*legato* articulation are used in florid singing. Tosi recognized two: *scivolato* (slurred) and *battuto* (detached). By the time of Garcia's *Traité* there were several variants, which he described and illustrated with musical examples. In *staccato*, the most heavily detached form of articulation, successive glottal stops resulted in momentary silences between the notes. In *sons piqués*, a lighter form of glottal articulation, the notes were not fully detached; Garcia maintained that this technique 'gives the phrase the effect of indecision and tenderness.' He also said that *sons martelés* (hammered sounds) 'have a good effect only in silvery and nimble voices; I would advise them only in women's voices,' and illustrated this with a musical example containing a reiterated single note (like Caccini's *trillo*) followed immediately by a descending passage in equally quick notes. He said the *marcato* sounds (*sons marqués*) 'suit all voices, but especially the basso profundo' (Garcia 1847, 2:29–30; 1975, 87–90). In *Hints on Singing* Garcia reduced his descriptions to five forms of vocalization: *legato*, *marcato*, *portamento*, *staccato*, and *aspirato* (Garcia 1894, 20). Francesco Lamperti described only four – *legato*, *portamento*, *picchettato*, and *martellato* – with *legato* being the most important. '*Legato* is the predominating quality, not only of agility, but of good singing in general; so the singer would do well not to study the others until he shall have mastered the art of singing *Legato*.' He recommended 'caution and moderation in the study of agility as the voice by too rapid exercises is apt to become tremulous and weak ...' (F. Lamperti 1916, 15).

Floridity

The expressive capabilities of florid singing have always been problematical. Just as there were supporters and detractors of *passaggi* and *trilli* in Caccini's era, there were also opposing views of floridity later on. Numerous eighteenth-century accounts of florid singing reveal that, as in Caccini's time, audiences were impressed by vocal agility. For instance, in a description of Farinelli's singing, Charles Burney said that the orchestra members 'were all gaping with wonder, as if thunderstruck' (MacClintock 1979, 26). Tosi, however, recognized that 'although a *passaggio* does not in itself possess the power to produce that sweetness which penetrates [the soul], it should be carefully considered as that thing which can help us admire the felicity of a flexible voice in a singer' (Tosi 1986, 30). The conflict between virtuosity and expression was also present in the nineteenth century. Francesco Lamperti defended the *canto d'agilità* when he said, 'It seems to me that the opponents of florid singing make a great mistake in the accusation they bring against it of being untrue, improbable, absurd, and worse, and as being contrary to all dramatic effect' (F. Lamperti 1984, 2). But Julius Stockhausen, writing in the same year, said, 'Such *coloratura* has nothing to do with expression, though in some comic operas they are often most attractive. It is only by great beauty of voice and a brilliant execution that such fireworks can be carried off successfully' (Stockhausen 1884, 117). J.J. Quantz, writing in 1752, seemed to prefer a full-throated approach to floridity: 'It is certainly true that if the sense of the words permits, and the singer possesses the capacity to produce passage-work in a lively, equal, round, and distinct manner, it is an exceptional ornament in singing ... Singers who have the capacity to produce passage-work roundly and distinctly, with all the force, and *none of the defects*, of the voice, are rare' (Quartz 1966, 330–1). In 1774 this remark was echoed by Giambattista Mancini, who said that agile singing 'should be sustained by the robustness of the chest, and accompanied by the gradation of the breath, the light action of the fauces, so that every note is heard distinctly ... One should not believe that this cantilena required detaching the note.' Perhaps this robust style is what he meant by the term *misto di granito*.[11] He added, 'It is a false opinion which many singers hold, that they cannot please or win merit unless they sing with agility' (57–8).

In the nineteenth century, Garcia again provided the most comprehensive treatment of florid singing (*canto fiorito*). 'This generic name includes every style which abounds in ornaments and colors at the same time. The florid style permits the singer to display the fertility of his imagination, and to make the most of the sonority and flexibility of his voice' (Garcia 1975, 192–3). Garcia recognized that light and heavy voices sang florid passages in different ways. In describing heavier forms of agile singing, he made specific reference to matters of timbre and breath pressure:

When the agility is performed pianissimo, it is necessary to hold back the expiration, and to expend only a thin stream of air. The pharynx, narrowed and shortened according to the conformation given to it by the timbre, elaborates and fashions the passages. The mouth is half opened. If one passes from the pianissimo to the mezzo-forte, one expends a little more air, but one maintains the action of the pharynx. Finally, in the forte, it is necessary to support the passages with a vigorous pressure of breath, a pressure which provokes a greater expenditure of air. The pharynx then offers the tone a more spacious route, more developed in height or in width, according to the timbre; the movements of which we have just spoken are less flexible and less frequent, and the mouth, for its part, presents to the tone an easier outlet. (Garcia 1984, 197)

It is important to remember that Garcia lived at a time when operatic styles were gradually turning away from vocal agility in favour of vocal strength. He noted the trade-offs that were necessary to accommodate this change, and made an important distinction by saying that 'agility itself is of two different natures: *di forza* (of power) and *di maniera* (of dexterity). These two natures are rarely found together in the same voice' (197). He explained that *di forza* required higher levels of breath pressure and airflow than *di maniera*, and that *di forza* was easier to execute, because it required less delicacy than *di maniera*. He noted that 'the more clear, white, thin, and supple the voices are, the more agile they can become, and *vice versa*' (10). He also discussed various sorts of articulation in passages, including tied sounds (*sons liés*), staccato sounds (*sons piqués*), detached sounds (*staccati*), marcato sounds (*sons marqués*), and hammered sounds (*sons martelés*). Thus he carried the discussion much further than the simple distinction made by eighteenth-century authors between 'beaten' and 'gliding' notes (Garcia 1975, 87–91).

Arguments concerning the expressive value of floridity extend from Caccini to the present. Owen Jander remarked, 'Excessive vocal display has been the object of repeated polemics throughout history ... History's recurring creeds against vocal ornamentation tend only to show, however, that audiences over the centuries have been persistently receptive to the delights of well-performed *fioratura*' (Jander 1980b, 338). Henry Pleasants maintains that 'most, if not all, the devices of *bel canto* originated in an expressive purpose.'

Brilliant roulades, or 'divisions,' lent themselves to the expression of fury, rage, vengeance and resolve, or, given the requisite harmony and figuration, jubilance and satisfaction. Trills and turns served to give emphasis to closes and cadences. Appoggiaturas brought dignity and gravity and sustenance to a long melodic line. Slurs, portamenti, and rapid scale passages, diatonic and chromatic, ascending and descending, could give weight and pathos to a climactic note. And embellishments could be fashioned according to situation and personality, thus becoming a constituent element of characterization. (Pleasants 1966, 21)

Many voice manuals admonished the singer to show good judgement in performing florid ornamentation. Mancini, for instance, in his discussion of vocal ornaments, wrote, 'In sum I say everything in one word, that all strength rests in perfect judgement, and understanding of the use of the graces of the art, which are in substance themselves the beauty of the art and the formation of the virtuoso style' (Mancini 1967, 53). Quantz echoed this when he said of singers, 'He who can truly fathom this art is not likely to be wanting in approval from his listeners, and his execution will always be *moving*. One should not imagine, however, that this fine discrimination can be acquired in a short time ... It comes only with the growth of feeling and judgment' (Quantz 1966, 126; see also 330–1).

The Trill

The chief ornament in florid singing in the eighteenth and nineteenth centuries was the trill – a swift, legato oscillation between two adjacent tones, as distinct from the earlier *trillo*. Quantz wrote, 'The singer must be able to execute a good shake that does not bleat' (Quantz 1996, 300). Tosi and others considered the trill an essential ornament in professional singing (Tosi 1986, 24). The trill was especially necessary in cadences, where its apparent fragility added a type of vocal instability that enhanced the tension-and-release of the harmonic cadence. Said Tosi, 'He who has a very beautiful trill, although deprived of every other ornament, always enjoys the advantage of conducting himself without lack of taste in Cadenzas, where it is for the most part essential. And he who lacks it (or possesses a defective trill) will never be a great singer, even though he knows much' (25). Tosi presented eight variants of the trill (covering a semitone or a tone; short or long; increasing or decreasing in speed; interpolating other notes; short and sharp at the beginning of a note, called *trillo mordente*). Tosi also discussed how the trill could be approached by an upper or lower *appoggiatura*, and how it could be combined with other ornaments (24–7). Johann Agricola elaborated on all these points in his 1757 translation of Tosi's treatise (J. Agricola 1995, 136–50).

Despite the importance of the trill, Tosi gave no practical advice or exercises on how to produce it. Rather, he admitted that the trill was a difficult ornament to teach:

Two very strong obstacles are encountered in forming the trill perfectly. The first embarrasses the Master, for there has not yet been found an infallible rule for him who teaches it; the second confounds the Scholar, for ungrateful nature does not allow it to many, but to few. The impatience of him who teaches it joins to the desperation of him who studies it, so much that the one abandons the pain, and the other the application. (Tosi 1986, 24, 29)

He also admonished singers who have mastered trills to apply them with discretion.

Giambattista Mancini relied heavily on Tosi in his own discussion of the trill. He too, considered the trill to be an 'indispensible necessity,' and exclaimed, 'O trill! Sustenance, decoration, and life of singing.' Even at this date (1774) he complained that the trill was 'ignored and neglected.' He exceeded Tosi in expressing frustration at the difficulty of finding a sure way to teach the trill, and said, 'I confess that this certain rule cannot be found at this moment in the author.' He repeated Tosi's description of eight kinds of trill, and urged 'perfect judgement.' He rejected both the 'goat-bleat' and the 'horse whinney' (Mancini 1967, 48–51). The old *trillo* of Caccini was well and truly dead.

Garcia went further than his predecesors in trying to explain how to produce the trill:

The trill is an alternating striking [*martelée*], rapid, and equal succession of two contiguous tones of a semitone or a whole tone ... The trill is only a regular oscillation from low to high and *vice versa* which the larynx receives. This convulsive oscillation takes its birth in the pharynx by a very similar oscillation of the muscles of that organ ... It is necessary to impart to the larynx a regular oscillatory up and down movement, similar to that of a piston working in the body of a pump, taking place in the pharynx, which serves as an envelope for the larynx. (Garcia 1847, 1:71–3; 1984, 158–60)

Garcia rejected the notion that the trill was a 'gift of nature,' and maintained that 'nothing is more erroneous than that opinion.' He added, 'I urge students to seek the trill through the spontaneous trembling of the throat, and not through the progressive movement of the two notes' (Garcia 1984, 163). He proceeded to describe various kinds of trills, with accompanying exercises and specific examples of how certain singers applied trills (Garcia 1847; 1:70–3, 2:44–6; 1984, 161–79; 1975, 125–9).

Among Garcia's disciples, Mathilde Marchesi provided examples of the trill in her *Méthod de chant*, but without an explanation of how to achieve it. She said merely, 'The shake is a regular oscillation of the larynx' (Marchesi 1970, 42–3). On the other hand, Stockhausen proposed a new and detailed method of attaining the trill. He discussed the seventeenth-century *trillo*, *gruppo*, and *ribattuta di gola* with reference to Caccini and Herbst, and noted that these techniques used glottal articulation (which he referred to as 'aspirated vocalization'). For the modern trill, he drew attention to the visible oscillation of the larynx which he compared to the throat of a nightingale:

For the execution of a correct trill, with increasing rapidity, we require the movement of the larynx which we observe in a nightingale's throat, and can also feel in our own throat if we put our finger on the shield-cartilage (commonly called Adam's apple), and sing repeated aspirated notes. It will then be observed that the aspiration seems gradually to produce a second note of a slightly lower pitch, which, if the throat be at all flexible, soon produces a minor shake [semitone trill]. It is therefore advisable to practise this until the movements of the larynx have grown rapid and easy. Once this is achieved it will only be a question of time till the major shake (whole tone trill] can also be produced. (Stockhausen 1884, 76)

He elaborated on this point by suggesting that the pupil first learn to sing the aspirated *trillo*, which, if prolonged, would lead to the modern trill. Yet he cautioned against the ugly bleating sound that Garcia called *hennissement* (neighing), and that Johann Agricola called the *trillo caprino* (goat's trill). Stockhausen's assertion that the trill grew naturally out of the *trillo* and *gruppo* is paradoxical, since the *trillo* and the trill are based on quite different mechanisms. Given his historical awareness of singing technique, it is possible that he was trying to reconcile the *trillo* with the trill, but the attempt was ill founded. He also provided a long series of exercises for the trill, along with musical examples taken from Schumann, Haydn, Handel, and even Wagner (78–83).

Francesco Lamperti also demonstrated his acquaintance with earlier authors when he cited Baini, Mancini, Manfredini, Bertarelli, and Benelli for their views on the trill. On the question of whether the trill is a natural gift or a learned artifice, he said:

My opinion is, that the shake properly so called is a natural gift; and I am not convinced by the statements of Garcia and Duprez (though I am sensible of the weight which attaches to such distinguished names) who declare that [Giuditta] Pasta acquired it by long practise. What she did acquire, is what I should call an *executive shake*, and I give it this name because it is to be gained by means of the same rules and exercises, which lead to the power of execution of other kinds of rapid passages; but this can never be mistaken for the shake properly so called, which is an exclusive gift of nature. Malibran and other well known singers possessed no natural shake, but acquired the executive shake. (F. Lamperti 1884, 31)

Giovanni Battista Lamperti echoed his father's views (G.B. Lamperti 1905, 18). Francesco's disciple William Shakespeare proposed yet another method of acquiring the trill, in which the pupil employed 'the rapid reiteration of the [syllable] lah on two notes, faster and faster, until the rapidity prevents the pronunciation of the *l*, and it becomes a trill, or the rapid succession of staccato Ahs, until the staccato becomes impossible, and a true rapid legato ensues, forming a trill' (Shakespeare 1910, 119). Shakespeare's suggestion, like Stockhausen's, seems quite impracticable.

It is apparent that there was a wide variety of opinion regarding the trill, and that some singers had a natural facility for trills while others had to approximate it by means other than the oscillation of the larynx. Nevertheless, laryngeal oscillation was clearly one of the most important vocal devices in idiomatic singing. While Tosi maintained that it was 'indispensible,' Francesco Lamperti argued that 'it is not indispensible. How often have I heard admirable artists, who touch the heart and evoke sympathy, without ever having recourse to the shake! I could name many of the first rank, but it is unnecessary' (F. Lamperti 1884, 31).

While the trill was widely admired as a vocal ornament, it was often overused. Leigh Hunt (the British critic whom we cited earlier for his biting comments on register breaks among tenors) said: 'Singers in general seem no more able to resist a shake when they are getting out of a song, than a dog when he gets out of the water' (Fenner 1972, 99). As with many other vocal matters, the trill was, and remains, a controversial vocal technique.

Tempo rubato

The singer's freedom to alter musical rhythms for the sake of expression was given a new name and a new definition by Pierfrancesco Tosi in *Opinioni de' cantori antichi* (1723). Apparently Tosi coined the term *il rubamento di tempo* (the stealing of time): 'He who does not know how to use *rubato* in singing ... remains deprived of the best taste and the greatest intelligence. Stealing the time in the pathetic [style of aria] is a glorious theft in one who sings better than others, provided that his comprehension and ingenuity make a good restitution' (Tosi 1986, 99). In a detailed new study of *rubato* called *Stolen Time: The History of Tempo Rubato*, Richard Hudson interprets Tosi's remarks to mean that the melody notes alone were stretched and shortened, while the accompaniment maintained a strict rhythmic beat. This differs from the type of *rubato* in which there is a rhythmic give-and-take of the entire musical texture by means of *accelerando*s and *ritardando*s (Hudson 1994, 1, 42–5). Hudson cites numerous eighteenth-century authors, including Johann Joachim Quantz, Johann Friederich Agricola, Friedrich Wilhelm Marpurg, Johann Adam Hiller, Johann Philipp Kirnberger, Johann Georg Sulzer, Johann Baptist Lasser, Roger North, and Charles Burney, all of whom indicate, with greater or lesser degrees of clarity, that *rubato* consisted of the singer's alteration of the notated rhythms while the accompaniment observed strict time (42–61). This was done either to accommodate accentuation of text or addition of ornaments and portamentos, or to simply add an expressive element of rhythmic tension to the music.

In the nineteenth century, Manuel Garcia provided the clearest description of the two practices of *rubato*:

In order to make the effect of the tempo rubato perceptible in singing, it is necessary to sustain the tempo of the accompaniment with precision. The singer, free on this condition to increase and decrease alternately the partial values, will be able to set off certain phrases in a new way. The accelerando and rallentando require that the accompaniment and the voice move together and slow down or speed up the movement as a whole. The tempo rubato, on the contrary, accords this liberty only to the voice.[12]

Garcia provided musical examples from operas by Donizetti, Mozart, Rossini, Zingarelli, and others, showing in musical notation an approximation of how some notes would rob others of part of their rhythmic value. He also stated that both his father Manuel Garcia I and the violinist Niccolò Paganini excelled in the use of the *rubato* applied within the musical phrase. He said, 'While the orchestra maintained the tempo regularly, they, on their part, abandoned themselves to their inspiration to rejoin with the bass only at the moment the harmony would change, or else at the very end of the phrase. But this means requires before everything an exquisite feeling of the *rhythm* and an imperturbable poise.'[13]

Rubato became associated with the piano playing of Frédéric Chopin, who apparently imitated the *rubato* of opera singers. Numerous accounts by Chopin's admirers and pupils document how he was influenced by the style of singing he heard in Bellini's operas and emulated this style in his *Nocturnes*.[14] Unfortunately, these pieces are rarely played with a true *tempo rubato*, but rather with *accelerando*s and *ritardando*s of the entire musical texture. Hudson calls the 'true' *rubato*, as described by Garcia and others, the earlier (melodic) *rubato*; the other practice (using *accelerando*s and *ritardando*s) he calls the later (structural) *rubato*. However, one might well argue that these terms are rather troublesome since Caccini's *sprezzatura* resembles Hudson's description of the later vibrato, thus muddying the waters somewhat.

Like Chopin, the celebrated French composer Camille Saint-Saëns learned *rubato* from singers, particularly Pauline Viardot, Manuel Garcia's sister. Viardot was a friend of Chopin, and occasionally studied piano with him during the summers from 1841 to 1845. As Hudson points out, 'she was thus in a unique position to understand the meaning of *tempo rubato* – both from the singer's point of view and from Chopin's' (Hudson 1994, 195). Saint-Saëns credited Viardot with teaching him the 'true secret of *tempo rubato*,' which he described as follows: 'In the true [*rubato*] the accompaniment remains undisturbed while the melody floats capriciously, rushes or retards, sooner or later to find again the support of the accompaniment.'[15]

The art of *rubato* apparently fell into disuse in the later nineteenth century, at least in German musical practice. Mathilda Marchesi berated German conductors for their lack of *rallentandos* and *rubato* (M. Marchesi 1898, 199). Her daughter Blanche complained that German opera conductors did not follow the singers, but rather, made the singers follow them. She maintained that this was a new development, and that the German conductors made music 'as strict as the military goose-step' (B. Marchesi 1923, 251). These statements suggest that not only the rhythmic tension of *rubato* but even the *accelerandos* and *ritardandos* of the entire musical texture had been lost.

Rhythmic flexibility held its own in other quarters. For example, in her father's singing, Marjory Kennedy-Fraser recalled a rhythmic fluctuation which she called *rubato* but which was more likely the use of *accelerando* and *ritardando:*

He used the *rubato* with great freshness and effect. The freshness I can vouch for. Having been his accompanist for so long, I know that every time he sang a song I had to be very much on the alert in this respect. All the world is conscious of rhythm in music and poetry, although all the world may not be able to produce it. All the world can be hypnotized by it and can respond to the thrill of the 'return of the beat' of a great swinging *rubato*, a *rubato* which has swung them out to mid-stream and then landed them safely on the other shore. Just as the *rubato* of the Scala orchestra could make the audience rise to its feet, so the daring but perfectly balanced phrasing of a fine Scots tune can thrill any audience to enthusiasm. (Kennedy-Fraser 1929, 66)

There are other examples of rhythmic flexibility. For instance, in Ireland there is a long tradition of 'old style' singing (*sean-nós*) in 'slow airs,' sung by a high female voice in a highly ornate style with no accompaniment and great rhythmic freedom. This may be a remnant of a medieval practice with certain Arabian influences (Acton 1978, 8). Vernacular styles of music, especially jazz, use *rubato* to a much greater extent than do classical styles. Perhaps this is because vernacular styles stay closer to the speech origins of song and allow for more rhythmic freedom.

Both *tempo rubato* and the speeding up and slowing down of the overall tempo have played an important role in idiomatic singing. There is a belief among some instrumental musicians that singers who do not adhere strictly to the beat or do not slavishly follow the accompaniment are sloppy musicians. Nevertheless, ever since Caccini's emphasis on *sprezzatura*, rhythmic flexibility and rhythmic tension have been a vital factor in idiomatic singing, even if such rhythmic play goes unappreciated by some listeners.

Categories of Expressive Song

Of course, not all songs are equally affective or full of passion. Rather, there are categories of song which differ from each other by both the degree and the kind of expressive vocal devices employed. This was already noted by Caccini in his complaint that singers 'indiscriminately' used *effetti* 'both in affective music (where they are more necessary) and in dance songs.'[16] He said that singers 'who thoroughly understand the ideas and the feelings of the words ... know how to distinguish where more affect is needed, and where less ...' (Caccini 1970, 48). In *Le nuove musiche*, he divided the songs into two categories: *madrigals* and *arias*. The through-composed madrigals were based on passionate texts and lent themselves to the use of affective vocal devices, the strophic arias were based on lighter poetry and made more use of *passaggi* but required fewer affective vocal devices.[17] Here again, it was incumbent on the singer to show good judgment in the use of affective singing techniques. The operas by Caccini, Jacopo Peri, and the other early Florentine composers contain not only affective songs and dance songs but also long sections of music in *stile recitativo*. It was here that the singers had the most opportunity to sing with *sprezzatura* and to use declamatory effects such as *esclamazioni*.

As the seventeenth century proceeded, opera passed from the princely court to the public opera house and castrato singers became the focus of virtuoso singing. Vocal music moved toward a more melodious style, and there was a growing distinction between recitative, arioso, and aria, with the aria being the chief vehicle of expressive singing. Toward the middle of the century, some of the affective and ornamental devices of the Florentines gave way to a more moderate form of expression. Musicologist Manfred Bukofzer maintained that the musical style that emerged between 1630 and 1640 in the works of Luigi Rossi in Rome and Pier Francesco Cavalli in Venice marked the beginning of *bel canto*. He remarked that musical elements in opera, oratorio, and cantata were now 'coordinated with, rather than subordinated to, the words,' and found that the 'exuberant *coloratura*' and 'garish virtuosity' of early opera and monody were replaced by a lilting melodic flow, simple harmony, and more restrained vocal idiom well suited to the penetrating quality and sustained power of the castrato singer. 'Bel-canto melodies were more highly polished and less ostentatiously affective than those in monody' (Bukofzer 1947, 120–3). His definition of *bel canto* was apparently based upon a particularly narrow view of what constitutes idiomatic and expressive singing.

In the eighteenth century, there was a methodical categorization of arias. Arias were classified according to the type of emotion being portrayed, the type of vocalism employed, and the quality of the accompaniment. In *Opinioni* (1723), Tosi devoted an entire chapter to arias (*Dell' Arie*), in which he decried the fact that *bravura* arias were gradually replacing the older style of *pathetic* arias. He complained that musicians paid lip-service to the *pathetic* aria, regarding it as 'the dearest delight of the ear, the sweetest passion of the soul, and the strongest foundation of harmony.' But, he said, 'they praise the pathetic and sing the allegro.' While the pathetic arias were sung *adagio*, with all the expressive power of *cantabile* and *portamento*, the *bravura* arias allowed the singer to make the greatest display of *passaggi*. 'Singers of today are not content until they have transformed all with horrid metamorphoses of such *passaggi* running unbridled to attack with reinforced violence their final notes' (Tosi 1986, 68). These final cadenzas especially rankled Tosi, and he devoted a separate chapter to them. He preferred *cantabile* cadenzas, characterized by the 'sweetness of the *portamento*, in *appoggiaturas*, in art, and in the intelligence of runs, going from one note to another with singular and unexpected strategems, with *tempo rubato*, and on the movement of the bass, which are the principal qualities indispensibly most essential for good singing, and which [even] the ingenious human being cannot find in their capricious cadenzas' (82). For Tosi, empty virtuosity was the bane of his time.

In 1763 there appeared a rather obscure tract by an author named John Brown (one of many John Browns, as the British Library catalogue amply illustrates!), called *Dissertation on the Rise, Union, and Power, the Progressions, Separations, and Corruptions, of Poetry and Music*. John Brown (1715–66) was an English clergyman, writer, amateur musician, and keen observer of musical practice, whose treatise was one of the earliest general histories of music.[18] Brown described the different classes of arias in considerable detail. Johann Adam Hiller (1728–1804) also described four types of arias: the *aria di bravura*, the *aria di strèpito*, the *aria d'espressione*, and the *aria di cantabile* (Hiller 1774, 213). These aria types were described in greater detail by Johann F. Christmann (1752–1817), a German clergyman, composer, and writer on music, in his *Elementarbuch der Tonkunst* (1782).[19]

Arias in opera are classified according to the respective character; an aria which is marked by difficult passages and impassioned melody is called an *aria di bravura* since it requires much boldness in its execution. If the voice has more declamation than flowing melody, and if the accompaniment is active and full, it is an *aria di strepito* [agitation], and an aria which contains many changes and digressions in the expression of various passions, and in which the tempo changes a number of times, is called an *aria d'espressione*. (Christman 1782–9, 242; trans. Ratner 1980, 280)

The descriptions of John Brown gained wider circulation when they were quoted at length by British music critic George Hogarth, in his well-known *Memoirs of the Opera in Italy, France, Germany, and England* (Hogarth 1851). Hogarth said that the classification of aria types was by no means arbitrary, but was 'founded on principles of taste.' Hogarth's five categories of arias can be summarized as follows:

1. The *aria di cantabile* is 'the only kind of song which gives the singer an opportunity of displaying all his powers of every description. The proper objects of this kind of air are sentiments of tenderness; and its proper expression is a pleasing sadness.' The *aria di cantabile* is slow, full of pathos, highly ornamented, and has a simple accompaniment.
2. The *aria di portamento* is comprised chiefly of sustained long notes that express 'the carriage or sustaining of the voice.' Here the tone quality is most important, 'for the beauty of sound itself, and of vocal sounds in particular, as being the finest of all sounds, is held by the Italians to be one of the chief sources of the pleasure derived from music. The subjects proper for this class of air are sentiments of dignity, but calm and undisturbed by passion ... The subject of the *portamento* is too grave and serious to admit of the degree of ornament which is essential to the *cantabile*.'
3. 'The *aria di mezzo carattere* is a species of air, which, though expressive neither of the dignity of the *portamento* nor of the pathos of the *cantabile*, is, however, serious and pleasing.' This type of aria covers a wider range of lesser sentiments than either the *aria di cantabile* or the *aria di portamento*. It is usually an *andante*, and the orchestra 'may on the whole contribute more to the general effect of the air.'
4. The *aria parlante*, which Hogarth calls a 'speaking air,' is fairly rapid and syllabic, with few ornaments. It is also called the *aria di nota e parole*, the *aria agitata*, and if it becomes more excited it is called *aria di*

strèpito or *aria infuriata*. It expresses emotions such as fear, joy, grief, or rage, and it often has a strong and animated accompaniment.

5. The *aria di bravura*, or *aria d'agilità*, offers the singer 'an opportunity of displaying extraordinary powers of voice and execution ... Such airs too frequently serve no other purpose than that of astonishing the ignorant, while they make the judicious grieve.' (This was the kind of 'wowism' that Tosi and many others so disliked.) (Hogarth 1851, 2:64–8)

What is significant about Hogarth's classification of arias is that it relates the expression of specific emotional qualities directly to idiomatic techniques of singing. *Cantabile, portamento, bravura, agilità* – these were the stock-in-trade of cultivated singers, and idiomatic singing techniques were inseparable from expressive song.

This relationship of emotional qualities to idiomatic singing techniques continued in the nineteenth century. The pedagogical treatises of Garaudé and Garcia gave specific instructions on how to apply idiomatic singing devices to various classes of arias. Garaudé wrote a chapter called 'On the Character of Diverse Pieces of Music,' which included not only a discussion of recitative, but of *cantabile, allegro, agitato, cavatina, rondo, canzonetta*, duos, trios, and ensembles, nocturnes, and romances. This was followed by the chapter 'On Style, Taste, and Expression.' Garaudé thus continued the tradition of linking vocal techniques to the style and expressive properties of the music of his day (Garaudé 1830, 119–52).

Manuel Garcia devoted much of Part Two of his *Traité* to a discussion of the variety of vocal styles for both recitative and arias. He used the term *canto spianato* for the 'broad' style that included *cantabile* and *portamento*. This style required the highest degree of art and training, including *legato*, smooth register change, shadings of loud and soft, clarity of articulation, tasteful use of timbres, limited but appropriate ornamentation, and 'pathetic' expression. The *canto spianato* category of arias included *largos, cantabiles*, and *andantes*, and Garcia provided numerous examples from the operatic repertoire to illustrate his remarks (Garcia 1847, 2:66–8; 1975, 186–92).

Garcia separated florid singing into several categories, each of which had its own character and was suitable for certain kinds of expression. While the florid style, like the *spianato* style, made use of the *messa di voce, tempo rubato, portamento*, and graduated dynamics, its principal effects were based on the tasteful use of *passaggi*. In this category Garcia placed the *canto di agilità*, the *canto di maniera* (which included the *canto di grazia* and the *canto di portamento*), and the *canto di bravura* (which included the *canto di forza*, the *canto di slancio*, and the *canto di sbalzo*). He described each of these in detail, citing specific pieces from the operatic repertoire, and even naming specific singers who excelled in these styles (68–70; 192–200), and he did the same for the *canto declamato* (dramatic style) (70; 200–1). In the *canto di agilità*, 'the treatment of the passages should be free, the performance light, and the voice used sparingly' (Garcia 1975, 194). The *canto di maniera* was suitable for singers with weak voices who did not possess extreme agility, but who could substitute short, elegant motives for longer and more difficult passages. The *canto di bravura* was like the *canto di agilità*, but 'with the addition of power and emotion.' When it was dominated by large intervals it took the name *canto di slancio* (197–8).

The long tradition of vocal treatises that discussed vocal techniques in the context of specific musical styles extended from Caccini to Garcia, but then gave way to pedagogical treatises that were simply manuals on 'how to sing.' After Garcia, authors such as Mathilda Marchesi, Julius Stockhausen, the Lampertis, and William Shakespeare restricted themselves largely to vocal techniques and did not relate those techniques to specific styles and composers. In turn stylistic criticism of a scholarly nature lost touch with the importance of performance practices – separation of disciplines that marked an unfortunate development, and that has worked to the disadvantage of both.

Modern Views of Vocal Idiom and Expression

The idea that singing can be expressive of emotion has long intrigued scholars. In some cases, this has led to theories suggesting that the origins of speech and music are found in the bodily gestures associated with human emotional behaviour. The mechanisms of tension-and-release that manifest themselves in bodily gestures can also affect the pitch, intensity, melodic contour, pacing, quality, and articulation of the voice. At the end of his book *On the Sensations of Tone* (1862), Helmholtz suggested that music, in its initial state, 'may have been originally an artistic imitation of the instinctive modulations of the voice that corresponds to various conditions of feelings.' By this he implied that certain characteristics of the speaking voice offer cues to 'corresponding psychical motives.' These, in turn, 'embrace really mechanical but involuntary muscular contraction' (Helmholtz 1895, 370–1). In *The Expression of the*

Emotions in Man and Animals (1872), Charles Darwin also related forms of vocalization to emotional states and to expression in music. His general theme is that human emotional behaviour is reflected in bodily gestures; vocalization is one example of such gestures (Darwin 1965, 86–93, 217 passim).

More recently this theme has been taken up by Peter Kivy, who describes a speech theory of musical expressiveness in which the gestures of emotional speech find expression in musical qualities, as seen in the *stile recitativo* of the Camerata. 'What Peri and Caccini were doing was evolving a kind of musical declamation which, by following the rise and fall of the speaking voice, as it expresses the emotions of the speaker, resulted in a musical line distinctly nonmelodic in nature' (Kivy 1980, 19). Kivy points out that Caccini's view was that this style of singing enabled a listener to recognize, and perhaps even share the emotion being projected, and takes the argument further by suggesting that purely musical factors, through association with physical gestures, can be expressive of some strong emotions, even without voice or text (65, 77, 83 passim).

Other authors from various disciplines have also pursued this line of thinking.[20] Voice researcher Johan Sundberg writes:

I invite you to the following speculation. We signal our attitudes and emotional states by means of a body language, i.e. patterns for physical motion. Such patterns are likely to characterize also the movement of the entire voice organ with its cartilages, bones, and muscles. However, it is these organs which control the acoustic sound characteristic of the voice, such as pitch, loudness, phonation type, etc. If the body language in a certain mood is characterized by the motion, the muscles regulating voice pitch must be assumed to move slowly too, and so all acoustic voice parameters will change slowly too. If so, the human voice can be regarded as an organ which converts body language into sound. Perhaps this is important to music; it implies that it is the existence of the human voice which enables us [in] the highly sophisticated interpretation of sound which seems to be a prerequisite for musical communication. (Sundberg 1985a, 102)

Elsewhere, Sundberg also commented on the more imponderable emotional elements of voice quality: 'Clearly there is something quite unusual about the voice of a first-class opera singer. Quite apart from the music, the intrinsic quality of such a voice can have a forceful impact on the listener' (Sundberg 1977a, 82).

Individual voice quality is also an important element in singing. Says

Owen Jander, 'Even without words ... the voice is capable of emotional utterance as unique, personal and identifiable as the cry of an infant to its mother. It is arguably the most subtle and flexible of musical instruments, and therein lies much of the fascination of the art of singing' (Jander 1980b, 338). The singer with a highly distinctive voice often has an advantage over singers whose voice quality is more anonymous or generic, and easy recognition of a singer's voice may play an important role in that singer's success.

The modern author who has most closely approximated Caccini's description of affect is Donald N. Ferguson. In his book *Music as Metaphor* he asserted that emotion is 'one of the behavior-patterns of a mind in action,' and that it 'involves a complex of nervous tensions and their attendant releases.' He continued, 'Two of those factors of experience, nervous excitement and motor release, are themselves manifestations of tension and motion ... Tension and motion can become elemental for expression if they are designed, not merely to effect cohesion essential to form, but also to *represent* familiar characteristics of feeling' (Ferguson 1960, 65, 67).

For Ferguson, the key to musical expressivity is found in 'tone-stress' and in 'ideal motion.' Tone-stress resides in the antagonistic forces that lead to vibration, while ideal motion is the musical gesture which is generated by tone-stress. In addition to these primary elements, Ferguson maintained that 'the most conspicuous secondary factors are timbre, register, *tempo rubato*, vibrato, shading, and phrasing' (81). He said that shading, 'although it is often an effect of color, is chiefly accomplished through dynamic gradations' (84). While Ferguson was not speaking specifically about the voice in his theory of musical expressivity, his ideas fit well with Caccini's. He noted that 'anyone who has the least familiarity with music will see that its whole substance, whether of tone or rhythm, appears in a constant and essential condition of varied stress' (68).

The common element that runs through the arguments of these authors is that human emotion is expressed not only through the tension-and-release of body language, but through analogous gestures of the human voice. Classical singing is regarded as a stylization and amplification of the characteristics of emotional speech, and results in voice qualities and vocal gestures that are a window on human feeling. Caccini's preface to *Le nuove musiche* is one of the earliest and best records of this theory of expression, and it still resonates in the works of Ferguson and Kivy.

Word-Note-*Tone* Relationships: A Case Study

As discussed earlier, critics and musicologists have paid little attention to the role of singing in their analysis of word-tone relationships in songs and arias. To illustrate this, I can think of no better example than the famous aria 'Che farò senza Euridice?' from Gluck's opera *Orfeo ed Euridice*, first performed in Italian in Vienna in 1762; a French version was subsequently presented in Paris in 1774. This aria has been harshly dealt with by some critics, from Eduard Hanslick in 1854 to Peter Kivy in 1980, because the sombre mood and character of the text is contradicted by Gluck's rather jaunty melody in a major mode (Kivy 1980, 73–6). Orpheus has just lost his betrothed for the second time because he turned to look at her as he was leading her out of the underworld. He sings his lament to the gods, saying, 'What will I do without Euridice?' Hanslick noted:

> At a time when thousands (among them were men like Jean-Jacques Rousseau) were moved to tears by the air from *Orpheus:*
> *J'ai perdu mon Euridice,*
> *Rien n'égals mon malheur.*
> [I have lost my Euridice,
> Nothing equals my sorrow.]
> Boyé [Pascal Boyer], a contemporary of Gluck, observed that precisely the same melody would accord equally well, if not better, with words conveying exactly the reverse, thus:
> *J'ai trouvé mon Euridice,*
> *Rien n'égale mon bonheur.*
> [I have found my Euridice,
> Nothing equals my joy.]

Hanslick went on to say, 'We, for our part, are not of the opinion that in this case the composer is quite free from blame, inasmuch as music most assuredly possesses accents which more truly express a feeling of profound sorrow' (Hanslick 1957, 32–4). This was because Gluck chose to set sad words with a lilting, upward-rising melody in the major mode, a *cantilena* far more suited to happy words than sad ones. One opera handbook says: 'It is a strange air – strange because, despite its pathetic words and the sense of agonized loss which it supposedly expresses, its straightforward, major-key tune has none of the purely musical features which normally convey pathos in singing' (Jacobs and Sadie 1964, 34).

Deryk Cooke, in *The Language of Music*, tried to explain this anomaly by saying, 'How can such a simple, diatonic, major melody express grief? In fact, it achieves a purely classical pathos, by suspending the tonic on the major seventh, as a 4–3 progression on the dominant, in the essentially pleasurable context of the major key. The pathos is even enhanced, in a purely classical way, by being in a major context; since this conveys the natural joy of life which is undermined by the pathetic suspension' (Cooke 1959, 83). Cooke is saying that the frequent use of the dissonant *appoggiatura* (the descending melodic semitone at the end of phrases), was sufficient to overcome the happier qualities of the tune and evoke sad sentiments. In fact, composers have often used such *appoggiaturas* to convey a musical 'sigh' (*Seufzer*). One familiar example is 'Porgi amor,' the doleful aria sung by the Countess in Mozart's *Le nozze di Figaro*, which is also in the major mode, and which also begins with a rising melodic line. However, the sighing *appoggiatura* alone cannot transform the character of *Che farò*; it requires something more.

In *The Corded Shell* (1980), Peter Kivy, whose field is philosophy and whose specialty is expression and meaning in music, responded to Cooke. Kivy could not accept Cooke's premise that Gluck's use of the dissonant appoggiatura was sufficient to overcome the moderately rapid tempo, the major key, and the diatonic melody that were conventionally associated with happiness. Like Hanslick, Kivy maintains that Gluck missed the mark with this aria (Kivy 1980, 140). Opera historian Robert Donington joined this chorus when he said, 'Though the tune is heart-melting, it is not particularly sad, with its C major tonality and its easy lilt ... Gluck had not Mozart's gift or Wagner's, of conveying musically a precise character or situation or feeling; he just conveys feeling in general' (Donington 1978, 78).

Some scholars have tried to explain away the problematical nature of *Che farò* by suggesting that Orpheus is beyond grief when he sings this aria. In 1936, musicologist Alfred Einstein wrote, 'Critics have thought it strange that Orpheus should at this ineffable moment sing an aria at all, and that *this* aria should be in C major and might well express the opposite meaning ... It is devoid of pathos because, as has been finely said, it transcends all expression' (Einstein 1962, 88, 96). Musicologist Joseph Kerman, in his book *Opera as Drama* (1988), echoed the view of Einstein, saying 'the aria is beyond grief, and represents a considered solution, a response to the catastrophe' (Kerman 1988, 33). He maintained that Hanslick's objection to *Che farò* missed the 'essential point,' which was that Orpheus was not really grief-stricken at all, but rather, was master of his situation, using 'self-control,' and 'lyric introspection' to gain a 'state of beatitude' (33–6). In this sense, Kerman maintained, the aria was successful precisely because its purpose was not to evoke sadness, but to *transcend* it. This strikes me as a rather specious argument, since it is hard to accept that the singers and audiences of Gluck's day, who were used to certain operatic conventions, would have regarded Orpheus in such a transcendental way, especially when the text is so clearly one of grief.

The common element in the criticisms of Hanslick, Cooke, Einstein, Kivy, Donington, and Kerman is the absence of any mention of the singer's role in projecting the sentiments of this aria. If, as Hanslick maintained, 'thousands were moved to tears by this aria,' then the expression of grief and despair was indeed communicated by singers who knew how to overcome the apparent weaknesses of the music by the expressive use of the voice. Gluck himself was acutely aware that this aria was treading a fine line between opposing emotional qualities, and that it was up to the performers to ensure that the proper expression was achieved. In 1770 he wrote: 'Little or nothing, apart from a slight alteration in the mode of expression, would be needed to turn my aria in *Orfeo*, 'Che farò senza Euridice?' into a puppet-dance. One note more or less sustained, failure to increase the tempo or make the voice louder, one appoggiatura out of place, a trill, a passage or roulade, can ruin a whole scene in such an opera' (Muller van Asow 1914, 217).

In a letter published in the *Journal de Paris* in 1777, Gluck again discussed the importance of the performers: 'Finally, I believed that the voices, the instruments, all the sounds, and even the silences, ought to have only one aim, namely, that of expression, and that the union of music and words ought to be so intimate that the poem would seem to be no less closely patterned after the music than the music after the poem' (trans. Weisstein 1969, 111). This statement makes it clear that Gluck considered vocal and instrumental performance, as well as word-tone relationships, to be essential elements in expressing passions and sentiments in song.

The first singer to perform the role of Orpheus was castrato Gaetano Guadagni (ca. 1725–92), who was praised by Hogarth for his performance of this aria: 'He produced a great impression by his action, and especially by the impassioned and exquisite manner in which he sang the aria "Che farò senza Euridice"' (Hogarth 1851, 2: 143). Manuel Garcia, in his *Traité* of 1847, described the timbre of the voice that he thought was suitable for this aria: 'Restrained threat, profound grief, and repressed despair take a hollow [*caverneux*] timbre ... Here the accents of grief are shaded, sometimes by a tint of melancholy, sometimes by bursts of sorrow, sometimes by a dark despair' (Garcia 1847, 2:56; 1975, 156). This seems to suggest that a dark vocal timbre will impart a sense of grief and despair, regardless of the salient quality of the music.

Hector Berlioz, in his book *Gluck and His Operas*, described the singing of mezzo-soprano Pauline Viardot, who sang the role of Orpheus in the 1859 revival of Gluck's opera. 'To speak, now, of Madame Viardot is to approach what forms a study in itself. Her talent is so complete and varied; it touches so many points of art; and is united to so much science, and to such an entrancing spontaneity, that it produces, at one and the same time, both astonishment and emotion; the result being that it strikes, and yet appeals to the heart; it overawes, and yet persuades' (Berlioz 1914, 14). After several more pages of adulation, he came to his account of '*J'ai perdu*':

Gluck has somewhere said, 'change the slightest shade of movement or of accent in that air, and you make a dance of it.' Mme Viardot makes of it precisely what is wanted to be; one of those prodigies of expression, wellnigh incompehensible for vulgar singers, and which are, alas! so often profaned. She delivered the theme in three different ways: firstly, with a contained grief, and in slow movement; then, after the episodal adagio:

> *Mortel silence!*
> *Vaine espérance!*
> [Deathly silence!
> Vain hope!]

in *sotto voce*, *pianissimo*, and with a trembling voice choked by a flood of tears; and, finally, after the second adagio, she took the theme with a more animated movement, in quitting the body of Euridice by the side of which she had been kneeling, and in throwing herself, mad with despair, towards the opposite side of the scene, with the bitter cries and sobs of a distracted grief. I shall not try to describe the transports of the audience at this overpowering scene ... (20)

It is clear from this account that Viardot used all the devices at her disposal to ensure that this aria was indeed expressive of grief and despair. Her performance would certainly not have suited Kerman's view of this aria as expressing 'self-control,' 'lyric introspection,' or a 'state of beatitude.'

While those early performances of 'Che farò' are, of course, lost to us, there is nevertheless a 1932 recorded performance by Italian tenor Tito Schipa that illustrates the role of idiomatic singing in capturing the affect of this aria.[21] Schipa has often been acknowledged as a singer who represented the old Italian school in the early decades of the twentieth century. His recording is remarkable in the way it captures Orpheus's sadness and despair. His voice infuses this melody with pathetic elements not readily apparent in the written notes. Schipa's voice has a dark and contained sound that fits Garcia's description of the proper timbre for this aria. One can readily hear characteristics of *appoggio*, with its 'held back' breath. The slight 'aftergrunts' heard at the end of phrases attest to the pent-up breath pressure, which, as suggested earlier, may evoke a feeling of pent-up emotion. Schipa sings in the chest register, but with frequent use of covered singing, especially on the climactic high notes. This cultivated vocal manoeuvre, with its internal tensions, adds to the expression of Orpheus's extreme emotional state. An even, steady vibrato enriches Schipa's sound and gives it a fragile tremulancy that might be equated with human emotional behaviour. He sings with a flawless *legato*, which suits the outpouring of emotion, and he sometimes uses low pitch onset and *portamento*, which add to the expressiveness and the intelligibility of the singing. Even the orchestra mimics his *portamento* as an expressive device.[22] Schipa's use of dynamic gradations on sustained tones, including crescendo, decrescendo, and a faultless *messa di voce*, further adds to the expressive quality of the singing. As well, he chose a slow tempo, which is appropriate for the mood of the text, and he uses tempo changes and *rallentandos* effectively to follow the ebb and flow of Orpheus's emotional state. Like Viardot, Schipa quickens the tempo with an *accelerando* in the final climactic section. He follows Gluck's admonition by avoiding empty vocal flourishes, and he certainly does not turn the aria into a 'puppet-dance.'

Schipa's combination of idiomatic vocal techniques fits Manuel Garcia's description of *canto spianato:*

This style, the most noble of all, but also the least zesty, because of the slowness of its movement and the simplicity of its forms, rests only on the shades of the emotion, and the variety of the musical chiaroscura. Here nothing can substitute for the correctness of the intonation, the expression of the voice, the purity and the effects of syllabication, the musical coloring. This style has for its principal resources the clarity of the articulation and the various degrees of energy which it includes; the breadth and the equality of the voice; the agreement, the fusion or the delicacy of the timbres; the use of drawn out sounds in all varieties; the finest shades of dynamics, potamentos, the *tempo rubato*. The artist who has obtained this result, so difficult to obtain with only these resources, completing their effect with the *cantabili*, knows how to phrase all kinds of songs. (Garcia 1847, 2:66; 1975, 186–7)

As sung by Schipa, 'Che farò senza Euridice' is indeed the grief-stricken piece that Gluck intended. The true measure of its success lies in the word-note-*tone* relationship, where the art and idiom of the singer is added to the art of the composer in order to ensure the effective portrayal of human emotion.

Conclusions

There is an expressive power in the trained singing voice that I like to refer to as the 'vocal aesthetic.' This is the power of the singer to astonish, charm, or move an audience in a way no other instrument can. Part of the power of expression, of course, is due to the presence of words, which convey their own meaning. But aside from linguistic communication, there is another level of expression that comes from the cultivated vocal techniques described above. These techniques include properties of timbre, range and registration, gradations of vocal intensity, vocal agility and floridity, pitch onset, *legato*, *portamento*, and other forms of articulation, trills, and rhythmic flexibility. Taken together, these techniques constitute what might be called a classical vocal 'idiom,' in that they are well suited to the trained singing voice, and distinguish it both from other forms of vocal usage and from instrumental idioms.

   While these techniques provide the means of singing expressively and can, to a degree, serve as critical criteria in assessing the effectiveness of musical performance, there remains a whole dimension of expressivity that does not yield to analysis. The true artist ultimately relies on his or her musical instincts and intuition in order to be expressive, and this results in a thousand nuances and imponderable elements of singing that elude our meager analytical templates and transcend our intellectual arguments. Despite the best vocal training and the best understanding of musical styles, truly expressive singing is ultimately a matter of the heart, and in this lies its mystery and its beauty.

7

Bel canto: Context and Controversy

Réprise: Toward a Definition of *Bel canto*

As noted in the Introduction, the term *bel canto* has been around for over
a century, but its meaning has remained obscure. Up to this point, I have
avoided the term as much as possible, letting it slip into the narrative
only when it could not be avoided. It seemed preferable to present the
materials of the previous chapters before hazarding my own definition,
which I now put before you:

Bel canto is a concept that takes into account two separate but related matters.
First, it is a highly refined method of using the singing voice in which the glottal
source, the vocal tract, and the respiratory system interact in such a way as to
create the qualities of *chiaroscuro*, *appoggio*, register equalization, malleability of
pitch and intensity, and a pleasing vibrato. The idiomatic use of this voice
includes various forms of vocal onset, *legato*, *portamento*, glottal articulation, crescendo, decrescendo, *messa di voce*, *mezza voce*, floridity and trills, and *tempo
rubato*. Second, *bel canto* refers to any style of music that employs this kind of
singing in a tasteful and expressive way. Historically, composers and singers
have created categories of recitative, song, and aria that took advantage of these
techniques, and that lent themselves to various types of vocal expression. *Bel
canto* has demonstrated its power to astonish, to charm, to amuse, and especially
to move the listener. As musical epochs and styles changed, the elements of *bel
canto* adapted to meet new musical demands, thereby ensuring the continuation
of *bel canto* into our own time.

The purpose of this chapter is to provide the historical context in
which *bel canto* originated and developed. We will return to the early

Baroque period, when virtuoso singers first gained celebrity with a new kind of solo repertoire that showed off their extraordinary vocal ability. These developments marked the establishment of 'the old Italian school,' the first of many so-called golden ages of singing. I will examine the castrato phenomenon, in which neutered males sang with high voices in heroic roles, sometimes forming their own 'schools' of singing. I will review the pervasiveness of the Italian manner of singing, and demonstrate how other national schools of singing were measured against this Italian model. I will discuss the recurring complaint from age to age that the art of good singing was in a state of decline, and show how this was related to the changing demands of new musical styles. And finally, I will make some brief observations on the so-called secrets of *bel canto*.

The Establishment of the Old Italian School of Singing

It is always a bit hazardous to put forward a case for the origins of any musical style (see Allen 1962, 183–5). Yet, there is extensive historical documentation that attests to the rise of an 'old Italian school of singing' in the late sixteenth and early seventeenth centuries. This period, of course, marked the origins of Baroque musical style. Specifically it marked a new manner of singing, beginning with the emergence of solo singing from late Renaissance polyphony, particularly the Italian madrigal, and it led to the introduction of new styles of solo singing in the *stile recitativo* and in songs called *monodies*. Court chronicles, letters, prefaces to operas and song collections, reminiscences, and other types of historical evidence provide a picture of the remarkable rise of a new class of professional virtuoso singers whose vocal prowess eclipsed amateur choristers, and who established principles of good singing that were to endure for centuries. What follows is a brief account of the origins of this new style of singing, and its establishment as the model for good singing – a model that became known to later generations as *bel canto*.

Virtuoso singing in the second half of the sixteenth century was at first not widespread, but was concentrated in a few cities of northern Italy that vied for the services of a small cadre of trained singers. The first significant activity took place in Venice in the 1550s and 1560s, especially with a circle of lady singers, or *cantatrici*, who were associated with the composer Baldisserra Donato.[1] It was the practice of these ladies to sing madrigals that had been composed as part-songs but were performed as solo songs, with lute, harp, or harpsichord accompaniment. The vocal part was embellished with various degrees of *passaggi*.

The letters of Pietro Aretino, Antonfrancesco Doni, and Andrea Calmo gave high praise to these singers. In a 1562 letter to the singer Signora Calandra, Calmo wrote, 'And as for your singing, I have never heard better: oh, what a beautiful voice, what style, what runs and divisions, what sweetness, enough to soften the cruelest, hardest, most wicked heart in the world! How excellent the words, the subject, the meaning, so acute, so elegant that poetry itself lags behind.'[2] These arrangements of madrigals are what Alfred Einstein referred to as 'pseudo-monodies' in his monumental study *The Italian Madrigal*.[3]

In the 1570s and 1580s the centre of virtuosic activity shifted to Ferrara and Mantua. It is difficult to speak of one of these cities without the other, since there was such an interplay of musical forces between them. Up to this time, virtuoso singers were scarce, and rival courts competed for their services (Canal 1879, 693). Musical life at the courts of the Este and Gonzaga families has been well documented through archival research, first by Angelo Solerti (1891) and Pietro Canal (1879), and more recently by Anthony Newcomb (1980) and Iain Fenlon (1980). The court of Alfonso II d'Este of Ferrara became famous for its *concerto delle donne*, in which certain ladies of the court gained special recognition for their fine singing, both in accompanied solo song and in duets and trios of florid music. Newcomb points to 1580 as a dividing line in the court's music, when Alfonzo II married the music-loving Margherita Gonzaga and formed the *concerto delle donne*. This group became known as *musica secreta*, and was intended for the inner court circle (Newcomb 1980, 21–2). 'Although there had been singing ladies in the Ferrarese court before 1580, the new group was significantly different from the group that had preceded it. The first group was made up of courtiers who happened to sing, the second of singers who, because of their musical abilities, were made courtiers' (7–8). Fenlon elaborates on this: 'What had been in 1571 merely an incidental feature of court entertainment seems to have been cultivated almost obsessively after 1580 ... The change was from an ensemble of aristocratic amateurs performing for their own pleasure to one of professional virtuosos who rehearsed and performed for an audience in a more formal sense' (Fenlon 1980, 126).

Much has been written about the celebrated female singers at the court and also the official court composer Luzzasco Luzzaschi (1545? – 1607), whose solos, duets, and trios with harpsichord accompaniment showed off the vocal abilities of these singing ladies.[4] One of the most celebrated of these singers was Lucretia Bendidio, whose singing was described in a letter: 'Gifted with a most beautiful voice and an expert in the art of music, she and her sister Isabella always had the main part in the grandiose concerts which, from 1571 to 1584, under the direction of the famous Luzzasco Luzzaschi and of Tarquinia Molza, delighted the court of Ferrara. The two Bendidio sisters and Anna Guarini, a cavalier's daughter who later joined the court, served as chamber musicians and amazed everyone by their improvised singing of any *motto* or composition that was suggested to them.'[5]

Newcomb has referred to this ornamented kind of accompanied madrigal as the 'luxuriant style' (Newcomb 1980, 48–9, 78–80). He said, 'In 1580 a single new element was added to this complicated compound of circumstances – a single element that, given the particular situation, had an extraordinarily powerful effect on the whole. This element was a high degree of musical and vocal training among the singers. The vocal amateurs of the 1570s were replaced by vocal virtuosi' (19). According to Newcomb, this element marked the emergence of a class of professional singers with extraordinary vocal and musical abilities. It is worth noting that this generation of professional singers in Ferrara was largely women, not men, falsettists, or castrati. In fact, there was a notable absence of male singers. Said Newcomb, 'Tenors were never an essential part of the *concerto delle donne*, which was the most striking feature of the *musica secreta*,' and Alfonso 'let pass the opportunity to lure both Caccini and Francesco Rasi during the late 1580s and early 1590s' (22–3). Vincenzo Giustiniani, who had heard many performances at the court, noted that the earlier style of singing that arose around 1575 was founded by basses (23, 46 *seq*). One such bass was Giulio Cesare Brancaccio, who was between 60 and 65 years old in 1580, when he was a part of the *musica secreta*; Torquato Tasso and Giovanni Battista Guarini wrote poems in his praise (185–6). However, as Einstein pointed out, there was a shift in taste toward high voices in the last two decades of the century. Brancaccio did not fit in with the new class of virtuoso female singers, and he was dismissed for refusing to sing with the ladies (Einstein 1949, 2:822–5, 832). The *concerto delle donne* flourished until the 1590s, when the ladies's voices started to deteriorate, and the luxuriant style, with its elaborate diminutions, gave way to genuine affective monody which emanated from Florence.

Vincenzo Gonzaga, who was a music lover, spent much time in Ferrara, even after he became Duke of Mantua in 1587. In 1589 he formed his own *concerto delle donne*, which sometimes engaged in musical competitions with the ladies of Ferrara (Newcomb 1980, 95–100). Vincenzo Giustiniani recalled the Mantuan performances in his *Discorso sopra la musica* (ca. 1628):

The ladies of Mantua and Ferrara were highly competent, and vied with each other not only in regard to the timbre and training of their voices but also in the design of exquisite passages [*passaggi*] delivered at opportune points, but not in excess. (Giovanni Luca [Conforto] of Rome, who also served at Ferrara, usually erred in this respect.) Furthermore, they moderated or increased their voices, loud or soft, heavy or light, according to the demands of the piece they were singing; now slow, breaking off sometimes with a gentle sigh, now singing long passages legato or detached, now groups, now leaps, now with long trills, now with short, or again with sweet running passages sung softly, to which one sometimes heard an echo answer unexpectedly. They accompanied the music and the sentiment with appropriate facial expressions, glances and gestures, with no awkward movements of the mouth or hands or body which might not express the feeling of the song. They made the words clear in such a way that one could hear even the last syllable of every word, which was never interrupted or suppressed by passages and other embellishments. They used many other particular devices which will be known to persons more experienced than I.[6]

Despite the time that had lapsed between this event and Giustiniani's recounting of it, Giustiniani's memory seems accurate, and Fenlon maintains that 'there is a strong body of evidence to support it' (Fenlon 1980, 127). The Mantuan *concerto delle donne* was disbanded after 1598 (135). Giustiniani's account of the singing ladies of Ferrara and Mantua certainly fits many of the criteria for *bel canto* as defined above. As well, it accords with Giulio Caccini's description of vocal techniques in the preface to *Le nuove musiche*.

This is more than a coincidence. Newcomb documents the 'cultural espionage' of Alessandro Striggio the elder on behalf of the Grand Duke Francesco de' Medici of Florence, and this espionage included Caccini as a central character. Striggio reported enthusiastically on the ladies of Ferrara,[7] and sent his own madrigals imitating their style to Caccini for his comment. Caccini sent notes to Striggio, admonishing him to include 'very difficult runs exploring the high and low registers ...' Caccini subsequently travelled with Giovanni Bardi and others to Ferrara in 1583 where he first heard the *concerto delle donne*. He called three of the ladies 'angels of paradise, for they sing so miraculously that it seems to me impossible to do better' (Newcomb 1980, 90). When he returned to Ferrara in 1592, he gave lessons to the three ladies in *accenti* and *passaggi*, and he also sang for the court. A poem by the resident poet of Ferrara, Torquato Tasso, describes the singing of an unidentified Giulio, whom Einstein claimed was Caccini.[8] It was at this time that Alfonso II tried to hire Caccini and his pupil Francesco Rasi. Antonio Brunelli wrote that when Caccini visited Ferrara in 1592 he gave a 'certain finesse' to the singing style of the ladies (Hitchcock 1973, 146). According to Striggio, the Grand Duke Francesco de' Medici formed his own *concerto* at Florence, and at least three sopranos were trained by Caccini. These singers were probably Vittoria Archilei, Laura Bovia of Bologna, and Lucia Caccini, Giulio's first wife (Newcomb 1980, 90–1). All this anticipates the shift in focus from Ferrara to Florence in the waning years of the sixteenth century.

It would be difficult to overestimate the role of Giulio Caccini as a seminal figure in the establishment of the old Italian school of singing. Although he was a bit of a rogue, had a huge ego, carried out unsavory court activities, and ultimately ended up as a gardener,[9] he was the most famous singer and voice teacher of his time, as well as a composer of opera and monody. We have already seen that the preface to his *Le nuove musiche* was a thorough account of the new 'noble manner of singing,' and served as the model for generations of later vocal pedagogues. His compositions helped to establish the *stile recitativo* as an important new narrative style, while his *arie* and *madrigali* were examples of a new style of affective songs and dance songs respectively. His large number of celebrated pupils is unique for that period, and he certainly ranks with Garcia and the Lampertis as one of the most successful and prolific voice teachers in music history.

Caccini was recognized as a fine singer, even as a child (Kirkendale 1993, 121). His singing was praised by Giovanni de' Bardi, his son Pietro de' Bardi, Severo Bonini, Vincenzo Giustiniani, Pietro della Valle, and many others.[10] Bonini, who may have been a pupil of Caccini, dedicated his *Madrigali, e canzonette spirituali* (1607) to him, and praised him as the inventor of this 'most noble manner of singing' (*nobilissima maniera di cantare*) (Kirkendale 1993, 168). Caccini's pupils included, by his own account, his first wife, Lucia, his second wife, Margharita, and his daughter Francesca, who herself became a well-known composer.[11] His other two children, Pompeo and Settimia, also performed from time to time in the Medici theatre festivals (Nagler 1964, 84, 88, 17, 143, 154, 173). Also in Florence was his celebrated pupil Vittoria Archilei, who was praised alike by Peri, Caccini, Cavallieri, and Bonini.[12] Peri called her 'the Euterpe [Greek Muse of music] of our age,' and said, 'This lady, who has always made my compositions seem worthy of her singing, adorns them not only with those groups and those long windings of the voice, simple and double, which the liveliness of her talent can invent at any moment (more to comply with the usage of our times than because she considers the beauty and force of our singing to lie in them), but also with those elegances and graces that cannot be written or, if written, cannot be learned from writing' (trans. Strunk 1950, 375). This indicates that some of the older practices of diminution were still hanging on while the more expressive devices of Caccini were taking hold.

There was also a certain Giuseppino – who may have been Giuseppe Cenci from the papal choir (Fortune 1954, 211). According to Della Valle, Giuseppino did not have a particularly beautiful voice, but he did have abundant *dispositione* and could sing *passaggi* as if they were second nature. His status as a singer was attested to by Giustiniani, who wrote, 'Giulio Caccini and Giuseppino, as I have shown already, were the ones who were almost the inventors of this style, or at least gave it good form; and then little by little it became more perfect, to such a point that it seems that little else can be added to it in the future' (Giustiniani 1962, 71). Another Caccini pupil, tenor Francesco Rasi, sang in Peri's *Euridice* and Gagliano's *Dafne*, two of the earliest operas. Bonini said that Rasi 'sang elegantly, and with great passion and spirit. He was a handsome, jovial man, and he had a delightfully smooth voice; there was in his divine, angelic singing something of his own majesty and cheerfulness' (Solerti 1903, 138; Fortune 1954, 211). Nigel Fortune, in an article on Italian singers of this period, commented, 'It seems that for sheer beauty of tone no one could touch Rasi' (Fortune 1954, 211). Also included in Caccini's stable of singers was Melchior Palentrotti who, according to Giustiniani, was a 'sweet and sensitive' singer (Giustiniani 1962, 71). Palentrotti had been a member of the papal choir, and he sang in Peri's *Euridice* and in Caccini's *Il rapimento di Cefalo* in 1600. Caccini reprinted Palentrotti's vocal part for the song 'Muove si dolce' with all its original ornamentation in *Le nuove musiche* (Caccini 1602, 20–1; 1970, 104–6). Della Valle mentioned Palentrotti for his *'eccellente dispositione'* (Solerti 1903, 162).

These singers were all at the court of Grand Duke Ferdinand de' Medici of Florence, and they were such an impressive group that they formed what one scholar, C. Lozzi (1902), called the first 'school' of singers. There were others who were Caccini's pupils. Aldobrando Trabocchi of Pienza, was described by Lozzi as having perhaps the best bass voice in Italy (Lozzi 1902, 315). Caterina Martinelli, who was praised by Gagliano, was advised when very young to stay in Florence at the school of Caccini rather than in Mantua, because the Tuscan singing was better than the Lombard (318). Her nickname, in fact, was Romanina, after Caccini's own nickname Romano. Adriana Basile of Naples (who was later appointed to the court of Mantua) and Giovanni Gualberto (a Florentine who sang in Monteverdi's *Orfeo* in Mantua) were probably also pupils of Caccini (318). There were others as well, whose names are less well known, but who are listed chronologically by Warren Kirkendale in his expansive book on Florentine court musicians (Kirkendale 1993, 166).

It was Caccini and his pupils and colleagues who brought the noble manner of singing to other parts of Italy. Pietro Della Valle credited Caccini's colleague and collaborator Emilio de' Cavalieri with bringing 'that good school of Florence' (*la buona scuola di Firenze*) to Rome. He compared the earlier group of singers – those who sang with many diminutions – to the more expressive Florentine style:

However, all those people, apart from *trilli* and *passaggi*, and a good placement of the voice, had in their singing practically nothing of the art of *piano* and *forte*, of making the voice crescendo little by little, of a graceful decrescendo, of the expression of the *affetti*, of reinforcing the meaning of the words with judgement, of making the voice become cheerful or melancholy, of becoming pitiful or bold as required, and of similar galanteries, which singers today can do so excellently ... (Della Valle 1640, in Solerti 1903, 162–3)

Giustiniani credited Vittoria Archilei with influencing Roman singing as well. He said she provided the example by which 'many others in Rome practiced this manner of singing, so that it prevailed on all musicians of the other cities and Princes already spoken of' (Giustiani 1962, 70). Characteristically, Caccini gave *himself* credit for taking his style to Rome:

The aforesaid madrigals and the air were performed in Signor Nero Neri's [Rome] house for many gentlemen assembled there (and notably Signor Lione Strozzi), and everyone can testify how I was urged to continue as I had begun, and was told that never before had anyone heard music for a solo voice, to a simple stringed instrument, with such power to move the affect of the soul as these madrigals. (This was both because of their new style and because, accustomed then to hearing as solos madrigals published for multiple voices, they did not think that a soprano part sung by itself alone could have any effect whatsoever, without the artful interrelationships of [all] the parts.)[13]

It is clear, then, that the 'old Italian school of singing' grew out of courtly music of the late sixteenth and early seventeenth centuries, first in the luxuriant style of pseudo-monody as sung by female virtuosos associated with Ferrara and Mantua, and then in the new 'noble manner of singing' of Giulio Caccini and his coterie in Florence. With Caccini, vocal technique and the new styles of recitative and monody were inextricably linked. Caccini was first and foremost a singer and singing teacher who rejected polyphony in favour of expressive solo singing with simple accompaniment, and he composed his own music in order to make the best use of his new techniques of singing. It was widely recognized that Caccini's vocal techniques and the Florentine style were the model for good singing, and that this style was carried to other cities. Later authors, including Praetorius (1619), Giustiniani (ca. 1628), Della Valle (1640), Herbst (1642), Bernhard (1650), G.B. Doni (1763), Charles Burney (1789), Manuel Garcia (1841), and Julius Stockhausen (1884), all credited the Florentines with the establishment of good singing. All this indicates that the early seventeenth-century school of Caccini represented the first golden age of singing. Bonini maintained that Gagliano, Giulio and Francesca Caccini, and Peri – all singers in the new *stile recitativo* – 'surpassed the ancients by far' (Bonini 1979, 57). Modern authors have supported this view.[14] In his book *The Early History of Singing*, W.J. Henderson wrote, 'History has long entitled the Handelian era "the golden age of bel canto," but if perhaps the sun of vocal virtuosity attained its high noon in Handel's day, it rose in its most bewildering glory in the first years of the seventeenth century' (Henderson 1921, 100).

The Castrato Phenomenon

Perhaps no aspect of the old Italian school has so fascinated readers as the phenomenon of castrato singers – eunuchs who were castrated at a young age for the sake of preserving the small larynx of a boy while developing the muscular strength and lung capacity of an adult. There had to be a large payoff for such a drastic measure as castration, and this payoff was found in the combination of vocal strength and floridity that the castrati possessed to a degree unmatched by normal singers. While the castrati also exhibited extended vocal ranges and a vocal timbre unlike that of normal singers, it was ultimately the combination of vocal power and flexibility that distinguished them. Despite the great success of the castrati, their lengthy domination of opera was an aberration, and they fell from favour as times and tastes changed. While the reader can look elsewhere for an account of their colourful lives and careers,[15] what I will discuss here is their mastery of those elements of singing that I have defined as *bel canto*. As well, I will present some modern views regarding the castrato phenomenon.

I believe it would be an exaggeration to suggest, as some authors have, that the castrati were the 'most important element' in the development of *bel canto*.[16] The principles of *bel canto* were well established before the rise of castrato singers, and the best pedagogical descriptions of *bel canto* techniques were written by Garcia and others at a time when the castrati were in a state of decline. It is likely that *bel canto* singing techniques would have developed even without the castrato phenomenon, but this is not to suggest that the castrati did not epitomize the *bel canto* ideals in a way that no other singers could.

The rise of the castrati was a gradual one. During the late sixteenth and early seventeenth centuries there were few castrati, either in the chapel or the court. Anthony Milner maintains that the presence of 'sacred capons' in chapel choirs dates back to 1553, and was authorized by a papal bull in 1589 (Milner 1973). Enrico Celani found references in records of the Papal Choir referring to Spanish castrati in 1588 and Italian eunuches in 1599.[17] As late as 1602, Lodovico Viadana, the choirmaster at the cathedral of Mantua, was still using boys and falsettists for the upper parts in choral music (see Strunk 1950, 42). However, by the 1580s, Duke Guglielmo employed several castrati at the court of Mantua. One of these, apparently, was a dreadful singer whose only notable quality was that he was a castrato – his upper register was weak, he was not precise, he had no *disposizione di gorga*, and he knew no pieces by heart. 'These animals,' wrote Guglielmo's secretary, are 'extremely scarce' and 'very fickle.' Their pay was no higher than that of any other singer. Guglielmo's efforts to hire castrati away from Ferrara and France for his court and his chapel failed, and he decided it would be easier to get one in Spain.[18] At about the same time that Guglielmo was having these difficulties, the ladies at the court of Ferrara sang everything by heart with astonishing voices,[19] and Caccini and company were gaining fame for their noble manner of singing in Florence. Guglielmo's successor, Francesco Gonzaga, also complained that 'we have very few sopranos [castrati] here, and those few not good' (Fenlon 1986, 12). Claudio Monteverdi, who composed his celebrated *Orfeo* in 1607 while he was court composer to Francesco, gave the title role to Francesco Rasi, while the role of Eurydice went to an unnamed 'little priest' who may have been a castrato, Padre Girolamo Bacchini (4). It is also known that another castrato in Mantua was a pupil of Caccini (12). The castrati during this period clearly played a secondary role to the normal singers of Mantua and Florence (Arnold 1985, 322). Canal maintained that 'the advantage of these new [castrato] voices did not begin to be known and appreciated properly until ornate music was introduced and the art of singing refined' (Canal 1879, 696).

With the growth of opera in the early seventeenth century, there was a dramatic increase in the importance of castrato singers. It was after the opening of the first public opera house in 1637 – San Cassiano in Venice – and the subsequent rapid spread of Italian opera throughout Italy and Europe, that the castrati gained their greatest fame and influence. They were challenged only by a few female singers, and they often earned far more than the composers whose operas they performed. Quantz regarded the early eighteenth century, with its celebrated castrati, as the 'highest pinnacle' of singing (Quantz 1966, 322). This view was reiterated by George Hogarth (1851, 1:273–4). Hogarth observed that, during the early eighteenth century, tenors and basses were 'performers of inferior note,' who sang only subordinate parts. Good roles for tenors were 'of a very rare occurrence.' Regarding basses he wrote, 'In tyrants, old men, or rough and harsh characters, the bass voice could be appropriately introduced: but it would seem that nothing more was required from the performance than force and energy, without any of the polish and cultivation which have been attained by the bass-singers of more recent times' (Hogarth 1851, 1:342). Stendahl placed the golden age of singing somewhat later, a view echoed by English voice teacher Shakespeare (1909).[20]

The use of castrati continued throughout much of the eighteenth century and into the nineteenth. But by the mid-eighteenth century the tide was already turning against them. The rise of the comic intermezzo and *opera buffa*, which required natural singers to play the stock characters drawn from the Italian *commedia del arte*, left no room for castrato voices. As well, the new philosophical outlook of the Enlightenment could not condone the cruelty and artifice surrounding the castrati. Jean-Jacques Rousseau's call for a *retournons à la nature* may well have nurtured the turn toward more realistic operatic subjects (such as in his own *opéra bouffe* of 1752, *Le devin du village*). The trend toward natural singers accelerated in the 1830s with the new type of romantic tenor who could sing the high notes with *voix couverte* rather than by switching to falsetto, and could rival a castrato's power if not his flexibility. Vocal strength and the *do di petto* soon replaced the vocal pyrotechnics of the castrato in the affections of the public. Mount-Edgcumbe noted that tenors had taken the place of the castrati, who had 'become so scarce that Italy can produce no more than two or three very good ones.'[21] Stendahl noted that Rossini lost faith in the last great castrato Vellutti, whom he accused of adding too much ornamentation to his arias (Pleasants 1966, 91–3). Heriot maintained that the last composer to write specifically for the castrato voice was Meyerbeer in his *Il Crociato in Eggito* of 1824 (Heriot 1956, 21). Nevertheless, for almost two centuries the castrati dominated Italian opera, and performed vocal feats that have become indelibly linked to *bel canto*.

We cannot know what the castrati sounded like, but there is no scarcity of written accounts of their vocal prowess. Raguenet, Hawkins, Burney, Quantz, Mount-Edgcumbe, Stendhal, and many other critics wrote detailed descriptions of castrato singing, from the glorious voices of Farinelli, Caffarelli, Carestini, Pacchierotti, Senesino, Nicolini, and Rubinelli, to the less-gifted eunuchs such as Velluti, and even to those whose mutilation led to no vocal advantage whatsoever. Even a small sampling of their remarks reveals the remarkable vocal skills of the castrati. The reader will notice the importance of vocal strength and floridity in these accounts.

In 1702 François Raguenet praised the Italian castrati over either male or female French singers, saying that the castrati expressed thoughts of love better than the hoarse voices of men, that their voices were stronger than those of women, and that they were easily heard over the orchestra. He compared their *passaggi* to the singing of nightingales, and noted that their voices lasted for thirty or forty years. He also admired their imitations of echoes, and their 'Swellings of prodigious Length' (Raguenet 1709, 37–9). (This last comment is likely a reference to their use of soft singing and the *messa di voce*.)

Robert Samber's *Eunuchism Display'd* (1718) was a translation of Charles d'Ancillon's *Traité des eunuques* of 1707 with Samber's own interpolations. This book described the mutilation of boys which could 'not only meliorate, but preserve the Voice, and it has been frequently known, that Eunuchs have had their voices perfectly well at 50 or 60 Years of Age. But if castration does better a good one, it yet never can give a Voice where there was none before, or make a bad one good.' Samber lamented the practice of cutting children in their 'most tender Infancy,' noting that of 200 Eunuchs, 'not one of them had a tolerable Voice ... and it is certain, nothing in Italy is so contemptible as a Eunuch that cannot sing' (Samber 1718, 38–9). Despite these misgivings, Samber heaped praise upon several castrati. He called Pasqualini 'the greatest Master of Vocal Musicke in the World ... For besides, that his Voice was an Octave, at least (and I speak within Compass) higher than any ones else, it had all the Warblings and Turns of a Nightingal [sic], but with only this difference, that it was much finer, and did not a Man know the contrary, he would have believed it impossible such a Tone could proceed from the Throat of any Thing that was human' (30–1). Samber was equally enthusiastic in his praise of the castrati Jeronimo and Pauluccio.

In 1776 historian John Hawkins lauded the singing of Farinelli and Senesino:

> The world had never seen two such singers upon the same stage as Senesino and Farinelli; the former was a just and graceful actor, and in the opinion of very good judges had the superiority of Farinelli in respect of tone of his voice; but the latter had so much the advantage in other respects, that few hesitated to pronounce him the greatest singer in the world; this opinion was grounded on the amazing compass of his voice, exceeding that of women, or any of his own class; his shake was just, and sweet beyond expression; and in the management of his voice, and the clear articulation of divisions and quick passages, he passed all description. (Hawkins 1875, 876)

Charles Burney's accounts of Senesino, Farinelli, and many others, make similar points regarding the vocal techniques of the castrati. Senesino 'had a powerful, clear, and sweet contralto voice, with a perfect intonation, and an excellent shake; his manner of singing was masterly, and his elocution unrivalled.' As well, he used judgment in his ornaments, which he sang from the chest, and he cut a majestic figure on stage (Burney 1775, 188). Regarding Farinelli, he wrote, 'There was none of Farinelli's excellencies by which he so far surpassed all other singers, and astonished the public, as his *messa di voce* or swell; which, by the natural formation of his lungs, and artificial economy of breath, he was able to protract to such a great length as to excite incredibility, even in those who heard him; who, though unable to detect the artifice, imagined him to have had the latent help of some instrument by which the tone was continued, while he renewed his powers by respiration' (Burney 1935, 2:739; MacClintock 1979, 262). Regarding his tone quality, Burney said, 'Farinelli, without the assistance of significant gestures or graceful attitudes, enchanted and astonished his hearers by the force, extent, and mellifluous tones of the mere organ, when he had nothing to execute, articulate, or express' (Burney 1935, 2:737; MacClintock 1979, 261). Quantz also noted Farinelli's 'penetrating, well-rounded, luscious, clear and even soprano' (Pleasants 1966, 73–4). Burney's friend, Mr Garrick, heard both Farinelli and Caffarelli in 1764, when Caffarelli was 64 years old. Garrick said that Caffarelli, 'though old, has pleased me more than all the singers I have heard. He *touched* me; and it was the first time that I have been touched since I came to Italy' (Burney 1935, 2:819).

Just one more encomium will be cited here, this one by Lord Richard Mount-Edgcumbe. Edgcumbe said that Pacchierotti was 'decidedly, in my opinion, the most perfect singer it ever fell to my lot to hear.' He continued:

Pacchierotti's voice was an extensive soprano, full and sweet in the highest degree; his powers of execution were great, but he had far too good taste and too good sense to make a display of them where it would have been misapplied, confining it to one bravura song (aria di agilità) in each opera, conscious that the chief delight of singing, and his own supreme excellence lay in touching expression, and exquisite pathos.

He went on to say that Pacchierotti was a thorough musician, singing in every style, varying his ornaments, but always judiciously. He was a perfect sight-reader, and a good actor despite his awkward figure. 'As a concert singer, and particularly in private society, he shone almost more than on the stage' (Mount-Edgcumbe 1823, 23–6).

Many more descriptions of the singing of castrati could be cited, but the important points have already been made. The art of the castrato was defined by a tone quality that was strong, penetrating, round, and sweet; by an astonishing flexibility and, in the best cases, good judgment in the singing of florid passages; by clear articulation; by an expanded range and united registers; by trills that outdid the nightingales; by the superb execution of the *messa di voce*; by breath economy and unbelievably long vocal phrases; and finally, by the ability to touch an audience, even by tone alone. The qualities listed above had already been established during the first golden age of singing in the early seventeenth century, but the castrati, with their physical advantages, brought these qualities to a new and higher level than previously seen.

The castrato phenomenon involved much more than simply good singing. It had deeper psychological and aesthetic implications as well. In a chapter titled 'Causes of the Castrati's Supremecy,' Heriot asked, 'Why was so strange and cruel a practice thought worth while, and why should audiences of succeeding generations have preferred these half-men with voices as high as women's, both to women themselves and to natural men? Since we have never heard their voices, it is impossible for us to judge of their beauty, which in itself no doubt made up for many other things: but there are other reasons which may still be investigated'

(Heriot 1956, 23). Heriot discussed the use of castrati in church choirs which disallowed women singers, and said 'the introduction of castrati on to the stage undoubtably arose from a similar reason,' namely, the linking of female theatrical performers with prostitution and licentiousness. He noted that the celebrated women singers of the early seventeenth century were respected members of courtly society, and that the performances of operas were princely affairs, not public events. 'The attitude of the Church towards the practice of castration continued to be absurdly inconsistent and unreasonable throughout the eighteenth century.' He also cited Goethe, who praised the castrati for their artifice in imitating female behaviour, thereby suggesting, according to Heriot, 'that the more artifice there is in art, the better' (26). Heriot maintained that the castrati had a more rigorous and solid training than other singers, and that they were better at improvisation and ornamentation than women singers, citing Tosi in support of this view. He reported on the relative unimportance of tenors and basses, and he elaborated on the physical advantages of the castrato singer, whose infantile larynx, coupled to an abnormally large chest, put the castrato in command of the voice to a degree unmatched in normal singers. But in the end, Heriot did not answer his own question as to *why* the castrato phenomenon occurred.

The question 'Why did it happen?' was taken up again in 'The Psychology of the Castrato Voice' by Paul J. Moses (1960). This article is little known to musical scholars, probably because it was written by a psychiatrist and published in a medical journal rather than a musical one. Moses' theory is a well-reasoned argument for the popularity of the castrati in the seventeenth and eighteenth centuries, based on his insights from psychoanalytical thought. Moses ascribed the emergence of castrato singing to 'wish fulfillment of hermaphroditic dreams, and ideals. The hermaphroditic idea is deeply rooted in the psyche of man. Myths express directly the collective unconscious (*Jung*), a deeper stratum than that of the personal unconscious. Note, too, the preoccupation of the Baroque at first with nothing but mythological material – the subject-matter of opera – with its scenes from the lives of Greek gods and demigods' (Moses 1960, 206). Moses discussed the theme of unity in the 'generative, active male element and the vegetative, passive female element,' and said:

All ancient peoples imagined the hermaphrodite as a supreme deity who ruled over life and death. This mystic, supernatural bisexuality, preserved throughout the centuries, probably originated in the physiological and psychological bisexuality of the human race. Specific vocal equivalents can be found in both normal and pathological expression. Without doubt, the Baroque expressed the height of hermaphroditic desires through the preponderance of the castrato voice, uniting the male and female ... The castrato voice cast a spell over its hearers for it had a unique nature. It expressed something unheard before or after. (206–7)

In comparing the castrato to the falsettist, Moses wrote, 'A high voice, purified through castration and therefore chaste, meant a young, heroic character. Such metacommunication could not occur in a falsettist who faked not voice but depersonalization. He was still a *man*, not purified, not casting the magic spell of the hermaphroditic ideal' (208). Moses developed these ideas with historical, social, physiological, and psychological reference points. His views were reiterated by voice doctor Friedrich Brodnitz, who wrote, 'Voices mirror not only individual characters but the spirit of a period as well. In this sense the voice of the castrato personifies the bisexual ideal with its unity of a female voice in a man's body. In the mythological atmosphere of the baroque opera the castrato portrayed gods and mythological persons who presented male and female characteristics in a vocal hermaphroditic combination' (Brodnitz 1975, 294). It was this 'mythological atmosphere' that gave way to the more realistic characters of the *opera buffa* in the mid-eighteenth century, and that signalled the decline of the castrato.

As an aside, it can be suggested that the phenomenon of hermaphroditism, bisexuality, and sexual ambiguity are still very much present in our popular music today, although our modern mythology is far removed from the Baroque variety. Many female pop singers, unlike their classically trained counterparts, sing largely in the chest voice, and sometimes even in the tenor range. A number of male pop singers use the falsetto register extensively. Sexual ambiguity has been further heightened in some singers by cosmetic surgery and modes of dress. All this is consistent with Moses' assertions regarding 'wish fulfillment of hermaphroditic dreams.' Can it be that Moses' theories are still applicable in a measure to our own time? Whether or not one accepts Moses' theory, it must be acknowledged that he ventured an analysis of the castrato phenomenon when musical scholars did not.

National Differences in Singing Styles

The early seventeenth century constituted the first golden age of singing, and the establishment of an Italian vocal tradition that would be passed along to later generations and would eventually be considered the fount of *bel canto*. The pre-eminence of Italian singing throughout those ages has been noted by many. In Giovanni Bontempi's *Historia musica* (1695) – one of the first real histories of music – there is an account of the singing of Baldassare Ferri, considered by Bontempi to be the most sublime singer of his age. Bontempi praised Ferri for his clear voice, his ease in making long and beautiful *passaggi* and *trilli*, his great economy of breath, his *maraviglie dell'arte*, his *soavité*, his skill at difficult intervals, his powers of expression, and his many other miraculous vocal qualities that were the hallmarks of Italian singing (Bontempi 1695, 110–11).

In his book *The Great Singers*, Henry Pleasants recognized several golden ages of singing, all of them dominated by Italians or by those trained in the Italian tradition, and he noted that 'there has been a continuity in the vocal art from the very beginning' (Pleasants 1966, 13). According to Pleasants, the first golden age of the eighteenth century extended from about 1720 to 1740 and included the famous voice teacher Nicolò Porpora and his celebrated castrato pupils Farinelli and Caffarelli. Other singers of this generation included Senesino, Bernacchi, and Carestini, and the prima donnas Faustina and Cuzzoni (13). Vocal historian Franz Häbock referred to Porpora as the leader of a Neapolitan school of singing, and Bernacchi as the leader of a Bologna school (Häbock 1927, 328–410). English music historian Charles Burney described many of these singers, and noted that the success of opera in London was due not to the poetry or even the music, but to the quality of Italian singing (Burney 1935, 2:680–1). Another golden age is said to have occurred around 1770–1790, during the vocal reign of the castrati Guadagni, Pacchierotti, Luigi Marchesi, and Crescentino, and the prima donnas Mara (Gertrude Elizabeth Schmeling), Todi (Luiza Rosa d'Aquiar), Brigitta Banti, and Angelica Catalani. Häbock considered Marchesi to be the leader of a Milan school, and Pacchierotti to be the leader of an influential Venetian school (Häbock 1927, 411–21). Following the decline of the castrati, the next golden age, around 1825–1840, included Manuel Garcia I, his daughters Maria Malibran and Pauline Viardot, Giulia Grisi, and rival tenors G.B. Rubini, Adolphe Nourrit, and Gilbert Duprez, the 'three tenors of the 1830s' (Pleasants 1995, 142–62). Pleasants considered the period from around 1880 to the First World War as the last golden age, represented by the gentlemen singers Victor Maurel, Francesco Tamagno, and Jean De Reszke, and the ladies Lillian Nordica, Nellie Melba, Marcella Sembrich, Emma Eames, and Ernestine Schumann-Heink (Pleasants 1996, 13–14). He went on to speak of 'an Italian afterglow,' which included Caruso, Tetrazzini, Galli-Curci, and Ponselle (284–300). But the list does not stop there. J.B. Steane picked up the thread where Pleasants left off, and discussed a number of late nineteenth- and twentieth-century singers who constituted both a golden age and a grand tradition (Steane 1992). Perhaps historian George Hogarth described the dominance of Italian singing best when he wrote, 'The Italian singers, from the very infancy of the musical drama, attained that superiority over those other countries which they have always preserved' (Hogarth 1851, 17).

Italian singing was the ideal against which all other singing was measured. When French, German, or English singing is discussed in the historical literature, it is almost always compared to the superiority of Italian singing. This is most pointed in discussions of French singing, from the seventeenth century onwards. For instance, in *Harmonie universelle* (1636), Marin Mersenne urged French voice teachers to travel to Italy 'where they pride themselves on their fine singing and knowing music better than do the French ... Those who are unable to travel should at least read Giulio Caccini ...' (Mersenne 1979, 173–4). In fact, Caccini's *Le nuove musiche* formed the basis of the chapter on singing in Mersenne's *Harmonie universelle*. He especially noted the affective manner in which Italians sang in the new *stile recitativo*:

As to the Italians, in their recitatives they observe many things of which ours are deprived, because they represent as much as they can the passions and affections of the soul and spirit, as, for example, anger, furor, disdain, rage, the frailties of the heart, and many other passions, with a violence so strange that one would almost say that they are touched by the same emotions they are representing in the song; whereas our French are content to tickle the ear, and have a perpetual sweetness in their songs, which deprives them of energy. (173)

In 1666 Jean Millet published *La belle methode ou l'art de bien chanter*, in which he showed that Italian types of vocal ornaments were applied to the French *airs de cour* of the mid-seventeenth-century. As a church musician, he did not include remarks on the voice itself. But just two years later, Bénigne de Bacilly provided a more detailed account of French singing in his *Rémarques curieuses* (1668). Whereas Caccini and others had little regard for the falsetto voice in male singing, Bacilly was more generous in his views:

In addition, I feel compelled to comment upon a certain widely-held opinion concerning the falsetto voice. (This particular opinion is an almost worthless one, but heard far and wide.) Whether because of a self-imposed attitude or because this type of voice might be considered to be in some sense contrary to nature's ways, it is very easy to pile abuse upon it and to make inappropriate remarks about falsettists (which are entirely untrue). On the other hand, with a little sober reflection, it is soon realized that the vocal art owes everything to this high falsetto voice, because of the fact that it can render certain *ports de voix*, intervals, and other vocal decorations in a fashion entirely different from that of the normal tenor voice. (Bacilly 1968, 23)

In general, Bacilly preferred small voices because of their greater flexi-bility in ornamentation, although even in small voices he looked for a full tone quality (Bacilly 1968, 23; Stanford 1979, 6). As well, Bacilly com-pared the French *airs de cour* with Italian operatic arias, saying, 'First of all, it must be established that in the musical world opinions differ greatly. Some persons are of the opinion that French airs cannot com-pare with the Italian, especially when sung by a French singer.' While he did not necessarily agree with this view, he added, 'Still others hold that Italian airs do not sound good when sung by a French singer and that they lose all their force and expressivity, so that all the delicacies and ornamentation which a talented French singer will add to an Italian air will amount to nothing' (Bacilly 1968, 42). Bacilly also acknowledged that the Italian language 'permits more freedom than the French, whose strictness (which is perhaps excessive) tends to hold composers in check and often prevents them from doing everything which their genius would inspire' (42). Bacilly was careful in his judgments, and appeared fair in his comparison of Italian and French singing.

Controversies regarding the relative merits of French versus Italian opera abounded throughout the eighteenth century. This was due to several factors: (1) the arguments between the supporters and detractors of Jean Baptiste Lully during the reign of Louis XIV; (2) the *Querelles des bouffons* in which supporters of Italian opera squared off against sup-porters of French opera; and (3) the stir created by *opera buffa* and the 'reform' operas of Gluck.[22] Two of the early combatants in this contro-versy, Abbé François Raguenet and Jean Laurent Le Cerf de la Viéville, argued over the operas of Lully, and in the course of those arguments touched upon important matters of singing style.

In 1702 Raguenet wrote *Parallèle des Italiens et des Français, en ce qui regarde la musique et les opéras*. This work was translated anonymously (probably by J.E. Galliard) and published in 1709 as *A Comparison between the French and Italian Music and Operas*. Raguenet preferred French recitative to Italian, saying that the Italian recitative 'is the same throughout, and can't properly be call'd Singing. Their Recitative is little better than downright speaking, without any Inflexion, or Modulation of the voice.' However, the translator disagreed, singling out Nicolini, Valentini, and others for their fine singing of recitatives (Raguenet 1709, 35). Raguenet said that the Italian language was better than the French for music because Italian had more sonorous vowels and no mute vowels, and hence, could be better understood than French (12). He admired the ability of Italian singers to make florid passages in unlikely places that would never occur to French singers, and to favour the vowel [a] for such passages (12, 16–18). 'The *Italians* Sing from their *Cradles*, they sing at all Times and Places; a Natural Uniform Song is too vulgar for their ears.' This, he said, accounted for the variety in Italian singing (19). Raguenet noted that the French made more use of basses than the Italians, and said that the Italian castrati kept their voices longer than women. He praised the Italians for their nicety, their echoes (soft singing), and their ability to express passions (6–7, 47).

In 1704–6, in response to Raguenet and others who had argued in favour of Italian opera over French, Jean Laurent Le Cerf de la Viéville, a musical amateur, published his *Comparaison de la musique italienne et de la musique françoise*. In this three-volume work he described a musical aesthetic of late seventeenth-century France that favoured simple, rational, and natural art over sensuous beauty (Cohen, 1980). He gave this description of an ideal voice:

A perfect voice would be sonorous, with a wide range, sweet, clear, alive, flexible. These six qualities which nature assembles in one voice but once a century are found ordinarily distributed by halves. A voice with a wide range and a lovely, touching sound is a large and beautiful voice. The sweeter it is, and big voices are generally less so than others, the more beautiful I find it. An alive and flexible voice is pretty and pleasant; the more it is clear in addition, the more I value it. Bacilly for his part was more interested in small voices than big ones. My friend and I, who prefer noble, bold, piercing voices, are of another taste.[23]

A particular type of 'bold, piercing' voice called the *haute-contre* emerged in France during the late seventeenth and the eighteenth centuries, and was associated especially with the operas of Rameau and even of Gluck.[24] The *haute-contre* voice may have been related to the Italian *tenor contraltino*, a voice higher than the normal tenor and similar in range to an alto. Early *haute-contre* singers, especially choristers, may have included castrati, but in opera the *haute-contre* was most often a high tenor. Scholars have produced evidence to show that, unlike the modern counter-tenor, the *haute-contre* did not usually resort to the falsetto register in order to achieve the upper notes, but instead used the full chest voice to reach pitches as high as *B*4 and *C*5 (Zaslaw 1974; Cyr 1977, 291–2). The most celebrated *haute-contre* in Rameau's operas was Pierre Jélyotte, whose singing was widely praised. Mary Cyr, in her study of the *haute-contre*, notes that 'one is accustomed today to think of the *haute-contre* as a high and light voice. Historical evidence does not support that contention, for the novelty of Jélyotte's singing included an ability to produce a strong sound in the high register.' She cites Josephe de Lalande who praised the singing of Jélyotte, saying, 'one takes more pleasure in hearing a large voice than a small one ...' – a view that was similar to Le Cerf's (Cyr 1977, 292). However, Jélyotte's successors were often criticized for shouting or using force in the upper reaches of the voice (292–3). As late as 1862 Hector Berlioz described such a voice as 'noisy, forced, and somewhat rare, called haute-contre; which, after all, is nothing but a high tenor' (Berlioz 1862; in Regier 1996, 37). Since the *haute-contre* singer was a natural tenor who had to sing well above the *passaggio*, it can be speculated that the forced and shouted high notes were probably belted in much the same way Broadway singers belt such tones today. Since it is clear that the falsetto was avoided, and since the covered tones of tenors were not yet cultivated in Rameau's day, the idea of belting is not unreasonable. While this is pure conjecture, it certainly adds an interesting new dimension to the history of belting.

In the later eighteenth century, the critical comments of Johann Joachim Quantz and Charles Burney drew large distinctions between Italian and French singing. In his flute manual of 1752, Quantz wrote:

The *French manner of singing* is not designed, like the Italian, to train great virtuosos. It does not at all exhaust the capacities of the human voice. They require facility of the tongue, for pronouncing the words, more than dexterity of the throat. That which should be added in the way of graces is prescribed by the composer; hence the performers do not have to understand harmony. They make hardly any use of passage-work, since they maintain that their language does not allow it. As the result of the lack of good singers, their arias are mostly written so that anyone who wants to may sing them; this affords satisfaction to the amateurs of music who do not know much, but offers good singers no particular advantage. The only distinctive quality of their singers is their acting ability, in which they are superior to other peoples. (Quantz 1966, 328–9)

Quantz also criticized French singers for their poor ability to unite the registers. 'The Italians and several other nations unite this falsetto with the chest voice, and make use of it to great advantage in singing: among the French, however, it is not customary, and for that reason their singing in the high register is often transformed into a disagreeable shrieking' (55). Quantz summarized by saying:

The *Italian manner of singing* is profound and artful; it at once moves and excites admiration; it stimulates the musical intellect; it is pleasing, charming, expressive, rich in taste and expression, and transports the listeners in an agreeable manner from one passion into another. The *French manner of singing* is more simple that artful, more spoken than sung, more forced than natural in the expression of the passions and in the use of the voice; in style and expression it is poor, and always uniform; it is more for amateurs than connoisseurs; it is better suited to drinking songs than to serious arias, diverting the senses, but leaving the musical intellect completely idle. (334)

In a journal of his travels to France, Charles Burney also berated French singing. On a journey to Paris in 1770, Burney attended a performance at the *Theatre Italien*, 'in which the singing was the worst part of the performance.' He noted that the songs were ill-performed, and the bravura execution poor. 'But the French voice never comes further than from the throat; there is no *voce di petto*, no true *portamento*, or direction of the voice, on any of the stages' (Burney 1773, 14). Also in Paris he described the singing as 'the screaming of tortured infernels. The Sopranos are squalled by Cats in the shape of women. M. le Gros, with a very fine Counter Tenor voice, becomes by his constant performance in the French serious Opera more and more intollerable every day' (310). In December 1770, Burney travelled to Lyon. 'In visiting the theatre, I was more disgusted than ever, at hearing French music, after the exquisite performances to which I had been accustomed in Italy ... There were many pretty passages in the music, but so ill sung, with so false an expression, such screaming, forcing, and trilling, as quite made me sick' (309). He wrote similarly harsh judgments of the singing in Lille (310).

In 1778 when Wolfgang Amadeus Mozart was in Paris with his mother, he met and worked with Joseph Le Gros, the director of the Concert spirituel. (Le Gros was also a *haute-contre*.) While in Paris, of course, he observed French singing, and on April 5 he wrote to his father, Leopold:

What annoys me most of all in this business is that our French gentlemen have only improved their *goût* to this extent that they can now listen to good stuff as well. But to expect them to realize that their own music is bad or at least to notice the difference – Heaven preserve us! And their singing! Good Lord! Let me never hear a Frenchwoman singing Italian arias. I can forgive her if she screeches out her French trash, but not if she ruins good music! It's simply unbearable. (Anderson 1985, 522)

Strong criticism of French singing continued into the nineteenth century. English music critic Henry F. Chorley maintained that poor French singing was related to the whole French temperament and culture, not just language (Chorley 1844, 1:30–1, 90 seq.). He described French voices as 'shrill and wiry, qualities which are more easily pardoned (who can explain why?) in French than in Italian voices' (Chorley 1862, 372). Richard Mount-Edgcumbe offered descriptions of many singers, often laudatory, but when it came to the French he said, 'Though some of their lighter pieces are pretty, the *grand opera* to all ears but French can only give *pain*.' Or again, 'Of French music the less that is said the better ... The *grand opera* was in no respect improved: that human ears can bear it is marvellous' (Mount-Edgcumbe 1823, 45, 90). Manuel Garcia noted that French singing of Italian music was recognizable for its pervasive nasality, which, he said, was 'incompatible with the pleasantness of the singing voice' (Garcia 1975, 10). This view was later echoed by Frederic Root, who felt that the French nasal vowels resulted 'in compelling good singers to make some distressing sounds' (Root 1894, 229).

These remarks and many others like them attest to the different aesthetic and taste, if not ability, of French singers. They may also reflect the 'no-love-lost' attitude of the English toward the French, with Burney qualifying as a Francophobe. The French took special interest in the language itself, with the subtleties of pronunciation and articulation having priority over the artifices of the singing voice. This was already apparent in Bérard's *L'art du chant* (1755); the chapter titled 'Pronunciation and Articulation Envisaged with Regard to Singing' is the largest chapter in the book, and outweighs the chapter discussing 'The Voice in Relation to Singing.' As well, French opera, with its emphasis on spectacle, *divertissement*, ballet, crowd and battle scenes, and ensemble singing, represented a different aesthetic from Italian opera, which placed a higher value on virtuosic solo singing. Seen in its own context, French singing may well have had charm, sweetness, and flexibility, but this differs from the passionate, full-throated singing that constituted *bel canto* as we have defined it.

In 1851 George Hogarth thought that the situation in France was improving: 'Till within a recent period the badness of French singing has been constantly remarked by all (except the French themselves) who have had occasion to speak of the music of that country.' He noted that this improvement began in the late eighteenth century with the singing of the tenor Pierre Garat, 'one of the greatest vocalists that France has produced.' Garat apparently learned to sing largely by imitating Italian singers in Paris. His voice was considered soft and sweet, with a three octave range, which strongly suggests the use of an extended falsetto register. He was an expert in singing the operas of Gluck, where he refused to add improvised ornamentation. He was also the teacher of Garaudé (Robinson 1980). Hogarth named certain contemporaneous French singers, including Nourrit and Duprez, both of whom studied in Italy (Hogarth 1851, 2:272–5). By this time the pedagogical works of Mengozzi, Garaudé and Garcia were *de rigueur*, and it may have been the influence of Italian vocal techniques that caused the improvement in French operatic singing.

The Germans did not escape comparison with Italian singing. Quantz devoted a lengthy passage to German singing, noting that it was still based in a choral tradition and was mostly associated with the church; while the cantors were good scholars, they had poor vocal training and were bad singers. He said that only 'a few Germans, by imitating the Italian style, have cast aside this defect.' He continued:

Thus as a rule they sing with a uniform volume of tone, without light and shade. They are hardly cognizant of the defects of the voice that stem from the nose and throat. Joining the chest voice to the falsetto is as unknown to them as it is to the French. As to the shake, they content themselves with what nature provides. They have little feeling for Italian flattery, which is effected by slurred notes and by diminishing and strengthening the tone. Their disagreeable, forced, and exceedingly noisy chest attacks, in which they make vigorous use of the faculty of the Germans for pronouncing the *h*, singing ha-ha-ha-ha for each note, make all the passage-work hacked up, and far removed from the Italian manner of executing passage-work with the chest voice. They do not tie the parts of the plain air to one another sufficiently, or join them together with retarding notes [appoggiaturas]; in consequence, their execution sounds very dry and plain. (Quantz 1966, 336)

Quantz despaired that 'good singing style may never become as general among the Germans as among the Italians, who have had the best institutions in this respect for a long time past' (337). Burney also found fault with German singing, which he found 'vulgar and ordinary' (Burney 1775, 154–5). He found the worst singing in cities like Leipzig, which did not have Italian opera companies close by to serve as examples. But he nevertheless found German singing better than French and, 'except the Italians, the German manner of singing is less vicious and vulgar, than that of any other people in Europe' (31, 42).

In the nineteenth century the criticism of German singing continued. In his journals of 1844, Chorley told of an 1839 Berlin performance of Weber's *Der Freischütz* in which 'there was not a *solo* singer on the stage who did not sing with an impaired and inferior style (Chorley 1844, 2:89). Chorley, like Burney before him, found that Germans, after the time of Mozart, 'despised the art of singing,' and placed their faith in the orchestra for the expression of ideas (Chorley 1862, 68–9). Root was less strident in his assessment of German singing:

The sphere of genuine musical interpretation is much stronger in Germany, than in Italy. In Italy their extremes in the matter of expression and their exaggerated style strike one as shallow and conventional, whereas in Germany one generally finds a genuine, deep, musical inspiration. The German ideals with regard to quality of tone, however, are much inferior to the Italians. Germans will even sacrifice intonation to declamation; and easily overlook poor quality of tone in an otherwise musicianly singer. (Root 1894, 228)

German operatic singing, then, grew out of a sacred choral tradition, and while its practitioners were respected for their erudition and profundity, they apparently could not sing very well. Historical sources often mention the importance of the orchestra in German opera, sometimes referring to the complexity of orchestral writing and counterpoint as 'science.' The implication here was that too much 'science' in the orchestral writing took away from the primacy of the singing voice in opera. We will return to this subject when discussing Wagner.

The inevitable comparison of national differences in singing styles extended to England as well. In Italy, theatre was opera. English theatre, of course, had descended from Shakespeare, Jonson, and Dryden, where acting and the spoken word reigned supreme. Henry Purcell, the chief composer of English theatre music in the seventeenth century, fashioned a uniquely English style of recitative, quasi-recitative, and florid singing.

George Hogarth, writing long after the fact, praised Purcell's style and his manner of capturing the English character, but he noted that the English singers were not in the same league as the Italians. The males were not 'much spoken of as singers, though they are described as excellent actors.' The women were better (Hogarth 1851, 1:143). For the most part, opera in England was imported from Italy, or composed in the Italian style by Handel and Johann Adolf Hasse. Handel brought the finest singers from Italy for his productions, as did his rival Niccolò Porpora.

The single most important author to compare Italian and English singing styles was Richard Mackenzie Bacon, an amateur musician, a keen observer of music in his time, and an engaging and sophisticated writer. His *Elements of Vocal Science, Being a Philosophical Enquiry into Some of the Principles of Singing* (1824), is a collection of critiques (letters) originally written for an English musical journal; Letter VII is titled 'On the Differences Between Italian and English Manner.' Bacon asserted at the outset that 'English vocalists never attain to the true Italian manner' (nor did the Italians attain to the English manner). He maintained that the Italian character, defined by strong emotions, ardent temperaments, and extravagant language led to the very essence of Italian singing, namely, 'that it is *dramatic*.' In contrast, 'We have nothing approaching to opera – by which I mean, a drama depending for its expression of sentiment and passion mainly upon music as a vehicle' (Bacon 1966, 53–4). That being said, Bacon turned to the technical aspects of singing. He maintained that the English tone was 'purer' than the Italian, being neither *di petto* nor *di testa*, but 'from a region somewhere between both, where it receives its last polish.' In elaborating on this, Bacon seems to suggest that English tone was closer to conversational speech than to the highly cultivated tone quality of Italian singers that sometimes sacrificed intelligibility to tone quality. 'They accommodate themselves to powerful expressions of passion – they shadow their tones according to the sentiment – now thickening and veiling them as it were – now rendering them light and brilliant and piercing' (54). In other words, the Italians made more use of *timbres* as an expressive vehicle. Bacon continued by saying that perhaps the most striking distinction between the two styles of singing was found in the use of *portamento*, 'an inarticulate gliding of the voice from one [note] to the other, whether, ascending or descending. This is in constant use with Italian singers, and sometimes with beautiful effect.' Bacon seems to include legato as well as portamento in this description. He found that this device 'appears not to accord with the genius of English expression ... This we conceive to be a national difference' (55). He also found differences in the trill (shake), which English singers varied in speed more than did the Italians. Regarding the singing of florid passages, Bacon noted that, whereas the Italians had earlier shown more judgement in the singing of embellishments, at this point in time the English showed greater propriety in the matter. In short, he was describing that well-known English 'reserve.' He summarized by saying:

Such are the principal intellectual and technical distinctions, as they appear to me, between Italian and English singing. The difference in their effects is easily to be traced to the causes. To the Italians belong passion, force, transition, variety, and general splendour. To the English, sensibility tempered by an invariable sense of propriety, purity, delicacy, and polish. The emotions raised by the first are strong, but liable to sudden disgusts and transient – the last are more equable, and please most on reflection; in few words, the one is theatrical, the other orchestral – the one lies as it were beyond, the other within the range of our natural domestic pleasures. Italian music is now also much more voluptuous than English, and its execution must partake of its intrinsic qualities. (59)

Probably the most troubling matter facing the English critics regarding Italian opera was the prevalence of the castrati. In his 1980 book *Italian Opera in London, 1760–1800,* musicologist Frederick C. Petty drew together a large number of English commentaries on Italian opera in England. He noted that, during the last half of the eighteenth century, English critics 'were almost unanimous in their condemnation of the castrato,' usually on humanitarian grounds. He quoted one critic who was seated behind two young ladies, both of whom were well acquainted with music and with the Italian language. These cultured young ladies, however, lost their English reserve when the castrato appeared. The critic noted that his 'advantageous figure' made a 'ridiculous contrast with his voice. This contrast has a surprising effect on the young ladies. They indulged themselves in loud peals of laughter, which neither the eyes of the whole audience, nor the remonstrances of a brother or a husband, who sat next to them, could either stop or even moderate' (Petty 1980, 82). The castrati were also subjected to strident satirical treatment, which today might well be considered out-of-bounds in terms of political correctness. One particularly unkind author wrote:

They have the look of a crocodile, the grin of an ape, the legs of a peacock, the paunch of a cow, the shape of an elephant, the brains of a goose, the throat of a pig, and the tail of a mouse. To crown the whole, if you sit but a few moments in their company, you will be sure of having your nostrils perfumed in a strange manner; for they have continually about them the odiferous effluvia of onion and garlick, so that you would swear, that they carry their dinner in their pockets. (83)

Castrati were often the subject of unflattering caricatures as well, with their long-boned physique and barrel chests being the focus of exaggeration.[25]

In conclusion, it can be said that the old Italian school of singing was truly an Italian affair. France, Germany, and England could emulate, incorporate, imitate, appreciate, or denigrate Italian singing, but in the end *bel canto* belonged to the Italians, who bequeathed this very special kind of singing to the rest of the world.

The Perennial 'Decline of the Art of Singing'

George Bernard Shaw said, 'The notion that singing has deteriorated in the present century is only a phase of the Good Old Times delusion ... Every musical period suffers from the illusion that it has lost the art of singing, and looks back to an imaginary golden age in which all singers had the secret of the *bel canto* taught by Italian magicians and practiced *in excelsis* at the great Opera Houses of Europe.' (Shaw 1960, 329). He wrote these words in 1950, when he was ninety-six years old, and had seen many generations of singers come and go.

As we have seen, there have been a number of so-called golden ages of singing from the early seventeenth century through to the late nineteenth century. Owen Jander (1980b, 344) considers even the 1920s and 1930s to have been a golden age. (My own choice for a golden age is the 1950s, when I first attended performances of the Metropolitan Opera and heard Tebaldi, Warren, Merrill, Tozzi, Peerce, Tucker, Milanov, Peters, Bergonzi, Corelli, and many others who opened my ears.) But for every supposed golden age, there was also a perceived period of decline in the art of singing. Of course, Shaw was right. It is human nature to recall the best of the past while complaining of the agonies of the present. But there is more than just the fallacy of the 'good old days' at work here. As has often been noted, the strongest force in the world is inertia, and this is certainly true in singing. Many of the comments regarding the decline of good singing are related to a time lag between a stylistic change brought about by composers and the ability of singers and singing teachers to adjust to this change. As well, the inevitable personal biases of some authors figure into the equation. It is this complex mix of factors that accounts for the perennial complaints about the decline of good singing.

In 1723 Tosi wrote, 'O you masters [voice teachers], Italy no longer hears the great voices of times past, particularly among the women, and to the confusion of the guilty, I will tell you why: Ignorance does not allow the parents to hear the very bad voices of their daughters, as poverty makes them believe that to sing and to grow wealthy are one and the same thing, and that to learn music a lovely face is enough' (Tosi 1986, 9; see also Tosi 1743, 15). But what Tosi failed to mention was that he was writing at the very time when the art of the castrato was at its apex with such singers as Bernacchi, Farinelli, and Carestini, and when women were at a decided disadvantage.[26]

Mancini made an equally disingenuous remark in 1774. After listing a great number of living singers, including Aprile, Guadagni, Niccolini, Rauzzini, and Pacchierotti, Mancini went on to complain that 'in Italy music is decadent, there are no more schools, nor great singers. There are still a few esteemed masters, and still some valorous scholars. I do not know to what else may be attributed the real cause, since the ancient systems have fallen into disuse, and the good customs of the ancient schools no longer regulate the Profession' (Mancini 1967, 12). Mancini was surely crying poverty in the midst of plenty.

As noted earlier, Quantz maintained that the art of singing reached its highest pinnacle during the first thirty years of the eighteenth century, especially with the school of Francesco Pistocchi, but then there was a change for the worse. He suggested that this change was due to the antagonism that existed between singers and instrumentalists regarding who could make the most improvised embellishments, and that this situation led to a 'bizarre and unbridled style ... The singers do not wish to grant that the instrumentalists can move the listeners as well as they do with singable ideas, and abrogate to themselves without any distinction a superiority over instrumentalists' (Quantz 1966, 322–3). We should keep in mind that Quantz made his remarks in 1752 in his manual on flute playing, and that his view was surely a biased one. He remarked that it was rare to find a singer who had all the qualities necessary for excellence. 'Hence you must be more indulgent in judging a singer than in judging an instrumentalist, and must be content if you find only some of the principles enumerated above together with various defects, not denying him the accustomed title of virtuoso because of this' (301). There is clearly an element of condescension in Quantz's remarks.

One of the most frequent complaints associated with the decline of good singing was that the accompaniment was too heavy. John Hawkins quoted an anonymous pamphlet from 1728, called *Avviso ai compositori, ed ai cantanti* (Advice to Composers and Singers), which complained of the increasing importance of instrumental music and accompaniments at the opera. The anonymous author said, 'Another irregularity is that of encumbering and overcharging the composition with too many symphonies. This custom has so much grown upon us within these late years, that if a stop be not put to it, the singer will be made to give place to the instruments, and the orchestra will be more regarded than the voices.' Hawkins added that audiences would have been content to hear the singing of Senesino, Cuzzoni, and Faustina during the whole performance, without instrumental music (Hawkins 1875, 874).

In 1772 Charles Burney met the great opera librettist Pietro Metastasio and the composer Johann Adolf Hasse, both of whom said that the good school of singing was dead. All three men laid the blame on the orchestra. Burney recalled Metastasio's views saying, 'He did not think that there was now one singer left who could sustain the voice in the manner the old singers were used to do. I endeavored to account for this, and he agreed with me, that theatrical music was become too instrumental; and that the cantatas of the beginning of this century, which were sung with no other accompaniment than a harpsichord or violoncello, required better singing than the present songs, in which the noisy accompaniments can hide defects as well as beauties, and give relief to the singer' (Burney 1775, 104). In similar fashion, Burney quoted Hasse: 'He thinks, with Metastasio, that the good school for singing is lost; and says, that since the time of Pistocco, Bernacchi, and Porpora, no great scholars have been made' (107). In 1773, Burney added his own view that in both England and Milan, the orchestras were too loud in the opera houses. 'Nothing but noise can be heard through noise; a delicate voice is suffocated' (Burney 1773, 77).

There may be a logical explanation for these complaints. The two sticking points seem to be the over-use of embellishments, fed by the competition between instrumentalists and singers, and the growth of the orchestra, which made it difficult to hear the singers. It seems likely that the light, flexible voice of the coloratura singer was incompatible with the growth of the orchestra. Since embellishments were not ordinarily written out by the composer, but were added extemporaneously by the singer, it would seem that singers were working against their own interests by adding such a high degree of embellishment. It would have been judicious for them to sacrifice some flexibility in order to cultivate a fuller and stronger tone. It is clear from the above accounts that singers were slow to make this adjustment, or, if they did make it, they were criticized for abandoning the older ways. This was a real 'Catch-22' situation for the singers. As well, there was a considerable time lag between the stylistic changes made by composers and the guidance given in vocal tutors. It wasn't until the late nineteenth century that voice treatises finally advocated a stronger tone, preferring the *canto spianato* to the *canto d'agilità*. By then, florid singing had largely disappeared, being regarded as meaningless warbling. Perhaps Shaw had something like this in mind when he wrote, 'Before we drop too many tears over this decadence of the art of singing, it is well to consider whether all that we have lost is worth regretting' (Shaw 1960, 99).

The litany of complaints about the decline of singing continued unabated in the nineteenth century. These complaints were shared equally by singers, voice teachers, music critics, composers, and even the new breed of laryngologist-voice teachers.[27] The great castrato Crescentini complained to the composer Louis Spohr in 1816 that the 'good old vocal school' had become ever rarer (Pleasants 1961, 169; 1966, 91). Spohr, in turn, vented his spleen on Rossini for his lack of skill in harmony and voice leading, and said that in his quest for novelty Rossini 'is robbing the voice of its charms and its virtues, or that he is actually degrading it when he imposes upon his singers roulades and passages which any instrumentalist could manage with greater accuracy and continuity ... With his "flowery song," regardless of the pleasure it excites, he is well on the way to putting an end to real song, of which not much is left in Italy anyway' (Pleasants 1961, 172–3). Mount-Edgcumbe found Rossini's accompaniments too loud and busy, and claimed the orchestra overpowered the singers. He said the decline of singing was due to the disappearance of the castrati, and that 'the good singers disappeared and remained unreplaced' (Mount-Edgcumbe 1823, viii–x). William Henderson noted that Rossini's orchestra led to louder singing. 'With Rossini entered the vocal *tour de force*, and with that began the demand for the Big Tone, the curse of today's singing' (Henderson 1906, 221). Related to this, of course, was the tenor's *ut de poitrine*, which, as we have seen, Rossini abhorred. Emil Behnke, like Rossini, preferred the high tenor notes to be sung in falsetto, and in the 1881 edition of his book he recounted a critique by Gloggner-Castelli of Duprez's use of the *ut de poitrine* in Rossini's *Guillaume Tell*:

Duprez may justly be considered one of the greatest dramatic singers of our time, and the main features of his method soon spread themselves all over Europe. After hearing of Duprez, and how the chest register could be cultivated even into the highest regions of the voice, the public were no longer contented with the use of falsetto ... Thus the school founded by Duprez, important in itself, has called into life a manner of singing, the ruinous consequences of which we see daily. (Behnke 1881, 5–6; quoted in Miller 1977, 111–12)

Despite the claim of 'ruinous consequences,' or the 'curse' of the big tone, history shows that a bigger tone and the use of covered high notes in preference to falsetto became permanently established in opera. Techniques that were considered at the time to contribute to a decline in singing turned out instead to constitute an important turning point in the history of operatic singing style.

Mount-Edgcumbe was among those who couldn't quite stomach these changes. He claimed that he had been 'passionately fond of music while music was really good, and having lived in what I considered one of its most flourishing periods, now, I lament to say at an end ... The remembrance of the past is therefore infinitely more agreeable than the enjoyment of the present' (Mount-Edgcumbe 1823, viii–x, 118–22). Henry Chorley said repeatedly that, during the 1800s, fewer and fewer good Italian singers could be found, either in London or in Italy itself (Chorley 1862, 387, 396). In discussing the operatic style of Bellini, Chorley said, 'The modern idea of accomplishment ... now denounces a shake as beneath the dignity of a hero, and a roulade to be nothing less meritricious than a dancer's pirouette' (53). This was written at a time when Bellini's *La Somnambula* was gaining favour.

Among the voice teachers of the nineteenth century, Garcia also displayed inertia in wanting to hang on to the older styles. In *Hints on Singing* (1894) he lamented the disappearance of the castrati, the decline of the florid style, and the tendency of composers to 'simplify the role of the voice and to rely more and more upon orchestal effect. Thus, singing is becoming as much a lost art as the manufacture of Mandarin china or the varnish used by the old [violin] masters' (Garcia 1894, iv). These remarks appeared at a time when Wagner's music dramas were in full flower. Mathilde Marchesi complained in 1898 that, with Wagner, the orchestra dominated, and that Wagner 'treats the voice merely as an additional wind instrument. Rossini was right when he said that singing nowadays was like storming a barricade' (M. Marchesi 1898, 287–8).

Francesco Lamperti was the most outspoken critic of the lot. In an essay titled 'On the Decadence of the Art of Singing,' he lamented the absence of castrati, the disappearance of the true contralto voice, and the forfeiting of agility in favour of declamation. He criticized the impresarios (who hired poorly trained singers), the raising of concert pitch, and the so-called syllabic style of Bellini and others. He was most severe in his condemnation of elaborate orchestral accompaniments, which he blamed on the Germans.[28] Further on in the same book, Lamperti wrote, 'Modern Music is altogether unfitted for the cultivation or preservation of the voice, and to its use we may in a great measure attribute the dearth there is of good singers' (F. Lamperti 1916, 27). He continued, 'In former times the great German composers came to Italy to study the pure Italian melody ... Nowadays composers go to Germany to learn a sort of mathematical and scientific music, which, though beautiful as symphonic music, is totally unsuited to opera' (28).

Of course, the unnamed German who was the target of Lamperti's scorn was Wagner. Toward the end of the nineteenth century, there developed what Hermann Klein called the 'Wagner craze,' which put *bel canto* 'in imminent danger of becoming lost' (Klein 1923, 8). This Wagner craze was fuelled by the writings of such critics as Eduard Hanslick and Henry Chorley. Said Hanslick:

What I have reproached him [Wagner] with is the violation of music by words, the unnaturalness and exaggeration of the expression, the annihilation of the singer and the art of singing by unvocal writing and orchestral din, the displacement of the melody of song by declamatory recitation, enervating monotony and measureless expansion, and finally, the unnatural, stilted expression of his diction, a diction which offends every feeling for fine speech. (quoted in Deas 1940, 21)

Chorley added Verdi to the villains. He spoke of the years 'during which singers' music has been stamped to bits as so much trash by the Wagners of New Germany, and banded into a premature destruction of its voice by the Verdis of infuriate Italy' (Chorley 1862, 398). Henderson saw ruin among both the Germans and the Italians. 'Be not deceived. Singers like Caruso cultivate the Big Tone quite as industriously as the Germans. The Italians are following the downward path that leads to mere noise' (Henderson 1906, 225).

However, not everyone subscribed to this negative view regarding the so-called decline of the art of singing, or the deleterious effects of the music of Verdi and Wagner on the human voice. It is remarkable that

one of the voices raised in defence of Verdi, Wagner, and the art of singing was that of Giovanni Battista Lamperti, who clearly did not agree
with his father or the other doomsayers. In an essay called 'Preventing
the Decadence of the Art of Singing' (1893), he focused on the necessity
of building a solid vocal technique as the way to preserve good singing.
Giovanni's view represented a radical change from the whining and
complaining of his predecessors. Rather than attacking all and sundry
for the sorry state of singing, he maintained that by adhering to traditional voice training the singer could adapt to any style. 'One part of the
lay-world says that there are no longer real voices, and the other that
there is no longer any talent. Neither is right. Voices still exist, and talent
too, but the things which have changed are the *study of the breath, of
vocalization* and *of classic repertory*, as cultivated by the singers of former
times. They used to study for four or five years before they dared to be
seen publically in a small role' (Brown 1957, 1). He added, 'It is wrong to
believe that after studying the Italian method of singing (the one and
only true method of good singing) it is impossible to interpret and sing
dramatic music' (10). In defending Verdi and Wagner, he said, 'This
period is swayed by a prejudice: everyone says the music of Verdi and
Wagner spoils the voice. That is not true of perfected voices. And here
we have the one cause of the deterioration of singing, which no one will
grasp and which is nevertheless so simple. The insufficiently cultivated
voice, which possesses neither the flexibility nor the art of breath-
supported legato, naturally quickly wears itself out' (3–4). He also said,
'Nowadays, after maltreating the larynx for a few months, a student
considers himself an artist, and attempts the most difficult feats. Neither
Verdi nor Wagner has ever said to singers: "In order to sing our music it
is not necessary to study the art of singing; it is sufficient to have a
strong voice and to be a good actor." On the contrary, when Verdi
talked to the Congress at Naples on the decadence of music, he said that
it was absolutely necessary to return to the serious study of former
times' (2). In *The Technics of Bel Canto* (1905), Lamperti reiterated his
view that 'only a singer with a perfectly trained voice can satisfy the
demands of the musical declamation ... A strong, thoroughly trained
organ will by no means, as many erroneously think, be ruined by Wagner's music; the fatal mistake is rather, that unripe artists undertake the
most difficult tasks before possessing the necessary ability' (G.B.
Lamperti 1905, 31–2, 35). Here, then, was a teacher who firmly maintained that the voice trained in the old Italian tradition was equally
suited to the new stylistic demands of Verdi and Wagner.[29]

Others thought similarly. George Bernard Shaw, in a neat twist, said in 1885 that one could not survive in Wagner without mastering the voice and using non-destructive (self-preserving) methods; hence, Wagner's music 'is bringing about a busy revival of the art of singing' (Shaw 1960, 100–1). Music critic W.J. Henderson (1906, 228–52) moderated his opinion about heavier singing styles and railed against those who thought Wagner's operas required a type of vocal declamation without beauty of tone. He echoed G.B. Lamperti when he wrote, 'Singers who possess the real old Italian method, not the false one practised all over Europe by half-trained singers in Wagner's early days, have proved that when Wagner's music is sung with opulent beauty of tone and with a perfect diction, it raises to heights of beauty and eloquence which the first exponents of it never attained' (248). He named several singers, including Lilli Lehmann that he considered to be good Wagnerians. Lehmann was known for being able to sing Mozart or Wagner equally well, and in her own book on singing, she agreed that singers must use their voices well for Wagner (Lehmann 1914, 168). In 1923, Blanche Marchesi, who also sang Wagner's music, wrote, 'Richard Wagner has been specially accused of having broken voices. I must emphatically deny this.' She then went on to a long defense of Wagner and, like G.B. Lamperti and Henderson, she blamed the singers themselves for their vocal problems (B. Marchesi 1923, 201–4).

What did Wagner think of all this? In the early years of his career, Wagner wrote an essay called 'Pasticcio, by Canto Spianato' (1834), in which he extolled 'the old Italian mode of song' with its sostenuto, dexterity, and character.' He criticized the modern school, especially in Germany. 'Today one hardly ever hears a truly beautiful and finished *trillo*; very rarely a perfect *mordente*; very seldom a well-rounded *coloratura*, a genuine unaffected, soul-stirring *portamento*, a complete equalization of the vocal register and perfect maintenance of intonation throughout the varying nuance of increase and diminution in the volume of sound' (Wagner 1899, 80). He criticized German composers for regarding the human voice 'as a mere portion of the instrumental mass,' and for allowing the instruments to 'gag' the singer. He said that the voice should not be characterized by force, but by a 'good, Italian cantabile style' (59–66). Here, then, is Wagner sounding very much like the *bel cantists*.

Was he serious? Hermann Klein certainly thought so. In his book *Great Women-Singers of My Time* (1931), Klein spoke of the impact of Wagner in England, beginning with the Albert Hall Festival of 1877 and the presentation of the *Ring* cycle in 1882. 'Well-trained, experienced artists, they offered living justification for Wagner's *dictum* that only singers reared in the old Italian school were capable of interpreting his music in the manner he had intended – that was, of combining his system of declamation with the art of the *bel canto* ... Music which we had regarded as unsingable flowed from the lips of these accredited interpreters with a freedom and ease wholly undreamt of in our philosophy' (Klein 1931, 186–7). The singers mentioned by Klein included Amalia Materna, Marianne Brandt, Rosa Sucher, Therese Vogl, and especially Lilli Lehmann, who started out as a light soprano and slowly matured into a Wagnerian (Klein 1931, 186–237; 1923, 16). This was proof positive that the principles of *bel canto* could be adapted to the operatic style of Wagner. In 1847 Wagner sent his niece Johanna to study with Garcia. She was the soprano who, two years earlier, had created the role of Elizabeth in *Tannhäuser* at the age of nineteen. She also studied with Pauline Viardot. According to both Mackinlay (Garcia's biographer) and Blanche Marchesi, Wagner apparently sent a letter to Garcia praising him as the best teacher of the old Italian method.[30] Mackinlay added that more than twenty-five years later, in 1876, Wagner invited Garcia to train the singers for the first Bayreuth Festival; Garcia declined the offer because he was so busy in London. If these stories are true, they add further evidence of Wagner's views regarding *bel canto*.

There is one further aspect to the question of the preservation of *bel canto* which should be mentioned here. With the establishment of a 'great repertoire' in the late nineteenth and the twentieth centuries, in which musical works from earlier periods found a permanent place in the operatic repertoire alongside newly composed works, singers were faced with a new problem: how to deal with a wide range of musical and vocal styles, both old and new. Whereas previous generations of singers had largely sung the music of their own day, in their own language, singers were now required to seek a technique that would serve equally the several historical styles in which they might sing. The versatility of Lilli Lehmann is a case in point.

This problem has now become further exacerbated. Today's aspiring singers must decide whether to pursue 'classical' singing (which requires long, rigorous, and expensive training) or to seek the rewards of vernacular styles of singing. At the end of the twentieth century, a new plurality exists in the world of singing. Some singers specialize in the opera of just one era, or just one style, or even just one composer. Some cultivate floridity over strength, or vice versa. Some are versatile enough to be considered 'all-purpose' singers who can perform in various operatic styles. The phenomenon of 'cross-over' singing, in which classically trained singers perform in vernacular styles (most crossover singers move from classical to popular music, not vice-versa) is another aspect of this plurality. But amidst a plethora of vocal styles, whenever a singer sings with *chiaroscuro*, with *appoggio*, with equalized registers, with flexibility and a pleasing vibrato, we immediately identify this with *bel canto* training.

The perennial complaints regarding the supposed decline of the art of singing have continued into the twentieth century,[31] despite the flourishing of good singing. It seems fitting to end this section by allowing George Bernard Shaw one last dig at Garcia. In 1950 Shaw wrote, 'Let us hear no more of a golden age of *bel canto*. We sing much better than our grandfathers. I have heard all the greatest tenors (except Giulini [Antonio Giuglini]) from Mario to Heddle Nash, and I know what I am writing about; for, like De Reszke, I was taught to sing by my mother, not by Garcia' (Shaw 1960, 329).

Coda: The 'Secrets' of *Bel canto*

I return now to a matter raised in the Introduction – the notion that the 'secrets' of *bel canto* have been lost, and that this loss is responsible for the decline in the art of singing. Hermann Klein wrote, 'Many people imagine that there is involved in the Italian method something in the nature of a great secret ... The true answer to that suggestion is that if trade secrets of the kind ever existed they were divulged by Manuel Garcia years ago' (Klein 1923, 19). And what did Garcia say of this? In *Hints on Singing*, following the description of ringing and veiled sounds caused by varying the strength of glottal closure, he wrote, 'Coupled with the theory of *timbres* and that of the breath, it puts the singer into possession of all the "tints" of the voice, and indeed initiates him into all the secrets of voice production' (Garcia 1894, 7). The 'secrets,' then, are found in the control and coordination of the breath, the voice source, and the vocal tract. These are the basic techniques Garcia described so well in his *Traité* of 1841 and repeated again and again throughout his long life.

This brings us full circle. Just as we began with an appraisal of Garcia, so also will we end with him. Our *coda* is provided by Blanche Marchesi, one of Garcia's staunchest supporters. With her colourful and high-flown style, she serves as the perfect counterpoise to the equally opinionated and flamboyant George Bernard Shaw. Marchesi wrote 'It would be utterly impossible to write anything serious about singing if one did not start with the consecrated name of Garcia. The Garcia family were the founders of the singing school in which knowledge of the physiology of the voice goes hand in hand with all the great traditions of style' (B. Marchesi 1923, 13). She proposed that 'the whole world should adopt the Garcia method,' and that 'There are only two methods: the good one and the bad. If the world knew the full truth it soon could be of my opinion' (266–7). Her final pronouncement is that ' if there ever was one who worked in the service of *bel canto*, adding to it the discovery of the actual secret vocal mechanism, it was he, Garcia the second' (B. Marchesi 1932, 156).

Appendix

The Groningen Protocols

This appendix may strike some readers as an oddity. Musicological monographs do not usually conclude with a technical section based on first-hand laboratory measurements. But as the well-known maxim goes, 'The proof of the pudding is in the eating.' The vocal theories presented by authors such as Garcia and the Lampertis are landmarks in the history of vocal pedagogy, and each generation must try anew to understand their meaning and significance. Modern voice science offers a means to reinterpret these theories in the context of objective data. This chapter takes a first cautious step in this direction.

Introduction

The following pages constitute a report on work that was carried out at the GroningenVoice Research Lab, in order to test some of Garcia's theories as discussed in the previous chapters. It represents the combined efforts of Professor Harm K. Schutte, who is the head of the Lab, his associate Donald G. Miller, and myself. The experimental procedures, or protocols, were suggested by me, using myself as the 'singer-subject.' All the technical work, using a variety of laboratory equipment, was done by Schutte and Miller. As well, Schutte created the graphics from the raw data, and Miller held my interpretations in check. Thus, while the writing is mine, this chapter belongs as much to them as to me.

I first went to Groningen in 1974, when Professor Janwillem van den Berg was the director of the Laboratory for Medical Physics at the University of Groningen, and Harm Schutte was his associate. At that time the Laboratory was well known for its work with subglottal pressure measurements of both voice patients and singers. I had been studying

the treatises of Francesco and Giovanni Battista Lamperti, who advocated singing with 'compressed breath,' which I interpreted as implying
high subglottal breath pressure. The role of subglottal pressures in singing was therefore of particular interest to me, but it was an open question what the optimum pressures might be. The measurements taken at
the Groningen Voice Research Lab confirmed that my breath pressures
registered levels as high as 100 cmH$_2$O – higher than might be considered typical. I was concerned that such pressures might have an adverse
effect on flexibility and voice quality, and wondered whether this level
of pressure was the right one for me. Schutte had encountered these
high pressures only in tenor high notes, and concluded that there was
insufficient reason to discard this singing method completely (Schutte
1980, 160). Nevertheless, I subsequently learned to lower the subglottal
pressure, so that I rarely reached 60 cmH$_2$O, even on high, loud notes,
and this seemed to have a positive effect on other aspects of my singing.

This experience was my initiation into experimental voice science and
its use for pedagogical purposes. My orientation was, and continues to
be, that of a singer, voice teacher, and musicologist, rather than a trained
voice scientist. But my growing experience in the laboratory has played
a major role in my understanding of singing.

My interest in voice science increased when I undertook a serious
study of Manuel Garcia's theories while on a sabbatical leave in England. Garcia's *Traité* described the different role of the voice source
as opposed to the vocal tract in singing, and instructed the pupil in how
to use 'all the tints of the voice.' I began to experiment with his techniques and learned to produce and compare different voice qualities. In
1991 I wrote an article on Garcia's *Traité* (Stark 1991), and subsequently
received an invitation to return to Groningen in order to test my interpretations of Garcia's theories in an objective way. My work there has
extended over a period of five years and six trips to the Netherlands,
totalling many weeks in the laboratory. The data presented here represents only a fraction of the research that was done, and of course I
expect the research to continue.

Schutte developed an experimental method for voice patients that he
called 'intra-individual comparison' (Schutte 1980, 94), in which paired
phonations of different qualities were produced by a single subject. I
thought that this procedure could be used equally well with singers. It
seemed more useful to base measurements upon such paired tones in an
individual singer (myself, in this case), than to attempt comparisons
between singers who were less familiar with Garcia's teachings, or who

were less able to control the physiological and acoustical parameters. This procedure had also been employed by Garcia, who used himself as subject in a similar fashion 150 years ago, with the aid of only a simple laryngeal mirror, a perceptive ear, and a good understanding of vocal anatomy and physiology. Garcia wrote, 'In our considerations, we will not concern ourselves with the different timbres which characterize and differentiate the voices of individuals, but only with the diverse timbres which the voice of the same individual presents' (Garcia 1984, li). In a way, then, this chapter is a *redux* of Garcia's theories and methods; I served as the singer-subject, and Schutte and Miller provided the laboratory expertise in carrying out the protocols.

During our period of research we conducted numerous paired-tone comparisons, in which we observed and measured contrasting types of glottal closure, closed quotients, airflow rates, subglottal breath pressures, voice quality, *messa di voce*, *mezza voce*, and respiratory control of vibrato. The methods used include visual examination of the vibrating vocal folds (using a rigid laryngoscope and videostroboscopy), breath pressure readings (using an esophageal balloon), airflow rates (using a pneumotachograph and airflow mask), and acoustical analysis (using a real-time spectrum analyzer).[1]

It must be emphasized that the research protocols were not intended to be comprehensive or definitive. Rather, they were a modest attempt to illuminate certain pedagogical concepts in a fairly objective way. The experiments depended on my ability to alter one parameter of vocal technique more or less independently of other parameters, using the paired-tone method. Strictly speaking, of course, this cannot be done, since altering one muscle group will necessarily affect another as well. But, in a relative way, different vocal functions can be isolated to a sufficient degree to allow for comparisons. It would probably not be possible to employ this method with a large group of singer-subjects, since specialized training would be necessary in order to ensure that they could alter parameters in approximately the same way. It should also be noted that singers will be more skillful at producing a tone in their habitual way than in a way that is somewhat alien to their normal technique. This could pose a problem with paired-tone comparisons using only one singer-subject because the singer will probably be more skilled at producing one of the tones than the other. However, this problem can be largely overcome by practice, and the paired tone-comparisons in our experiments show a consistency that lends credibility to the results.

Glottal Settings

When Manuel Garcia invented the laryngoscope in 1855, he used a hand mirror to direct light from the sun or from a lantern to a laryngeal mirror which he used to view his own larynx.[2] It must be assumed that he became very skillful at this, judging from the detail of his written observations. Modern technology has now developed two new types of laryngoscopes: (1) a flexible scope containing optic fibres that can be inserted through a nasal passage and turned at the nasopharynx to aim at the larynx, and (2) a rigid type without optic fibres that is placed in the oropharynx and focused on the larynx. We chose the rigid scope because it has the advantage of a larger, better illuminated, and sharper image. This laryngoscope was connected to a stroboscope, in which a 1 Hz difference between the frequencies of the voice and the light source results in an illusory slow motion of the vocal folds that works well with periodic vibration. The stroboscopic images were recorded on video tape, and could be played back frame by frame. We used videostroboscopy to visually record loose versus firm phonation. By means of a connect frame-grabber, we were able to print out single frames from the video, and to make still photographs of these frames.

Garcia described two glottal settings, which he referred to as the 'five-fifths glottis' and the 'three-fifths glottis' respectively (Garcia 1984, 205). He maintained that in the five-fifths setting, both the membranous and the cartilagenous portions of the glottis participated in the vibration, while in the three-fifths setting, the arytenoid cartilages were 'pinched' firmly together along the midline, and only the membranous portion of the vocal folds vibrated. While the details of his assertions are open to question, at the very least he associated a shortened glottis with strong adductory forces.

In our observations, we compared loose and firm phonation using a variety of pitches in both chest voice and falsetto. Single tones were recorded using videolaryngostroboscopy, alternating between loose and firm phonation. But this procedure caused a problem, in that each single tone was followed by an inhalation; this resulted in a change in the positioning of the laryngoscope, causing a slight mismatch between the images of the two separate phonation, thereby making precise comparisons impossible. We finally arrived at a better method, in which a single long tone was begun with loose phonation and abruptly changed to firm phonation halfway through its duration without an intervening inhalation. This ensured a more stable position of the laryngoscope for the paired tones, and produced uniform pictures for comparison.

The differences between the two glottal settings as seen from above are remarkable, and involve far more than just glottal length. The vocal manoeuvre of changing from the loose glottal setting to the firm one shows several details. First, the laryngeal entrance, or 'collar' of the larynx, becomes smaller by several actions that influence the position of the epiglottis, the aryepiglottic folds, and the apexes of the arytenoid cartilages. This change in the size of the larynx collar forms a compact aryepiglottic region called a 'vestibule' which some researchers have identified as an important resonance chamber (Sundberg 1977a). The apexes are brought closer together by the contraction of the interarytenoid muscles, and the false vocal folds move inwards medially toward the glottis. In my case, firm glottal closure caused the apexes to obscure the posterior portion of the glottis, since the apex region (dorsal part of the collar) lies at a higher (superior) level than the dorsal part of the lower (caudal) lying glottis. This sometimes made it difficult or impossible to determine the positions of the vocal processes. The difficulty of seeing the entire glottis during phonation suggests the possibility that Garcia's theory of the three-fifths versus five-fifths glottis may have been based on assumptions that went beyond his actual observations with the laryngoscope.

In our observations, during loose phonation the vocal processes of the arytenoid cartilages remained adducted, but the cartilagenous portion of the glottis sometimes separated, creating a posterior chink (known as the 'short triangle') that resulted in the waste of unphonated air. Unlike Garcia's description, the cartilagenous portion of the glottis was never actually involved in phonation. This may be because I habitually sing with firm glottal closure, and even my loose closure is still strong enough to keep the vocal processes adducted. In most other ways our observations were consistent with Garcia's. His note 'when we pinch the glottis strongly, we synergistically bring about a certain contraction, a kind of condensation of the tissues of the pharynx,' may have been a reference to the circular narrowing of the collar of the larynx and the movement inwards of the false vocal folds (Garcia 1847, 2:54; 1975, 152–3). This was also apparent in our observations. Garcia noted that the glottis became 'no more than a linear or elliptical slit' (1847, 2:54; 1975, 152–3). Our observations showed a glottis which indeed appeared narrower, in that the lateral excursion of the vocal folds was smaller.

Garcia also noted that the firm closure of the arytenoids created 'deep contact' of the vocal folds. 'This deep contact, which continues even after the apophoses [vocal processes] no longer partake in the vibrations, gives a deep tension to the membranes, increases the depth of their contact, and, as a necessary consequence, augments the resistance they present to the air' (Garcia 1855, 408). In our observations, the different vibrational patterns of the vocal folds during loose and firm phonation were immediately apparent. During firm phonation, there was a clear lateral phase difference and deep contact of the vocal folds, and there were mucosal waves that appeared as a rippling of the mucosal covering of the folds. As well, there was a 'zipper' effect as the folds opened from the anterior to the posterior portion of the glottis. Greater resistance to the air was confirmed by our measurements of subglottal pressure and airflow rates.

Thus, while our results differed from Garcia's in details of glottal length and the action of the cartilagenous portion of the glottis, other important distinctions between loose and firm glottal closure were in agreement with his. Firm phonation resulted in a shorter and narrower glottis, made deeper contact of the vocal folds, and showed a tautness in the region of the collar of the larynx and the false vocal cords. Firm phonation also increased glottal resistance to the breath and reduced airflow rates. Unfortunately, very little of this can be illustrated by reproducing individual frames of the videostroboscopy. These features only become clear with careful examination of the slow-motion video and other measurements. However, the still photographs can illustrate certain aspects of loose versus firm phonation.

Figure A.1 illustrates loose and firm glottal phonation at the point of maximal opening of the folds during the vibratory cycle. These photographs illustrate that, the glottis was shorter in firm phonation than in loose phonation, but not in the ratio of three-fifths to five-fifths. Rather, a portion of the membranous folds immediately forward of the vocal processes remained adducted during phonation, and did not vibrate. This is consistent with Pressman's 'damping factor' (Pressman 1941, 1942). More obvious is that in firm phonation the glottis seems narrower.

As noted in chapter 1, firm glottal closure, with its strong muscular contractions, has been interpreted by some observers as an example of hyperfunction that could lead to vocal damage. However, I have a perfectly healthy larynx, despite many years of singing with firm phonation. This raises the question of whether current clinical definitions of vocal hyperfunction are adequate to distinguish between the normal vigorous activity associated with operatic singing and the types of vocal behaviour that are demonstrably abusive to the larynx. It can be argued that firm glottal closure when skillfully executed does not constitute a form of vocal abuse, but is rather an extraordinary use of the vocal muscles that is necessary in some kinds of singing.

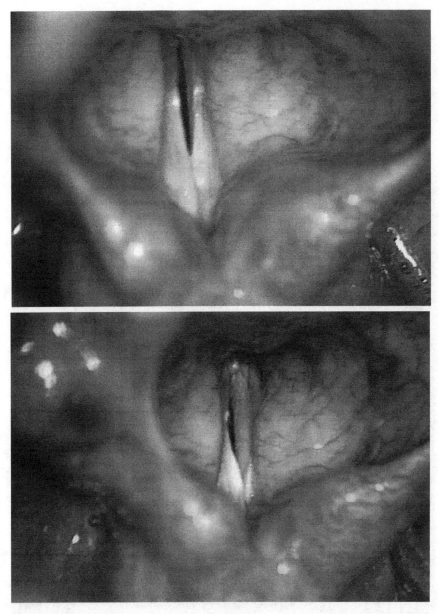

Figure A.1 Visual observations of glottal settings: videostroposcopic frames using rigid laryngoscope showing loose phonation (top) and firm phonation (bottom).

Closed Quotients

Garcia did not have the means to determine the percentage of time in each glottal cycle that the folds remained open or closed, nor could he measure airflow or subglottal pressure. Hence, his remarks on these matters were subjective. In *Observations on the Human Voice* (1855), he included a section on 'Pressure of the Air,' in which he stated, 'The intensity of the sound can only depend on the quantity of air which goes to each *sharp* explosion. I say *sharp* explosion, as an express condition; the glottis should close itself perfectly after every vibration; for if the air found a constant passage, as in the notes of the falsetto, then the greatest movements of the glottis, and the greatest waste of air, would produce precisely the weakest tones' (Garcia 1855, 409). Elsewhere he wrote, 'it is necessary to conclude that the brilliance of the voice results from the firm closure of the glottis after each pulsation. This procedure also has the advantage of bringing about a great economy of air' (Garcia 1984, 27). These statements imply complete glottal closure with no leakage of breath, which is consistent with bright timbre and low airflow rates.

Nowadays the measurement of closed and open quotients during singing can be made with an electroglottograph, in which a weak electrical current passes between two round metal plates placed externally on either side of the thyroid cartilage. With some singers the larynx lies too deep in the neck for the electroglottograph to be effective, and this was unfortunately the case with me. No amount of manipulation of the contact plates would result in a clear reading. It was therefore necessary to find an alternative means for estimating the closed quotient.

We adopted a method of timing the open and closed glottis by counting the number of frames on the videostroboscopic tape during each series of consecutive stroboscopic periods (that is, each complete cycle of vibration), in order to calculate the closed quotient. A similar method was recently reported by researcher Peak Woo (1996). It was a laborious process, and subject to artifacts and cycle-to-cycle variations resulting from the strobe effect, but nevertheless it appeared to give a satisfactory estimate of the closed quotient. The results were consistent with measurements made by videokymography – a digital technique for high-speed visualization of vibration recently developed in the Groningen Voice Research Lab (Švec, Schutte, and Miller 1996). Stroboscopic measurements were taken on both loose and firm phonation on three different pitches: $Bb3$, $Eb4$, and $G4$.

Figures A.2A and A.2B illustrate the closed quotient percentages dur-

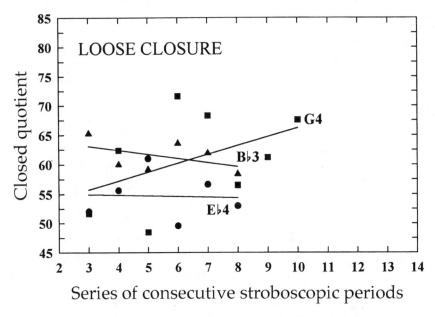

Figure A.2A Closed quotients using loose closure: *Bb3* (triangles), *Eb4* (circles), *G4* (squares).

ing loose and firm phonation. Each number on the x-axis represents one glottal cycle as seen with the stroboscope. The lines showing linear regression represent an averaging of the data for the purpose of showing trends; a rising regression line indicates an increasing closed quotient, while a falling regression line indicates a diminishing one.

In general, firm phonation resulted in larger closed quotients than did loose phonation. Using loose glottal closure, the closed quotients ranged from about 54 to 68 per cent; while in firm phonation the closed quotients ranged from about 60 to 75 per cent, with the higher pitches having the larger closed quotients. In Figure A.2A in (loose closure) the data shows more 'scatter' and is less easy to graph or plot. Here the closed quotient on *Eb4* is nearly stable, while there is a slightly reduced closed quotient on *Bb3*. It will also be observed that, while singing with loose closure, only 9 or 10 stroboscopic periods were recorded (as opposed to 13 periods for firm closure). This can be explained by the higher airflow rates necessary in loose phonation, which necessarily reduces the duration of the phonation.

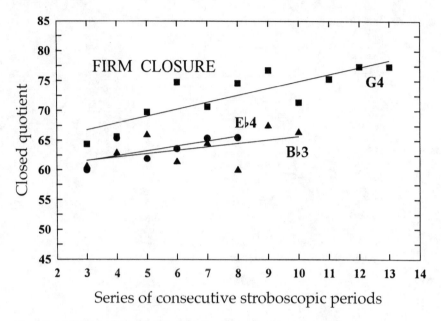

Figure A.2B Closed quotients using firm closure: *Bb3* (triangles), *Eb4* (circles), *G4* (squares).

Figure A.2B shows little difference between *Bb3* and *Eb4* during firm glottal closure, but there is a very large closed quotient of 75 per cent on *G4*, which lies above the *passaggio*. It will be seen that the closed quotients of all three notes increased with the duration of the phonations. This may be due both to fine glottal adjustments as the tones progress and to the tendency to apply stronger adduction as the breath supply is reduced. One of the peculiarities revealed by examination of the stroboscopic images during closed quotient was that, just as it appeared that the glottis was about to open, this opening movement seemed to be postponed, and the closure was extended. It is unclear how this is done or what causes it.

Airflow Rates

It will be recalled that Garcia, in his discussion of glottal closure, maintained that a strong glottal pinch (*pinçon fortement la glotte*) resulted in 'the fourfold or fivefold duration of the breath' compared to loose glottal

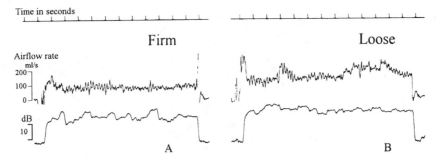

Figure A.3 Airflow measurements: a diatonic scale (*G3–D4*) sung up and down on the vowel [a], at *mezzo-forte* level, using loose and firm phonation.

closure (Garcia 1847, 1:15, 2:54). His *coup de la glotte* and glottal pinch were intended to ensure low airflow rates and a bright timbre. His estimates of airflow were based on how long a tone could be sustained on a single breath – a ready test that requires no equipment other than a timepiece. Today airflow rates can be precisely measured with a pneumotachograph, an instrument that uses an airflow mask that fits over the nose and mouth of the singer. As the breath passes through a fine mesh screen, its volume is measured in millilitres-per-second (ml/s). With this apparatus we undertook numerous measurements of paired tones, using loose and firm phonation. The results of one of those experiments, shown in Figure A.3, are typical of the other experiments.

In this protocol, it would have been easy to skew the results by purposely singing the examples of loose phonation with an overly breathy tone. This is apparently what Garcia did, using an 'enormous expenditure of air,' in order to achieve his large difference between the two glottal settings (Garcia 1847, 1:54; 1984, 152–3). We decided instead that the examples of loose phonation should have a 'usable' tone quality without audible breath. However, one aspect of this protocol was slightly problematic, namely, that the airflow mask muffles the tone and affects aural feedback. This means that the singer is not as fully in control as during normal singing.

In general, our measurements corroborated Garcia's observation that strong glottal closure reduces the rate of airflow. We used the scale *G3–D4*, which is in the comfortable middle part of the voice. The scale was sung up and down twice for each phonation. During firm phonation the airflow stabilized at about 100 ml/s, but during loose phonation it sometimes exceeded 200 ml/s. For purposes of comparison, a flow rate of 200 ml/s is rather common, but a flow rate of 100 ml/s can be considered quite low. As well, the airflow was steadier in firm phonation. The decibel levels were nearly the same in firm and loose phonation. The termination of the tone in the two examples is of some interest. When using firm phonation, I ended the scale with a quick release of subglottal pressure. This method of release, often used by operatic singers, is sometimes referred to as 'aftergrunt.' With loose phonation, however, I ended the tone by stopping the breath. This stoppage shows clearly in the graph.

Subglottal Pressures

Throughout his works, Garcia called attention to the relationship between glottal resistance and breath pressure. He noted that greater pressure was necessary in order to produce greater intensity, and that the higher the pressure, the greater the glottal resistance: 'It is necessary to pinch the glottis in proportion to the amount of pressure one gives the air' (Garcia 1847, 1:15; 1855, 15; 1984, 27). For Garcia, of course, this statement was based on sensation rather than measurement. Later labels relating to the balance between breath pressure and glottal resistance include *lutte vocale, appoggio, Stütze,* and *Stauprinzip.* In all of these, it was recognized that the regulation of subglottal pressure was an essential element in vocal technique.

Nowadays it is possible to make pressure measurements by several means (Schutte 1992). Some of these methods, such as passing a pressure-sensitive needle between the tracheal rings below the larynx, or passing a catheter through the glottis, are obviously not favoured among singers. A more commonly used method calculates subglottal pressure from intra-esophageal pressure, which is measured by inserting a flexible catheter fitted with an esophageal balloon through a nasal passage to the nasopharynx, then past the epiglottis where it is swallowed into the esophagus. While this sounds dreadful, it is easily tolerated by most singers, and normal singing is not greatly affected. Subglottal pressures can be reliably derived using this method if esophageal pressure changes also take lung volume into account (Schutte 1992, 129). Pressure is calibrated with a U-tube manometer and is expressed in centimetres of water pressure (cmH_2O), as measured with an electronic pressure transducer. For audio recording, a condenser microphone was placed 30 cm in front of the mouth. Using this method,

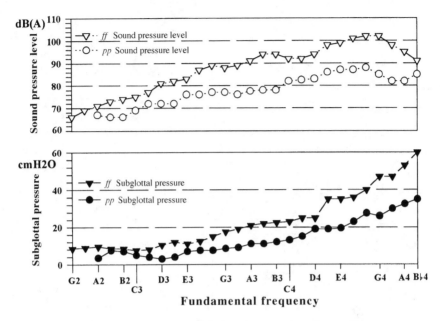

Figure A.4 Pressure phonetogram: subglottal pressure and sound pressure levels as a function of pitch, during singing at *ff* and *pp* levels.

we measured subglottal pressure and sound pressure levels in numerous paired tones, using five pitches and two intensity levels.

Pressure phonetograms, as developed in Groningen for trained singers, record both subglottal pressures and sound pressure levels, and show the relationship between them. In Figure A.4 the upper and lower graphs are based on a series of tones that were sung with firm phonation only (since this is my normal way of singing). The series of tones was sung twice, once at the dynamic level of *pianissimo* (*pp*), and once at *fortissimo* (*ff*). In trained singers, a difference of 5 to 15dB between the two dynamic levels can be considered typical; a maximum sound pressure level of about 100dB is within the normal range, although this is on the low side for opera singers. The phonetogram in Figure A.4 exhibits a three-stage slope. At the lower pitch levels (*G2–D3*), subglottal pressures are fairly uniform; in the middle portion of the voice (*E3–D4*) pressures rise gradually; at *E4* a 'pressure event' takes place in which there is a significant increase in pressure. This may be related to the glottal squeeze that becomes stronger as the *passaggio* is approached. Above the *passaggio*, from about *F4–Bb4*, there is a marked rise in subglottal pressure, reaching a maximum of about 60 cmH$_2$O when singing *fortissimo*. This is a strong contrast to the subglottal pressures measured in 1974, which produced consistently higher subglottal pressures, sometimes reaching 100 cmH$_2$O.[3]

It is not unusual for the dB level to fall off after the *passaggio* is reached, possibly because of the acoustical change which accompanies the covering manoeuvre: the dominant resonance just below the *passaggio* is F_1–H_2, but above the *passaggio* it changes to F_2–H_3, which represents a change in voice quality. Presumably singers trade intensity for quality. Maintaining the F_1–H_2 resonance on the highest pitches would result in a 'yelling' or 'belting' quality that is not acceptable in classical singing styles. (This is illustrated in Figure A.5E.)

Voice Quality

Readers will recall from chapter 2 that, for classical singing, the ideal voice quality has long been known as *chiaroscuro*. One interpretation of this bright-dark tone is that it gains its brightness from strong high-frequency components and its darkness mainly from a lowered F_1. Garcia referred to the brightness of the tone as *éclat*. This *éclat* originates at the voice source, since strong glottal closure produces the 'sharp explosions' that give acoustic energy to the higher partials. When these partials occur in proximity to a formant of the vocal tract, the result is a band of 'brightness' that can take more than one form. The brightness is often due to the presence of a strong singer's formant, which is a clustering of F_3, F_4, and sometimes F_5; in other cases it is due to a dominant F_2–H_3 or F_2–H_4 resonance.

We conducted a number of paired-tone measurements comparing loose and firm glottal closure, using an FFT real-time spectrum analyzer. We made long-time-average-spectra of a chromatic scale pattern which was measured over its duration of about five seconds. In Figures A.5A, A.5B, and A.5C we measured the vowels [a], [i], and [u] on a chromatic scale from *G3–D4*, using both loose and firm phonation. The use of a chromatic scale ensured that the long-time-average-spectrum would be a satisfactory average of all the notes within the interval of a fifth.

Figure A.5A clearly establishes the acoustical difference between loose and firm phonation. The vowel articulation is virtually the same for both loose and firm phonation (the first two formant frequencies are

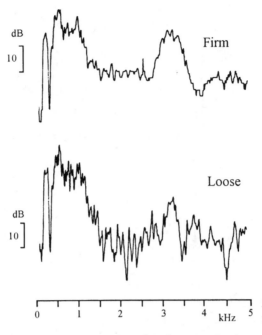

Figure A.5A Long-time-average-spectra: paired tones using loose and firm phonation, sung on a chromatic scale, *G3–D4*, using the vowel [a].

unchanged). The difference in sound is due both to the greater high-frequency energy in the source spectrum, and to the compactness of the singer's formant in firm phonation. The compactness occurs as the higher formants are brought into greater proximity with one another, while the higher decibel level of the singer's formant implies greater high-frequency energy in the source spectrum. In this example the singer's formant occurs at about 3300 Hz, and it has greater intensity relative to the vowel formants than does the example using loose phonation.

Figure A.5B illustrates the same tendencies on the vowel [i]. Here the example using firm phonation has a distribution of energy between F_2, F_3, and F_4, in which the acoustic component resonated by F_4 nearly equals that of H_1. The example using loose phonation shows a ragged slope with a clear falling-off of acoustic energy among the upper harmonics.

In Figure A.5C the vowel [u] shows even more clearly the correlation between firm phonation and a stronger, more compact singer's for-

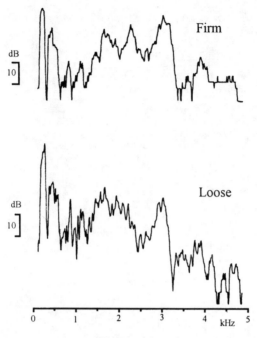

Figure A.5B Long-time-average-spectra: paired tones, using loose and firm phonation, sung on a chromatic scale, *G3–D4*, using the vowel [i].

mant. In firm phonation the singer's formant is the dominant resonance. In loose phonation the singer's formant is less compact, with a gap appearing between F_3 and F_4. The steep slope shows more than a 30dB dip between the fundamental and the singer's formant. This spectrogram is a clear illustration of radical difference in sound between the two examples.

All three of the above examples measured the acoustic effects of firm phonation in chest voice. Figure A.5D measures the effects in falsetto using a different procedure. The following example presents a comparison of loose and firm phonation on the vowel [u] while singing an ascending and descending diatonic 5-note scale from *F4* to *C5*. The scale was repeated twice on one breath for this measurement.

The difference between loose and firm phonation is as remarkable in falsetto as it is in chest voice. In loose phonation the spectrum had a steep and uniform slope, with virtually no singer's formant; instead, the

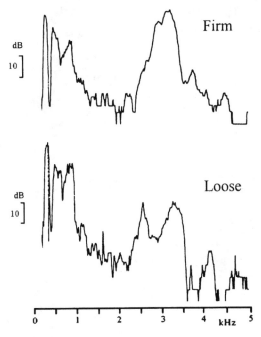

Figure A.5C Long-time-average-spectra: paired tones, using loose and firm phonation, sung on a chromatic scale, *G3–D4*, using the vowel [u].

acoustic energy is concentrated in the fundamental. This is typical of the 'hooty' quality of falsetto. But in firm phonation, with its high-energy partials, the spectrum shows a strong F_2 as well as a strong and compact singer's formant.

The final example of this series, Figure A.5E, measures a 'belt-to-sing' manoeuvre. This manoeuvre was arrived at spontaneously. I demonstrated a 'yell' on a high pitch which I described as using strong glottal closure, high subglottal pressure, a high larynx, and a 'straight tone.' The resulting tone can be referred to as 'male belt' (Miller and Schutte 1994, 163). Midway through the phonation I employed the covering manoeuvre by abruptly changing the position of the vocal tract, especially lowering the larynx and darkening the vowel. This adjustment of the vocal tract produced a marked change in the voice quality and was also accompanied by the appearance of vibrato.

In Figure A.5E, the first half of the phonation (the belt) is represented

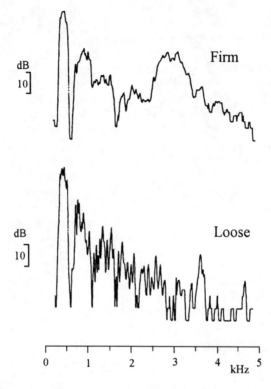

Figure A.5D Long-time-average-spectra: paired tones sung in falsetto, using loose and firm phonation, sung on a diatonic scale ascending and descending, *F4–C5*, using the vowel [u].

in the lower graph, and the covered tone is shown in the upper. In the belt, the dominant resonance is F_1–H_2, with the higher frequencies displaying a fairly flat slope. This is characteristic of a yell; there is no vibrato. In the subsequent covered tone, F_1 falls between H_1 and H_2 and loses its role as the dominant resonance. Now the dominant resonance becomes F_2–H_4. The vibrato appears with this laryngeal adjustment. As discussed earlier, there is a drop of about 15dB from the belted to the covered tone, but what is lost in intensity is gained in quality. This same manoeuvre (not shown) was measured on the pitch *Ab4* with nearly identical results. The dominant F_2–H_4 resonance is characteristic for me on high notes with a front vowel, and is a form of brightness that is as effective as the singer's formant in creating 'edge' to the tone.

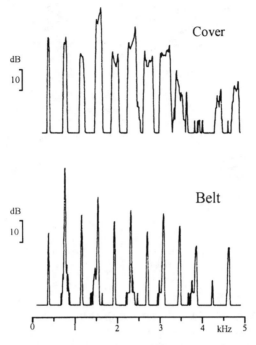

Figure A.5E Spectrograms of the 'belt-to-cover manoeuvre,' performed on a single phonation, on the vowel [e], G4.

In general, these spectrograms illustrate the fact that firm phonation, with its strong glottal closure and large closed quotient, consistently produces strong high-frequency components that can be amplified by certain formants of the vocal tract. The 'brightness' or 'edge' of the tone manifests itself in a compact singer's formant, in a strong F_2 resonance, or a combination of the two. Either resonance might well qualify for Garcia's description of *éclat*. A similar phenomenon occurs in both chest voice and falsetto.

Messa di voce

The *messa di voce* is sometimes considered the ultimate test of a good vocal technique, since it requires a fine coordination of laryngeal, respiratory, and resonance factors. Readers will recall from chapter 4 that Garcia described a method of performing the *messa di voce* in which the exercise began *pianissimo* in falsetto (which, to Garcia, meant loose glottal closure), changed to chest voice (firm glottal closure) for the crescendo, and then changed back to falsetto for the decrescendo. This will be referred to as the 'Garcia method.' A different approach was described by Garaudé and the Lampertis, in which the entire exercise was produced with strong glottal closure, while the *crescendo-decrescendo* was largely governed by varying the breath pressure. This will be referred to as the 'Lamperti method.'

It should be noted that the instructions provided by Garcia and the Lampertis point to only a few of the elements involved in this complex vocal manoeuvre. In a studio situation, the teacher would have included other unspecified adjustments necessary for the *messa di voce* in the instructions to the pupil. In our protocol, the attempt to recreate both the Garcia and the Lamperti methods of producing the *messa di voce* is approximate at best, and makes no pretense at being definitive, but does attempt to demonstrate in an objective way that the *messa di voce* can indeed be executed in two essentially different ways, depending on glottal closure and airflow rates.

Figure A.6 illustrates my approximation of the Garcia method and the Lamperti method of producing the *messa di voce*. The results show that there are indeed clear differences. With the Garcia method (A), the esophageal pressure rises from about 10 cmH_2O to about 20–5 cmH_2O at the apex before returning to 10 cmH_2O. With the Lamperti method (B), there is a prephonatory increase in pressure. Upon onset, pressure falls briefly before the voice becomes audible, then rises to the apex of about 20–5 cmH_2O before falling again for the decrescendo.

The airflow rate with the Garcia method begins at about 200 ml/s, drops to less than 100 ml/s as glottal resistance increases during the crescendo, then returns to almost 200 ml/s at the end. With the Lamperti method, airflow begins at less than 50 ml/s; only after phonation is well stabilized does the airflow increase to about 150 ml/s. At the end of the exercise, the rate drops to zero with the glottal stop before exhalation releases the breath pressure. This release is clearly indicated in the graph by the sharply rising line. Despite these differences, both examples show the rise and fall of the sound pressure level which is characteristic of the *messa di voce*; the Lamperti method is marginally higher at the apex.

Mezza voce

The technique of singing with *mezza voce* (half voice) is not well

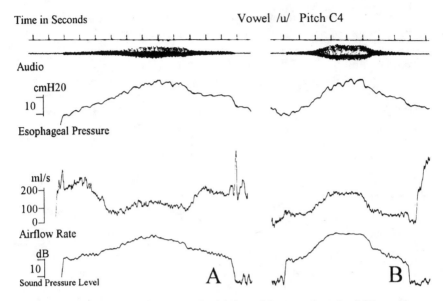

Figure A.6 *Messa di voce*: Garcia method (A), and Lamperti method (B) on the vowel [u], *C4*.

described in the pedagogical or scientific literature. The term is in the parlance of many singers and teachers, and the technique is an important one for opera and concert singers. Yet, it is infrequently referred to in singing manuals, and when it does occur, it is usually mentioned only in passing, as if the reader already knows how it is produced. In other words, *mezza voce* is a technique that is taken for granted and not explained. Garcia may have been the first to offer a technical description of *mezza voce*. As we observed in chapter 3, Garcia raised the matter of *mezza voce* in his discussion of *voix mixte*, or *mezzo petto*. He maintained that tenors could extend the chest register upwards, avoiding falsetto, while singing *piano* and *mezza voce*, and that this could be achieved by 'reducing the ventricles and the pharynx to a purely passive role,' by 'reducing the number of vibrating partials,' and by narrowing 'more and more the column of air' (Garcia 1847, 2:58; 1975, 161–2). Using today's language, this could be restated as disengaging the vocal tract to make it as passive as possible, thereby reducing the resonances of the vocal tract, while keeping airflow rates low.

While Garcia's description of *mezza voce* was imperfect, it served as a starting point for our experiments. I practised the *mezza voce* according to Garcia's description (as I interpreted it). I aimed at reducing the resonances of the vocal tract by using a weaker glottal closure than for full voice, thinking this would lessen the high-frequency components in the tone. I also found that by keeping the larynx at its position of rest or slightly lower, the tone quality became darker, presumably because of the lowered formants. I also tried to keep the airflow to a minimum as Garcia suggested. The vocal manoeuvres used to produce *mezza voce* were complex but easily learned.

Using our usual paired-tone procedure, we compared 'full voice' and *mezza voce* in several ways: (1) videostroboscopic frames (using a rigid laryngoscope); (2) pressure phonetograms; (3) airflow rates; (4) closed quotients; (5) spectrograms.

For this procedure I sang a long tone on the pitch $E4$, using quasi [i], the 'vowel of laryngoscopy.' I began in full voice and then changed abruptly to *mezza voce* halfway through the phonation without any intervening inhalation. This ensured a stable position of the rigid laryngoscope, and produced acceptably uniform pictures. As in Figure A.1, the still photos in Figure A.7A can reveal only a small number of the features that were observed on the videotape. What follows, then, is a verbal description of the 'full voice to *mezza voce* manoeuvre,' with particular reference to the still photos.

During the full voice phonation, the glottis appeared short and narrow, with a long closed phase, as was seen earlier with firm phonation. During the shift from full voice to *mezza voce*, the larynx descended noticeably, thus increasing the distance between the larynx and the laryngoscope. At the same time the aryepiglottic folds drew inward, changing the shape of the collar of the larynx from fairly round to oval, and the false vocal folds moved away from each other. This would presumably reduce the space in the venticles of Morgagni, and would therefore have an effect on voice quality. During the *mezza voce* phonation, it appeared that the glottis was further diminished, both latitudinally and longitudinally. It seemed that the changed shape of the collar, together with the changed position of the false vocal folds, were major factors in the production of *mezza voce*. The firmly closed position of the arytenoids was stable throughout the entire phonation, and it appeared that the membranous portion of the vocal folds just anterior of the vocal processes remained closed throughout the glottal cycle. There was also a curious (and unexplained) strobe effect: with each phonation, during

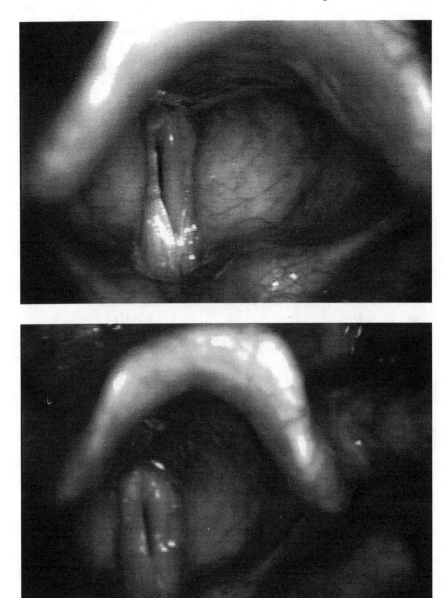

Figure A.7A Visual observations of full voice to *mezza voce* manoeuvre: video-stroboscopic frames using rigid laryngoscope, on the vowel quasi [i], *E4*.

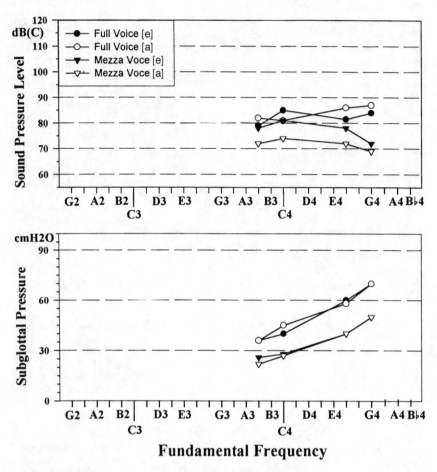

Figure A.7B Pressure phonetogram: subglottal pressure and sound pressure levels on the vowels [e] and [a], singing *Bb4, C4, F4, and G4* full voice and *mezza voce*.

the singing of *mezza voce* the glottal cycle appeared to double in speed. This was a regularly occurring and predictable phenomenon.

The still photographs reproduced here were selected for their maximal glottal openings. Although the laryngoscope was off-axis, the comparison is clearly seen. The shortened glottis (which is typical for me, even in full voice) was shortened (squeezed) even more in *mezza voce*. Since the placement of the rigid laryngoscope was stable during the

Pitch	Phonation	Vowel	SBL (bB)	P$_{sub}$(cmH2O)	Airflow (ml/s)
F4	Full voice	[e]	82	56	70
F4	Full voice	[a]	84	56	75
F4	Mezza voce	[e]	73	38	75
F4	Mezza voce	[a]	74	38	80
G4	Full voice	[e]	87	60	80
G4	Full voice	[a]	85	72	90
G4	Mezza voce	[e]	75	40	70
G4	Mezza voce	[a]	74	50	100

Figure A.7C Airflow measurements: full voice and *mezza voce* on the vowels [e] and [a], singing *F4* and *G4*.

manoeuvre, the full voice photo is closer to the camera; the *mezza voce* photo shows the lower position of the larynx.

Figure A.7B shows the subglottal pressure and the sound pressure levels for paired tones on the vowels [e] and [a] using full voice and *mezza voce*. The subglottal pressures are consistently higher when singing with full voice than when singing with *mezza voce*, using either vowel. The difference ranges from just over 10 cmH$_2$O to just over 20 cmH$_2$O, with the higher pitches having the greater difference. The sound pressure levels show a greater difference for the vowel [a] than for [e], with a spread of about 2 to13dB for [e] and about 10 to 18dB for [a]; the higher pitches show a greater difference for both vowels.

In this protocol several measurements were taken simultaneously: subglottal pressure was measured with an esophageal balloon and U-tube manometer; sound pressure levels were measured with a microphone; airflow rates were measured with a pneumotachograph. I began each sung example without the mask, taking advantage of aural feedback to establish the desired phonation. Once stability was established, I applied the mask and maintained the tone for several seconds while airflow was measured. I then removed the mask while continuing the tone, in order to ensure that the phonation had remained stable. Repeated trials demonstrated that this technique was reliable.

Figure A.7C presents the data in a table, showing pitch, type of phonation, vowel, sound pressure level, subglottal pressure, and rate of air-

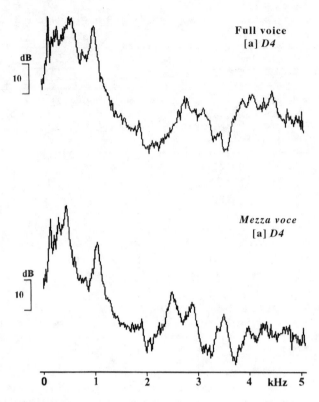

Figure A.7D Spectrograms of full voice and *mezza voce*: four examples using the vowels [a] and [e], singing *D4*, *F4*. First example.

flow. The airflow rates were remarkably low for both full voice and *mezza voce*, and remained within a range of 70 to 100 ml/s. While these rates are commensurate with the low airflow rates measured earlier in my singing, they are significantly lower than the normal rates for tenors (which typically range between 150 to 200 ml/s). The table indicates that subglottal pressure, sound pressure levels, and airflow rates were all lower for *mezza voce* than for full voice.

For spectrograms and closed quotient measurements we used the new *VoceVista* hardware/software package, which incorporates two electronic signals (real time spectral analysis and electroglottography). In this case the electroglottograph gave satisfactory results. This proto-col also used paired tones in order to compare full voice with *mezza voce* on the vowels [e] and [a] using the pitches *D4* and *F4*. The four

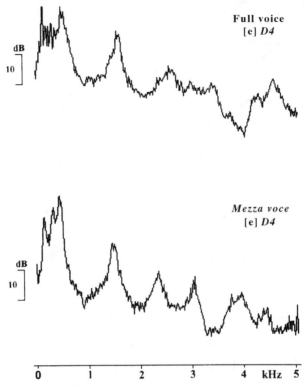

Figure A.7D Second example.

spectrograms in Figure A.7D clearly show the reduction in the resonances of the vocal tract when singing *mezza voce* as compared to full
voice. This is especially apparent in the regions of F_2 and the singer's
formant, which characteristically give the tenor voice its 'edge.' The
closed quotients are presented as a table. The data shown in Figure
A.7E illustrate that full voice consistently had a larger closed quotient
than *mezza voce*.

Respiratory Control of Vibrato

Garcia and others apparently rejected the vibrato in the artistic voice.
However, there is reason to question whether he and other opponents of
the vibrato meant to reject all vibrato, or only vibrato that deviated from
certain acceptable norms of rate, extent, intensity, and timbre. As shown

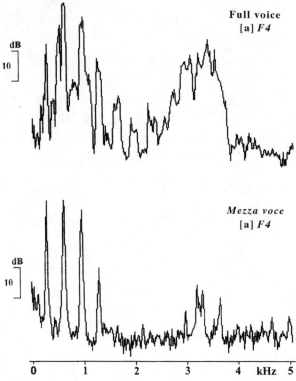

Figure A.7D Third example.

in chapter 5, some modern researchers have suggested that singers can control some aspects of vibrato by 'pumping' the chest apparatus, that is, by modulating the subglottal pressure slightly in synchrony with the vibrato. This is a way to coordinate the respiratory, laryngeal, and resonance systems, and influence the character of the vibrato.

In this pilot study, we attempted to measure the influence of chest-pumping on the vibrato. We compared two sung tones on the vowel [a], on the pitch E♭4. In the first example (A), the 'normal' vibrato was not consciously controlled by the singer, but was simply allowed to function 'on its own.' In the second example (B), the singer used a slight chest-pumping action which caused a modulation in the breath pressure that affected the vibrato.

Figure A.8 shows that both forms of vibrato had a stable sound pressure level, although (B) rose slightly toward the end of the phonation. The fluctuation of the sound pressure level for each cycle of the vibrato

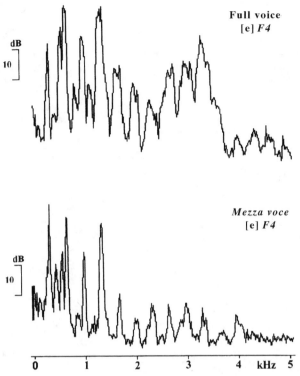

Figure A.7D Fourth example.

is seen more clearly in (B) where chest-pumping is used. This can probably be attributed to the undulations of the breath pressure (shown here
as esophageal pressure), which are more marked in (B) than in (A).
There may also be an acoustical factor present, as the undulating frequency modulation causes the harmonics to approach certain formants,
thereby boosting their intensity.

Example (A) shows a modulation of esophageal pressure of about 1
cmH_2O, and (B) has a modulation of about 2.5 cmH_2O. Example (A) also
shows a higher amplitude of airflow than (B). In both examples the airflow took more than two seconds to stabilize and become regular. This
may have been due to the aural feedback problem caused by the mask,
which caused a longer reaction time than in normal singing. The vibrato
rate was slightly affected by chest-pumping; example (A) had a rate of
about 4.6 undulations per second, and (B) was marginally faster, at
about 4.9.

Pitch	Vowel	Phonation	Closed Quotient
D4	[a]	Full voice	76%
D4	[a]	*Mezza voce*	53%
D4	[e]	Full voice	83%
D4	[e]	*Mezza voce*	53%
F4	[a]	Full voice	74%
F4	[a]	*Mezza voce*	61%
F4	[e]	Full voice	63%
F4	[e]	*Mezza voce*	60 %

Figure A.7E Closed quotients of full voice and *mezza voce*: using the vowels [a] and [e], singing *D4* and *E4*, using the *VoceVista* program.

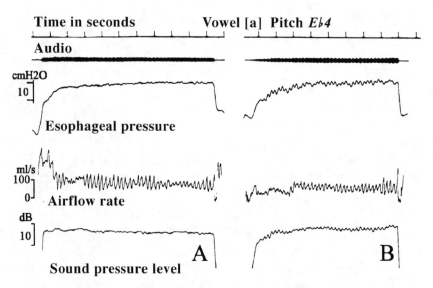

Figure A.8 Respiratory control of vibrato: normal vibrato (A) and vibrato with chest-pumping (B), sung on *E♭4* using the vowel [a].

Conclusions

The Groningen protocols described above must be regarded as anecdotal, in that they are based on my own singing, using myself as a control. The experiments probably cannot be replicated by others, due to individual differences in vocal technique and training among singers. While the protocols were based on pedagogical concepts, especially those of Garcia and the Lampertis, it is not possible to tell how closely my approximations of paired tones came to meeting the ideals of these teachers.

The focus of Garcia's vocal method was strong glottal closure, which gave brightness and breath economy to the tone. Our experiments showed that there are clear differences between loose and firm glottal settings. Videostroboscopy revealed the differences in glottal length and closed quotients between the two settings. Airflow rates were shown to differ significantly between the two settings. Glottal resistance in firm phonation resulted in higher subglottal pressures. Strong high-frequency components during firm phonation gave the tone brightness, while the relative weakness of those components during loose phonation made the tone veiled or dull, as Garcia described. In the comparison of full voice and *mezza voce* it was seen that the high-frequency components were greatly diminished in *mezza voce*. When a tone has a lowered F_1, as well as a singer's formant or a dominant F_2, it may satisfy the historical description of *chiaroscuro*. One protocol demonstrated the contrast between a belted tone and a covered tone on a single phonation, illustrating the effects of laryngeal lowering on the resonances of the vocal tract. Regarding the *messa di voce*, it was demonstrated that this manoeuvre can be performed in two essentially different ways, as implied by the descriptions of Garcia and the Lampertis, with glottal closure and airflow rates being the main parameters for comparison. Finally, it was shown that the vibrato, which is often considered merely a laryngeal phenomenon, can be influenced by small periodic undulations in the subglottal pressure which are produced by chest-pumping.

In a general way, then, the results of the protocols presented here seem to be consistent with some of the main vocal theories discussed in the previous chapters. Not everyone will agree with this, which is understandable in a field as controversial as vocal technique. But perhaps some singer-scholars will be motivated to enter the laboratory environment themselves and seek answers to some of these issues. This would represent an important advance over mere verbal debate about the meaning of historical treatises on singing. The voice is resistant to giving up its secrets, but every new venture may contribute to our understanding of singing.

Notes

Introduction

1 Pleasants 1966, 19–20; see also Duey 1951, 3–12.
2 Goldschmidt 1890; Chrysander 1891–4; Pleasants 1966.
3 Haas 1929; Bukofzer 1947; *Rosensteil* 1982, 325; Neumann 1978, 27.
4 Della Corte 1933.
5 Duey 1951; Foreman 1969; Celletti 1991.
6 Hitchcock 1988, 43ff.
7 R. Miller 1986b, 195.
8 Foreman 1969, 1–3; see also Reid 1950, 155.

1: The *coup de la glotte*: A Stroke of Genius

1 For biographical information see Mackinlay 1908; Paschke 1986–7; Garcia 1984, ii–xi; Mackenzie 1890, 128; Fuchs 1958; Timberlake 1989–90.
2 Goldschmidt 1890, 1891, 1901–4, 1907.
3 For details, including children's voices, see Titze 1994, 178–82, and Titze 1988, 31.
4 Van den Berg 1960, 1968b; Luchsinger and Arnold 1965, 72; Zemlin 1968, 136–57; Baken 1971; Laver 1980, 106–9.
5 Mackenzie 1890, 11. Mackenzie's book was first published in 1886. The seventh edition (1890) is especially valuable in that it includes Mackenzie's responses to Garcia's criticisms.
6 See Vennard and Isshiki 1964.
7 Browne and Behnke 1904, 153–4; see also Vennard and Isshiki 1964, 15–16.
8 Zemlin 1968, 175–6; Luchsinger and Arnold 1965, 85; R. Miller 1977, 2–4.

9 Van den Berg 1958. See also Vennard 1961; Zemlin 1968, 175; Broad 1973, 141–3; Catford 1977, 32–6.

10 Sundberg 1987, 39, 80–92. See also Gauffin and Sundberg 1980; Leanderson, Sundberg, and von Euler 1985.

11 Benade 1976, 380–1; Large 1972; Large, Iwata, and von Leden 1970; Lieberman 1986a, 32; Luchsinger and Arnold 1965, 66–7; Reed 1982; Rothenburg 1981; Schutte 1980, 3–4; Sundberg 1973; Sundberg 1977a; Sundberg 1980; Sundberg 1981; Sundberg 1987, 79; Troup 1982; van den Berg 1956, 47; van den Berg 1958; van den Berg 1960; Wyke 1974a, 76–89, 91, 288; Zemlin 1968, 177–83.

12 Laver 1980, 97–9. For a more detailed discussion, see Titze 1994, 94–100.

13 Titze 1994, 248; Winckel 1952, 95; Mårtensson and Skoglund 1964, 332; Broad 1973, 161.

2: *Chiaroscuro*: The Tractable Tract

1 Edward Foreman's translation, *Practical Reflections on Figured Singing* (Mancini 1967), compares the editions of 1774 and 1777.

2 See Sanford 1979, 1–22, for a review of the early treatises.

3 See Cerone 1613, chapter 78. Cerone acknowledges his source with a marginal note 'Lod. Zac 68.'

4 See Pleasants 1995 and 1966, 165–70.

5 Chorley, 1844, 1:62–76. See also Pleasants 1995 and 1966, 161–5.

6 See Titze 1994, 136–68, for a detailed discussion of this matter.

7 Miller and Schutte 1990, 231. See also Sundberg 1977a.

8 Bartholomew 1934, 1945; Winckel 1953; Vennard 1967, 119–20.

9 Zemlin 1968, 133–5; Sundberg 1974; Luchsinger and Arnold 1965, 78; Vennard 1967, 108; Shipp 1977.

10 For more sources, see Fields 1947, Burgin 1973, and Monahan 1978.

11 See Hines 1994 for interviews with some of these singers.

3: Registers: Some Tough Breaks

1 For a review of the literature, see Mackenzie 1890, 237–56; Large 1972; Large 1973b; Fields 1947; Fields 1973; Broad 1973; Burgin 1973; Monahan 1978; Mörner, Fransson, and Fant 1964.

2 See Vicentino 1555, 80; Maffei 1562, 26; Giustiniani 1962, 71; Ulrich 1912, 80.

3 Translated in Strunk 1950, 299.

4 Translated in Strunk 1950, 317.

5 Galliard's translation is available in a facsimile edition 1968. There is also a

fine edition by Edward Foreman 1986 which includes the original Italian side-by-side with the English translation, along with bibliographical details.

6 This German version has recently been translated into English as *Introduction to the Art of Singing* by Julianne C. Baird (1995).

7 See biographical details in Tosi 1986, xvi–xxi; see also Hawkins 1875, 823–4; Tosi 1743, viii–ix; Häbock 1927, 342.

8 Häbock 1923, 1927; Heriot 1956; Pleasants 1966.

9 'A Record of Singers' 1982, HLM 7252.

10 Mancini 1967; for further bibliographical and biographical information, see pages v–vi.

11 Vogler 1778, 18 *seq*; Lasser 1798, 45–6; Engelbrunner 1803, 103–9.

12 Petri 1767, 206; translation in Sanford 1979, 43–4.

13 Stendahl/Coe 1956, 373; see also Chorley 1862, 87–8.

14 Hiller 1780, 6–7. See also Häbock 1927, 96–7, and Duey 1950, 119–120.

15 Martini 1792, 5; Sanford 1979, 46.

16 Mengozzi 1803, 12; Garaudé 1830, 22.

17 Quoted in Pleasants 1966, 167.

18 At the *26th Annual Symposium: Care of the Professional Voice* (Philadelphia, 6 June 1997) Mr Tran Kuang Hai gave a remarkable demonstration of overtone singing by singing the tune 'Ode to Joy' over a drone.

19 Browne and Behnke 1904, 129–37; see also Monahan 1978, 148.

20 Shakespeare 1924, 38; see also 1910, 40.

21 Oncley 1973; Hollien, Gould, and Johnson 1976.

22 Van den Berg 1960 and 1968b. See also Luchsinger and Arnold 1965, 79–80.

23 Large 1968; Colton 1972, 1973b; Colton and Hollien 1973b; Levarie and Levy 1980; Sundberg 1973, 1987.

24 Colton 1973a; Colton and Hollien 1973a; Hollien 1974; Lieberman 1968a, 31–2.

25 Rothenberg 1981; Sundberg 1981; Lieberman 1968a, 31–2.

26 Preissler 1939, 65–85; Luchsinger and Arnold 1965, 95; Deinse, Frateur, and Keizer 1974, 431.

27 Keidar, Hurtig, and Titze 1987, 232; Appelman 1967, 93; Large 1968, 1969, 1973a; Lerman and Duffy 1970; Colton 1972, 1973a, 1973b; Colton and Hollien 1973a, 1973b.

28 For a review of the literature, see Fischer 1993, 180–3; Large 1972; Bunch 1977; Luchsinger and Arnold 1965, 103–7.

29 Sonninen 1968, 80–6; Luchsinger and Arnold 1965, 76–7; Shipp 1975, 1977; Honda and Baer 1982, 66.

30 Sullivan 1989; Miles and Hollien 1990; Schutte and D.G. Miller 1993; D.G. Miller and Schutte 1994.

31 Van den Berg 1962, 95–6; see also van den Berg 1960, 23.

32 See Kelsey 1950, 58–9; Vennard 1967, 65–6; R. Miller 1977, 106–7; 1986, 118, 136–42; Proctor 1980b, 111.

33 Van den Berg 1960; Large, Iwata, and von Leden 1970, 393.

34 See Sundberg 1977a, 1977b, 1980, 1985a, 1987; Benade 1976; D.G. Miller and Schutte 1990, 1994

35 D.G. Miller 1994, 31; Schutte and Miller 1986, 390–1.

36 Van den Berg 1960, 25; Hollien 1968, 1971, 1974; Hollien, Girard, and Coleman 1977; Hollien and Keister 1978.

37 Rubin and Hirt 1960, 1317; van den Berg 1968a, 21; Catford 1977, 103.

4: *Appoggio*: The Breath Be Dammed!

1 See Duey 1951, 174; F. Lamperti 1884, 1; Lamperti 1916, 5.

2 See, for example, Vennard 1967, 18–35.

3 Translated in Fortune 1954, 215; the entire preface is printed in Goldschmidt 1890, 76 ff.

4 For a review of these other works, see Sanford 1979, 80, and Duey 1951, 148.

5 See, for example, Corri 1810 and Nathan 1836.

6 W.E. Brown 1957, 43. See also G.B. Lamperti 1905, 6–7.

7 W.E. Brown 1957, 134. Compare this to Fischer 1993, 177.

8 See the discussion in Fischer 1993, 10–12, and in Jander 1980b, 343–4.

9 See Fucito and Beyer 1922, 118, 127, and Hines 1994, 60, 102, 222, 304.

10 See Titze 1994, 263–9, for details of subglottal formants.

11 Hixon and Hoffman 1979, 9–10; Leanderson and Sundberg 1988, 11.

12 See Leanderson and Sundberg 1988; Bouhuys 1977; Bouhuys, Mead, and Proctor 1968; Bouhuys, Proctor, and Mead 1966; Proctor 1974, 52–3; Proctor 1980a, 73, 107–8; Sears 1977, 87–90.

13 Proctor 1974, 53; see also Luchsinger and Arnold 1965, 13; Bouhuys, Proctor, and Mead 1966.

14 Wyke 1974d, 297. See also Hixon 1987, 362–3; Mead, Hixon, and Goldman 1974, 58; Proctor 1974, 52–3; Proctor 1980a, 107–8.

15 Proctor 1974, 52–3; Proctor 1980a, 72–82; Baken 1980, 10–12.

16 Leanderson and Sundberg 1988; Leanderson, Sundberg, and von Euler 1985, 1987a, 1987b.

17 Leanderson, Sundberg, von Euler, and Lagerkrantz 1984, 218.

18 For a description of the experimental methods used in determining subglottal pressures, see Proctor 1980a, 36–7; van den Berg 1956a; Schutte 1992; Schutte 1980; Lieberman 1968b.

19 Catford 1977, 29; Khambata 1977, 63; Proctor 1980a, 36, 93; Sears 1977, 84; see also Ladefoged, in Wyke 1974a, 477.

20 Sears 1977, 82; van den Berg 1958, 241; Cavagna and Margaria 1968; Schutte 1980; Catford 1977, 26–36.

21 Proctor 1980a, 55, 62, 79; Proctor 1974, 47; see also Proctor and Ladefoged in Wyke 1974a, 476–7.

22 See Proctor 1980a, 69; Schutte 1980, 20–5; Cavagna and Margaria 1968, 162; Leanderson and Sundberg 1988, 7–8.

23 Zemlin 1968, 204; Rubin, LeCover, and Vennard 1967; Schutte 1980, 149–55; Large 1972, 32.

24 Large and Iwata 1971; Large and Iwata 1976; Large 1980b.

25 See, for example, Proctor 1980a, 108–10.

26 Wyke 1974a, 477–8; see also *Transcripts* 1980, 40.

27 Bishop 1974; Wyke 1974a, 68–9; Wilder 1980b, 13; Campbell 1974, 3.

28 Wyke 1974a, 68–9; Gould and Okamura 1974a, 356–9; Horii and Weinberg 1980, 62–3.

29 See R. Miller 1977, 28; Hines 1994.

5: Vocal Tremulousness: The Pulse of Singing

1 Zacconi 1592, fol. 60; see also MacClintock 1979, 73, for an alternative translation.

2 Ganassi 1959, 9; see also chapters 23 and 24.

3 Manfredini 1775, 7; see also Mancini 1967, 120.

4 For recordings of these singers, see *A Record of Singers*, HML 7252 and HML 7255.

5 Hamlet and Palmer 1974; Hakes, Shipp, and Doherty 1987; Shipp and Hakes 1986; Hakes, Doherty, and Shipp 1990.

6 See Seashore 1932 and 1936. For summaries see also Seashore 1938, 32–53; Seashore 1947, 55–70; Kwalwasser 1926.

7 For a review of the literature, see Large and Iwata 1976, 42–4; Large 1980b; Campbell and Michel 1980, 50–1.

8 See, for example, Bartholomew 1934, 293; Luchsinger and Arnold 1965, 93; Mason and Zemlin 1966, Large and Iwata 1971; E. Schubert 1983, 183; Rothman and Arroyo 1987.

9 See Sundberg 1987, 168; Rothenberg, D.G. Miller, and Molitor 1988; for a recent update on the state of research in vibrato, see Dejonckere, Hirano, and Sundberg 1995.

10 Schoen 1922, 256; see also Zemlin 1968, 204–5.

11 Seashore 1932, 367; also see Zemlin 1968, 205.

12 Mason 1971; Damsté, Reinders, and Tempelaars 1983, 17; Ramig and Shipp 1987, 166; Shipp, Leanderson, and Sundberg 1980b; Titze 1994, 289.

13 Schoen 1922, 257–8; Shipp, Sundberg, and Haglund 1985, 117; Hsiao, Solomon, Luschei, and Titze 1994.

14 Thomas Shipp in *Transcripts* 1985, 1:123; see also Sundberg 1985a, 98.

15 Winkel 1953, 245; Luchsinger and Arnold 1965, 92; Shipp, Sundberg, and Haglund 1983, 116; Sundberg 1985a, 98, 1987, 104; Schutte and Miller 1991, 217; Titze 1994, 291.

16 Shipp, Leanderson, and Sundberg 1980b, 46; Titze 1994, 291; Rothman 1986.

17 Titze 1994, 291; see also 'Discussion on Vibrato' 1987, 170.

18 Bartholomew 1934, 293–4; Luchsinger and Arnold 1965, 94; Wyke 1974a, 261; Sundberg 1987, 164; Kwalwasser 1926, 223.

19 Bartholomew 1945, 22–4; Vennard 1967, 205; Oncley 1971, 136; Sundberg 1980, 85; Sundberg 1987, 164, 183.

20 Bartholomew 1934, 293; Luchsinger and Arnold 1965, 15; Mason and Zemlin 1966, 16–17; Zemlin 1968, 205; Smith 1970; Zantema and van den Berg 1956; Appelman 1967, 23; 1971; Appelman and Smith 1986.

21 Sundberg 1980, 85; see also 'Discussion of Vibrato' 1987, 169.

22 Bartholomew 1934, 293; Sundberg 1987, 163.

23 Winckel 1953; Luchsinger and Arnold 1965, 94; Shipp and Hakes 1986.

24 Vennard 1967, 202; Vennard and von Leden 1967, 19–26.

25 See the panel discussion in *Transcripts* 1980, 64.

26 Vennard 1967, 197; see also Neilson in *Transcripts* 1980, 1:62.

27 Seashore 1932, 108–9. See also Metfessel 1926.

28 Bartholomew 1945, 24–6, 144; Luchsinger and Arnold 1965, 92; Rothman, Nielson, and Hicks 1980, 53; Schillinger 1948, 18.

29 *Transcripts* 1985, 1:122; see also Shipp and Hakes 1986, 72.

30 *Transcripts* 1985, 1:118; Sundberg 1995, 54.

6: Idiom and Expression: The Soul of Singing

1 See H.M. Brown 1976; Ferand 1956, 1961, 1966; Horsley 1951; Kuhn 1902.

2 Luzzaschi 1601; see Newcomb 1980, 1:20–52; Fenlon 1980, 1:124–7; Einstein 1949, 2:844–7; Solerti 1891, lxxiv–lxxv, passim.

3 For a listing of these, see Sartori 1952.

4 For a translation of excerpts from their writings, see Strunk 1950.

5 Zacconi 1592, fol. 56; Bovicelli 1594, 8–9; Praetorius 1619, 3:231; Bernhard 1973, 17–18.

6 See the excerpts printed in Solerti 1903.

7 Printed in Solerti 1903, 51; translated in Strunk 1950, 371.

8 Printed in Solerti 1903, 76–89; see also Fortune 1980, 27.

9 For more on this subject, see Palisca 1956 and Arnold and Fortune 1968, 133–226.

10 See Monahan 1978, 215–16; Garaudé 1830, 30–8; Garcia 1975, 82–6; Stockhausen 1884, 37; Mackenzie 1890, 101–2.

11 Mancini 1967, 135–6; see also Foreman's comments on p. 8.

12 Garcia 1847, 2:24; 1975, 75–6; see also Garcia 1894, 62.

13 Garcia 1847, 2:24–5; 1975, 75–7. See also Hudson 1994, 65–81.

14 Bellman 1989; Hudson 1994, 189–237.

15 Hudson 1994, 195; Bellman 1989, 67.

16 Regarding dance songs, see Bukofzer 1947, 38–42; Aldrich 1966.

17 See Palisca 1981, 22–7; Fortune 1953.

18 See *New Grove* 1980, 3:343–4; Ratner 1980, 280–1.

19 See *New Grove* 1980, 4:374.

20 See Paget 1930; Merleau-Ponty 1962, 184–95; Winckel 1967, 157; Coker 1972, 10–20, 230; Proctor 1980b, 2; Fonagy 1981; Levarie and Levy 1980, 72–9.

21 *Tito Schipa: Opera and Song Recital*. Angel COLH 117, side 2, band 1.

22 See Sherman 1996 for more information on orchestral portamento.

7: *Bel canto*: Context and Controversy

1 Donato and his music are discussed in Einstein 1949, 1:448–453.

2 Calmo 1888, 295; translated in Einstein 1949, 2:843.

3 See chapter 12, 'Pseudo-Monody and Monody,' in Einstein 1949, 2:836–49.

4 Luzzaschi 1601. See also Newcomb 1980, 7–23, 49–50, 67–89, 183–4; Fenlon 1982, 161–81; Einstein 1949, chapters 11 and 12; Solerti 1891; Solerti 1895, vol. 1; MacClintock 1979, 28–9.

5 Valdrighi 1884, as translated in Einstein 1949, 2:539–40; see also 2:825–6.

6 Giustiniani 1962, 69–70; quoted in Fenlon 1980, 126–7.

7 Striggio's letters are printed in Gandolfi 1913, 527–38; portions are translated in Einstein 1949, 2:846–7.

8 The poem is printed in Einstein 1949, 844.

9 For the most recent account of Caccini, see Kirkendale 1993, 119–80; for other biographical information, see H.M. Brown 1981.

10 Comments by Giovanni de' Bardi (1580) and Pietro de' Bardi (1634) are translated in Strunk 1950 (pp. 290–301 and 363–6 respectively). See also Bonini 1979, 140–4; Giustiniani 1962, 71; Della Valle 1903, 143–7.

11 Caccini 1602, iv; Caccini 1970, 51; Silbert 1946, 50–62.

12 Comments by Peri and Caccini are translated in Strunk 1950 (pp. 375 and 371

respectively). For comments by Cavallieri, see Solerti 1902, 812. For comments by Bonini, see Solerti 1903, 137.

13 Caccini 1602, i–ii; Caccini 1970, 45–6. For a different translation, see Strunk 1950, 379.
14 See H.M. Brown 1981; Willier 1983.
15 Häbock 1923, 1927; Duey 1951; Heriot 1956; Pleasants 1966.
16 Duey 1951, 44. See also Foreman 1969; Celletti 1991, 7–8, 108–14.
17 Celani 1907, 86, 766. See also Canal 1879, 695.
18 Canal 1879, 696–7. See also Celani 1907, 766.
19 According to Giovanni Battista Doni (1763, 2:245), the ladies had memorized a repertoire of 330 pieces.
20 Stendahl 1956, 366; Shakespeare 1910, 'Preface.'
21 See Arundell 1957, 309; Lang 1966, 170 seq.
22 For source readings on these controversies, see Strunk 1950.
23 Le Cerf de la Viéville 1704–6, 1:333; translated in Sanford 1979, 6–7.
24 For a thorough discussion of the haute-contre, see Regier 1996.
25 For further examples, see Pleasants 1966 and Petty 1980.
26 See Foreman's remarks in Tosi 1986, 116, n 1.
27 Regarding the latter, see Seiler 1881, 15; Behnke 1883, 1–7; Mackenzie 1890, 115.
28 F. Lamperti 1916, 5–8. Lamperti first published this essay as the preface in his Guida teorica-practica-elementare per lo studio del canto (1864). See also F. Lamperti 1884, 23–6.
29 For more on Verdi, see Gatti 1955, 132–3; Pleasants 1966, 290–1; Nicolaisen 1980, 60–7.
30 Mackinlay 1908, 163–5; B. Marchesi 1935, 155–6.
31 See, for instance, Kelsey 1950, 10 and 1954, 45.

Appendix: The Groningen Protocols

1 For a description of the various laboratory procedures used in voice research, see Baken 1996.
2 See the drawings in Garcia 1984, xxii–xxiii.
3 See Schutte 1980, 147–62. I am referred to as 'Subject 13, a Canadian tenor.'

References

Acton, Charles. 1978. *Irish Music and Musicians*. Dublin: Eason and Son.

Agricola, Johann Friedrich. 1995. *Introduction to the Art of Singing*. Translated by Julianne C. Baird. Cambridge Musical Texts and Monographs. Cambridge and New York: Cambridge University Press. [This work is a translation of and commentary on Pierfrancesco Tosi's *Opinioni de cantori* (1757), first published in German as *Anleitung zur Singekunst* (Berlin, 1757). Facsimile reprint, ed. Erwin Jacobi (Celle: Moeck, 1966).]

Agricola, Martin. 1545. *Musica Instrumentalis Deudsch*. Wittemberg: Rhau.

Aldrich, Putnam. 1966. *Rhythm in Seventeenth-century Italian Monody*. New York: W.W. Norton.

Allen, Warren Dwight. 1962. *Philosophies of Music History*. New York: Dover. [First published in 1939.]

Anderson, Emily, ed. 1985. *The Letters of Mozart and His Family*. Third edition (revised). New York: W.W. Norton.

Apel, Willi. 1969. *Harvard Dictionary of Music*. 2nd edition, revised and enlarged. Cambridge: Harvard University Press.

Appelman, Ralph D. 1967. *The Science of Vocal Pedagogy*. Bloomington: Indiana University Press.

– . 1971. 'Cinefluoroscopic Observations of Abdominal Muscular Functions in their Relation to the Support-Vibrato Syndrome in Singing.' Abstract of paper presented at the Acoustical Society of America conference, 6 November 1970. *Journal of the Acoustical Society of America* 49: 137.

Appelman, Ralph D., and Ethel Smith. 1986. 'Cineflouroscopic and Electromyographic Observations of Abdominal Muscular Function in its Support of Vibrato.' In *Transcripts of the Fourteenth Symposium: Care of the Professional Voice* 1: 79–82. New York: The Voice Foundation.

Armin, Georg. 1909. *Das Stauprinzip und die Lehre vom Dualismus der menschlichen Stimme*. Strassburg im Elsaß: Carl Bongard.

– . 1930. *Enrico Caruso: Eine Untersuchung der Stimme Carusos und ihre Verhältnis zum Stauprincip in Spiegel eigenen Erlebnisses*. Leipzig: Kistner & Siegel.

– . 1931. *Die Technik der Breitspannung: Ein Beitrag über die horizontal-vertikalen Spannkräfte beim Aufbau der Stimme nach dem 'Stauprinzip.'* Berlin-Wilmersdorf: Verlag der Gesellschaft für Stimmkultur.

– . 1946. *Die Meisterregeln der Stimmbildungskunst*. Berlin-Wilmersdorf: Gesellschaft für Stimmkultur. [Renamed: Leutenberg i. Thür: Landhaus Marga].

– . [n.d.] *Von der Urkraft der Stimme*. Third edition. Lippstadt: Kistner & Siegel.

Arnold, Denis. 1970. 'Monteverdi's Singers.' *The Musical Times* 111: 982–5.

– . 1985. 'Performing Practice.' In *The New Monteverdi Companion*, edited by Denis Arnold and Nigel Fortune. London: Faber & Faber, 319–6.

Arnold, Denis, and Nigel Fortune. 1968. *The Monteverdi Companion*. New York: W.W. Norton.

Arundell, Denis. 1957. *The Critic at the Opera: Contemporary Comments on Opera in London over Three Centuries*. London: Ernest Benn.

Bacilly, Bénigne de. 1968. *Commentary upon the Art of Proper Singing*. Translated and edited by Austin B. Caswell. New York: Institute of Medieval Music. [First published in French as *Remarques curieuses sur l'art bien chanter* (Paris, 1668; 2nd edition 1679).]

Bacon, Richard Mackenzie. 1966. *Elements of Vocal Science: Being a Philosophical Enquiry into Some of the Principles of Singing*. New edition with notes and introduction by Edward Foreman. Champaign, Illinois: Pro Musica Press. [First published London: Baldwin, Cradock & Joy, 1824.]

Baken, R.J. 1971. 'Neuromuscular Spindles in the Intrinsic Muscles of a Human Larynx.' *Folia Phoniatrica* 23: 204–10.

– . 1980. 'Respiratory Mechanisms: Introduction and Overview.' In *Transcripts of the Eighth Symposium: Care of the Professional Voice* 2: 9–13. New York: The Voice Foundation.

– . 1996. *Clinical Measurement of Speech and Voice*. San Diego: Singular Publishing Group.

Barbier, Patrick. 1989. *Triomf en Tragiek der Castraten*. Utrecht: A.W. Bruna Uitgevers.

Bardi, Giovanni de'. [*ca.* 1580]. *Discorso mandato a Giulio Caccini*. Translated in Strunk 1950, 290–301.

Bartholomew, Wilmer T. 1934. 'A Physical Definition of "Good Voice Quality" in the Male Voice.' Reprinted in Large 1980a, 299–306. [First published in *Journal of the Acoustical Society of America* 6: 25–33.]

– . 1945. *Acoustics of Music*. New York: Prentice-Hall.

– . 1983. 'Terminology in Voice Teaching.' *Journal of Research in Singing* 6(2): 1–6. [Paper presented at the Convention of the National Association of Teachers of Singing in St. Louis, Missouri, 28 December 1953.]

Bassani, Giovanni Battista. 1585. *Ricercate, passaggi et cadentie*. Venezia: Appresso Giacomo Vincenzi & Ricciardo Amadino.

Bataille, Charles. 1861. *Nouvelles recherches sur la phonation: Mémoire présenté et lu à l'Académie des sciences le 15 avril 1861*. Paris: Victor Masson et fils.

Behnke, Emil. 1880. *The Mechanism of the Human Voice*. London: J. Curwen & Sons.

– . 1881. *The Mechanism of the Human Voice*. Second edition. London: J. Curwen & Sons.

– . 1883. *The Mechanism of the Human Voice*. Third edition. London: J. Curwen & Sons.

Bell, A. Melville. 1867. *Visible Speech: The Science of Universal Alphabetics*. London: Marshall.

Bellman, Jonathan. 1989. 'Chopin and the Cantabile Style.' *Historical Performances* 2(2): 63–71.

Benade, Arthur H. 1976. *Fundamentals of Musical Acoustics*. London and New York: Oxford University Press.

Bérard, Jean-Baptiste. 1969. *L'art du chant*. Translated with commentary by Sidney Murray. Milwaukee: Pro Musica Press. [First published Paris: Dessaint & Saillant, 1755.]

Berlioz, Hector. 1914. *Gluck and His Operas, with an Account of their Relation to Musical Art*. Translated by Edward Evans from Berlioz's *À travers chant*. London: W.M. Reeves. [Portion translated in MacClintock 1979, 414–32. *À travers chant* first published Paris, 1862.]

– . 1963. *Evenings in the Orchestra*. Translated from the French by C.R. Fortescue. Harmondsworth: Penguin Books. [First published in French as *Les soirées de l'orchestre* (Paris, 1852).]

Bernhard, Christoph. *ca.* 1650. *Von der Singe-Kunst oder Maniera*.

– . 1973. 'The Treatises of Christoph Bernhard.' Translated by Walter Hilsa. *The Music Forum* 3: 13–29. [Includes translation of *Von der Singe-Kunst oder Maniera* (*ca.* 1650).]

Bishop, Beverly. 1974. 'Abdominal Muscle Activity During Respiration.' In Wyke 1974a, 12–24.

Bonini, Severo. 1979. *Discorsi e regole*. A bilingual edition, translated and edited by Maryann Bonino. Provo, Utah: Brigham Young University Press. [Manuscript *ca.* 1640–50]

Bontempi, Giovanni Andrea Angelini. 1695. *Historia Musica*. Perugia: Costantini.

Bouhuys, Arend. 1977. *The Physiology of Breathing*. New York: Grune and Stratton.

Bouhuys, A., D. Proctor, and J. Mead. 1966. 'Kinetic Aspects of Singing.' *Journal of Applied Physiology* 21(2): 483–96. Reprinted in Large 1980a, 58–87.

Bouhuys, A., J. Mead, D. Proctor, and K. Stevens. 1968. 'Pressure Flow Events During Singing.' *Annals of the American Academy of Science* 155: 165–76.

Bovicelli, Giovanni Battista. 1594. *Regole, passagi di musica*. Venezia: Giacomo Vincenzi. [Facsimile reprint edited by Nanie Bridgman, *Documenta Musicologica*, I. Reihe. (Kassel: Bärenreiter, 1957).]

Brand-Seltei, Erna. 1972. *Belcanto: Eine Kulturgeschichte der Gesangskunst*. Wilhelmshaven: Heinrichshofens Verlag.

Bridgman, Nanie. 1956. 'Girolamo Camillo Maffei et sa lettre sur le chant.' *Revue de musicologie* 38: 3–34.

Broad, David J. 1973. 'Phonation.' In Minifie, Hixon, and Williams 1973, 127–68.

Brodnitz, Friedrich S. 1965. *Vocal Rehabilitation*. Third edition. Rochester, Minnesota: American Academy of Ophthalmology and Otolaryngology.

– . 1975. 'The Age of the Castrato Voice.' *Journal of Speech and Hearing Disorders* 40: 291–5.

Brown, Howard Mayer. 1976. *Embellishing 16th-century Music*. Early Music Series, I. London: Oxford University Press.

– . 1981. 'The Geography of Florentine Monody: Caccini at Home and Abroad.' *Early Music* 9: 147–68.

Brown John. 1763. *Dissertation on the Rise, Union, and Power, the Progressions, Separations, and Corruptions, of Poetry and Music*. London: L. Davis & C. Reymers.

Brown, William Earl. 1957. *Vocal Wisdom: Maxims of Giovanni Battista Lamperti*. Enlarged edition. New York: Arno Press. [First published in 1931.]

Browne, Lennox. 1876. *Medical Hints on the Production and Management of the Singing Voice*. London: Chappell & Co.

Browne, Lennox, and Emil Behnke. 1904. *Voice, Song and Speech: A Practical Guide for Singers and Speakers from the Combined View of Surgeon and Voice Trainer*. New York: G.P. Putnam's Sons.

Bruns, Paul. 1922. *Carusos Technik*. Charlottenburg: Verlag Walter Göritz.

– . 1929. *Minimalluft und Stütze*. Berlin-Charlottenburg: Walter Göritz.

Buelow, George J. 1983, 'Johann Mattheson and the Invention of the Affektenlehre.' In *New Mattheson Studies*, edited by George Buelow and H.J. Marx. Cambridge: Cambridge University Press, 393–407.

Bukofzer, Manfred. 1947. *Music in the Baroque Era*. New York: W.W. Norton.

Bunch, M. 1977. 'A Survey of the Research on Covered and Open Voice Qualities.' *Bulletin of the National Association of Teachers of Singing* (February): 11–18.

Burgin, John Carrol. 1973. *Teaching Singing*. Metuchen, NJ: Scarecrow Press.

Burney, Charles. 1770. *Music, Men, and Manners in France and Italy*. British Museum add. MS 35122. [Edited with an introduction by H. Edmund Poole (London: The Folio Society, 1969). Portions reprinted in MacClintock 1979, 364–7.]

– . 1773. *The Present state of Music in France and Italy*. Second edition, corrected. London: T. Becket and Co. [Reprint edition, *Dr. Burney's Musical Tours in Europe*, vol. 1, edited by Percy A. Scholes (London: Oxford University Press, 1959).]

– . 1775. *The Present state of Music in Germany, the Netherlands, and United Provinces*. Second edition, corrected. London: T. Becket and Co. [Reprint edition, *Dr. Burney's Musical Tours in Europe*, vol. 2, edited by Percy A. Scholes (London: Oxford University Press, 1959). Portions reprinted in MacClintock 1979, 368–72.]

– . 1935. *A General History of Music*. Edition with critical and historical notes by Frank Mercer. London: G.T. Foulis. [First published London, 1789. Portions reprinted in MacClintock 1979, 256–66.]

Caccini, Giulio. 1602. *Le nuove musiche*. Firenze: Marescotti. [Facsimile edition New York: Performers' Facsimiles 35, n.d.]

– . 1614. *Nuove musiche e nuova maniera di scriverle*. Fiorenza: Appresso Zanobi Pignoni e Compagni.

– . 1970. *Le nuove musiche*. English translation by H. Wiley Hitchcock. Madison, WI: A-R Editions. [Translation of Caccini 1602.]

– . 1978. *Nuove musiche e nuova maniera di scriverle*. English translation by H. Wiley Hitchcock. Madison, WI: A-R Editions. [Translation of Caccini 1614]

Calmo, Andrea. 1888. *Le lettere di Messer Andrea Calmo ... Introduzione ed illustrazioni di Vittorio Rossi*. Torino: Loeschler.

Campbell, E.J.M. 1974. 'Muscular Activity in Normal and Abnormal Ventilation.' In Wyke 1974a, 3–11.

Campbell, William M., and John Michel. 1980. 'The Effects of Auditory Masking on Vocal Vibrato.' In *Transcripts of the Eighth Symposium: Care of the Professional Voice* 1: 50–6. New York: The Voice Foundation.

Canal, Pietro. 1879. *Della musica in Mantova: Notizie tratte principalmente dall'Archivio Gonzaga*. Extracted from *Memorie del reale istituto veneto di scienze, lettere ed arti* XXI, 655–744. [Also published separately with different pagination, Venezia: Presso la segretaria del R. Instituto, 1884.]

Castiglione, Baldassare. 1528. *Il libro del cortegiano*. Firenze: Heredi di Philippo di Giunta.

Catford, J.C. 1964. 'Phonation Types: The Classification of Some Laryngeal Components of Speech Production.' In *In Honour of Daniel Jones*, edited by Abercrombie, Fry, MacCarthy, Scott, and Trim. London: Longmans.

– . 1977. *Fundamental Problems in Phoniatrics.* Bloomington: Indiana University Press.

Cavagno, Giovanni A., and Rodolfo Margaria. 1968. 'Airflow Rates and Efficiency Changes during Phonation.' In *Annals of the New York Academy of Science* 155: 152–63.

Celani, Enrico. 1907, 1909. 'I cantori della cappella pontifica nei secoli xvi–xvii.' *Rivista Musicale Italiana* 14 (1907): 83–104, 752–90; 16 (1909): 55–112.

Celletti, Rodolfo. 1979. 'On Verdi's Vocal Writing.' In *The Verdi Companion*, edited by William Weaver and Martin Chusid. New York: W.W. Norton.

– . 1991. *A History of Bel Canto.* Translated by Frederick Fuller. Oxford: Clarendon Press. [First published as *Storia del Belcanto*. Fiesole: Discanto edizione, 1983. Translated into German by Federica Pauli as *Geschichte des Belcanto*. Kassel: Bärenreiter, 1989.]

Cerone, Domenico Pietro. 1613. *El melopeo y maestro: Tractado de musica theorica y pratica.* Napoles: Por I.B. Gargano, y L. Nucci. [Facsimile reprint: *Biblioteca musica Bononiensis*, sezione 2, n. 25. Bologna: Forni, 1969.]

Chorley, Henry F. 1844. *Music and Manners in France and Germany.* 3 vols. London: Longman, Brown, Green, & Longmans.

– . 1926. *Thirty Years' Musical Recollections*, edited with an introduction by Ernest Newman. New York and London: Alfred A. Knopf. [First published London, 1862.]

Christmann, Johann F. 1772–89. *Elementarbuch der Tonkunst.* Speyer.

Chrysander, Friedrich. 1891–4. 'Lodovico Zacconi als Lehrer des Kunstgesanges.' *Vierteljahrsschrift für Musikwissenschaft* 7: 337–96; 9: 249–310; 10: 531–67.

Clippinger, David Alva. 1910. *Systematic Voice Training.* Chicago: Gamble Hinged Music.

Cohen, Albert. 1980. 'Le Cerf de la Viéville, Jean Laurent.' In *The New Grove Dictionary of Music and Musicians* 10: 584.

Coker, Wilson. 1972. *Music and Meaning: A Theoretical Introduction to Musical Aesthetics.* New York: Free Press.

Colton, Raymond H. 1972. 'Spectral Characteristics of the Modal and Falsetto Registers.' *Folia Phoniatrica* 24: 337–44.

– . 1973a. 'Vocal Intensity in the Modal and Falsetto Registers.' *Folia Phoniatrica* 25: 62–70.

– . 1973b. 'Some Acoustic Parameters Related to the Perception of Modal-Falsetto Voice Quality.' *Folia Phoniatrica* 25: 302–11.

Colton, Raymond H., and Harry Hollien. 1973a. 'Physiology of Vocal Registers in Singers and Non-Singers.' In Large 1973b, 105–36.

– . 1973b. 'Perceptual Differentiation of the Modal and Falsetto Registers.' *Folia Phoniatrica* 25: 270–80.

Conforto, Giovanni Luca. 1593. *Breve et facile maniera d'essercitarsi a far passaggi*. Roma. [Facsimile edition with German translation by Johannes Wolf (Berlin: M. Breslauer, 1922).]

Cooke, Deryck. 1959. *The Language of Music*. London: Oxford University Press.

Cooper, Morton. 1973. *Modern Techniques of Vocal Rehabilitation*. Springfield, IL: Charles C. Thomas, Publisher.

Corri, Domenico. 1810. *The Singer's Preceptor, or Corri's Treatise on Vocal Music*. London: Chappell & Co.

Crescentini, Girolamo. *ca.* 1810. *Raccolta di esercizi per il canto all'uso del vocalizzo*. Paris: Imbault [Second publication London: T. Boosey, *ca.* 1848.]

Critchley, MacDonald, and R.A. Hensen, eds. 1977. *Music and the Brain*. London: William Heinemann.

Curtis, Henry Holbrook. 1909. *Voice Building and Tone Placing*. Third edition. London: J. Curwen & Sons. [First edition, 1896.]

– . 1918. *Thirty Years' Experience with Singers*. New York: [n.p.].

Curwen, John. 1875. *The Teacher's Manual of the Tonic Sol-Fa Method*. Fifth edition. London: J. Curwen & Sons.

Cyr, Mary. 1977. 'On Performing 18th-century Haute-Contre Roles.' *Musical Times* 118: 291–5.

– . 1980. 'Eighteenth-century French and Italian Singing: Rameau's Writing for the Voice.' *Music and Letters* 61: 318–38.

Dahlhaus, Carl. 1983. *Foundations of Music History*. Translated from the German by J.B. Robinson. Cambridge: Cambridge University Press.

dalla Casa, Girolamo. 1584. *Il vero modo di diminuir*. 2 vols. Venezia: Appresso Angelo Gardano.

Damsté, P.H., A. Reinders, and S. Tempelaars. 1983. 'Why Should Voices Quiver?' *Journal of Research in Singing* 6(2): 16–21.

Darwin, Charles. 1965. *The Expression of the Emotions in Man and Animals*. Chicago: University of Chicago Press. [First published in 1872.]

Deas, S. 1940. *In Defense of Hanslick*. London: Williams & Norgate. [Revised edition, 1972.]

Deinse, J.B. van, L. Frateur, and J. Keizer. 1974. 'Problems of the Singing Voice.' *Folia Phoniatrica* 26: 428–34.

Dejonckere, P.H., Minoru Hirano, and Johan Sundberg, eds. 1995. *Vibrato*. San Diego and London: Singular Publishing Group.

Della Corte, Andrea. 1933. *Canto e bel canto*. Torino: G.B. Paravia.

Della Valle, Pietro. 1640. *Della musica dell'età nostra*. [Originally published as part of G.B. Doni's *Trattati di musica* (Firenze, 1763). Reprinted in Solerti 1903, 148–79.]

Diday, Y.R., and Pétrequin. 1840. 'Mémoire sur une nouvelle espèce de voix chantée.' *Gazette Médicale de Paris* 8: 307–14.

'Discussion on Vibrato.' 1987. *Journal of Voice* 1 (2): 168–71.

Dmitrev, L. and A. Kiselev. 1979. 'Relationship between the Formant Structure of Different Types of Singing Voices and the Dimensions of Supraglottic Cavities.' *Folia Phoniatrica* 31: 238–41.

Dodart, Denis. 1700–7. 'Sur les causes de la voix de l'hommes, et de ses différens tons.' *Histoire de l'académie royale des sciences de Paris* 10 (1700): 244; 16(1706): 136–8, 388–410; 17 (1707): 66–81.

Doni, Giovanni Battista. 1763. *Lyra Barberina amphicordos: accedunt eiusdem opera.* Edited by A.F. Gori and G.B. Passeri. 2 vols. [*Trattati I* and *Trattati II*]. Firenze: Ant Franc. Gorius. [Facsimile edition with critical notes by Claude V. Palisca, *Biblioteca musica Bononiensis*, sezione 2, n.151 (Bologna: A.M.I.S., 1981). Portion reprinted in Solerti 1903, 186–228.]

Donington, Robert. 1978. *The Opera.* New York: Harcourt Brace Jovanovich.

– . 1982. *Baroque Music: Style and Performance.* New York: W.W. Norton.

Duey, Philip A. 1951. *Bel Canto in its Golden Age.* New York: King's Crown Press.

Duprez, Gibert-Louis. 1880. *Souvenirs d'un chanteur.* Bibliothèque contemporaine. Paris: Calmann Lévy. [Reprinted in *Voix d'opéra: Écrits de chanteurs du XIXe siècle* (Paris: M. de Maule, 1988).]

Einstein, Alfred. 1949. *The Italian Madrigal.* Translated by A.H. Krappe, R. Sessions, and O. Strunk. 3 vols. Princeton, NJ: Princeton University Press.

– . 1962. *Gluck.* Translated by Eric Blom. New York: Collier Books. [First published in German in 1936.]

Ellis, Alexander J. 1877. *Pronunciation for Singers.* London: J. Curwen & Sons.

Engelbrunner, Nina d'Aubigny von. 1803. *Briefe an Natalie über den Gesang.* Leipzig: Leopold Voss. [Second edition, improved and expanded, 1824.]

Falck, Georg. 1688. *Idea boni Cantoris, dass ist Getreu und gründliche Anleitung.* Nuremberg.

Fant, Gunnar. 1960. *Acoustic Theory of Speech Production.* The Hague: Mouton. [Second edition, 1970.]

Faure, Jean-Baptiste. 1866. *La voix et le chant: Traité pratique.* Paris: Heugel.

Fenlon, Iain. 1980. *Music and Patronage in Sixteenth-century Mantua.* 2 vols. Cambridge: Cambridge University Press.

– . 1982. 'Review of *The Madrigal at Ferrara, 1579–1597* by Anthony Newcombe.' *Journal of the American Musicological Society* 35(1): 167–81.

– . 1986. 'The Mantuan "Orfeo."' In *Claudio Monteverdi's Orfeo*, edited by John Whenham. Cambridge Opera Handbooks. Cambridge: Cambridge University Press.

Fenner, Theodore. 1972. *Leigh Hunt and Opera Criticism: The 'Examiner' Years, 1808–1821.* Lawrence, KS: University Press of Kansas.

Ferand, Ernest T. 1956. 'Improvised Vocal Counterpoint in the Late Renaissance and Early Baroque.' *Annales Musicologique* 4: 129–74.

– . 1961. *Improvisation in Nine Centuries of Western Music*. Anthology of Music, vol. 12. Köln: Arno Volk Verlag.

– . 1966. 'Didactic Embellishment Literature in the Late Renaissance: A Survey of Sources.' In *Aspects of Medieval and Renaissance Music*, edited by Jan LaRue. New York: W.W. Norton, 154–72.

Ferguson, Donald N. 1960. *Music as Metaphor: The Elements of Expression*. Minneapolis: University of Minnesota Press.

Ferrari, Giacomo Gotifredo. 1818. *Brevi trattato de canto Italiano*. London: Schulze & Dean. [English translation by W. Shield, *A Concise Treatise on Italian Singing* (London: Schulze & Dean, 1818).]

Ferrein, Antoine. 1741. 'De la formation de la voix de l'homme.' *Histoire de l'académie royale des sciences de Paris* 51: 409–32.

Fields, Victor Alexander. 1947. *Training the Singing Voice*. New York: King's Crown Press.

Finck, Hermann. 1556. *Practica musica*. Wittenberg: Georg Rhaw. [Portion translated in MacClintock 1979, 61–7.]

Fischer, Peter-Michael. 1993. *Die Stimme des Sängers*. Stuttgart und Weimar: Verlag J.B. Metzler.

Fónagy, Ivan. 1981. 'Emotions, Voice and Music.' In *Research Aspects on Singing*. Stockholm: Royal Swedish Academy of Music.

Foreman, Edward Vaught. 1969. *A Comparison of Selected Italian Vocal Tutors of the Period circa 1550–1800*. D.M.A. Thesis, University of Illinois. Ann Arbor: University Microfilms.

Fortune, Nigel. 1953. 'Italian Secular Monody from 1600 to 1635.' *The Musical Quarterly* 34: 171–95.

– . 1954. 'Italian 17th-century Singing.' *Music and Letters* 35, 206–19.

– . 1968. 'Solo Song and Cantata.' In *New Oxford Dictionary of Music* 4: 125–217.

– . 1980. 'Sprezzatura.' In *The New Grove Dictionary of Music and Musicians*, 18: 27–8.

Friderici, Daniel. 1614. *Musica figuralis oder newe Singekunst*. [Reprint edited by Ernst Langelütje (Berlin: R. Gaertner, 1901).]

Froeschels, Emil. 1943. 'Hygiene of the Voice.' *Archives of Otolaryngology* 38: 122–30.

Fuchs, Viktor. 1958. 'Manuel Garcia, Centenarian.' *Opera Annual* 5: 67–72.

Fucito, Salvatore, and Barnet J. Beyer. 1922. *Caruso and the Art of Singing*. New York: Frederick A. Stokes.

Galilei, Vincenzo. 1581. *Dialogo della musica antica e moderna*. Firenze: Girogio Marescotti. [Facsimile reprint, ed. Fabiol Fano, in *Instituzioni e monumenti*, 4 (Roma: Reale accademia d'Italia, 1934). Portions translated in Strunk 1950, 302–22.]

Ganassi dal Fontego, Sylvestro di. 1535. *Opera intitulata Fontegara*. Venezia: Silvestro. [Facsimile reprint. Milan: Balletino Bibliografico Musicale, 1934.]

– . 1542. *Regola rubertina: Regola che insegni sonar di viola darcho tastada*. 2 vols. Venetia. [Facsimile edition by M. Schneider. 2 vols. Leipzig: Kistner & Siegel, 1924.]

– . 1959. *Opera intitulata Fontegara*. English translation by Dorothy Swainson. Berlin-Lichterfelde: R. Lieneu. [This translation was made from a 1956 German translation by Hildemarie Peter.]

Gandalfi, Riccardo. 1913. 'Lettere inedite scritte da musicisti e letterati, appartenenti alla seconda metà del secolo xvi, estratte dal R. Archiviio di Stato in Firenze.' *Rivista musicale italiana* 20: 527–54.

Garaudé, Alexis de. [*ca.* 1830]. *Méthode complète de chant*. Paris: [by the author]. [Second edition, 1852.]

Garcia, Manuel. 1847. *Traité complet de l'art du chant*. En deux parties: première partie, 2ᵉ édition; seconde partie, 1ᵉ édition. Genève: Minkoff Éditeur. [Reprint with an introduction by L.J. Rondeleux. Includes *Mémoires sur la voix humaine* (1840).]

– . 1855. 'Observations on the Human Voice.' *Proceedings of the Royal Society* 3: 399–408. [Reprinted in Large 1980a, 123–33.]

– . 1894. *Hints on Singing*. Translated from the French by Beata Garcia. New and revised edition [by Hermann Klein]. London: E. Ascherberg. [Reprint edition: New York: Joseph Patelson Music House, 1982.]

– . 1975. *A Complete Treatise on the Art of Singing: Part Two*. The editions of 1841 and 1872 collated, edited, and translated by Donald V. Paschke. New York: Da Capo Press. [English translation of Garcia 1847, part 2.]

– . 1984. *A Complete Treatise on the Art of Singing: Part One*. The editions of 1841 and 1872 collated, edited, and translated by Donald V. Paschke. New York: Da Capo Press. [English translation of Garcia 1847, part 1.]

Gårtner, J. 1981. *The Vibrato, with Particular Consideration Given to the Situation of the Flutist*. Regensburg: Gustav Bosse Verlag.

Gatti, Carlo. 1931. *Verdi*. 2 vols. Milano: Edizioni Alpes.

– . 1955. *Verdi, the Man and His Music*. Translated by Elizabeth Abbott. New York: G.B. Putnam's Sons.

Gauffin, J., and J. Sundberg. 1980. 'Data on the Glottal Voice Source Behavior in Vowel Production.' *Transmission Laboratory Quarterly Progress and Status Report* (KTH, Stockholm) 2–3: 61–70.

Gautier, H., J.E. Remmers, and D. Bartlett Jr. 1973. 'Control of the Duration of Expiration.' *Respiratory Physiology* 18: 205–21.

Geering, Arnold. 1955. 'Gesangspädagogik.' In *Die Musik in Geschichte und Gegenwart*, vol. 4, columns 1908–1934.

Giustiniani, Vincenzo. 1962. *Discorso sopra la musica*. Translated and edited by Carol MacClintock. Musicological Studies and Documents, 9. [n.p.]: American Institute of Musicology. [Manuscript, *ca.* 1628. MacClintock's translation is also published in *Musica Disciplina* 15 (1961): 209–25.]

Godt, Irving. 1984. 'New Voices and Old Theory.' *The Journal of Musicology* 3(3): 312–19.

Goldschmidt, Hugo. 1890. *Die italienische Gesangsmethode im 17. Jahrhunderts und ihre Bedeutung für die Gegenwart*. Breslau: Schlesische Buchdrückerei.

– . 1891. 'Verzierungen, Veränderungen und Passagien im 16. und 17. Jahrhundert, und ihre musikalische Bedeutung besprochen nach zwei bisher unbekannten Quellen.' *Monatshefte für Musikgeschichte* 23: 111–26.

– . 1901–4. *Studien zur Geschichte der italienische Oper*. 2 vols. Leipzig: Breitkopf und Härtel.

– . 1907. *Die Lehre von der vokalen Ornamentik, erster Band: das 17. und 18. Jahrhundert bis in die Zeit Glucks*. Charlottenburg: Paul Lehsten.

Gould, Wilbur J. 1970. 'The Effect of Respiratory and Postural Mechanisms upon the Action of the Vocal Folds.' Paper presented at Collegia Medicorum Theatre, Barcelona, Spain, November 1970.

– . 1971a. 'The Value of Voice Analysis in Singers.' Paper presented at the 15th International Congress of Phoniatrics, Buenos Aires, August 1971.

– . 1971b. 'Voice Production and Postural Mechanisms.' Paper presented at the 15th International Congress of Phoniatrics, Buenos Aires, August 1971.

– . 1971c. 'Effect of Respiratory and Postural Mechanisms upon Action of the Vocal Cords.' *Folia Phoniatrica* 23: 211–24.

– . 1974. 'Respiratory Training of the Singer.' *Folia Phoniatrica* 26: 275–86.

– . 1977. 'The Effect of Voice Training on Lung Volumes in Singers, and the Possible Relationship to the Damping Factor of Pressman.' *Journal of Research in Singing* 1(1): 3–15.

– . 1980. 'Interrelationship between Voice and Laryngeal Mucosal Reflexes.' In *Transcripts of the Eighth Symposium: Care of the Professional Voice* 2: 54–7. New York: The Voice Foundation.

Gould, Wilbur J., and Hiroshi Okamura. 1974. 'Interrelationships between Voice and Mucosal Reflexes.' In Wyke 1974a, 347–59.

Greenlee, Robert. 1983. 'The Articulation Techniques of Florid Singing in the Renaissance: An Introduction.' *Journal of Performance Practice* 1: 1–18.

Haas, Robert. 1929. *Die Musik des Barocks*. Handbuch der Musikwissenschaft, vol. 2, edited by Ernst Bücken. Leipzig: C.G. Röder.

Häbock, Franz. 1908. 'Die physiologischen Grundlagen der Altitalienischen Gesangsschule.' *Die Musik* Jahrgang 8: 337–47.

– . [1923]. *Die Gesangskunst der Kastraten; erster Notenband: A. Die Kunst des Cavaliere Carlo Broschi Farinelli. B. Farinellis berühmte Arien.* Wien: Universal.

– . 1927. *Die Kastraten und ihre Gesangskunst.* Edited by Martina Häbock. Berlin and Leipzig: Deutsche Verlags-Anstadt in Stuttgart.

Hakes, J., T. Shipp, and E.T. Doherty. 1987. 'Acoustic Properties of Straight Tone, Vibrato, Trill, and Trillo.' *Journal of Voice* 1(2): 148–56.

Hakes, J., E.T. Doherty, and T. Shipp. 1990. 'Trillo Rates Exhibited by Professional Early Music Singers.' *Journal of Voice* 4(4): 305–8.

Hamlet, S.L., and J.M. Palmer. 1974. 'Investigation of Laryngeal Trills Using the Transmission of Ultrasound through the Larynx.' *Folia Phoniatrica* 26: 362–77.

Hanslick, Eduard. 1957. *The Beautiful in Music.* Translated by Gustave Cohen. Indianapolis and New York: Bobbs-Merrill. [First published in German as *Vom Musikalisch-Schönen* (Leipzig, 1854).]

Hartlieb, K. 1953. 'Schädigungen der äusseren Kehlkopf-Muskeln als Ursachen für Störungen der Sängerstimme.' *Folia Phoniatrica* 5: 146–66.

Hawkins, John. 1875. *A General History of the Science and Practice of Music.* A New Edition, with the Author's Posthumous Notes. London: Novello, Ewer & Co. [First published London, 1776.]

Helmholtz, Hermann. 1954. *On the Sensations of Tone as a Physiological basis for the Theory of Music.* [Reprint of] Second English edition, translated, thoroughly revised and corrected ... by Alexander J. Ellis, with a new introduction by Henry Margenau. New York: Dover. [First published London: Longmans, Green, 1885. Originally published in German, 1862.]

Henderson, William James. 1906. *The Art of the Singer: Practical Hints About Vocal Technics and Style.* New York: G. Scribner's Sons.

– . 1921. *The Early History of Singing.* New York: Longmans, Green and Co.

Herbert-Caesari, Edgar F. 1936. *The Science and Sensations of Vocal Tone.* London: J.M. Dent & Sons.

Herbst, Johann Andreas. 1642. *Musica practica sive instructio pro symphoniacis.* Nuremberg: J. Dümlers.

Heriot, Angus. 1956. *The Castrati in Opera.* London: Secker and Warburg. [Reprint edition, New York: Da Capo Press, 1975.]

Hertegård, S., J. Gauffin, and P.-E. Lindestad. 1995. 'A Comparison of Subglottal and Intraoral Pressure Measurements during Phonation.' *Journal of Voice* 9(2): 149–55.

Hibberd, Lloyd. 1946. 'On "Instrumental Style" in Early Melody.' *The Musical Quarterly* 32: 107–30.

Hiller, Johann Adam. 1774. *Anweisung zum musikalisch-richtigen Gesange.* Leipzig: J.F. Junius.

– . 1780. *Anweisung zum musikalisch-zierlichen Gesange.* Leipzig: F. Junius.

Hines, Jerome. 1994. *Great Singers on Great Singing*. Seventh edition. New York: Limelight Edition. [First published in 1982.]

Hitchcock, H. Wiley. 1970. 'Vocal Ornamentation in Caccini's *Nuove musiche*.' *The Musical Quarterly* 61: 389–404.

– . 1973. 'A New Biographical Source for Caccini?' *Journal of the American Musicological Society* 26: 145–7

– . 1974. 'Caccini's 'Other' *Nuove musiche*.' *Journal of the American Musicological Society* 27: 438–60.

– . 1988. *Music in the United States: A Historical Introduction*. 3rd edition. Englewood Cliffs, NJ: Prentice Hall.

Hixon, Thomas J. 1973. 'Respiratory Function in Speech.' In Minifie, Hixon, and Williams 1973, 73–126.

– . 1987. *Respiratory Function in Speech and Song*. London: Taylor & Francis.

Hixon, Thomas J., and Cynthia Hoffman. 1979. 'Chest Wall Shape in Singing.' In *Transcripts of the Seventh Symposium: Care of the Professional Voice*, 1: 9–10. New York: The Voice Foundation.

Hixon, Thomas J., Peter J. Watson, and Jeannette D. Hoit. 1986. 'Prephonatory Chest Wall Posturing.' *Transcripts of the Fourteenth Symposium: Care of the Professional Voice* 1: 61–2. New York: The Voice Foundation.

Hixon, Thomas J., and Gary Weismer. 1995. 'Perspectives on the Edinburgh Study of Speech Breathing.' *Journal of Speech and Hearing Research* 38: 42–60.

Hodges, Sheila. 1993. 'A Nest of Nightingales.' *The Music Review* 54(2): 79–94.

Hogarth, George. 1851. *Memoirs of the Opera in Italy, France, Germany, and England*. A new edition. 2 vols. London: Richard Bentley. [Reprint edition, New York: Plenum Publishing, 1972.]

Hollien, Harry. 1968. 'Vocal Fry as a Phonational Register.' *Journal of Speech and Hearing Research* 11: 600–4.

– . 1971. 'Three Major Vocal Registers: A Proposal.' In *Proceedings of the Seventh International Congress of Phonetic Sciences* 320–31. The Hague: Mouton.

– . 1974. 'On Vocal Registers.' *Journal of Phonetics* 2: 125–43.

Hollien, Harry, Gary T. Girard, and Robert F. Coleman. 1977. 'Vocal Fold Vibratory Patterns of Pulse Register Phonation.' *Folia Phoniatrica* 29: 200–5.

Hollien, Harry, W.J. Gould, and Beverly Johnson. 1976. 'A Two-Level Concept of Vocal Registers.' In *XVI International Congress of Logopedics and Phoniatrics*, 188–94. Basel: Karger.

Hollien, Harry, and Elwood Keister. 1978. 'Pilot Data on Frequency Production Abilities of Singers and Non-Singers.' *Journal of Research in Singing* 1(2): 15–23.

Honda, Kiyoshi, and Thomas Baer. 1982. 'External Frame Function, Pitch Control, and Vowel Production.' In *Transcripts of the Tenth Symposium: Care of the Professional Voice* 1: 66–73. New York: The Voice Foundation.

Horii, Yoshiyuki. 1989. 'Acoustic Analysis of Vocal Vibrato: A Theoretical Interpretation of Data.' *Journal of Voice* 3: 36–43.

Horii, Yoshiyuki, and Bernd Weinberg. 1980. 'Sensory Contributions to the Control of Phonation.' In *Transcripts of the Eighth Symposium: Care of the Professional Voice* 2: 58–65. New York: The Voice Foundation.

Horsley, Imogene. 1951. 'Improvised Embellishment in the Performance of Renaissance Polyphonic Music.' *Journal of the American Musicological Society* 4: 3–19.

– . 1963. 'The Diminutions in Composition and Theory of Composition.' *Acta Musicologica* 35: 124–53.

Hsiao, Tzu-Yu, Nancy Pearl Solomon, Erich S. Luschei, and Ingo Titze. 1994. 'Modulation of Fundamental Frequency by Laryngeal Muscles during Vibrato.' *Journal of Voice* 8(3): 224–9.

Hudson, Richard. 1994. *Stolen Time: The History of Tempo Rubato*. Oxford: Clarendon Press.

Husler, Frederick, and Yvonne Rodd-Marling. 1965. *Singing: The Physical Nature of the Organ*. London: Faber & Faber.

Husson, Raoul. 1960. *La voix chantée*. Collection des Sciences et Techniques d'aujourd'hui. Paris: Gauthier-Villars.

– . 1962. *Le chant*. Paris: Presses Universitaires de France.

Ivey, Donald. 1970. *Song: Anatomy, Imagery, and Styles*. New York: The Free Press.

Jacobs, Arthur, and Stanley Sadie, eds. 1964. *The Pan Book of Opera*. London: Pan Books.

Jander, Owen. 1980a. 'Bel Canto.' In *The New Grove Dictionary of Music and Musicians* 2: 240.

– . 1980b. 'Singing.' In *The New Grove Dictionary of Music and Musicians* 17: 338–46.

Kay, Elster. 1963. *Bel canto and the Sixth Sense*. London: Dobson.

Keidar, Anat, Ingo Titze, and Craig Timberlake. 1985. 'Vibrato Characteristics of Tenors Singing High C's.' *Transcripts of the Thirteenth Symposium: Care of the Professional Voice* 1: 105–10. New York: The Voice Foundation.

Keidar, Anat, Richard Hurtig, and Ingo R. Titze. 1987. 'The Perceptual Nature of Vocal Register Change.' *Journal of Voice* 1(3): 223–33.

Kelsey, Franklyn. 1950. *The Foundations of Singing*. London: Williams and Northgate.

– . 1954. 'Voice Training.' In *Grove's Dictionary of Music and Musicians*. Fifth edition, edited by Eric Blom, 9: 43–66.

Kennedy-Fraser, Marjory. 1909. *Songs of the Hebrides*. London: Boosey.

– . 1929. *A Life of Song*. London: Oxford University Press.

Kerman, Joseph. 1988. *Opera as Drama*. New and revised edition. Berkeley: University of California Press.

Kesting, Jürgen. 1993. *Die Grossen Sänger unseres Jahrhunderts*. Düsseldorf: Econ Verlag.

Khambata, A. S. 1977. 'Anatomy and Physiology of Voice Production: The Phenomenal Voice.' In Critchley and Henson 1977, 59–77.

Kirby, Frank E. 1961. 'Hermann Finck on Methods of Performance.' *Music and Letters* 42: 212–20.

Kirkendale, Warren. 1993. *The Court Musicians in Florence During the Principate of the Medici*. Firenze: Olschki.

Kitajima, K., and K. Tanaka. 1993. 'Intraoral Pressure in the Evaluation of Laryngeal Function.' *Acta Otolaryngologica* (Stockholm) 113: 553–9.

Kivy, Peter. 1980. *The Corded Shell: Reflections on Musical Expression*. Princeton Essays on the Arts, no. 9. Princeton, NJ: Princeton University Press.

Klein, Hermann. 1903. *Thirty Years of Musical Life in London, 1870–1900*. London: Heinemann.

– . 1923. *The Bel Canto, with Particular Reference to the Singing of Mozart*. London: Humphrey Milford, Oxford University Press.

– . 1931. *Great Women-Singers of My Time*. London: G. Routledge & Sons.

Koestler, Arthur. 1989. *The Act of Creation*. London: Penguin. [First published London: Hutchison, 1964.]

Kuhn, Max. 1902. *Die Verzierungskunst in der Gesangs-Musik des 16.-17. Jahrhunderts (1535–1650)*. Publikationen der Internationalen Musikgesellschaft, Heft 7. Leipzig: Breitkopf und Härtel.

Kwalwasser, Jacob. 1926. 'The Vibrato.' *Psychological Monographs* 36: 84–108. [Reprinted in Large 1980a, 202–28.]

Lamperti, Francesco. 1864. *Guida teorica-practica-elementare per lo studio del canto*. Milan: T. di Ricordi.

– . 1884. *The Art of Singing According to Ancient Tradition and Personal Experience*. Translated by W. Jekyll. London: G. Ricordi. [English translation of *L'arte del canto in ordine alla tradizione classiche ed particolare experienza*. Milano: G. Ricordi, 1883.]

– . 1916. *The Art of Singing*. Translated by J.C. Griffith. New York: G. Schirmer. [This work is a version of Francesco Lamberti's *A Treatise on the Art of Singing*. Earlier editions: New York: E. Schuberth, 1871; London: G. Ricordi, 1877; New York: G. Schirmer, 1890.]

Lamperti, Giovanni Battista. 1905. *The Technics of Bel Canto*. Translated by Theodore Baker. New York: G. Schirmer.

Lang, Paul Henry. 1966. *George Friderick Handel*. New York: W.W. Norton.

Large, John. 1968. 'An Acoustical Study of Isoparametric Tones in the Female

Chest and Middle Registers in Singing.' *Bulletin of the National Association of Teachers of Singing* (December): 12–15.

– . 1969. 'A Method for the Selection of Samples for Acoustical and Perceptual Studies of Voice Registers.' *Bulletin of the National Association of Teachers of Singing* (February): 40–2.

– . 1972. 'Towards an Integrated Physiologic-Acoustic Theory of Vocal Registers.' *Bulletin of the National Association of Teachers of Singing* 28(3): 18–25, 30–6.

– . 1973a. 'Acoustic Study of Register Equalization in Singing.' *Folia Phoniatrica* 25: 39–61.

– , ed. 1973b. *Vocal Registers in Singing*. Edited and with an Introduction by John Large. The Hague: Mouton.

– . 1974. 'Acoustic-Perceptual Evaluation of Register Equalization.' *Bulletin of the National Association of Teachers of Singing* (October): 20–7, 40.

– , ed. 1980a. *Contributions of Voice Research to Singing*. Houston: College-Hill Press.

– . 1980b. 'An Air Flow Study of Vocal Vibrato.' In *Transcripts of the Eighth Symposium: Care of the Professional Voice* 1: 39–45. New York: The Voice Foundation.

Large, John, and Shigenoba Iwata. 1971. 'Aerodynamic Study of Vibrato and Voluntary "Straight Tone" in Singing.' *Folia Phoniatrica* 23: 50–65. [Reprinted in Large. 1980a, 271–90.]

– . 1976. 'The Significance of Air Flow Modulations in Vocal Vibrato.' *Journal of the National Association of Teachers of Singing* (Feb–Mar): 42–7.

Large, John, Shigenoba Iwata, and Hans von Leden. 1970. 'The Primary Female Register Transition in Singing.' *Folia Phoniatrica* 22: 385–96.

– . 1972. 'The Male Operatic Head Register versus Falsetto.' *Folia Phoniatrica* 24: 19–29.

Large, John, and Thomas Murry. 1978. 'Studies for the Marchesi Model for Female Registration.' *Journal of Research in Singing* 1(2): 1–14.

Lasser, Johann Baptist. 1798. *Vollständige Anleitung zur Singkunst sowohl für den Alt*. München: Gedruckt mit Hübschmannchen Schriften.

Laver, John. 1980. *The Phonetic Description of Voice Quality*. Series: Cambridge Studies in Linguistics, no. 31. Cambridge: Cambridge University Press.

Leanderson, Rolf, and Johann Sundberg. 1988. 'Breathing for Singing.' *Journal of Voice* 2(1): 2–12.

Leanderson, Rolf, Johan Sundberg, and Curt von Euler. 1985. 'Effects of Diaphragm Activity on Phonation during Singing.' In *Transcripts of the Thirteenth Symposium: Care of the Professional Voice*, 1: 165–9. New York: The Voice Foundation.

– . 1987a. 'Role of Diaphragmatic Activity during Singing: A Study of Transdiaphragmatic Pressure.' *Journal of Applied Psysiology* 6(1): 259–70.

– . 1987b. 'Breathing Muscle Activity and Subglottal Pressure Dynamics in Singing and Speech.' *Journal of Voice* 1(2): 259–61.

Leanderson, Rolf, Johan Sundberg, Curt von Euler, and Hugo Lagerkrantz. 1983. 'Diaphragmatic Control of the Subglottal Pressures During Singing.' In *Transcripts of the Twelfth Symposium: Care of the Professional Voice* 2: 216–20. New York: The Voice Foundation.

Le Cerf de la Viéville, Jean Laurent. 1704–6. *Comparaison de la musique italienne e de la musique françoise.* 3 vols. Bruxelle: F. Foppens. [Portion translated in Strunk 1950, 489–510.]

Lehmann, Lilli. 1914. *How to Sing.* Translated from the German by Richard Aldrich. New and revised edition. New York: MacMillan. [First published as *Meine Gesangskunst* in 1902.]

Lerman, J., and R. Duffy. 1970. 'Recognition of Falsetto Voice Quality.' *Folia Phoniatrica* 22: 21–7.

Levarie, Siegmund, and Ernst Levy. 1980. *Tone: A Study in Musical Acoustics.* Second edition. Kent, OH: Kent State University Press.

Lieberman, Philip. 1968a. 'Vocal Cord Motion in Man.' *Annals of the New York Academy of Sciences* 155: 28–38.

– . 1968b. 'Direct Comparison of Subglottal and Esophageal Pressure During Speech.' *Journal of the Acoustical Society of America* 43: 1157–64.

– . 1977. *Speech Physiology and Acoustic Phonetics.* New York: Macmillan.

Lindblom, B.E.F., and Johan Sundberg. 1971. 'Acoustic Consequences of Lip, Tongue, Jaw and Larynx Movement.' *Journal of the Acoustical Society of America* 50: 1166–79.

Lozzi, C. 1902. 'La musica e specialmente il melodramma alla Corte Medicea.' *Rivista Musicale Italiana* 9: 297–338.

Luchsinger, Richard, and Godfrey E. Arnold. 1965. *Voice-Speech-Language.* Translated from the German by G.E. Arnold and Evelyn Rose Finkbeiner. Belmont, CA: Wadsworth Publishing Co.

Lunn, Charles. 1878. *The Philosophy of Voice: Showing the Right and Wrong Action of Voice in Speech and Song.* Fourth edition. London: Baillière, Tindall & Cox.

– . 1904. *The Voice: Its Downfall, Its Training, and Its Use. A Manual for Teachers, Singers, and Students.* London: Reynolds & Co.

Luzzaschi, Luzzasco. 1601. *Madrigali per cantare e sonare a uno, due e tre soprani.* Rome: S. Verovio. [Reprint edited by Adriano Cavicchi, Monumenti di musica italiana, serie 2, vol. 2. (Kassel: Bärenreiter, 1965).]

Maatz, Richard. 1937. 'Die Atemstütze im Kunstgesang.' In *Archiv Sprach-Stimmphysiologie und Sprach-und Stimmheilkunde,* 110–27.

MacClintock, Carol. 1976. 'Caccini's Trillo: A Re-examination.' *Bulletin of the National Association of Teachers of Singing* 33: 37–44.

– . 1979. *Readings in the History of Music in Performance*. Bloomington: Indiana University Press.

Mackenzie, Morrell. 1890. *The Hygiene of the Vocal Organs*. Seventh edition. New York: Edgar S. Werner. [First published 1886.]

Mackinlay, M. Sterling. 1908. *Garcia the Centenarian and His Time*. Edinburgh and London: William Blackwood & Sons.

Mackworth Young, Gerard. 1953. *What Happens in Singing*. London: Newman Neame.

Madelaine, Stéphan de la. 1864. *Theories completes du chant*. Second edition. Paris: Arneauld de Vresse. [First edition, 1852.]

Maffei, Giovanni Camillo. 1562. *Delle lettere ... libri due, un discorso della voce e del modo, d'apparar di cantar Garganta senza maestro*. Napoli: Apprò Raymuso Amato. [English translation of 'Letter I' in MacClintock 1979, 38–61; French translation of 'Letter 1' in Bridgman 1956.]

Mancini, Giambattista. 1967. *Practical Reflections on Figured Singing: The Editions of 1774 and 1777 Compared*. Translated and edited by Edward Foreman. Champaign, IL: Pro Musica Press. [Originally published as *Pensieri e riflessioni pratiche sopra il canto figurato* (Vienna, 1774; second edition 1777).]

Mandl, Louis. 1876. *Hygiène de la voix*. Paris and London: J.B. Baillière et Fils.

Manfredini, Vincenzo. 1775. *Regole armoniche, o siano precetti ragionati per apprendere i principi della musica*. Venezia: G. Zerletti. [Facsimile edition, New York: Broude Brothers, 1966.]

– . 1797. *Regole armoniche, o siano precetti ragionati per apprendere i principi della musica*. 2nd edition. Venezia: G. Zerlotti. [A second edition of Manfredini 1775, much enlarged with new sections on singing and counterpoint.]

Marcello, Benedetto. 1720. *Il teatro alla moda*. [Venezia]: Borghi di Belisania per A. Liconte. [Portion translated in Strunk 1950, 518–34.]

– 1948–9. 'Il teatro alla moda.' Translated by Reinhard G. Pauly. *The Musical Quarterly* 34: 371–403; 35: 85–105.

Marchesi, Blanche. 1923. *Singer's Pilgrimage*. Boston: Small, Maynard. [Reprint edition, New York: Da Capo Press, 1978.]

– . 1932. *The Singer's Catechism and Creed*. London: J.M. Dent & Sons.

Marchesi, Mathilde Graumann. 1877. *Méthode de chant théorique et pratique. (École Marchesi)*. Deuxième édition. Paris: L. Grus.

– . 1898. *Marchesi and Music: Passages from the Life of a Famous Singing-Teacher*. New York and London: Harper & Bros. [Reprint edition, New York: Da Capo Press, 1978.]

– . 1970. *Theoretical and Practical Vocal Method*. Reprint with introduction by

Philip L. Miller. New York: Dover. [An English version of Marchesi 1877, first published London: Enoch & Sons (n.d.).]

Mårtensson, A., and C.R. Skoglund. 1964. 'Contraction Properties of Intrinsic Laryngeal Muscles.' *Acta Physiologica Scandinavica* 60: 318–36.

Martienssen-Lohmann, Franziska. 1993. *Der Wissenden Sänger: Gesangslexikon in Skizzen.* Zurich: Atlantis Musikbuch-Verlag. [First published in 1956.]

Marpurg, Friedrich Wilhelm. 1763. *Anleitung zur Musik überhaupt und zur Singkunst besonders mit Uebungsexampeln erläutert.* Berlin. [Facsimile edition, Leipzig: Zentralantiquariat des Deutschen Demokratischen Republik, 1975.]

Mason, Robert M. 1971. 'Physiological Components of Vocal Vibrato.' Abstract of a paper presented at the Acoustical Society of America conference, 6 November 1970. *Journal of the Acoustical Society of America* 49: 136.

Mason, Robert M., and Willard Zemlin. 1966. 'The Phenomenon of Vocal Vibrato.' Reprinted in Large 1980a, 241–62. [First published in *Bulletin of the National Association of Teachers of Singing* 22(3): 12–17, 37.]

Martini, Jean Paul Egide. 1792. *Mélopée moderne: Ou l'art du chant, réduit en principes.* Paris: Chez Naderman.

Mattheson, Johann. 1739. *Der Volkommene Capellmeister.* Hamburg.

–. 1981. *Der Volkommene Capellmeister.* Revised translation with critical commentary by Ernest C. Harris. Ann Arbor, MI: UMI Research Press.

McLane, Marian. 1985. 'Artistic Vibrato and Tremolo: A Survey of the Literature.' *Journal of Research in Singing* 8(2): 21–43; 9(1): 11–42.

Mead, J., T.J. Hixon, and M.D. Goldman. 1974. 'The Configuration of the Chest Wall During Speech.' In Wyke 1974a, 58–67.

Mengozzi, Bernardo. 1803. *Méthode de chant du Conservatoire de musique.* Paris. [Second edition, Florence: Giglio, 1807.]

Merleau-Ponty, Maurice. 1962. *Phenomenology of Perception.* Translated by Colin Smith. London: Routledge & Kegan Paul. [First French edition, 1945.]

Mersenne, Marin. 1636. *Harmonie universelle.* Paris: Cramoisy. [Translation of 'The Sixth Book on the Art of Singing Well' in MacClintock 1979, 171–5.]

–. 1957. *Harmonie universelle: The Books on Instruments.* Translated by Roger E. Chapman. The Hague: M. Mijhoff.

Metfessel, Milton. 1926. 'Sonance as a Form of Tonal Fusion.' *Psychological Review* 33: 459–66.

–. 1929. 'The Vibrato in Celebrated Voices.' *The Scientific Monthly* 28: 217–19.

–. 1932. 'The Vibrato in Artistic Voices.' In *University of Iowa Studies in the Psychology of Music* 1: 14–117.

Michel, John F. 1978. 'The Accuracy of Prephonatory Laryngeal Adjustments.' In *Transcripts of the Sixth Symposium: Care of the Professional Voice*, 21–2. New York: The Voice Foundation.

286   References

– . 1983. 'Scooping.' In *Transcripts of the Eleventh Symposium: Care of the Professional Voice* 1: 100–2. New York: The Voice Foundation.

Miles, Beth, and Harry Hollien. 1990. 'Wither Belting?' *Journal of Voice* 4: 1, 64–70

Miller, Donald G. 1994. *Singing Technique*. Groningen: [the author].

Miller, Donald G., and H.K. Schutte. 1990. 'Formant Tuning in a Professional Baritone.' *Journal of Voice* 4(3): 231–7.

– . 1993. 'Physical Definition of the Flageolet Register.' *Journal of Voice* 7(3): 206–12.

– . 1994. 'Toward a Definition of Male "Head" Register, Passaggio, and "Cover" in Western Operatic Singing.' *Folia Phoniatrica et Logopaedica* 46: 157–70.

Miller, Richard L. 1959. 'Nature of the Vocal Cord Wave.' *Journal of the Acoustical Society of America* 31: 667–77.

– . 1977. *English, French, German and Italian Techniques of Singing*. Metuchen, NJ: The Scarecrow Press.

– . 1986a. *The Structure of Singing: System and Art in Vocal Technique*. New York: Schirmer.

– . 1986b. 'Quality in the Singing Voice,' In *Transcripts of the Fourteenth Symposium: Care of the Professional Voice*. New York: The Voice Foundation

Millet, Jean. 1666. *La belle methode ou l'art de bien chanter*. Lyon: Jean Gregoire. [Reprint edition, with an introduction by Albert Cohen. New York: Da Capo Press, 1973.]

Milner, Anthony. 1973. 'The Sacred Capons.' *Musical Times* 114: 250–2.

Minifie, Fred D., Thomas J. Hixon, and Frederick Williams, eds. 1973. *Normal Aspects of Speech, Hearing, and Language*. Englewood Cliffs, NJ: Prentice-Hall.

Mirollo, James V. 1962. *The Poet of the Marvelous: Giambattista Marino*. New York: Columbia University Press.

Monahan, Brent Jeffrey. 1978. *The Art of Singing*. Metuchen, NJ: Scarecrow Press.

Montéclair, Michel Pignolet de. 1736. *Principes de musique*. Paris

Mörner, M., F. Frannson, and G. Fant. 1964. 'Voice Registers.' *Speech Transmission Laboratory Quarterly Progress and Status Report* 4: 18–20.

Moses, Paul J. 1960. 'The Psychology of the Castrato Voice.' *Folia Phoniatrica* 12: 204–16.

Mount-Edgcumbe, Richard. 1823. *Musical Reminiscences of an Old Amateur for Fifty Years from 1773 to 1823*. London: W. Clarke.

Mozart, Leopold. 1756. *Versuch einer gründliche Violinschule*. [Facsimile of the 1787 edition, Leipzig: Breitkopf und Härtel. Portion translated in MacClintock 1979, 326–38.]

Mueller von Asow, Hedwig, and Erich H. Mueller von Asow. 1962. *The Collected Correspondence and Papers of Christoph Willibald Gluck*. Translated by Stewart Thomson. London: Barrie and Rockliffe.

Müller, Adolphe. 1844. *Vollständige Gesang-Schule*. Wien: Tobias Haslingers Witwe und Sohn.

Müller, Johann. 1837. *Handbuch der Physiologie der Menschen*. Band II. Coblenz: Hölschner.

Myer, Edmund. 1891. *Vocal Reinforcement*. Boston: Boston Music Co.

– . 1897. *Position and Action in Singing*. New York: E.S. Werner.

Myers, Denise, and John Michel. 1987. 'Vibrato and Pitch Transitions.' *Journal of Voice* 1(2): 157–61.

Mylius, Wolfgang. 1686. *Rudimental musices, das ist: Eine Kurtze und grundrichtige Anweisung zur Singe Kunst*. Gotha.

Nadoleczny, M. 1923. *Untersuchung über den Kunstgesang*. Berlin: Springer.

Nadoleczny-Millioud, M., and R. Zimmermann. 1938. 'Categories et registres de la voix.' *Revue française de phoniatrie* 21: 21–31.

Nagler, A. M. 1964. *Theater Festivals of the Medici, 1539–1637*. Translated by George Hickenlooper. New Haven, CT: Yale University Press.

Nathan, Isaac. 1836. *Musurgia Vocalis: An Essay on the History and Theory of Music, etc.* Second edition, enlarged. London: Fentum. [First edition published in 1823 under the title Essay on the History and Theory of Music.]

Neumann, Frederick. 1978. *Ornamentation in Baroque and Post-Baroque Music*. Princeton, NJ: Princeton University Press.

Newcomb, Anthony. 1980. *The Madrigal at Ferrara, 1579–1597*. 2 vols. Princeton, NJ: Princeton University Press.

New Grove Dictionary of Music and Musicians, The. 1980. Edited by Stanley Sadie. 20 vols. London: Macmillan.

Nicolaisen, Jay. 1980. *Italian Opera in Transition, 1871–1893*. Ann Arbor, MI: UMI Research Press.

North, Roger. 1959. *Roger North on Music: Being a Selection from his Essays Written during the Years c.1695–1728*. Transcribed from the manuscripts and edited by John Wilson. London: Novello.

Oncley, Paul B. 1971. 'Frequency, Amplitude, and Waveform Modulation in the Vocal Vibrato.' Abstract of paper presented at the Acoustical Society of America conference, 6 November 1970. *Journal of the Acoustical Society of America* 49: 136.

– . 1973. 'Dual Concept of Singing Registers.' In Large 1973b, 35–44.

Ortiz, Diego. 1553. *Tratado de glosas*. Roma: Valerio Dorico & Lodovico degli Arrighi. [Reprint edition edited by Max Schneider. Kassel: Bärenreiter, 1936.]

Page, Christopher. 1987. *Voices and Instruments of the Middle Ages*. London: J.M. Dent & Sons.

Paget, Richard. 1930. *Human Speech*. New York: Harcourt, Brace & Co.

Palisca, Claude V. 1956. 'Vincenzo Galilei's Counterpoint Treatise: A Code for the *Seconda Pratica.*' *Journal of the American Musicological Society* 9: 81–96.

– . 1960. 'Vincenzo Galilei and Some Links between "Pseudo-Monody" and Monody.' *The Musical Quarterly* 46: 344–60.

– . 1981. *Baroque Music.* Englewood Cliffs, NJ: Prentice-Hall.

Paschke, Donald V. 1986–7. 'Manuel Garcia: Method and Controversy.' *Journal of Research in Singing* 10(1): 49–58; 10(2): 51–6.

Pauly, Reinhard G. 1948. 'Benedetto Marcello's Satire on Early 18th-century Opera.' *The Musical Quarterly* 34(2): 222–33.

Peterson, G.E., and H.L. Barney. 1952. 'Control Methods Used in a Study of the Vowels.' *Journal of the Acoustical Society of America* 24: 175–84.

Petri, Johann Samuel. 1767. *Anleitung zur practischen Musik.* Lauban: J.C. Wirthgen.

Petty, Frederick C. 1980. *Italian Opera in London, 1760–1800.* Ann Arbor, MI: UMI Research Press.

Pirrotta, Nino. 1954. 'Temperaments and Tendencies in the Florentine Camerata.' *The Musical Quarterly* 40: 169–89.

– . 1968. 'Early Opera and Aria.' In *New Looks at Italian Opera*, edited by William Austin, 39–107. Ithaca, NY: Cornell University Press.

Pleasants, Henry. 1961. *The Musical Journeys of Louis Spohr.* Translated, selected, and edited from Louis Spohr's *Selbstbiographie.* Oklahoma City: University of Oklahoma Press.

– . 1966. *The Great Singers.* New York: Simon and Schuster.

– . 1995. *The Great Tenor Tragedy: The Last Days of Adolphe Nourrit as Told (Mostly) by Himself.* Portland, OR: Amadeus Press.

Praetorius, Michael. 1619. *Syntagma musicum.* Tom III, Wolfenbüttel. [Facsimile edition edited by Willibald Gurlitt, Documenta Musicologica (Kassel: Bären-reiter, 1958–1959). Part 3, chapter 9, translated in MacClintock 1979, 163–70.]

Preissler, W. 1939. 'Stimmumfänge und Gattungen der menschliche Stimme.' *Archiv Sprach-Stimmphysiologie und Sprach- und Stimmheilkunde* 3: 65–85.

Pressman, Joel J. 1941. 'Sphincters of the Larynx.' *Archives of Otolaryngology* 33: 221–36.

– . 1942. 'Physiology of the Vocal Folds in Phonation and Respiration.' *Archives of Otolaryngology* 35: 355–98.

Proctor, Donald F. 1974. 'Breathing Mechanics During Phonation and Singing.' In Wyke 1974a, 39–57.

– . 1980a. *Breathing, Speech, and Song.* Wien: Springer-Verlag.

– . 1980b. 'Breath, the Power Source for the Voice.' In *Transcripts of the Fourteenth Symposium: Care of the Professional Voice* 2: 14–18. New York: The Voice Foundation

Punt, Norman. 1952. *The Singer's and Actor's Throat.* London: Heinemann.

Quantz, Johann Joachim. 1966. *On Playing the Flute*. Translated by Edward R. Reilly. London: Faber. [First published as *Versuch einer Anweisung die Flöte transversière zu Spielen* (Berlin, 1752). Chapter 18, sections 11–12 translated in MacClintock 1979, 357–9.]

Raguenet, François. 1702. *Parallèle des Italiens et des Français, en ce qui regarde la musique et les opéras*. [Portion translated in Strunk 1950, 473–88.]

– . 1709. *A Comparison between the French and Italian Music and Operas*. London. [Translation of Raguenet 1702, attributed to J.E. Galliard. Reprint edition with an introduction by Charles Cudworth (Farnsborough, England: Gregg International, 1968).]

– . 1946. 'A Comparison between the French and Italian Music.' *The Musical Quarterly* 32. 1946: 411–36. [Translation by Oliver Strunk of Raguenet 1702.]

Ramig, Lorraine A., and Thomas Shipp. 1987. 'Comparative Measures of Vocal Tremor and Vocal Vibrato.' *Journal of Voice* 1(2): 162–7.

Randel, Don Michael, ed. 1986. *The New Harvard Dictionary of Music*. Cambridge: Harvard University Press.

Ratner, Leonard G. 1980. *Classic Music*. New York: Schirmer Books.

Record of Singers, A: The HMV Treasury. 1982. EMI HML 7252–7263. [Record 7252 includes selections sung by Emma Eames, Blanche Marchesi, Nellie Melba, and Alessandro Moreschi; record 7255 includes a selection by Emma Calvé.]

Reed, V. William. 1982. 'The Electroglottograph in Voice Teaching.' In *Transcripts of the Tenth Symposium: Care of the Professional Voice* 2: 58–65. New York: The Voice Foundation.

Regier, Marvin Paul. 1996. *The Haute-Contre Solo Voice: Tessitura and Timbre*. D.M.A. Dissertation, University of Oregon.

Reid, Cornelius L. 1950. *Bel Canto: Principles and Practices*. New York: Coleman-Ross. [Reprint edition, New York: Joseph Patelson Music House, 1971.]

Robinson, Philip. 1980. 'Garat, Pierre.' In *The New Grove Dictionary of Music and Musicians*, 7: 150.

Root, Frederic W. 1894. [Untitled interview with Manuel Garcia II]. *The Musical Herald* (London), 1 August 1894, 227–30.

Rosensteil, Leonie, ed. 1982. *The Schirmer History of Music*. New York: Schirmer; London: Collier Macmillan.

Rossetti, Biagio. 1529. *Libellus de rudimentis Musices*. Verona: Fratres de Nicolinis de Sabio. [Critical text edited by Albert Seay (Colorado Springs: Colorado College Music Press, 1981).]

Rothenberg, Martin. 1981. 'The Voice Source in Singing.' In *Research Aspects on Singing*. Stockholm: Royal Swedish Academy of Music, 80–96.

– . 1986. '"Cosi fan Tutte," and What it Means: or, Nonlinear Source Tract

Acoustic Interaction in the Soprano Voice and some Implications for the Definition of Vocal Efficiency.' In *Laryngeal Function in Phonation and Respiration*, edited by Thomas Baer, Clarence Sasaki, and Catherine S. Harris. Vocal Fold Physiology, Series 1. San Diego: College-Hill Press/Raven Press.

Rothenberg, M., D.G. Miller, and R. Molitor. 1988. 'Aerodynamic Investigations of Sources of Vibrato.' *Folia Phoniatrica* 40: 244–60.

Rothman, Howard B. 1986. 'Varying Vibrato: Is It Rate or Extent?' In *Transcripts of the Fourteenth Symposium: Care of the Professional Voice* 1: 75–8. New York: The Voice Foundation.

Rothman, Howard B., and A. Antonio Arroyo. 1987. 'Acoustic Variability in Vibrato and its Perceptual Significance.' *Journal of Voice* 1(2): 123–41.

Rothman, Howard B., Kenneth Nielson, and James W. Hicks, Jr. 1980. 'Perceptual Classification of Voice Movements.' In *Transcripts of the Eighth Symposium: Care of the Professional Voice* 1: 57–9. New York: The Voice Foundation.

Rothman, Howard B., and Craig Timberlake. 1985. 'Perceptual Evaluation of Singer's Vibrato.' In *Transcripts of the Thirteenth Symposium: Care of the Professional Voice* 1: 11–115. New York: The Voice Foundation.

Rousseau, Jean. 1687. *Traité de la viole.* Paris: Ballard.

– 1691. *Methode claire, certaine et facile, pour apprendre à chanteur la musique.* Amsterdam: P.& J. Blaeu. [First published in Paris, 1678]

Rubin, Henry J., and Charles C. Hirt. 1960. 'The Falsetto: A High Speed Cinematographic Study.' *The Laryngoscope* 70: 1305–24.

Rubin, Henry J., M. Le Cover, and William Vennard. 1967. 'Vocal Intensity, Subglottic Pressure and Air Flow Relationships in Singers.' *Folia Phoniatrica* 19: 393–413. [Reprinted in Large 1980, 88–107.]

Rzhevkin, S.N. 1956. 'Certain Results of the Analysis of a Singer's Voice.' *Soviet Physics-Acoustics* 2: 215–20. [Reprinted in Large 1980, 329–38.]

[Samber, Robert]. 1718. *Eunuchism Display'd: A Translation, with Interpolations, of Charles d'Ancillon's Traité des eunuques, 1707.* London: E. Curll.

Sanford, Sally. 1979. *Seventeenth and Eighteenth Century Vocal Style and Technique.* Doctoral Dissertation, Stanford University.

Sartori, Claudio. 1952. *Bibliografia della musica strumentale italiana.* Firenze: Leo Olschi.

Sataloff, Robert Thayer. 1991. *Professional Voice: The Science and Art of Clinical Voice.* New York: Raven Press. [Second edition, San Diego: Singular Publishing Group, 1997.]

Saviotti, A. 1919. 'Un'artista del cinquecento.' *Bolletino senese di storia patria (Siena)* 26: Fasc. 2, 105–34.

Scherer, Ronald C., and Ingo R. Titze. 1982. 'A New Look at van den Berg's Glottal Aerodynamics.' *Transcripts of the Tenth Symposium: Care of the Professional Voice* 1: 74–81. New York: The Voice Foundation.

Schilling, Rudolph. 1925. 'Untersuchung über die Atembewegung beim Sprechen und Singen.' *Monatschrift Ohrenheilkunde* 59: 51–80; 134–53; 313–43; 454–67; 643–68.

Schillinger, Joseph. 1948. *The Mathematical Basis of the Arts*. New York: Philosophical Library. [Reprint edition, New York: Da Capo Press, 1976.]

Schipa, Tito. [n.d.]. *Tito Schipa: Opera and Song Recital*. In series *Great Recordings of the Century*. Angel COLH 117.

Schoen, Max. 1922. 'An Experimental Study of the Pitch Factor in Artistic Singing.' *Psychological Monographs* 31: 230–59.

Schubert, Earl D. 1983. 'On Hearing Your Own Performance.' *Transcripts of the Eleventh Symposium: Care of the Professional Voice* 1: 161–85. New York: The Voice Foundation.

Schutte, Harm K. 1980. *The Efficiency of Voice Production*. Groningen: Kemper.

– . 1992. 'Integrated Aerodynamic Measurements.' *Journal of Voice* 6(2): 127–34.

Schutte, Harm K., and Donald G. Miller. 1986. 'The Effect of F_0/F_1 Coincidence in Soprano High Notes on Pressure at the Glottis.' *Journal of Voice* 14: 385–92.

– . 1991. 'Acoustic Detail of Vibrato Cycle in Tenor High Notes.' *Journal of Voice* 5(3): 217–23

– . 1993. 'Belting and Pop, Nonclassical Approaches to the Female Middle Voice: Some Preliminary Considerations.' *Journal of Voice* 7(2): 142–50.

– . 1996. 'Resonance Strategies for Tenor High Notes.' Paper presented at the 25th annual Symposium: Care of the Professional Voice. Philadelphia, 3–9 June 1996.

Schutte, Harm K., Donald G. Miller, and James A. Stark. 1997. 'Longitudinal Study of Subglottal Pressures in Tenor Singing.' Paper presented at the 26th annual Symposium: Care of the Professional Voice. Philadelphia, 3 June 1997.

Schutte, Harm K., Donald G. Miller, and Jan G. Švec. 1995. 'Measurement of Formant Frequencies and Bandwidths in Singing.' *Journal of Voice* 9(3): 290–6.

Scotto di Carlo, Nicole. 1979. 'Perturbing Effects of Overarticulation in Singing.' *Journal of Research in Singing* 2(2): 10–27.

Sears, T.A. 1977. 'Some Neural and Mechanical Aspects of Singing.' In Critchley and Henson 1977, 78–94.

Seashore, Carl E., ed. 1932. *The Vibrato*. University of Iowa Studies in the Psychology of Music, vol. I. Iowa City: University of Iowa Press.

– , ed. 1936. *Psychology of the Vibrato in Voice and Instrument*. University of Iowa Studies in the Psychology of Music, vol. 3. Iowa City: University of Iowa Press.

– . 1938. *Psychology of Music*. New York: McGraw Hill. [Reprint edition, New York: Dover, 1967.]

– . 1947. *In Search of Beauty in Music: A Scientific Approach to Musical Esthetics*. New York: Ronald Press Co.

Seidner, Wolfram, and Jürgen Wendler. 1997. *Die Sängerstimme: Phoniatrische Grundlagen der Gesangsausbildung*. Berlin: Henschel Velag.

Seiler, Emma. 1872. *The Voice in Singing*. Translated by W.H. Furners. A new edition, revised and enlarged. Philadelphia: J.B. Lippincott. [English translation of *Altes un Neues über die Ausbildung des Gesangorganes mit besonderer Rücksicht auf die Frauenstimme* (Leipzig: L. Voss, 1861). First English edition, 1868.]

– . 1881. *The Voice in Singing*. Translated by W.H. Furners. Philadelphia: J.B. Lippincott.

Shakespeare, William. 1899. *The Art of Singing, Based on the Principles of the Old Italian Singing Masters*. London: Metzler & Co.; Boston: O Ditson; New York: C.H. Ditson

– . 1910. *The Art of Singing ... Entirely Rewritten*. London: Metzler & Co. [Reprinted London: J.B. Cramer, (n.d.)]

– . 1924. *Plain Words on Singing*. London: G.P. Putnam's Sons.

Shaw, George Bernard. 1932. *Music in London, 1890–1894*. 3 vols. London: Constable and Company.

– . 1960. *How to Become a Music Critic*. Edited, with an introduction by Dan H. Lawrence. London: Rupert Hart-Davis.

Shipp, Thomas. 1975. 'Vertical Laryngeal Position during Continuous and Discrete Vocal Frequency Change.' *Journal of Speech and Hearing Research* 18: 707–18.

– . 1977. 'Vertical Laryngeal Position in Singing.' In *Journal of Research in Singing* 1(1): 16–24.

– . 1979. 'Vertical Laryngeal Position in Singers with the Jaw Stabilized.' In *Transcripts of the Seventh Symposium: Care of the Professional Voice* 1: 44–7. New York: The Voice Foundation.

– . 1987. 'Vertical Laryngeal Position: Research Findings and Application for Singers.' *Journal of Voice* 1(3): 217–19.

Shipp, Thomas, and Jean Hakes. 1986. 'Voice Frequency Oscillations During Vibrato, Trill, and Trillo.' In *Transcripts of the Fourteenth Symposium: Care of the Professional Voice* 1: 72–4e. New York: The Voice Foundation.

Shipp, Thomas, Rolf Leanderson, and Stig Haglund. 1983. 'Contribution of the Cricothyroid Muscle to Vocal Vibrato.' *Transcripts of the Eleventh Symposium: Care of the Professional Voice* 1: 131–3. New York: The Voice Foundation.

Shipp, Thomas, Rolf Leanderson, and Johan Sundberg. 1980a. 'Some Acoustical Characteristics of Vocal Vibrato.' *Journal of Research in Singing* 4(1): 18–25.

– . 1980b. 'Vocal Vibrato.' In *Transcripts of the Eighth Symposium: Care of the Professional Voice* 1: 46–9. New York: The Voice Foundation.

Shipp, Thomas, Johan Sundberg, and Stig Haglund. 1985. 'A Model of Frequency Vibrato.' In *Transcripts of the Thirteenth Symposium: Care of the Professional Voice* 1: 116–17. New York: The Voice Symposium.

Silbert, Doris. 1946. 'Francesca Caccini, called La Cecchina.' *The Musical Quarterly* 32: 50–62.

Silva, Giulio. 1922. 'The Beginnings of the Art of Bel Canto.' *The Musical Quarterly* 7: 53–68.

Smith, Ethel Clossen. 1970. 'An Electromyographic Investigation of the Relationship between Abdominal Muscular Effort and the Rate of Vocal Vibrato.' *Bulletin of the National Association of Teachers of Singing* (May–June): 2–17.

Solerti, Angelo, ed. 1891. *Ferrara e la corte Estense nella seconda metà del secolo decimosesto.* Città di Castello: S. Lapi.

– . 1902. 'Laura Guidoccioni Lucchesini ed Emilio de' Cavalieri; i primi tentativi del melodramma.' *Rivista Musicale Italiana* 9: 797–829.

– , ed. 1903. *Le origini del melodramma.* Torino: Fratelli Bocca. [Reprint edition: Hildesheim: Georg Olms Verlag, 1969.]

– . 1905. 'Lettere inedite sulla musica di Pietro della Valle a G.B. Doni ed una veglia drammatica-musicale del medesimo.' *Rivista Musicale Italiana* 12: 271–338.

Sonninen, Aatto. 1956. 'The Role of the External Laryngeal Muscles in Length Adjustments of the Vocal Cords in Singing.' In *Acta Otolaryngologica*, Supplementum 130.

– . 1961. 'Parastasis-Gram of the Vocal Folds and the Dimensions of the Voice.' In *Proceedings of the Fourth International Congress of Phonetic Sciences*, 250–8. The Hague: Mouton & Co. [Reprinted in Large 1980, 134–45.]

– . 1968. 'The External Frame Function in the Control of Pitch in the Human Voice.' *Annals of the New York Academy of Sciences* 155: 68–89.

Southern, Richard William. 1953. *The Making of the Middle Ages.* New Haven: Yale University Press.

Stanley, Douglas. 1945. *Your Voice: Applied Science of Vocal Art.* New York: Pitman.

Stark, James A. 1971. 'Giulio Caccini and the "Noble Manner of Singing."' *Journal of the Canadian Association of University Schools of Music* 1(2): 39–53.

– . 1991. "Garcia in Persective: His *Traité* After 150 Years.' *Journal of Research in Singing* 15(1): 2–55.

– . 1995. 'On the Role of Vocal Idioms in Singing.' *Canadian University Music Review* 15: 70–90.

Steane, J.B. 1992. *Voices: Singers and Critics.* Portland, Oregon: Amadeus Press.

– . 1993. *The Grand Tradition: Seventy Years of Singing on Record, 1900 to 1970.* Second edition. Portland, Oregon: Amadeus Press. [First edition published in 1974.]

Stein, Deborah, and Robert Spillman. 1996. *Poetry into Song: Performance and Analysis of Lieder.* New York: Oxford University Press.

Stendahl [Henri Beyle]. 1956. *Life of Rossini.* Translated by Richard N. Coe. London: John Calder. [First published in 1824.]

Stockhausen, Julius. 1884. *A Method of Singing.* Translated by Sophie Löwe. London: Novello. [English translation of *Julius Stockhausens Gesangs-methode,* Leipzig: Peters, 1884.]

Stone, Edgar. 1980. 'Francesco and Giovanni Battista Lamperti: A Comparative Study of Their Vocal Pedagogy.' *Bulletin of the National Association of Teachers of Singing* (March/April): 20–5, 30.

Strunk, Oliver. 1950. *Source Readings in Music History.* New York: W.W. Norton.

Sullivan, Jan. 1989. 'How to Teach the Belt/Pop Voice.' *Journal of Research in Singing* 13(1): 41–58.

Sundberg, Johan. 1973. 'The Source Spectrum in Professional Singing.' *Folia Phoniatrica* 25: 71–90.

– . 1974. 'Articulatory Interpretation of the "Singing Formant."' *Journal of the Acoustical Society of America* 55: 838–44.

– . 1977a. 'The Acoustics of the Singing Voice.' *Scientific American* (March): 82–91.

– . 1977b. 'Studies of the Soprano Voice.' *Journal of Research in Singing* 1(1): 25–35.

– . 1980. 'Acoustics: The Voice.' In *The New Grove Dictionary of Music and Musicians,* 1: 82–7.

– . 1981. 'The Voice as Sound Generator.' In *Research Aspects of Singing.* Stockholm: Royal Swedish Academy of Music.

– . 1982. 'Effect of the Vibrato and the "Singing Formant" on Pitch.' *Journal of Research in Singing* 5(2): 3–17.

– . 1985a. 'Using Acoustic Research for Understanding Various Aspects of the Singing Voice.' *Transcripts of the Thirteenth Symposium: Care of the Professional Voice* 1: 90–104. New York: The Voice Foundation.

– . 1985b. 'Supraglottal Contributions to Vocal Loudness and Projection.' *Transcripts of the Thirteenth Symposium: Care of the Professional Voice* 1: 202–11. New York: The Voice Foundation.

– . 1987. *The Science of the Singing Voice.* DeKalb, IL: Northern Illinois Press.

– . 1991. *The Science of Musical Sounds.* San Diego: Academic Press.

– . 1995. 'Acoustic and Psychoacoustic Aspects of Vocal Vibrato.' In Dejonckere, Hirano, and Sundberg 1995, 35–62.

Sundberg, J., Rolf M. Leanderson, and Curt von Euler. 1989. 'Activity Relationships between Diaphragm and Cricothyroid Muscles.' *Journal of Voice* 3(3): 225–32.

Švec, Jan G., and Harm K. Schutte. 1996. 'Videokymogrophy: High-Speed Line Scanning of Vocal Fold Vibrations.' *Journal of Voice* 10(2): 201–5.

Švec, Jan G., Harm K. Schutte, and Donald G. Miller. 1996. 'A Subharmonic Vibratory Pattern in Normal Vocal Folds.' *Journal of Speech and Hearing Research* 39: 135–43.

Taruskin, Richard. 1995. *Text and Act: Essays on Music and Performance.* New York and Oxford: Oxford University Press.

Taylor, David C. 1916. *New Light on the Old Italian Method.* New York: H.W. Gray Co.

Ternström, S., ed. 1986. 'Acoustics in Choir Singing.' In *Acoustics for Choir and Orchestra.* Stockholm: Swedish Academy of Music.

– . 1991. 'Physical and Acoustic Factors that Interact with the Singer to Produce the Choral Sound.' *Journal of Voice* 5(2): 128–43.

Timberlake, Craig. 1989. 'The Case for Manuel Garcia, II.' *Journal of the National Association of Teachers of Singing* 46(1): 19–22; 46(2): 23–8.

Titze, Ingo R. 1980. 'The Concept of Muscular Isometrics for Optimizing Vocal Intensity and Efficiency.' *Transcripts of the Eighth Symposium: Care of the Professional Voice* 1: 23–8. New York: The Voice Foundation.

– . 1994. *Principles of Voice Production.* Englewood Cliffs, NJ: Prentice Hall.

– . 1996. 'More on Messa di Voce.' *Journal of Singing* 52(4): 37–8.

– . 1998. 'Male-Female Differences in the Larynx.' *Journal of the National Association of Teachers of Singing* (Jan–Feb): 31

Tosi, Pierfrancesco. 1723. *Opinioni de' cantori antichi e moderni o sieno osservazioni sopra il canto figurato.* Bologna: Lelio dalla Volpe.

– . 1743. *Observations on the Florid Song.* Translated by J.E. Galliard. London: Wilcox. [Translation of Tosi 1723. Reprint edition, New York: Johnson Reprint, 1967.]

– . 1757. *Anleitung zur Singekunst.* [Translation of Tosi 1723: see J.F. Agricola 1757.]

– . 1986. *Opinions of Singers Ancient and Modern or Observations on Figured Singing.* Translated by Edward Foreman. Minneapolis: Pro Musica Press. [Translation of Tosi 1723.]

Transcripts of the Eighth Symposium: Care of the Professional Voice. 1980. New York: The Voice Foundation.

Transcripts of the Eleventh Symposium: Care of the Professional Voice. 1983. New York: The Voice Foundation.

Transcripts of the Thirteenth Symposium: Care of the Professional Voice. 1985. New York: The Voice Foundation.

Transcripts of the Fourteenth Symposium: Care of the Professional Voice. 1986. New York: The Voice Foundation.

Treitler, Leo.' 1982. 'Structural and Critical Analysis.' In *Musicology in the 1980s*, edited by D.K. Holoman and C.V. Palisca. New York: Da Capo Press, 67–77.

Troup, Gordon. 1982. 'The Physics of the Singing Voice.' *Journal of Research in Singing* 6(1): 1–26.

Ulrich, Bernhard. 1973. *Concerning the Principles of Voice Training During the A Cappella Period and until the Beginning of Opera (1474–1640)*. Translated by John W. Seale. Minneapolis: Pro Musica Press. [First published as *Die Grundsätze der Stimmbildung während der A Cappella Periode und zur Zeit des Aufkommens der Oper 1474–1646* (Leipzig: Breitkopf und Härtel, 1912).]

Vaccai, Nicola. 1840. *12 Ariette per camera in chiave di violino per l'insegnamento del bel canto italiano*. Milan.

Valdrighi, Luigi Francesco. 1884. *Cappelle, concerte e musiche di Casa d'Este, dal secolo XV. al XVIII*. Modena: Vincenzi.

Van den Berg, Janwillem. 1955. 'Transmission of the Vocal Cavities.' *Journal of the Acoustical Society of America* 27: 161–8.

– . 1956a. 'Direct and Indirect Determination of the Mean Subglottic Pressure.' *Folia Phoniatrica* 8: 1–24.

– . 1956b. 'Physiology and Physics of Voice Production.' *Acta Physiologica Pharmocology Nederland* 5: 40–55.

– . 1958. 'Myoelastic-Aerodynamic Theory of Voice Production.' *Journal of Speech Research* 3: 227–44.

– . 1959. 'Toward an Objective Vocabulary for Voice Pedagogy.' *Bulletin of the National Association of Teachers of Singing* (February): 10–15.

– . 1960. 'Vocal Ligaments Versus Registers.' *Current Problems in Phoniatrics and Logopedics* 1: 19–34.

– . 1962. 'Modern Research in Experimental Phoniatrics.' *Folia Phoniatrica* 14: 81–149

– . 1968a. 'Sound Production in Isolated Human Larynges.' *Annals of the New York Academy of Sciences* 155: 18–26.

– . 1968b. 'Register Problems.' *Annals of the New York Academy of Sciences* 155: 129–35.

– . 1968c. 'Mechanism of the Larynx and the Laryngeal Vibration.' In *Manual of Phonetics*, edited by Bertol Malmberg. The Hague and London: North-Holland Publishing Company, 278–308.

Vennard, William. 1961. 'The Bernoulli Effect in Singing.' *Bulletin of the National Association of Teachers of Singing* (February): 8–11.

– . 1964. 'An Experiment to Evaluate the Importance of Nasal Resonance in Singing.' *Folia Phoniatrica* 16: 146–53.

– . 1967. *Singing: the Mechanism and the Technic*. Revised edition, greatly enlarged. New York: Carl Fischer. [First edition, 1949.]

– . 1971. 'The Relation between Vibrato and Vocal Ornamentation.' Abstract of paper presented at the Acoustical Society of America conference, 6 November 1970. *Journal of the Acoustical Society of America* 49: 137.

Vennard William, Minoru Hirano, and John Ohala. 1970a. 'Laryngeal Synergy in Singing.' *Bulletin of the National Association of Teachers of Singing* (October): 16–21.

– . 1970b. 'Chest, Head, and Falsetto.' *Bulletin of the National Association of Teachers of Singing* (December): 30–7.

Vennard, William, and Nobuhiko Isshiki. 1964. 'Coupe de Glotte – A Misunderstood Expression.' *Bulletin of the National Association of Teachers of Singing* (February): 15–18.

Vennard, William, and Hans von Leden. 1967. 'The Importance of Intensity Modulation in the Perception of a Trill.' *Folia Phoniatricia* 19: 19–26.

Vicentino, Nicolà. 1555. *L'antica musica ridotta alla moderna prattica*. Roma: A. Barre. [Facsimile reprint, edited by Edward E. Lowinsky. Documenta musicologica 1. Reihe, 17. Kassel: Bärenreiter, 1959.]

Vogler, Georg Joseph (Abbé). 1778. *Kurpfälzische Tonschule*. Mannheim: Schwan & Götz.

von Leden, Hans. 1983. 'The Cultural History of the Human Voice.' In *Transcripts of the Eleventh Symposium: Care of the Professional Voice* 2: 116–23. New York: The Voice Foundation.

Wagner, Richard. 1834. 'Pasticcio, by Canto Spianato.' In *Richard Wagner's Prose Works*, vol. 8, translated by William Ashton Ellis. London: Kegan Paul, Trench, Trübner & Co., 1899.

Walker, J.S. 1988. 'An Investigation of the Whistle Register in the Female Voice.' *Journal of Voice* 2: 140–50.

Ward, W. Dixon. 1970. 'Musical Perception.' In *Foundations of Modern Auditory Theory*, vol. 1, edited by Jerry V. Tobias. New York: Academic Press.

Weisstein, Ulrich, ed. 1969. *The Essence of Opera*. New York: W.W. Norton. [First published in 1964.]

White, Ernest George. 1938. *Sinus Tone Production*. London: J.M. Dent & Sons.

Widdicombe, J.G. 1974. 'Pulmonary Reflex Mechanisms in Ventilatory Regulation.' In Wyke 1974a, 131–44.

Wieck, Friedrich. 1875. *Piano and Song*. Translated by M.P. Nichols. Boston: Lockwood, Brooks and Co. [Reprint edition, New York: Da Capo Press, 1982. First published as *Clavier und Gesang* (Leipzig, 1853).]

Wilder, Carol N. 1980a. 'Chest Wall Preparation for Phonation in Trained Speakers.' In *Transcripts of the Eighth Symposium: Care of the Professional Voice* 2: 25–32. New York: The Voice Foundation.

– . 1980b. 'Prephonatory Chest Wall Adjustments in Trained Singers.' *Journal of Research in Singing* 3(2): 1–16.

Willier, Stephen. 1983. 'Rhythmic Variants in Early Manuscript Versions of Caccini's Monodies.' *Journal of the American Musicological Society* 36: 481–97.

Wilson, John, ed. 1959. *Roger North on Music*. London: Novello and Company Ltd.

Winckel, Fritz. 1952. 'Elektroakustische Untersuchungen an der menschliche Stimme.' *Folia Phoniatrica* 4: 93–113.

– . 1953. 'Physikalische Kriterien für die objective Stimmbeurteilung.' *Folia Phoniatrica* 5: 232–52.

– . 1959. 'Die naturwissenschaftlichen Grundlagen der musikalischen Lautperzeption.' *Acta Musicologica* 31: 186–92.

– . 1967. *Music, Sound and Sensation*. Translated by Thomas Binkley. New York: Dover Publications. [First published in 1960 as *Phänomene des musikalischen Hörens*.]

Woo, Peak. 1996. 'Quantification of Videostrobolaryngoscopic Findings – Measurements of the Normal Glottal Cycle.' *The Laryngoscope* 1063 : Part 2 (March, 1996), Supplement No. 79. St. Louis: The American Laryngological, Rhinological and Otological Society, Inc.

Wyke, Barry D. 1974a. *Ventilatory and Phonatory Control Systems*. London: Oxford University Press.

– . 1974b. 'Respiratory Activity of Intrinsic Laryngeal Muscles: An Experimental Study.' In Wyke 1974a, 408–29.

– . 1974c. 'Laryngeal Myotatic Reflexes and Phonation.' *Folia Phoniatrica* 26: 249–64.

– . 1974d. 'Laryngeal Neuromuscular Control Systems in Singing: A Review of Current Concepts.' *Folia Phoniatrica* 26: 295–306.

– . 1980. 'Neurological Aspects of Phonatory Control Systems in the Larynx: A Review of Current Concepts.' In *Transcripts of the Eighth Symposium: Care of the Professional Voice* 2: 42–53. New York: The Voice Foundation.

Zacconi, Lodovico. 1592. *Prattica di musica utile et necessario si al compositore*. Venezia: Girolamo Polo. [Second edition, Venetia: B. Carampello, 1596. Facsimile reprint edition, Bologna: Forni, 1966. Chapter 66 translated in MacClintock 1979, 68–75.]

Zantema, J.T., and Janwillem van den Berg. 1956. 'Zur Erzeugung des Vibratos der Singstimme.' *Zeitschrift für Phonetik und allgemeine Sprachwissenschaft* 9(4): 336–43.

Zaslaw, Neal. 1974. 'The Enigma of the Haute-Contre.' *The Musical Times* 115: 939–41.

Zemlin, Willard R. 1968. *Speech and Hearing Science: Anatomy and Physiology*. Englewood Cliffs, NJ: Prentice-Hall.

— . 1988. *Speech and Hearing Science: Anatomy and Physiology*. Third edition. Englewood Cliffs, NJ: Prentice-Hall.

— . 1998. *Speech and Hearing Science: Anatomy and Physiology*. Fourth edition. Boston: Allyn and Bacon.

Index

References to figures are shown in italic type.

'Che farò senza Euridice,' 183–8;
Orfeo ed Euridice, 183; reform
operas, 207; use of *haute-contre*, 208;
on vocal expressivity, 185
Gluck and His Operas (Berlioz), 186
Godt, Irving, 150
Goethe, Johann Wolfgang von, 203
golden ages of singing and *bel canto*,
   xix, 197, 202, 204–6, 216
Goldschmidt, Hugo, xix
Gonzaga, Francesco, 198
Gonzaga, Margherita, 191
Gonzaga, Vincenzo (Duke of Man-
   tua), 192
Gonzaga family, court of, 191
gorgie, 123, 124, 155
Gould, Wilbur J., 22, 25
Gounod, Charles, 55
grave register, 67
grazia, 162
Great Singers, The (Pleasants), 205
Great Women-Singers of My Time
   (Klein), 223–4
Grisi, Giulia, 205
Groningen Voice Research Lab, 50,
   227, 234; Groningen protocols,
   257
groppetto, 123, 124–5, 125
*Grove's Dictionary of Music and Musi-
   cians* (1954 ed.), 148
gruppo (or *groppo*), 123, 124, 125–6,
   155, 160, 171
Guadagni, Gaetano, 185, 205, 217
Gualberto, Giovanni, 196
Guarini, Anna, 192
Guarini, Giovanni Battista, 192
Guglielmo, duke of Mantua, 198
*Guida teorica-pratica-elementare per lo
   studio del canto* (F. Lamperti), 42,
   266n28

Guidotti, Alessandro, 160
Guillaume Tell (Rossini), 41, 219
Haas, Robert, xix
Häbock, Franz, 64, 205
Haglund, Stig, 143
half breath (*mezzo-respiro*), 97, 99, 117
half-chest voice (*voce di mezzo petto*),
   68, 73, 74, 80
half voice (*mezza voce*), 75, 246–53
Handel, George Frideric, 171, 214
Hanslick, Eduard, 183, 184, 221
hard onset (or attack), 17, 21
harmonics, xiii, 47
Harmonie universelle (Mersenne), 126,
   206
Harvard Dictionary of Music, xix
Hasse, Faustina (née Bordini), 218
Hasse, Johann Adolf, 214, 218
haute-contre, 208–9, 210
Hawkins, John, 5, 200, 201, 218
Haydn, Franz Joseph, 171
Hayes, Catherine, 6
head voice (head register, *registre de
   tête, voix de tête, voce di testa*), 35, 52;
   in four-register theory, 66; Garcia's
   concept, 39, 68–73; legitimate, 85;
   male operatic, 85; *registre de fausset-
   tête*, 68, 71; in three-register theory,
   64, 67, 77, 80; in two-register theory, 57, 58, 60–2, 77; use for high
   notes, 60; use in *messa di voce*, 97,
   98; *voce piena in testa*, 85; *Vollton der
   Kopfstimme*, 85; *vs.* falsetto, 39, 59,
   61, 62, 64, 73; weakness, 62. *See also*
   register(s)
Heldentenöre, 108
Helmholtz, Hermann, xxii, 40, 45–7,
   50, 54, 56, 78, 180
Henderson, William James, 19–20,
   137, 197, 219, 223